Nuria Calduch-Benages
For Wisdom's Sake

Beihefte zur Zeitschrift für die alttestamentliche Wissenschaft

Edited by
John Barton, Reinhard G. Kratz, Nathan MacDonald,
Sara Milstein and Markus Witte

Volume 499

Nuria Calduch-Benages

For Wisdom's Sake

Collected Essays on the Book of Ben Sira

DE GRUYTER

ISBN 978-3-11-048650-6
e-ISBN (PDF) 978-3-11-049231-6
e-ISBN (EPUB) 978-3-11-049193-7
ISSN 0934-2575

Library of Congress Control Number: 2021931812

Bibliographic information published by the Deutsche Nationalbibliothek
The Deutsche Nationalbibliothek lists this publication in the Deutsche Nationalbibliografie;
detailed bibliographic data are available in the Internet at http://dnb.dnb.de.

MIX
Papier aus verantwor-
tungsvollen Quellen
FSC
www.fsc.org   FSC® C083411

Preface

Twenty-five years have passed since I defended my doctoral thesis on Sir 2,1–18 under the direction of Prof. Maurice Gilbert SJ at the Pontifical Biblical Institute in Rome. Since then, my interest in the book of Ben Sira has grown, and most of my research has concentrated on various aspects of this intriguing work.

For Wisdom's Sake brings together all my studies on Sirach that have been published in English from 1997 to 2018. Most have appeared in joint works or Festschrifts. I have also included the translation of two texts, a Spanish article first published in the journal *Gregorianum* (1997) and one in Italian that appeared in *Ogni Scrittura è ispirata* (2013), a collection of essays by professors from the Pontifical Biblical Institute and the Pontifical Gregorian University. Thus, although the volume is basically composed of studies published previously, it also offers some novelties, at least for English-speaking readers.

In trying to organize all of the material, I have opted for the following classification: studies that deal with introductory issues such as, for example, the canon and inspiration; thematic essays presented in chronological order (on trial, authority, divorce, animal imagery, women in the praise of ancestors, polygamy, good and bad wives, garment imagery, exodal traditions); and studies that concentrate on specific passages (Sir 2,1; 6,22; 21,1–10; 22,27–23,6; 23,27; 24,22; 31(34Hb),1–8; 42,15–43,33; 43,27–33).

All of the articles in this collection faithfully reproduce the content of the original publications, but they have been carefully revised from a formal and literary point of view in order to give coherence to the volume. Some errors and inaccuracies in the original text have been corrected, some additional information has been added in footnotes between square brackets, and some outdated information has been deleted. However, repetitions concerning Sir 25,8 and 42,13 have been unavoidable. When quoting Sirach 33–36, I have followed the numbering adopted in J. Ziegler's edition. All translations of texts in French, German, Italian, and Spanish are mine. Whenever possible, I have favoured the use of gender-neutral language.

The completion of this book would not have been possible without the help and support of many people who from the beginning have encouraged and helped me to carry it out. My sincere thanks go first to Dr. Martin X. Moleski SJ, who has had the patience and generosity to read and correct most of the texts, and also to professors Michael W. Duggan, Jeremy Corley, and Dean Bechard SJ for their corrections and very helpful suggestions. I am grateful to the publishers E. J. Brill, Walter de Gruyter, Catholic Biblical Association of America, Society of Biblical Literature, and J. B. C. Mohr (Paul Siebeck) for permission to republish

https://doi.org/10.1515/9783110492316-001

these articles. A very special thanks goes to Dr. Sophie Wagenhofer, Senior Acquisitions Editor for Religion at de Gruyter, who from the very beginning has encouraged me to carry out this project and has made possible the publication of this volume in *Beihefte zur Zeitschrift für die alttestamentliche Wissenschaft* (BZAW).

I would like to conclude this preface with a message of encouragement addressed to the new generations of Bible scholars, in particular my doctoral candidates who are working tirelessly to attain the goal. With Ben Sira, I say to you: "See that I have not worked for myself alone, but for all who seek wisdom" (Sir 24,34).

Nuria Calduch-Benages
Rome, 31st of July 2020

Contents

Part III. **Essays on Specific Passages**

X ─── Contents

First Publications

1. Sirach and the Biblical Canon. Translation of a Spanish original: Ben Sira y el canon de las Escrituras: Greg 78 (1997) 359–370 = in: Nuria CALDUCH-BENAGES, Pan de sensatez y agua de sabiduría. Estudios sobre el libro de Ben Sira (ABE. Artículos selectos 1), Estella: Verbo Divino, 2019, 19–31.
2. Sirach and Inspiration. Translation of an Italian original: Il Siracide, un libro deuterocanonico molto particolare, in: Peter DUBOVSKÝ—Jean-Pierre SONNET (eds.), Ogni Scrittura è ispirata. Nuove prospettive sull'ispirazione biblica (Lectio 5), Cinisello Balsamo (Milano): GBPress—Edizioni San Paolo, 2013, 124–135.
3. Trial Motif in the Book of Ben Sira, with Special Reference to 2,1–6, in: Pancratius C. BEENTJES (ed.), The Book of Ben Sira in Modern Research. Proceedings of the First International Ben Sira Conference 28–31 July 1996 Soesterberg, Netherlands (BZAW 255), Berlin—New York: Walter de Gruyter, 1997, 135–151.
4. Fear of the Powerful or Respect for Authority?, in: Renate EGGER-WENZEL—Ingrid KRAMMER (eds.), Der Einzelne und seine Gemeinschaft bei Ben Sira. Festschrift Prof. Friedrich V. Reiterer (BZAW 270), Berlin—New York: Walter de Gruyter, 1998, 87–102.
5. "Cut Her Away from Your Flesh". Divorce in Ben Sira, in: Géza G. XERAVITS—József ZSENGELLÉR (eds.), Studies in the Book of Ben Sira. Papers of the Third International Conference on the Deuterocanonical Books, Shime'on Centre, Pápa, Hungary, 18–20 May, 2006 (JSJSup 127), Leiden: Brill, 2008, 81–95.
6. Animal Imagery in the Hebrew Text of Ben Sirach, in: Jean-Sébastien REY—Jan JOOSTEN (eds.), The Texts and Versions of the Book of Ben Sira. Transmission and Interpretation (JSJSup 150), Leiden: Brill, 2011, 55–71.
7. The Absence of Named Women from Ben Sira's Praise of the Ancestors, in: Jeremy CORLEY—Harm VAN GROL (eds.), Rewriting Biblical History. Essays on Chronicles and Ben Sira in Honor of Pancratius C. Beentjes (DCLS 7), Berlin: Walter de Gruyter, 2011, 301–317.
8. Polygamy in Ben Sira?, in: Angelo PASSARO (ed.), Family and Kinship in the Deuterocanonical and Cognate Literature (DCLY 2012/13), Berlin—Boston: Walter de Gruyter, 2013, 127–138.
9. Good and Bad Wives in the Book of Ben Sira: A Harmless Classification?, in: Christl M. MAIER—Nuria CALDUCH-BENAGES (eds.), The Writings and Later Wisdom Books (The Bible and Women. Hebrew Bible/Old Testament 1.3), Atlanta, GA: Society of Biblical Literature, 2014, 109–125.
10. Garment Imagery in the Book of Ben Sira, in: Markus WITTE—Sven BEHNKE (eds.), The Metaphorical Use of Language in Deuterocanonical and Cognate Literature (DCLY 2014/15), Berlin—Munich—Boston: Walter de Gruyter, 2015, 257–278.
11. The Exodus Traditions in the Book of Ben Sira, in: Judith GÄRTNER—Barbara SCHMITZ (eds.), Exodus. Rezeptionen in deuterokanonischer und frühjüdischer Literatur (DCLS 32), Berlin: Walter de Gruyter, 2016, 117–130.
12. Amid Trials: Ben Sira 2,1 and James 1,2, in: Jeremy CORLEY—Vincent SKEMP (eds.), Intertextual Studies in Ben Sira and Tobit. Essays in Honor of Alexander A. Di Lella, O.F.M. (CBQMS 38), Washington DC: The Catholic Biblical Association of America, 2005, 255–263.

https://doi.org/10.1515/9783110492316-002

13. A Wordplay on the Term *mûsar* (Sir 6,22), in: Renate EGGER-WENZEL—Karin SCHÖPFLING—Johannes Friedrich DIEHL (eds.), Weisheit als Lebensgrundlage. Festschrift für Friedrich V. Reiterer zum 65. Geburtstag (DCLS 15), Berlin—Boston: Walter de Gruyter, 2013, 13–26.
14. Poetic Imagery in the Book of Ben Sira: A Case Study of Sir 21,1–10, in: James K. AITKEN—Renate EGGER-WENZEL—Stefan C. REIF (eds.), Discovering, Deciphering and Dissenting. Ben Sira Manuscripts after 120 Years (DCLY 2018), Berlin: Walter de Gruyter, 2018, 267–284.
15. Emotions in the Prayer of Sirach 22,27–23,6, in: Stefan C. REIF—Renate EGGER-WENZEL (eds.), Ancient Jewish Prayers and Emotions. Emotions Associated with Jewish Prayer in and around the Second Temple Period (DCLS 26), Berlin: Walter de Gruyter, 2015, 145–160.
16. Ben Sira 23,27—A Pivotal Verse, in: Nuria CALDUCH-BENAGES (ed.), Wisdom for Life. Essays Offered to Honor Prof. Maurice Gilbert, SJ on the Occasion of His Eightieth Birthday (BZAW 445), Berlin: Walter de Gruyter, 2014, 186–200.
17. Ben Sira 24,22—Decoding a Metaphor, in: Andrea TASCHL-ERBER—Irmtraud FISCHER (eds.), Vermittelte Gegenwart. Konzeptionen der Gottespräsenz von der Zeit des Zweiten Tempels bis Anfang des 2. Jahrhunderts n. Chr. (WUNT 367), Tübingen: Mohr Siebeck, 2016, 57–72.
18. Dreams and Folly in Sir 34(31),1–8, in: Irmtraud FISCHER—Ursula RAPP—Johannes SCHILLER (eds.), Auf den Spuren der schriftgelehrten Weisen. Festschrift für Johannes Marböck (BZAW 331), Berlin—New York: Walter de Gruyter, 2003, 241–252.
19. The Hymn to the Creation (Sir 42,15–43,33): A Polemic Text?, in: Angelo PASSARO—Giuseppe BELLIA (eds.), The Wisdom of Ben Sira. Studies on Tradition, Redaction, and Theology (DCLS 1), Berlin—New York: Walter de Gruyter, 2008, 119–138.
20. God Creator of All (Sir 43,27–33), in: Renate EGGER-WENZEL (ed.), Ben Sira's God. Proceedings of the International Ben Sira Conference, Durham—Ushaw College 2002 (BZAW 321), Berlin—New York: Walter de Gruyter, 2002, 79–100.

Abbreviations

AB	Anchor Bible
ABE	Asociación Bíblica Española
AnBib	Analecta Biblica
AOAT	Alter Orient und Altes Testament
ASAW	Abhandlungen der Sächsischen Akademie der Wissenschaften
ASP	American Studies in Papyrology
ATD	Das Alte Testament Deutsch
ATSAT	Arbeiten zur Text und Sprache im Alten Testament
BAC	Biblioteca de Autores Cristianos
BBB	Bönner biblische Beiträge
BEATAJ	Beiträge zur Erforschung des Alten Testaments und des antiken Judentum
Bijdr	Bijdragen
BeO	Bibbia e Oriente
BET	Beiträge zur biblischen Exegese und Theologie
BETL	Bibliotheca Ephemeridum Theologicarum Lovaniensium
BHS	Biblia Hebraica Stuttgartensia
Bib	Biblica
BibInt	Biblical Interpretation
BibOr	Biblica et Orientalia
BJ	Biblia de Jerusalén
BJS	Brown Judaic Studies
BKAT	Biblischer Kommentar, Altes Testament
BN	Biblische Notizen
BVC	Bible et vie chrétienne
BZ	Biblische Zeitschrift
BZAW	Beiträge zur Zeitschrift für die alttestamentliche Wissenschaft
BZNW	Beiträge zur Zeitschrift für die neutestamentliche Wissenschaft
BWANT	Beiträge zur Wissenschaft vom Alten und Neuen Testament
CAF	Comicorum Atticorum Fragmenta
CBET	Contributions to Biblical Exegesis and Theology
CBQ	Catholic Biblical Quarterly
CBQMS	Catholic Biblical Quarterly Monograph Series
CCSL	Corpus Christianorum: Series Latina
CMG	Corpus Medicorum Graecorum
CNEB	The Cambridge Bible Commentary on the New English Bible
CSEL	Corpus Scriptorum Ecclesiasticorum Latinorum
DBSup	Dictionnaire de la Bible. Supplément. Edited by Louis Pirot and André Robert, Paris: Letouzey et Ané, 1928–
DCLS	Deuterocanonical and Cognate Literature Studies
DCLY	Deuterocanonical and Cognate Literature Yearbook
DSD	Dead Sea Discoveries
ÉBib	Études bibliques
EHAT	Exegetisches Handbuch zum Alten Testament
EHS.T	Europäische Hochschulschriften. Theologie

https://doi.org/10.1515/9783110492316-003

ENA	Elkan Nathan Adler Collection (Library of Jewish Theological Seminary, New York)
EstBíb	Estudios Bíblicos
ETL	Ephemerides Theologicae Lovanienses
ExpTim	Expository Times
FAT	Forschung zum Alten Testament
FCB	Feminist Companion to the Bible
FRLANT	Forschungen zur Religion und Literatur des Alten und Neuen Testaments
Greg	Gregorianum
GCS	Die griechischen christlichen Schriftsteller der ersten [drei] Jahrhunderte
GCT	Gender, Culture, Theory
HBS	Herders biblische Studien
Hen	Henoch
HthK.AT	Herders theologischer Kommentar zum Alten Testament
HTR	Harvard Theological Review
HTS	Harvard Theological Studies
HUCA	Hebrew Union College Annual
JBL	Journal of Biblical Literature
JBR	Journal of Bible and Religion
JJS	Journal of Jewish Studies
JNSL	Journal of Northwest Semitic Languages
JQR	Jewish Quarterly Review
JSJ	Journal for the Study of Judaism in the Persian, Hellenistic, and Roman Periods
JSJSup	Journal for the Study of Judaism Supplement Series
JSNTSup	Journal for the Study of New Testament Supplement Series
JSOTSup	Journal for the Study of Old Testament Supplement Series
LD	Lectio Divina
LHB/OTS	The Library of Hebrew Bible/Old Testament Studies
LoB	Leggere oggi la Bibbia
LPTB	Linzer philosophisch-theologische Beiträge
MilS	Milltown Studies
NAB	New American Bible
NBE	Nueva Biblia Española
NEB	Neue Echter Bibel
NICOT	New International Commentary of the Old Testament
NIGTC	New International Greek Testament Commentary
NRT	La nouvelle revue théologique
NTA.NF	Neutestamentliche Abhandlungen. Neue Folge
NTS	New Testament Studies
ÖBS	Österreichiche Biblische Studien
OBO	Orbis Biblicus et Orientalis
OTE	Old Testament Essays
OTL	Old Testament Library
OTMes	Old Testament Message
OTS	Oudtestamentiche Studiën
ParSpV	Parola Spirito e Vita
PaVi	Parole di vita

PG	Patrologia graeca. Edited by Jacques-Paul Migne. 162 vols., Paris: Garnier Fratres, 1857–1903
QD	Questiones Disputatae
RAC	Reallexikon für Antike und Christentum. Edited by Theodor Klauser et al., Stuttgart: Hiersemann, 1950–
RB	Revue biblique
REB	Revised English Bible
RevQ	Revue de Qumrân
RIDA	Revue internationale des droits de l'antiquité
RivB	Rivista biblica italiana
RSR	Recherches de science religieuse
RTL	Revue théologique de Louvain
Sal	Salesianum
SBFLA	Studi biblici Francescani Liber Annus
SBLDS	Society of Biblical Literature Dissertation Series
SBLEJL	Society of Biblical Literature Early Judaism and its Literature
SBLMS	Society of Biblical Literature Monograph Series
SBLSP	Society of Biblical Literature Seminar Papers
SBLSymS	Society of Biblical Literature Symposium Series
SC	Sources chrétiennes
ScEs	Science et esprit
SemeiaSt	Semeia Studies
SJLA	Studies in Judaism in Late Antiquity
SOTSMS	Society for Old Testament Studies Monograph Series
SSN	Studia Semitica Neerlandica
STDJ	Studies on the Texts of the Desert of Juda
SVTP	Studia in Veteris Testamenti Pseudepigraphica
TAPS.NS	Transactions of the American Philosophical Society. New Series
Thf	Theoforum
TPQ	Theologisch-praktische Quartalschrift
TQ	Theologische Quartalschrift
Trans	Transeuphratène
TSAJ	Texte und Studien zum antiken Judentum
TThSt	Trierer theologische Studien
TZ	Theologische Zeitschrift
VetChr	Vetera Christianorum
VT	Vetus Testamentum
VTS	Supplements to Vetus Testamentum
WMANT	Wissenschaftliche Monographien zum Alten und Neuen Testament
WOO	Wiener Offene Orientalistik
WUNT	Wissenschaftliche Untersuchungen zum Neuen Testament
ZAW	Zeitschrift für die alttestamentliche Wissenschaft

A	codex Alexandrinus
AD	*anno domini*

abs.	absolute
adj.	adjective
Arm	Armenian version of Sirach
B	codex Vaticanus
b	MSS 249 – 254 – 603 – 754 (cf. Ziegler's edition)
BC	before Christ
BCE	before the Common Era
C	codex Ephraemi rescriptus
ca.	*circa*, approximately
cf.	*confer*, compare
ch(s).	chapter(s)
Clem.	Clement of Alexandria (Corpus Berolinense)
cod. Vat. Gr.	codex Vaticanus Graece
col.	column
e.g.	*exempli gratia*, for example
ead.	*eadem*, the same (f.)
ed(s).	editor(s)
esp.	especially
ET	English translation
et al.	*et alii*, and others
f.	feminine
fig.	figuratively
frag.	fragment
Gk	Greek version
GkI	short form of the Greek version of Sirach
GkII	long form of the Greek version of Sirach
Hb	Hebrew text
HbI	short form of the Hebrew text of Sirach
HbII	long form of the Hebrew text of Sirach
ibid.	*ibidem*, in the same place
i.e.	*id est*, that is
id.	*idem*, the same (m.)
impf.	imperfect
impv.	imperative
indic.	indicative
inf.	infinitive
L	Lucianic recension (MSS 248 – 493 – 637) (cf. Ziegler's edition)
L'	*L* + *l* (MSS 106 – 130 – 545 – 705) (cf. Ziegler's edition)
Lat	Latin version of Sirach (VL-Vulg.)
lit.	literally
LXX	Septuagint (the Greek OT)
m.	masculine
Mal.	Malachias Monacus (MS from the Real Biblioteca de San Lorenzo de El Escorial, Ω-I-7)
MS(S)	manuscript(s)
MS A	manuscript A (Sirach)
MS B	manuscript B (Sirach)

MS Bmg	manuscript B marginal (Sirach)
MS C	manuscript C (Sirach)
MS D	manuscript D (Sirach)
MS E	manuscript E (Sirach)
MS F	manuscript F (Sirach)
MS Mas	Masada manuscript (Sirach)
MT	Masoretic Text
neut.	neuter
no(s).	number(s)
NT	New Testament
O	Origenic recension (MS 253-Syh) (cf. Ziegler's edition)
orig.	original
OT	Old Testament
p(p).	page(s)
pass.	passive
per.	person
pl.	plural
ptc.	participle
repr.	reprinted
rev.	revised
S	codex Sinaiticus
sg.	singular
Syh	Syro-Hexaplaric version of Sirach
Syr	Syriac version of Sirach
trans.	translator, translated by
V	codex Venetus
v(v).	verse(s)
viz.	*videlicet*, namely
VL	Vetus Latina
vol(s).	volume(s)
vs.	versus
Vulg.	Vulgate

Part I. **Introductory Questions**

Ben Sira and the Canon of the Scriptures

The book of Ben Sira, also known as Sirach or Ecclesiasticus, is a very controversial book. Roman Catholics consider it deuterocanonical (sacred and inspired by God), while for Jews and Protestants it belongs to the Apocrypha, i.e. the books they do not accept as canonical. Situated on the border of the canon, this book of wisdom is as quickly introduced into the canon as it is excluded[1]. Our purpose is to study the importance of the book for the Jews and for Christians in antiquity after the rabbis excluded it from the Jewish canon.

Our method will be as follows: firstly, we will begin with a brief presentation of the textual history of the book; secondly, we will consider its place in Rabbinic Judaism and, thereafter, in the primitive Church; and, finally, we will attempt to draw some conclusions.

1 The Textual History of the Book of Ben Sira[2]

The Hebrew text we have in our possession is fragmentary and strewn in various manuscripts. The Greek, Latin and Syrian versions, on the other hand, have preserved the integral text of the book. We shall now very briefly see the different forms the text presents.

1.1 Hebrew I (HbI)

The book was originally written in Hebrew by Jesus, son of Sira towards 180 AD in Jerusalem[3], and addressed to the young disciples who went to his school (cf. Sir 51,23). Unfortunately, this text was lost, but we neither know when nor how.

For centuries, the only two ways to access to the work of Ben Sira were via the numerous quotations in rabbinic literature and the translations into Greek, Syriac and, above all, Latin. This situation radically changed in 1896: Solomon Schechter, at that time professor at the Cambridge University, discovered, on a page of an ancient manuscript bought in the East by Mrs. Agnes Smith Lewis

---

1 Cf. RÜGER, Siracide, 47–67.
2 For the bibliography relative to this section, cf. CALDUCH-BENAGES, Crisol.
3 This date, which is generally accepted, is based on two elements: on the one hand, the praise of the high priest Simon II (Sir 50,1–24), who was contemporary of Ben Sira, and, on the other hand, the absolute silence of the sage about the crisis of 167–164 BC.

https://doi.org/10.1515/9783110492316-004

and Mrs. Margaret Dunlop Gibson, the Hebrew text of Sir 39,15–40,7. Other equally important discoveries followed.

Between 1896 and 1900, experts identified many fragments of the book of Ben Sira. Like the first one, these fragments came from the Karaite synagogue of Old Cairo. They belong to four manuscripts (A, B, C and D) dated between the 10th and the 12th centuries AD. In 1931, Joseph Marcus discovered a fifth manuscript among the fragments of the Adler Collection at the Hebrew Theological Seminary of America, the so-called MS E. Some twenty years later, other discoveries were made at Qumran. In 1952, fragments of the book of Ben Sira were found in the second cave (2Q18), and three years later a scroll with an important fragment of our book was discovered in cave 11 (11QPs[a]). The latter is dated from before 69 AD. In 1958 and 1960, two discoveries of Jefim Schirmann completed respectively the texts of MSS B and C. In 1964, the excavations at Masada recovered a very deteriorated leather scroll (26 pieces) containing fragments of Sir 39,27–43,30, dated before 73 AD. Finally, in 1982, Alexander Scheiber found a part of a sixth manuscript (MS F), previously unknown. He published it in a Hungarian review that was scarcely noticed in international circles. His work made little impression until it was treated in Alexander Di Lella's commentary, which came out in 1987. The author then published the manuscript in a better-known biblical journal.

At present, we estimate that we have two thirds (68%) of the Hebrew text assembled from six manuscripts discovered in the *genizah* in Cairo and the fragments from Qumran and Masada[4]. Unfortunately, a large part of the text is still missing: Sir 1,1–3,5; 16,28–30,10 and 38,27–39,14. Among the lost sections, the most outstanding ones are: chapters 1–2 (on Wisdom and fear-of-the-Lord), chapter 24 (the praise of Wisdom) and 38,27–39,14 (a portrait of the sage).

1.2 Greek I (GkI)

The grandson of Ben Sira translated the work into Greek—this information is furnished by the anonymous author of the Prologue—during his stay in Egypt to in-

---

4 Cf. BEENTJES, Preliminary Remarks, 471–484. At the First International Ben Sira Conference, celebrated from 28 to 31 July 1996 in Soesterberg, near Utrecht (Netherlands), on the occasion of the centennial of the discovery of the first Hebrew manuscripts of the Hebrew text of Ben Sira, P.C. Beentjes announced that a new edition of the Hebrew text of Ben Sira would soon be published in the form of a synopsis [For updated information about this edition and the recent discoveries, cf. note 8 in our next study: Sirach and Inspiration].

struct the Jews of the Diaspora[5]. He accomplished his task between the years 132 and 117 (under the reign of Ptolomeus VII, Evergetes II: 170–164 and 146–117 AD)[6]. The text of this version is called GkI or short form of the text. It is attested by the large uncial codices (A, B, C, and S), written metrically by lines, and other minor ones.

1.3 Hebrew II (HbII)

The manuscripts found in Cairo do not present a unified text. On one hand, many passages are repeated in two (this is most frequent) or more manuscripts; and, on the other hand, the large number of variations lead exegetes to believe in the existence of a long form of the Hebrew text, called HbII. Dated between 50 and 150 AD it is characterized by its additions, and its best illustration is MS A. Concerning the origin of HbII, there are diverging opinions: Hart considers HbII to be a revised form of HbI that should be attributed to the Pharisees, whereas Kearns, basing himself on a consideration of the eschatology of the long form, defends its Essene origin. This second form of the Hebrew text—we only have a few samples of it—is the version on which GkII, VL and, in a confusing way, also the Syriac, version depend.

1.4 Greek II (GkII)

The long form of the Greek version, composed between the 1st century and the middle of the 2nd century AD, is called GkII and is represented by various minor manuscripts, among which the well-known codex 248 (cod. Vat. Gr. 347) stands out. The author did not provide a new translation, independent of GkI. On the contrary, he added to the original base text of GkI a word or groups of words (1,30e; 2,11a), lines (2,5c.9c; 12,6c; 16,18c; 18,33c) or entire verses (1,5.7; 3,19.25; 10,21; 11,15–16). With the exception of some lines of Greek origin, coming from the Alexandrine school of Aristobulus, the majority of them depend on the long form of the Hebrew text (HbII), which may have existed in one or more versions at the time that this compilation was produced.

---

5 For a general presentation of the translator and his work, see CADBURY, Grandson, 219–225.
6 These dates, now generally accepted by the majority of the authors, suppose that the Prologue is authentic. Nevertheless, cf. DIEBNER, Großvater, 1–37.

2 The Book of Ben Sira in Rabbinic Judaism

When the Rabbinic Pharisees definitively closed the Jewish canon, at the Synod of Jamnia in 90 AD, the book of Ben Sira officially lost the character of a sacred book[7]. However, in spite of its exclusion from the canon, the work of the sage continued to be widely read among the Jews for several generations. In fact, the book of Ben Sira is the only non-canonical work of the Talmud used as Sacred Scripture and classified among the hagiographers.

The Jewish canon, according to the information provided by Flavius Josephus[8], contains 22 books (Genesis, Exodus, Leviticus, Numbers, Deuteronomy; Joshua, Judges with Ruth, Samuel, Kings, Chronicles, Ezra with Nehemiah, Esther, Job, Isaiah, Jeremiah with Lamentations, Ezekiel, the minor prophets, Daniel; Psalms, Proverbs, Canticle, Qohelet). Their canonicity is based on the fact that they were composed during the period between Moses and Artaxerxes, i.e. before the end of the prophetic succession in Israel. According to t. Soṭah 13,2, "When Haggai, Zechariah and Malachi, the last prophets, died, ... the Holy Spirit disappeared from Israel".

Therefore, all the books written after the disappearance of the Holy Spirit are books that "do not contaminate the hands" because they are not sacred or canonical books. According to m. Yad. 2,13: "the Gospels and the books of the heretics do not contaminate the hands. The books of Ben Sira[9] and all the books that have been written later on do not contaminate the hands".

Another way of designating this category of books is the expression "exterior books" (those that do not form a part of the canon) in contrast to the "interior books" (the canonical ones); see R. Aqiba, below.

Despite this rigorous distinction between canonical and non-canonical (interior and exterior) books, the book of Ben Sira, along with other works not included in the canon, remained popular with many Jews, who continued to consider it and use it as Sacred Scripture.

Having come to this point and in order to gain a clearer vision of the situation of our book in Rabbinic Judaism and its successive evolution, it would be

---

7 Cf. LEWIS, Jabneh, 125–132; NEWMAN, Jamnia, 310–350; SCHÄFFER, Synode, 54–64; 116–124 and, in contrast, LEIMANN, Canonization, esp. 120–124.
8 C. Ap. 1,38–41.
9 According to Gilbert, these books refer to diverse forms of the book or to some collections. Cf. GILBERT, Introduction, 40.

important to distinguish between the period of the Tannaim—the repeaters (1ˢᵗ and 2ⁿᵈ century AD)—and the Amoraim—interpreters (8ᵗʰ century AD)[10].

At the time of the Tannaim, Ben Sira was probably a part of the scriptural canon. Let us look at some important proofs:

- In m. 'Abot 4,4, R. Levitas of Jamnia says: "Humiliate yourself extremely before others because what is waiting for man is the worm". The sentence is a quotation of Sir 7,17Hb: "More and more, humble your pride; what awaits man is worms"[11].
- In b. Pesaḥ. 113b, we hear: "Our rabbis have taught us: 'There are four things reason cannot support: a poor man who is proud, a rich man who acts lowly, an old man who commits adultery, the leader of a community who is a tyrant. Others add: that a man divorces once, twice, from his wife and takes her back again as his wife". This text is clearly an adaptation of Sir 25,2: "My soul hates three kinds of men, and I am greatly offended at their life: a beggar who is proud, a rich man who is a liar, and an adulterous old man who lacks good sense".
- In b. Yebam. 63b we find: "It is written in the book of Ben Sira: A good wife makes a happy husband! The number of his days will be doubled". Sir 26,1 says precisely: "Happy is the husband of a good wife; the number of his days will be doubled".

Despite these proofs, and others we must leave aside for lack of space and time, we must not neglect the discordant voice of the famous R. Aqiba († 135 AD) who spoke out against the book of Ben Sira in no uncertain terms. His opinion concerning the canonicity of Ben Sira as it appears in y. Sanh. 28a is forcefully expressed: "R. Aqiba adds: whoever reads the exterior books, books such as Ben Sira and the books of Ben Leaga ... has no part in the future world. ... A Tannait taught: this means the books of the heretics" (cf. m. Sanh. 10,1).

The hidden reasons behind this so strongly contrasting position have been thoroughly studied by Jacques Trublet in his article about the Hebrew canon[12]. According to him, it may be that R. Aqiba prohibited reading Ben Sira both because the book was popular among the Sadducees and Qumran and because it was used by authors of the New Testament. In other words, the fear in face of the

---

10 For this section, we are following Trublet, Constitution, 77–187, esp. 156–163, and use various of the texts he quotes.
11 The Greek version adds new elements: "Humble yourself greatly, for the punishment of the ungodly is fire and worms".
12 Cf. Trublet, Constitution, 158–161.

sectarian currents menacing Jewish orthodoxy incited the great Rabbi to take drastic measures for the sake of security.

Despite the opinion of R. Aqiba, who was a highly influential authority for other masters, the book of Ben Sira became very popular at the time of the Amoraim. Ignoring the teaching of R. Aqiba, the "repeaters" reintroduced the book of Ben Sira into their canon. We will now present some illustrative examples:

- In b. Sanh. 100b, R. Joseph († 333) declares in relation to a teaching concerning the heretic books: "It is forbidden to read the book of Ben Sira". However, later, after a long conversation with his disciple R. Abaye († 338/339), he admits: "The beautiful words that we find in it [the book of Ben Sira], we can teach them".

- In b. B. Qam. 92b, Rabah ben Meir, in his answer to a question asked by Rabah, places Ben Sira among the hagiographers: "[This idea] is written in the Torah, it is repeated in the Prophets and is mentioned for the third time in the Hagiographers: All the fools live close to someone who resembles them, and the man close to his like". The text of our sage says: "Every creature loves its own kind, and every person his or her neighbor" (Sir 13,15; cf. also 27,9).

- In b. Ḥag. 13a, in respect to the speculations about the division of heaven, R. Aha ben Jacob says: "You are allowed to go to this point in your speculations, but no further. This is what the book of Ben Sira says: Do not try to penetrate what is incomprehensible, nor to search for what is hidden from you. Give your attention only to what you are permitted to examine: you must not occupy yourself with secret things". Let us see what the text of Ben Sira actually says: "Seek not what is too difficult for you, nor investigate what is beyond your power. Reflect upon what has been assigned to you, for you do not need what is hidden" (Sir 3,21–22).

Once again, we have seen, through a few examples, the prominence given to our book in Jewish circles with the exception of R. Aqiba. Unfortunately, this popularity gradually diminished with the passing of time until, in the end, the book practically disappeared, probably at the time when the Talmud was compiled in the Jewish academies of the 5th century AD.

Let us now go on to the third part of our study, in which we will follow the tracks of Sirach in the life of the Church.

3 The Book of Ben Sira in the Primitive Church

The book of Ben Sira was very popular during the first centuries of Christianity. This is proven by its repercussion in the New Testament[13] and in the writings of the Church Fathers[14]. At the end of the 2nd and beginning of the 3rd centuries, the Church—in the East and in the West—practically recognizes the canonicity of Sirach: Tertullian and Cyprian, in Africa, and Clement of Alexandria in Egypt quote the texts of Sirach as Sacred Scripture. Here are a few examples.

TERTULLIAN
Nat. 2,2: Initium, inquit, sapientiae metus in deum (Sir 1,16)[15].

CYPRIAN
Test. 2,1: Ite apud eundem in Ecclesiastico (Sir 24,3 – 6.19; Vulg. 24,5 – 11.25.26)[16].

CLEMENT
Paed. 3,58,2: Κατὰ τὴν γραφὴν (Sir 21,21)[17].

This peaceful situation becomes troubled towards 170. Melito of Sardis went to Palestine in order to make a detailed study of the number and the order of the Old Testament books. When he returned, he opted for the Jewish canon (already fixed at that time) with its 22 books (Esther and the deuterocanonical books left aside). However, in spite of this clear preference for the Jewish canon, Melito continued quoting the deuterocanonical books in his writings[18]. Hence, it appears evident that the Christian canon (different from the Jewish one) still had not been officially established.

In Palestine and the surrounding regions, the situation is delicate: the cohabitation of the Jews and Christians clearly showed the canonical discrepancies. Origen (185 – 254) played a major role. He had a thorough knowledge of the Scriptures used in Alexandria and the Scriptures of the Jews. At the beginning of his Commentary on the Psalms he gave the list of the 22 books of the

---

13 Cf. CALDUCH-BENAGES, Nuevo Testamento, 305 – 316, esp. 306 – 307. The apostolic period, on the contrary, is much more obscure; cf. GILBERT, Introduction, 42 (on Did. 4,5; Barn. 19,9a = Sir 4,31 and Did. 1,6 = Sir 12,1a) and SKEHAN, Didache 1,6, 533 – 536.
14 For a global view, cf. VATTTIONI, Ecclesiastico, XXXII–LX; GILBERT, Introduction, 41 – 47.
15 CSEL 20,95.
16 CSEL 31/1,62.
17 SC 158,122.
18 In his Treatise on the Passover (SC 132,60 – 127), Melito quotes the book of Wisdom (18 times) and Sirach (twice).

Jewish canon without mentioning the deuterocanonical ones[19]. This silence may have reflected his reticence about those books that were not integrated into the Jewish canon[20], i.e. the "exterior books". According to Eusebius, Origen made the following assertion: "And besides these there are the Maccabees, which are entitled Σαρβὴθ Σαρβανὲ Ἐλ"[21]. However, in spite of his doubts, Origen quotes Sirach as Sacred Scripture:

> Hom. Gen. 12,5: Audi enim quid dicit Scriptura (Sir 22,19)[22].
>
> Hom. Jer. 16,6: λεγούσης τῆς γραφῆς (Sir 8,5)[23].

Origen paves the way for us to understand the different opinions of the Fathers of the 4th century and the beginning of the 5th. This period is characterized by disagreements about the canonicity of the book of Ben Sira.

Cyril of Jerusalem (315?–387), in his fourth Catechetical lecture: "De decem dogmatibus" (written in the course of 350) devoted one section to Holy Scripture[24]. In this passage, he asserted the inspired nature of the Old and the New Testament, categorically prohibited the reading of apocryphal books (ἀμφιβαλλόμενα, "converted books") and recognized the books accepted by everyone (παρὰ πᾶσιν ὁμολογούμενα), i.e. the 22 books of the Old Testament according to the Jewish canon. However, these books are not to be read in the order of the Hebrew text, but in that of the inspired version of the LXX (including Baruch, the Letter of Jeremiah and probably the Greek additions of Esther and Daniel). Thus, thanks to the LXX, the Jewish books became a part of the Christian tradition. Cyril quotes Sirach eight times and without any introduction, except in one of his Mystagogical catecheses: Καὶ πῶς εἴρηται ἀλλαχοῦ (Sir 31[34Hb],9–10)[25].

A few years later (367), Athanasius, after having spoken about the exterior books (ἕτερα βίβλια τούτων ἔξωθεν) in his 39th Festal Letter[26], discussed the meaning of the term "apocrypha" used by Cyril in his 4th Catechetical lecture. According to Athanasius, this word does not designate the deuterocanonical books but rather recent works composed by wicked men and heretics who attempt "to

---

19 PG 12,1084BC.
20 On this subject, cf. RUWET, Antilegomena, 18–54.
21 Hist. eccl. 6,25,27–29 (PL 20,518A). However, in his letter to Julian the African (Ep. Afr. 8–9), Origen expressed himself much more explicitly; cf. SC 302,532–535.
22 SC 7/1,308.
23 SC 238,148.
24 PG 33,494C–502A.
25 Catech. myst. 5,17 (SC 126,164).
26 Ep. fest. 39 (PG 26,143B–1440A).

mix them up with the divinely inspired Scripture" (ἐπιμίξαι ταῦτα τῇ θεοπνύστῳ Γραφῇ). He immediately presented the list of the 22 books of the Jewish canon (excluding Esther and including Baruch and the Letter of Jeremiah). Further on, he indicates the non-canonical books. Now, here comes the surprise: he recommends reading these writings to those "who wish for instruction in the word of godliness" (βουλομένοις κατηχεῖσθαι τὸν τῆς εὐσεβείας λόγον)[27]. The books mentioned are: Wisdom, Sirach, Esther, Judith, Tobias, the Didache of the Apostles and the Pastor of Hermas. In practice, Athanasius also considered Sirach as Sacred Scripture:

Ep. Aeg. Lib. 3: τὰ ὑπὸ τοῦ Πνεύματος εἰς αὐτον εἰρημένα (Ps 49,16) καὶ (Sir 15,9)[28].

C. Ar. 2,79: Εἰ δὲ ἐστιν, ὥσπερ οὖν καὶ ὁ τοῦ Σιράχ φησὶν (Sir 1,9–10)[29].

Epiphanius of Salamina (ca. 315–403) retained the distinction between the canonical books and those only destined for the instruction of catechumens (useful and beneficial books). The later are not a part of Scripture "because they were not placed in the chest that is in the Ark of the Covenant"[30]. On the contrary, in the Panarion (Adversus haereses), he considered Sirach to be a sacred text: "… [having gone through] the books of Wisdom, that is the books of Solomon and of the son of Sira, and in a word, all the books of the Scriptures…"[31]. In practice, Epiphanius quotes Sirach as Sacred Scripture:

Pan. 33,8: (Sir 13,16) φησὶν ἡ φραφή.

Pan. 42,11: τίς αὐτῷ κρημνὸν περιποιεῖ, πληρῶν τὸ γεγραμμένον, τὸ· (Sir 14,5)[32].

In the Church of Cappadocia, Gregory of Nazianzus (330–390) faithfully followed the teaching of Athanasius[33]. In his poem, *De Veteris Scripturae libris*, he reproduces the list of the 22 book of the Old Testament according to the Jewish canon and then, after indicating the books of the New Testament, concludes:

---

27 Cf. RUWET, Canon, 12–13. The author believes that Athanasius is echoing a practice already in force in the Church of Antioch: have the catechumens read the easier books.
28 PG 25,541C–544A.
29 PG 26,313BC.
30 Mens. et pond. 4: Διὸ δὲ ἐν τῷ Ἀαρὼν ἀνετέθησαν, τοῦ τε ἐν τῇ τῆς διαθήκης κιβωτῷ (PG 43,244C).
31 Pan. 76,22: … ἔν τε ταῖς Σοφίαις Σολομῶντός τέ φημὶ καὶ υἱοῦ Σειράχ, καὶ πάσαις ἁπλῶς γραφαῖς θείαις… (GCS III,369).
32 GCS I,458 and GCS II,152.
33 Cf. GILBERT, Grégoire, 307–314.

"You have them all. If another book is found outside of these, it is not a part of the authentic ones"[34]. In spite of this final assertion, in practice Gregory did not question the authenticity of Sirach and quoted it as Sacred Scripture:

> Sermo 4,12: ...καὶ ἀνυπονόητον κοσμῶν διαδήματι παρὰ τῆς θείας καὶ τοῦτο λαμβάνω Γραφῆς (Sir 11,5b)[35].

> Sermo 32,21: εἰ ἔστι σοι λόγος συνέσεως, ἀποκρίθητί, φησι, καὶ οὐδεις ὁ κωλίσων· εἰ δὲ μὴ, δεσμὸς κείσθω σοῖς χείλεσι (Sir 5,12)[36].

Jerome, in his "Praefatio in libros Salomonis iuxta LXX interpretes", admitted to Paula and Eustachio that he does not want to translate the books of Wisdom and Sirach[37]. In his "Praefatio in libros Samuel et Malachim"—the so-called "Prologus galeatus", written in 391—he enumerated the 22 books of the OT according to the Jewish canon. He placed the other writings among the apocrypha[38]. Six years later (397), in the "Praefatio in libros Salomonis", he asserted that in the view of the Church the books of Wisdom and Sirach are not canonical. In any case, he recommended their reading for the spiritual edification of the Christian people (in the liturgy). Nevertheless, these books (like Judith, Tobit and Maccabees) were not to be used as authoritative sources to resolve dogmatic disputes[39].

This strong stance contrasts with Jerome's practice. In many cases, he quotes Sirach as Sacred Scripture[40]. This is the case, for example, in his Treatise against Jovinianus, where after quoting Sir 26,6 without any introduction, he goes on to the text of Sir 2,1 with the well-known formula: *et in alio loco scribitur*[41].

We are going to end this historical survey with a very significant fact: while Jerome excluded the apocryphal books from the canon, the African churches of

---

34 See the original text: Πάσας ἔχεις. Εἴ τι δὲ τούτων ἐκτὸς, οὐκ ἐν γνησίαις (PG 37,474A).
35 SC 309,104.
36 SC 318,128.
37 Porro in eo libro, quia a plurisque Sapientia Salomonis inscribitur, et in Ecclesiastico, quem esse Jesu filii Sirach, nullus ignorat, calamo temperavi: tantummodo canonicas Scripturas vobis emendare desiderans, et studium meum certis, magis quam dubiis comendar (PL 29,427A–428A).
38 Ut scire valeamus quidquid extra hos est, inter ἀπόκρυφα esse ponendum. Igitur Sapientia, quae vulgo Salomonis inscribitur, et Jesu filii Sirach liber et Judith, et Tobias, et Pastor, non sunt in Canone (PL 28,600B–602A).
39 Sicut ergo Judith et Tobi, et Machabaeorum libros legit quidem Ecclesia, sed inter canonicas Scripturas non recipit: sic et haec duo volumina legat ad edificationem plebis, non ad auctoritatem ecclesiasticorum dogmatum confirmandum (PL 28,1308A).
40 Cf. VATTIONI, San Gerolamo, 131–149; GILBERT, Jérôme, 109–120.
41 Jov. 2,3 (PL 23,300A).

the same period recognized their canonicity. The list of the canonical Scriptures of the Council of Hippo (393) mentioned "the five books of Solomon" (Wisdom and Sirach were implicitly included). The same list continued to be in force at the third Council of Carthage (397). The position of Augustine on this subject is in perfect harmony with the principles indicated at the mentioned councils. He participated in them as a priest in Hippo and as a bishop in Carthage[42].

Our brief survey shows that the first Christian centuries included some who followed the canon of the Hebrew scriptures while others used the broader canon derived from the Septuagint. The book of Ben Sira had broad support from both groups as worthy of attention.

A dozen centuries later, the Council of Florence (1442), in the "Decretum pro Iacobitis", adopted the list from the third Council of Carthage[43]. The same line was followed by the Council of Trent (1546). In the "Decretum de libris sacris et de traditionibus recipiendis" once again reproduces the list of the canon of the Council of Florence and, in addition, rejects all distinctions of categories between the books of the Hebrew canon and the writings found only in the Greek or Latin Bible:

> (Ecclesia) omnes libros tam Veteris quam Novi Testamenti, cum utriusque unus Deus sit auctor, nec non traditiones ipsas, tum ad fidem, tum ad mores pertinentes, tamquam vel oretenus a Christo, vel a Spiritu Sancto dictatas et continua successione in Ecclesia catholica conservatas, pari pietatis affectu ac reverentia suscipit et veneratur[44].

4 Concluding Reflections

Both in the Jewish and in the Christian circles, we have found the attitude towards the canonicity of the book of Ben Sira to be very inconsistent. Many authors who, in theory denied the sacred character of the book, in practice quoted it as Sacred Scripture and used it to re-enforce their views, teachings and even social behavior. In fact, the rigid distinction between the interior and exterior books leaves much to be desired, because many works belong both to the first group as well as to the second one. In others words, they are situated on the fringe of the canon. The case we have presented is a good example of this.

According to the declaration of the Council of Trent (see above), the canonicity of Sirach is guaranteed. Now, let us remember that the work of Ben Sira has

---

42 Cf. ZARB, De historia canonis, 184–187.
43 Cf. DENZINGER–SCHÖNMETZER, Enchiridon, no. 1335.
44 Cf. DENZINGER–SCHÖNMETZER, Enchiridon, nos. 1501–1505.

been transmitted to us, without counting the versions, in two different languages (Hebrew and Greek) and in two different textual forms (the short form: HbI-GkI and the long form: HbII-GkII). Hence, we may ask: Which text is canonical?[45] Is it the short text written by Ben Sira and translated into Greek by his grandson or the long version, the augmented revision of the first text, which is the work of anonymous authors? Do we need to choose one and exclude the other? The Council of Trent did not make any allusion to the book of Sirach, but when it speaks of *libros integros cum omnibus suis partibus*[46], we can understand that the judgment applies to both versions of the text.

Speaking of the canon inevitably leads to the discussion of inspiration. In our case, which text—or texts—are to be treated as inspired by the Holy Spirit? Is it only the Greek text transmitted by the Church or also all the portions of the Hebrew manuscripts found in Cairo, Qumran and Masada? If we cannot deny the inspiration of the sage Ben Sira, author of the lost Hebrew original, we cannot deny that of his grandson either, because the latter did not limit himself to translating the work of his grandfather; rather, he adapted it to the circumstances of that moment, by both deepening and modifying its theological contents. Moreover, we cannot deny the inspiration of the long form, which is generally more profound, spiritual and appealing to Christians than the first text; and in addition, this long form is quoted by the Church Fathers (Clement of Alexandria and Cyprian).

Hence, should we talk about an inspired double text or of two equally inspired stages of the text? We are inclined towards the second answer and conclude by making ours the words of Maurice Gilbert: "There are two stages of the book of Ben Sira, and both are canonical, because both one and the other are inspired"[47].

---

45 Cf. GILBERT, Ecclésiastique, 233 – 250.

46 Cf. DENZINGER–SCHÖNMETZER, Enchiridon, no. 1504: Si quis autem libros ipsos integros cum omnibus suis partibus, prout in Ecclesia catholica legi consueverunt et in veteri vulgata latina editione habentur, pro sacris et canonicis non susceperit, et traditiones praedictas sciens et prudens contempserit: anathema sit.

47 GILBERT, Ecclésiastique, 248: "Il y a deux états du livre de Ben Sira, et ces deux états sont l'un et l'autre canoniques, parce que l'un et l'autre sont inspirés".

Sirach and Inspiration

Sirach (Ecclesiasticus or the book of Ben Sira)[1] is a very unusual deuterocanonical book on account of its complex textual evolution. Written in Hebrew and then translated into Greek, as well as into Latin and Syriac, it presents two different forms of the text, one long, one short, and that in both Hebrew and Greek. In the face of this textual situation, several questions arise regarding the theme of our study: Must we choose between the two textual forms? If so, which form is preferable? Which is canonical? Which is inspired? Both of them? If we abide by the definition of Trent (*libros ipsos integros cum omnibus suis partibus, prout in Ecclesia catholica legi consueverunt et in veteri vulgata latina edizione habentur*), then both forms of the text can be held to be canonical and inspired. Moreover, with the mention of the Vulgate, there is reference, even if implicit, to the long text which is used in the liturgy[2]. However, let us analyse the question more closely.

1 Brief History of the Evolution of the Text

The sage Ben Sira wrote his book in Hebrew (HbI) around 185 BC in Jerusalem where he ran a kind of school or academy for the young men of well-to-do families. In 132 BC, his grandson, who had gone to Alexandria in Egypt, decided to translate his grandfather's work into Greek (GkI) for the Jews of the diaspora, as he explains in his Prologue[3]:

> In the thirty-eighth year of King Euergetes, I too came to Egypt and stayed for a while; having discovered that the writing is of great educational value, I thought it necessary to use it and to translate it with scrupulous care (lines 27–30).

In the 1st century, the Hebrew original was enlarged with additions that were probably Essene in origin (HbII). During the 1st century and the first half of the 2nd century AD, this text was translated into Greek and enlarged with Greek and Alexandrian additions, some of them coming from the school of

---

1 For a status quaestionis of research on Sirach, cf. GILBERT, Études, 161–181.
2 Cf. GILBERT, Ecclésiastique, 233–250; CALDUCH-BENAGES, Canon, 359–370.
3 In the great uncial codices: Vaticanus and Sinaiticus of the 4th century, and Alexandrinus of the 5th century. Cf. ZIEGLER, Sapientia, 123–126.

https://doi.org/10.1515/9783110492316-005

Aristobulus, a Jewish-Hellenistic philosopher of the 2nd century AD (GkII)[4]. This contains 135 cola more than GkI. Before 200 AD, a Christian from North Africa translated GkII + GkI (chs. 1–43 + 51) into Latin (Vetus Latina)[5]. This text was then incorporated into the Vulgate because Jerome refused to translate the Hebrew text of Ben Sira, which he said that he had seen, although we do not know whether he was referring to HbI or HbII. Then, in the 3rd century AD, there appeared the Syriac version, the Peshitta, made from a Hebrew text, probably HbII[6], and, in the 7th century, the Syriac version of the Greek Hexaplaric text of the school of Origen (MS 253), that is, of GkII.

Excluded from the Jewish canon on the grounds that it was written after the disappearance of the prophetic spirit[7], the Hebrew text of Ben Sira continued nonetheless to enjoy a certain amount of consideration, as is inferred from the numerous citations in the rabbinic and Talmudic literature. Be that as it may, the book disappeared mysteriously, perhaps in the 5th century with the birth of the Talmudic schools, and it was preserved only in the grandson's translation and in the successive translations cited above.

Thanks to the discoveries begun in 1896 in the Genizah of the Cairo synagogue and later continued at Qumran, Masada and in the Taylor-Schechter Genizah Research Unit in the Cambridge University Library, today we have available almost 70 % of the Hebrew text distributed among several medieval manuscripts (A, B, C, D, E, F) plus those from Qumran, dated before 69 AD and the one from Masada, from before 73 AD[8].

In the vernacular editions of the Bible, the text recorded is generally the translation of the Greek version of Sirach or short text (GkI), because it is the text of the Septuagint (and, besides, it is a complete text). Only in some editions does the long text of the Greek version appear (GkII) or is marked out in italics

---

4 In the Lucianic recension (MSS 248, 493 e 637) and in the Origenic recension (MS 253) to which are added the "Sacra Parallella" attributed to John Damascene (676–749 AD). Cf. PRATO, Lumière, 317–346.

5 THIELE (ed.), Sirach. From Sir 25 on, the edition has been prepared by Anthony Forte.

6 CALDUCH-BENAGES—J. FERRER—J. LIESEN, Wisdom of the Scribe.

7 Cf. t. Soṭah 13,2: "When Haggai, Zechariah and Malachi, the last prophets died, the Holy Spirit disappeared from Israel". Ben Sira is, therefore, an excluded book which does not defile/soil the hands (since it is not a sacred book, the rites of ablution before and after its reading are not required). Rabbi Aqiba, who died in 135 AD, was a great opponent of Sirach. Cf. TRUBLET, Constitution, 77–187.

8 Cf. BEENTJES, Book; ID., Errata, 375–377. Obviously, this edition does not record the recent discoveries in 2007 (fragments of MS C), cf. ELIZUR, A New Fragment, 17–28; RÉY, Bifeuillet, 387–416; in 2011 (fragments of MS D), cf. ELIZUR, Two New Leaves, 13–29; and in 2015 (a small fragment of MS A), cf. REYMOND, New Hebrew Text, 83–98.

(cf. the Bible of the Italian Episcopal Conference, 2008; la Biblia de Jerusalén, 1998; la Sagrada Biblia of the Spanish Episcopal Conference, 2010) or else in notes (New Revised Standard Version).

2 The Content of the Book and Inspiration

Let us now consider some elements regarding the content of the book which to some extent are evidence of the inspiration of the text, first in the short form and then in the long one.

2.1 The Short Form

2.1.1 Authority of the Sage and of Wisdom

The first element to be dealt with is the authority of the sage and of Wisdom. In Sirach, as in the rest of the sapiential literature, there are no formulae of revelation as in the prophetic books ("oracle of the Lord" or "thus says the Lord"), or accounts of a calling, or signs from God. However, the sage/father/master addresses his disciples/sons with authoritative words. His authority is based not just on his experience and his knowledge of scripture and of tradition, but also on his personal relationship with God in assiduous and fervent prayer. The sage is a person who is dedicated first and foremost to "meditating on the law of the Most High", and it is precisely the Most High, if he considers it appropriate, who will give him a "spirit of understanding" (cf. Is 11,2) and "words of wisdom" so as to be able to direct his pupils in their humane and religious education:

5	τὴν καρδίαν αὐτοῦ ἐπιδώσει ὀρθρίσαι
	πρὸς κύριον τὸν ποιήσαντα αὐτὸν
	καὶ ἔναντι ὑψίστου δεηθήσεται·
	καὶ ἀνοίξει στόμα αὐτοῦ ἐν προσευχῇ
	καὶ περὶ τῶν ἁμαρτιῶν αὐτοῦ δεηθήσεται.
6	ἐὰν κύριος ὁ μέγας θελήσῃ,
	πνεύματι συνέσεως ἐμπλησθήσεται·
	αὐτὸς ἀνομβρήσει ῥήματα σοφίας αὐτοῦ
	καὶ ἐν προσευχῇ ἐξομολογήσεται κυρίῳ·
7	αὐτὸς κατευθυνεῖ βουλὴν καὶ ἐπιστήμην
	καὶ ἐν τοῖς ἀποκρύφοις αὐτοῦ διανοηθήσεται·
8	αὐτὸς ἐκφανεῖ παιδείαν διδασκαλίας αὐτοῦ
	καὶ ἐν νόμῳ διαθήκης κυρίου καυχήσεται.

5   Early in the morning, he directs his heart
    to the Lord, who has created him,
    and he prays before the Most High;
    and he opens his mouth in prayer,
    and he makes supplication for his sins.
6   If this is the will of the great Lord,
    he will be filled with the spirit of understanding;
    like rain he will pour forth words of wisdom,
    and in prayer he will render praise to the Lord;
7   he will direct his counsel and his knowledge,
    and he will meditate on the mysteries of God;
8   he will make the doctrine of his teaching to shine,
    and he will make his boast in the covenant of the Lord (Sir 39,5 – 8).

Wisdom too, that mysterious figure who escapes all definition, speaks and acts with an authority which comes from on high: "I came out of the mouth of the Most High and like a mist I covered the earth" (Sir 24,3). She is, therefore, being presented as the word of God which fills the universe. Moreover, we do not find any other character in the Old Testament who is presented as the source of life and salvation. A self-referential discourse of this kind is found uniquely on the lips of Wisdom. Lady Wisdom speaks in the first person and of her own accord in inviting, exhorting, teaching, motivating, stimulating and attracting those who desire her, love her and seek her: "Those who eat me will hunger for more; those who drink me will still be thirsty" (Sir 24,20).

2.1.2 Wisdom, Fear-of-the-Lord and the Law
The second relevant element is the trio "wisdom, fear-of-the-Lord and the Law", which are the three pillars on which the theological content of the book leans. In Sir 19,20 we read: "All wisdom is fear-of-the-Lord, and in all wisdom there is the practice of the law". To obtain the wisdom that comes from God, there is need of the-fear-of-the-Lord, an interior disposition which allows the pupil to come near to God and which is made concrete in the observance of the divine law. In this way, one who seeks Wisdom seeks God, and one who finds Wisdom finds God.

In other words, by contrast with Hellenistic wisdom, the wisdom taught by Ben Sira is profoundly religious, anchored in the tradition of a people who believe in the one God, creator of the universe.

2.1.3 Appeal to Tradition
Third, by appealing to tradition, Ben Sira connects himself with his people's past in a way that is direct, incisive, and effective for his young disciples. His teaching

is not the exclusive fruit of personal reflection and experience but is guaranteed and supported by a long tradition which, in its narratives and in its prayers, proclaims untiringly the infinite wisdom, love and mercy of the Lord. The history of Israel and the teaching of the sage converge in the same theological and didactic objective: to convince the pupil that the Lord does not disappoint the one who trusts in him, does not abandon the one who fears him, and does not forsake the one who calls upon him.

10 ἐμβλέψατε εἰς ἀρχαίας γενεὰς καὶ ἴδετε·
     τίς ἐνεπίστευσεν κυρίῳ καὶ κατῃσχύνθη;
     ἢ τίς ἐνέμεινεν τῷ φόβῳ αὐτοῦ καὶ ἐγκατελείφθη;
     ἢ τίς ἐπεκαλέσατο αὐτόν, καὶ ὑπερεῖδεν αὐτόν;
11 διότι οἰκτίρμων καὶ ἐλεήμων ὁ κύριος
     καὶ ἀφίησιν ἁμαρτίας καὶ σῴζει ἐν καιρῷ θλίψεως.

10 Consider the ancient generations and reflect:
     Who trusted in the Lord and turned out disappointed?
     Or who persevered in his fear and was abandoned?
     Or who called on him and was overlooked?
11 For the Lord is compassionate and merciful,
     he forgives sins and saves in time of tribulation (Sir 2,10–11; cf. 44–50)[9].

2.2 The Long Form

2.2.1 Its Anthropological and Spiritual Character

The long form presents an anthropological and spiritual character that is very marked. In his doctoral thesis on the Greek additions in Sirach, Severino Bussino has recently demonstrated that a great part of the additions "are concerned, in the first place, with discourse on [humanity], in particular with regard to [its] relationship with God, to right conduct chiefly in connection with the gifts and the action of God rather than at the level of social relationships which, however, are not absent"[10]. An example is to be found in Sir 2,5c:

ἐν νόσοις καὶ πενίᾳ ἐπ'αὐτῷ πεποιθὼς γίνου.

In sickness and in poverty, place your trust in him.

---

9 For what concerns Sir 2,10–11, cf. CALDUCH-BENAGES, Crisol, 123–148 and EAD., Gioiello, 80–96.
10 BUSSINO, Additions, 416–417.

This addition is inserted just before the conclusion of Sir 2,1–6, a passage composed of two strophes: vv. 1–3 (the pupil facing trial) and vv. 4–6 (the divine help). Even if 2,5c contains vocabulary foreign to chapter 2 and does not fit well into the argumentation of 2,4–6 (apodosis, motivation, conclusion), its object is to underline the salvific action of the Lord with regard to those who have placed their trust in him[11]. The advice of a general character in 2,4 ("Accept whatever is brought upon you, and in changes that humble you be patient") is made concrete by reflecting on two situations of great human suffering: illness and poverty. With these two concrete examples, the author of the gloss places the emphasis on the trust that is to be placed in God and in his help, in particular in times of the greatest tribulation[12].

2.2.2 Its Theological Dimension

The theological dimension of the text asserts that God is present and active in the lives of those who seek Wisdom:

μαστιγῶν ἐλεῶν τύπτων ἰώμενος
κύριος ἐν οἰκτιρμῷ καὶ παιδείᾳ διεφύλαξεν

Striking, pardoning, smiting, healing,
the Lord kept watch with mercy and discipline (Sir 16,10cd).

These verses have been inserted by way of a summary at the end of Sir 16,1–16 ("God chastises the ungodly"), a section which completes the one devoted to the question of human freedom (15,1–20). After the allusion to some episodes in the history of Israel (16,5–10ab), the addition "describes God's action by means of a series of contrasting binomes"[13] (cf. 18,13 and 16,11cd): on the one hand, he strikes and smites; on the other hand, he pardons and heals. Like a good pedagogue, God responds to human action in a just way: with mercy or discipline according to the circumstances of the case[14].

---

11 Cf. CALDUCH-BENAGES, Crisol, 68–69.
12 Cf. BUSSINO, Additions, 69–72.
13 ROSSETTI, Aggiunte, 634.
14 Cf. BUSSINO, Additions, 169–176.

2.2.3 The Love of God

GkII puts the emphasis on the love of God (by contrast with the short form) understood as the love of God for humans and the love of humans for God. A significant example is Sir 25,12ab:

φόβος κυρίου ἀρχὴ ἀγαπήσεως αὐτοῦ,
πίστις δὲ ἀρχὴ κολλήσεως αὐτοῦ.

The fear of the Lord is the beginning of love for him
and trust is the beginning of cleaving to him.

The series of ten beatitudes in Sir 25,7–10 ends thus: "The fear-of-the-Lord is worth more than anything; who can be compared to the one who possesses it?" (v. 10b). Not satisfied with this conclusion, the author of the gloss adds a further comment in which he plays on a double parallelism: fear of God/trust in God and love for God/closeness to God. He stresses four religious dispositions required of those who seek Wisdom: the faithful one who fears God expresses this fear in love and reveals this trust in clinging to him personally. In this way, the author of the gloss draws on the teaching of the sage that authentic fear-of-the-Lord is always to be understood as a necessary correlative of love for and intimacy with God[15].

2.2.4 Life Post Mortem

The life of the hereafter, a novelty where the shorter form is concerned, is present in at least eight cola where the eschatological component is inserted within the relationship between humanity and God. We take Sir 16,22c as an example:

καὶ ἐξέτασις ἁπάντων ἐν τελευτῇ.

And the examination of everything (will take place) at the end.

In Sir 16,17–23, Ben Sira is responding to the objection that God pays no attention to human affairs (v. 17). His response is developed in two stages, vv. 18–19 and vv. 20–22, then comes to a conclusion in v. 23. Verse 22 is certainly obscure: "Who will announce the acts of justice or who will await them, if the covenant is still far off?". The works of justice which people perform seem to have no effect where God is concerned (no one announces them; no one awaits them), because the fulfillment of the covenant (διαθήκη) is thought to be remote and inconsequential. The Greek term διαθήκη translates the Hebrew חק ("statute", "law")

---

15 Cf. CALDUCH-BENAGES, Crisol, 205–207; BUSSINO, Additions, 381–390.

which, in 14,12, refers to death ("the statute of Sheol"). This is also the understanding of the author of the gloss in 22c, who wishes to explain Ben Sira's teaching further by mentioning the role of God at the Last Judgement. Making use of a vocabulary typical of the book of Wisdom, he affirms that, at the end, everything will be subjected to the judgement of God, even if this is not apparent at the present time[16].

3 The Testimony of Tradition

After having examined the content of our book, which does not claim direct inspiration by God, we pass on now to the question of how it was received by the Church. The patristic citations confirm that Sirach was cited by the Fathers both in the short form (GkI) and the long one (GkII and Vetus Latina), in confirmation of the inspired character of both. In the words of M. Gilbert: "That is equivalent to saying that the Church acknowledges two traditions, but also that the canonicity and inspiration of the long text cannot be denied"[17].

We shall see some examples taken from the Greek and Latin Fathers[18]. Clement of Alexandria and Cyprian of Carthage confirm the sacred and inspired character of the long form of Sirach by using the formulas "according to Scripture" or "as Scripture says". The former quotes the long form in Greek (Sir 26,22 in Paed. 2,98,2), the latter in Latin (Sir 24,25b in Test. 2,1)[19].

Later, Jerome, even though he was generally unfavourable to the deuterocanonical books[20], cites Sirach more than 40 times, but, instead of using the Vetus Latina, he follows GkI, the short form, which he translates into Latin. For example, in his Treatise against Jovinianus, after citing Sir 26,6 without any introduction, he uses the well-known formula *et in alio loco scribitur* (Jov. 2,3) to introduce Sir 21,1. On the other hand, his contemporary, John Chrysostom quotes the long text (Sir 2,5c in Adv. Jud. 8,6)[21].

We conclude this brief selection of examples with Augustine who cites both the short (Sir 15,11–17 in Grat. 1,2,3) and the long forms (Sir 3,7a in Spec. 240).

---

16 Cf. BUSSINO, Additions, 194–197.
17 GILBERT, Études, 180.
18 Cf. GILBERT, Jesus Sirach, 888–904; CALDUCH-BENAGES, Padres, 199–215.
19 Cf., respectively, SC 108,186 and CCL 3,28.
20 Cf. his "Praefatio in libros Salomonis iuxta LXX interpretes" (PL 29,427A–428A), where he admits he refused to translate the books of Wisdom and Sirach. For the Wisdom of Solomon, cf. POCK, Sapientia Salomonis.
21 Cf., respectively, PL 23,300A and PG 48,936.

4 Concluding Reflections

Twenty-five years ago, in a famous study on the canonicity and inspiration of the two textual forms ("les deux états du texte") of Sirach[22], M. Gilbert defended the possibility that there could be two different inspired texts for one and the same biblical book. There are two key points around which he develops his analysis: the Church has never defined in what language a text is canonical and inspired nor even (where there is more than one text) which form of the text is canonical and inspired. Taking our cue from Gilbert's careful argument and from the results of our own research, we will suggest a similar conclusion.

Which is, or what are, the texts of Sirach which are inspired by the Spirit? Are they the texts which contain the short form or the texts which contain the long form? One thing is certain: we cannot deny the inspiration of the original author, Ben Sira, even if today we only have a fragmentary Hebrew text of his work. However, we cannot deny the inspiration of his grandson, who did not limit himself to translating his grandfather's work into Greek but adapted it to new historical circumstances and enriched it by adding his own theological re-flection. Moreover, we cannot deny the inspiration of the long form of the text which is generally more profound from the anthropological and spiritual point of view than the short text, nearer to Christian thought, and directly quoted by Fathers of the Church.

Independently of the language, therefore, the two forms of the book of Ben Sira (the short one written by the sage and translated by his grandson, on the one hand, and the successive additions found in the long text transmitted by Church tradition, on the other) are both to be held as canonical and inspired.

Even if the conclusion we have reached is about the book of Sirach, which we have taken as an example of the problem of inspiration in the deutero-can-onical corpus, it is valid also for the books of Tobit, Daniel and Esther, and, ul-timately, for all the other biblical writings which are found in multiple textual forms[23].

---

22 GILBERT, Ecclésiastique, 233–250.
23 Cf. BOGAERT, Formes, 66–77.

Part II. **Thematic Essays**

Trial Motif in the Book of Ben Sira with Special Reference to Sir 2,1–6

Human beings are subject to trials, challenges, and dangers from the time they are conceived in their mother's womb until death, the final test of human character. Life challenges them to resist dangers, obstacles, limitations, and the threat of suffering and death. Active resistance requires three things: a real defense of the higher values, an untiring struggle to put them into practice, and constant reflection on their nature and their effect on history. Trials arise from both outer and inner sources. On the one hand, human beings must face all kinds of external threats to their personal integrity. On the other hand, they also need to deal with the self-made limitations that derive from failing to develop their own personal powers.

The purpose of this paper is to explore the motif of trial in the Book of Ben Sira. The sage reflects upon various kinds of trials that humans endure, but his perspective is always oriented toward a spiritual dimension. For Ben Sira, the reality of being put to the test touches the most intimate level of human existence and opens a door to a personal encounter with the Creator. We will approach the subject by studying the most significant texts of the sage's work beginning with Sir 2,1–6.

1 Prepare Yourself for Testing (Sir 2,1–6)

From a thematic point of view, Sir 1–2 develops gradually and logically. The book opens with a beautiful poem about Wisdom, which appears as God's attribute, as the world's quality and as the gift of God to those who love him. It is followed by another poem about the close relationship between wisdom and fear-of-God. With attractive imagery, the author describes fear-of-God as the beginning, fullness, crown and root of Wisdom. The presentation of the two pillars of the book (wisdom and fear-of-God) is suddenly interrupted by a parenetic section. The parenesis opens with a frontal attack on impatience—and proceeds with a presentation of the necessary qualities to reach wisdom (patience, loyalty to the Law, sincerity and humility).

I acknowledge the help of Jan Liesen, who translated the Spanish original into English.

https://doi.org/10.1515/9783110492316-006

At this point in the introductory chapters, the field is prepared for the first and main condition for the disciple to meet wisdom, i.e. the fear-of-God[1]. Sir 1 narrates in a poetic way the origin of wisdom and her close relationship with fear-of-God. However, in the second chapter, Ben Sira shifts to a personal level and describes the disciple's attitude towards God. In other words, Sir 2 complements the former exposition with a deeply religious poem illustrating the relationship between God and the faithful. As the sapiential discourse progresses, the features of fear-of-God become more precise and its demands more explicit. What does it really mean to fear God? What are its benefits and its disadvantages? Ben Sira answers such questions by unfolding a vision of authentic spiritual life, which rounds off the presentation of wisdom that began in Sir 1. Moral, social and cultural themes are treated throughout the book after these fundamental concerns are introduced. The conclusion of Sir 1 – 2 is evident: the search for wisdom is a religious task that has a profound impact on all aspects of life.

Sir 2,1 – 18 is a lively exhortation, addressed to those who come forward as disciples of wisdom. It is organized into four sections: a. the presence of trials (vv. 1 – 6); b. the divine mercy (vv. 7 – 14); c. the behaviour of the faithful person (vv. 15 – 17); and d. in the hands of the Lord (v. 18)[2]. In this parenetic appeal, the sage introduces the young disciples to his program of wisdom with extraordinary pedagogic skill. His program is complex, but well planned and accurately articulated. It encompasses clear objectives, strong motivations, adequate means, examples to imitate, and obstacles and difficulties to overcome. It presupposes freedom of choice; it envisages final results; it looks forward to rewards and punishments.

Ben Sira opens his exhortation with a peculiar invitation (Τέκνον, εἰ προσέρχῃ δουλεύειν κυρίῳ, ἑτοίμασον τὴν ψυχήν σου εἰς πειρασμόν, "My son, if you come to serve the Lord, prepare your soul for testing"). This peculiar initial formulation announces the *Leitmotiv* of his parenesis, which is the inevitability of trials. At first sight, Ben Sira's words seem unreasonably severe, especially if we consider the youthfulness of his audience. However, the sage's bluntness has the almost irresistible attraction of a challenge. Formulating his invitation with a conditional clause, he locates his remarks within the domain of freedom, which encourages the disciple to make personal commitment to the life of wisdom. This context of freedom is characteristic of the wisdom school and is made explicit in

---

1 See IRWIN, Fear of God, 551 – 559. Based on the points of contact between Sir 1 – 2 (esp. 2,1 – 18) and Sir 6,5 – 17 (about friendship), Irwin concludes that a clear analogy exists between fear-of-God and friendship.
2 Cf. CALDUCH-BENAGES, Crisol. However, cf. SCHRÄDER, Leiden, 192.

Sir 6,32–33[3] and 15,15–17. Here too, Ben Sira introduces his teaching with the typical formula "if you want" (Hb: תחפץ אם; Gk: ἐὰν θέλῃς)[4].

Therefore, we can say that the warning "prepare yourself for testing" (2,1b) sets the stage and opens the curtains for the presentation of Ben Sira's educational program. From now on, the sage starts his teaching. Syntactically, the protasis ("If you come to serve the Lord") is followed by an extended apodosis consisting of six warnings. The first four warnings ("prepare your soul for testing; direct your heart; be steadfast; do not hurry in time of affliction") refer to the inner life of the disciple and the last two warnings concern his relationship with God ("cling to him and forsake him not"). Through the use of a synthetic parallelism, the author gives a strong conclusive quality to 2,3a, while emphasizing the first imperative of the colon. In other words, Ben Sira says that the key to enduring trials is to cling to the Lord.

Ben Sira interrupts the list of imperatives that make up the apodosis and inserts a final clause in 2,3b. This clause seems to express the purpose of the whole apodosis proleptically: "so that you grow at your end"[5]. After the interruption, Ben Sira continues the sequence of imperatives which started in 2,1b with δέξαι ("accept") and μακροθύμησον ("be patient", lit. "be great-hearted"). First, he encourages the disciple to accept "whatever befalls him". Because God is the implied subject of the verb (ἐπαχθῇ), this short sentence amounts to an unconditional approval of divine designs. Second, he exhorts the disciple to μακροθυμία, and this exhortation represents a double action. On the one hand, the disciple must practise the virtue of patience—if he wants to overcome trials; on the other hand, trial itself becomes a teacher of patience. This dynamic character of patience and the educational value of testing contrast sharply with the profane usage of μακροθυμία in some Greek authors. For example, Menander says: ἄνθρωπος ὢν μηδέποτε τὴν ἀλυπίαν αὐτοῦ παρὰ θεῶν, ἀλλὰ τὴν μακροθυμίαν, "being a person, do not ask the gods for the absence of pain, but for resignation"[6].

---

3 DI LELLA, Search, 190.

4 Paralleled by Matt 19,17: εἰ δὲ θέλεις εἰς τὴν ζωὴν εἰσελθεῖν, "If you want to enter into (eternal) life" and 19,21: εἰ θέλεις τέλειος εἶναι, "if you want to be perfect".

5 The meaning of ἐπ' ἐσχάτον σου is disputed. My view is that this expression does not refer here to eternal life, or the day of death, or the end of time, but to the time after a trial, when the tribulation or affliction has been overcome. In Syr: "so that you become wise in your ways".

6 Frag. 549 (CAF 3,167). In STRABO, μακροθυμία means "tenacity" (Geogr. 5,4,10) and in ARTEMIDORUS, "delay" (Onir. 2,25,9). Other authors, on the contrary, use it to describe the positive effects of suffering: ARETAEOS, Liber 3. Cur. Diut. 1,1 (CMG 2,36,12); PLUTARCH, Luc. 32,I,513a; 33,I,514c, and JOSEPHUS, B.J. 4,37. An example in the Bible is 1 Macc 8,4.

In order to justify the two elements of the extended apodosis ("accept whatever befalls you" and "be patient") the passage includes a wisdom saying which functions as a clause of justification (*Begründungssatz*). At this point the passage changes strategy and allows popular wisdom to take over. An anonymous representative of the wisdom of Israel voices a powerful message. The persuasive quality of the justification rests in its truth based on experience: ἐν πυρὶ δοκιμάζεται χρυσός, "gold is tested with fire". The passage builds the wisdom argument by transposing the experiencial truth of nature to the human sphere: καὶ ἄνθρωποι δεκτοὶ ἐν καμίνῳ ταπεινώσεως, "and acceptable people (are tested) in the crucible of humiliation". The result of the intertwining of natural phenomena with human life is a proverb with a typically chiastic disposition of its elements.

Sir 2,5 is the only instance in the Book of Ben Sira in which the image of the crucible is used to illustrate the idea of testing[7]. This image of the melting of metals is reminiscent of a literary motif that is very common in prophetic books (Jer 6,28 – 30; 11,4; Isa 1,22.25; 48,10; Ezek 22,17 – 22; Zech 13,9; Mal 3,3). Whereas the prophetic tradition applies the metaphor of the crucible to Israel, Ben Sira and the Psalms apply it to the individual (Ps 26[25],2 and 17[16],3; 66[65],10). In Sir 2,5, the logical direct object of divine testing is not the chosen people, but the ἄνθρωποι δεκτοί, "acceptable people". God tests them with fire (ἐν καμίνῳ), not to make them suffer but because they are as precious as gold for him, a noble metal of great value. A person, even when righteous, has to pass through a crucible in order to be purified (as gold is purified) as described in Prov 17,3[8].

This first section of Sir 2 concludes with v. 6, of which the most relevant feature is the emphasis on the relationship with God (πίστευσον αὐτῷ, καὶ ἀντιλήμψεταί σου· εὔθυνον τὰς ὁδούς σου καὶ ἔλπισον ἐπ' αὐτόν, "trust God and he will help you; make straight your ways and hope in him"). Here the sage's teaching reaches a high point when he speaks of the relationship with God, which consists of two main elements. On the one hand, this relationship involves the active

---

7 In 27,4 – 7 Ben Sira describes the human dimension of testing with the following images: a sieve (Amos 9,9), the kiln of the potter (cf. Jer 18; Is 29,16; 45,9) and the cultivation of a tree (Prov 1,31; 11,30; 12,14; 13,2; 18,20; 27,18). Cf. HADOT, Penchant mauvais, 141 – 145 and BEENTJES, Jesus, zoon van Sirach, 80 – 85.

8 Melting of metals as a metaphor for spiritual purification also occurs in the Qumran documents: 1QS IV, 20: "then God will purify by means of his truth all the works of humans and will purify for himself the human configuration"; 1QH V, 16: "you have brought him [the poor] to the test as gold is subjected to the action of the fire and as refined silver in the oven of the refiners so that he may be purified seven times"; 1QH VI, 8: "you will refine them [the Jews who stayed in Jerusalem] so that they may be purified from the offense".

collaboration of the disciple both in his inner attitude and his outer actions; on the other hand, the unconditional help of God. In short, the trust and hope in God combined with particular dedication and effort opens up the way for God's intervention in favour of the disciple. When trial comes to the disciple, the helpful hand of God offers a new horizon of hope, the shape of which becomes visible in the following verses.

At this point, let us look back to where we started our analysis. In 2,1b, the text does not specify the origin of trial. In fact, the Lord is not the grammatical subject of the verse. The origin of trial is given later in 2,5.9 (and also in vv. 10 – 11). In spite of this lack of explicit information, the disciple can already infer that both trial and liberation come from the Lord. This is what Ben Sira affirms in Sir 36(33Hb),1: "no evil can harm the one who fears the Lord; in trial, he will deliver him again and again". At first this affirmation appears to be a contradiction, but in fact it reveals the teaching (מוסר) of God, whose method combines firmness and affection at the right moment (cf. Deut 8,5).

We now know who the agent of testing is, and who is being tested, but we are still unaware of the nature of the trial. In various passages dispersed throughout his book, Ben Sira provides us with some indications of what the trials are (Sir 4,17Gk: fear, dread, and discipline; Sir 31[34Hb],10: mortal dangers; Sir 44,20: sacrificing a son). The sage concludes with his personal experience in Sir 51,1–12, where he speaks of the ultimate trial of death. Sir 2, however, does not treat of any particular trial in detail but treats the reality of testing in general terms[9].

2 Testing as an Educational Strategy (Sir 4,11–19)

Sir 4,11–19 is the second of a series of "wisdom poems", which are spread throughout the book[10]. For the first time, Wisdom decides to speak out (as also in chapter 24) in order to address her sons or disciples[11].

The poem opens with a general statement on the educational action of Wisdom (v. 11). She carries out two complementary tasks: teaching (למד) and admonishing (עוד). Wisdom does not limit herself to imparting instruction, but also

---

9 GkII, on the contrary, is much more explicit: "In sickness and poverty put your trust in him" (Sir 2,5c).
10 Cf. Marböck, Weisheit im Wandel; Rickenbacher, Weisheitsperikopen. For this section, we follow the Hebrew text of MS A in the main.
11 The principle ideas of this section are expounded in more detail in Calduch-Benages, Prueba, 25 – 48.

stimulates the disciple to open his mind to new horizons. In other words, Wisdom's teaching is not academic but oriented to life.

This general opening statement is followed by three verses (vv. 12 – 14) dealing with the different stages which the disciple has to go through in the learning process in Wisdom's school: loving, searching, persevering and serving. A gift from the Lord corresponds to each stage: life, favour, glory, and blessing. It follows that love of Wisdom and love of God are two inseparable realities.

After this introduction, Wisdom speaks in the 1st person singular (the Greek version has the 3rd person singular), in order to instruct the disciples about her method. As a skilled teacher, she begins by arousing enthusiasm in the disciple with a promise of a final reward (vv. 15 – 16 in Gk). Actually, she offers a double reward: first, the disciple responding positively to Wisdom's teaching will be allowed to live in the inner rooms of her house and; second, he will be allowed to pronounce judgment in the tribunal. Thus, intimacy and familiarity as well as social status and responsibility will be the disciple's recompense.

In v. 17, Wisdom speaks about her method of training her students using the metaphor of a journey. Studying wisdom is like walking on a long and arduous road, as once the Israelites did in the desert (Deut 8). Formerly, YHWH walked with his people; now Wisdom walks with her disciple (אלך עמו) without him realizing it (בהתנכר). Although YHWH guided and protected his people in the wilderness, he also tested them with hard trials but without withdrawing his protection from them (Exod 16,4; 20,20). In our text, Wisdom behaves in a similar way. She is an unusual travelling companion, who deliberately and systematically puts the disciple to the test, without abandoning him. Testing, in fact, is presented as a necessary and painful step on the road, but never as the final goal of the road or an end in itself. If the disciple's heart is to be filled with Wisdom, she must make her presence known and reveal her secrets to him. (v. 18). However, if the disciple deviates from the path set out by Wisdom, he will be severely punished by being bound with chains and handed over to torturers (v. 19).

The four cola of v. 17 deserve closer scrutiny. In the first colon, Wisdom walks with the disciple. Every day, experience shows that walking in the company of another person favours (or even can create) a relationship, and the deeper the relationship, the more pleasant the journey will be. The exchange of mutual empathy is normally expressed with words, gestures, and even silence. In v. 17a there is a remarkable detail worth investigating. Wisdom walks with the disciple "cunningly" (בהתנכר; Gk: διεστραμμένως, "by tortuous roads"), or "in disguise", using P. Skehan's translation, without the disciple realizing her presence. Wisdom hides herself but remains close at hand and continues to care for the disciple. She deliberately renders herself invisible to the disciple's eyes in order

to see what he is made of[12]. The disappearance of Wisdom places the disciple in
a critical situation. Because Wisdom hides her presence the disciple is obliged to
reflect on himself, his attitudes, and his actions, and above all else to take personal responsibility for his journey.

In the second colon ("first I shall probe him with trials"), the explicit mention of trial (בנסיונות) is reminiscent of Sir 2,1–6, esp. of 2,1b (εἰς πειρασμόν),
where the idea that enduring trials is central to growth in wisdom makes its
first appearance[13]. The indoctrination in the school of Wisdom resembles that
in the school of fear-of-God. If disciples who are suffering trials learn to fear
the Lord, they will reach the wisdom that comes from the one who alone is
wise (1,8). In the same way, disciples who gained Wisdom through being tested
actually serve the Lord (4,14, "whoever serves her, serves the Lord"). Sir 2,1–6
insists that the Lord comes to the aid of a youth undergoing a trial, but in
Sir 4,11–19 no mention is made of such support from Wisdom, which makes Wisdom seems more demanding than God himself. Her presence and aid are real,
but veiled and easily overlooked. According to her, allowing the students to
work through crises is an essential part of their education.

3 Trial of Endurance (Sir 6,18–37)

The starting point for our reading of the third text about undergoing trials is to
appreciate the fact that inquiry is a proper human activity. In a certain sense, all
human searching is motivated by a profound desire to discover. It is equally well
known that making discoveries requires time and effort. For any inquiry to be
sustained over a long period of time, one must be guided by a sincere motivation
to persevere in the quest. This experience is well expressed as a proverb in several languages: "Quien no sabe aguantar, no sabe alcanzar", "No pain, no gain",
"Ohne Fleiß, kein Preis". Ben Sira applies this fact of life to the disciple's search
for Wisdom in a suggestive poem (Sir 6,18–37) composed of three stanzas. In this

---

12 Jesus used precisely this educational strategy on the road to Emmaus: as he walked with the
two disciples and explained the Holy Sriptures to them, their eyes were prevented from recognizing him (Luke 24,15–16), but their hearts were burning with excitement as he taught them
(Luke 24,32).
13 According to Haspecker, Sir 2,1–5; 4,17 and 6,18–22 are basically identical (HASPECKER, Gottesfurcht, 217 note 9). The way of teaching Wisdom is the way of teaching about God and Wisdom's teaching is education in fear-of-God.

section, we will deal with only the first two of them (6,18–22 and 6,23–31), because they are most relevant to our theme.[14]

After assuring the student that paying attention to the sage's teaching will bear good fruit in years to come ("My son, if you concentrate on instruction in your youth, you will find Wisdom in your old age"), the sage describes the pedagogical principles of Wisdom with a stream of images (Sir 6,19–22).

Through the images of ploughman and sower, of fields and fruits, Ben Sira invokes the agricultural context in order to illustrate the learning process. The relationship between a farmer and his field is bipolar. On the one hand, it is characterized by love, closeness, gratitude, and hope; on the other hand, it requires work, fatigue, sweat, continuous effort and patience. However, the sage subtly emphasizes the first aspect. The work is not excessive, the harvest will come soon, and the fruits will be abundant. The same is true for Wisdom and her disciple. As the farmer cultivates the land in order to eat its produce, so the disciple has to cultivate his mind and heart diligently in order to enjoy the fruits of Wisdom.

The sage's realism comes to the surface in Sir 6,20–21. Since he already has spoken of the disciple's search for Wisdom, contrasts the qualities necessary to bear good fruit with those of the fool. This is expressed in a new set of images. In the preceding verses, Ben Sira utilized agricultural images, but now he shifts to mineral imagery. The insensitive fool does not give himself to Wisdom's course of instruction. He finds her rough, burdensome, and uncomfortable. For him Wisdom is like a heavy stone, a touchstone (אבן משא, λίθος δοκιμασίας), which bears down on his shoulders and puts him to the test[15]. Not understanding the value of the lesson in endurance, the fool loses no time in shaking it off. All the wealth of vitality and fecundity that was associated with the first group of images has now disappeared to give way to the sterility and inertia of stones.

In the second stanza (Sir 6,23–31), the sage is concerned with the difficulties of learning Wisdom and describes them with images taken from slavery, hunting, and love. The disciple is like a slave caught in a net, constrained with shackles and burdened with the yoke of Wisdom. He is like a tireless hunter, who tracks the trail of his prey. He is like the lover passionately in search of his beloved (as in Sir 14,20–24)[16]. Slave, hunter and lover, the disciple has to pass through many hard trials to attain his desired goal. But if he really longs to become wise and

---

14 Our reading of these stanzas is based mainly on the Hebrew text.

15 This probably refers to a Greek custom, common among young men, in order to prove their virility: the sport of lifting heavy stones.

16 GILBERT, Sequela, 53–70.

persistently searches for Wisdom, the moment will arrive when oppressive slavery, fatiguing pursuit, and unrequited love stop being an unbearable weight and instead become a reason for peace and joy. Then Wisdom's net is transformed into a secure refuge, her chains into a glorious robe, her yoke into a golden ornament, and her bonds into purple threads. In v. 31, the symbolism of clothing is like a golden brooch; it is the finishing touch to the exuberant series of images. With this metaphor, the sage expresses the profound harmony between the disciple and Wisdom: "you will wear her as a splendid robe; as a wreath of honour, you will crown yourself with her".

In this way, Ben Sira has illustrated artistically how the search for Wisdom is in fact a true trial of endurance, without speaking explicitly of trial.

4 Trial of Travelling (Sir 31[34Hb],9 – 17)

Though geography does not seem to interest Ben Sira, it provides him another analogy for his concept of trial. In three instances of his wisdom book (Sir 31[34Hb],9 – 17; 39,4; 51,13aGk), he describes travelling in a favourable way. He considers it as a fount of experience, knowledge and wisdom[17]. For the sage, the connection between travelling and wisdom is unquestionable. Travelling is enriching in every way: the person who travels increases his or her cultural treasure and comes closer to wisdom with each journey.

Of the three texts referred to above, the most significant is undoubtedly the first, i.e. Sir 31(34Hb),9 – 17. This text ingeniously contrasts with the preceding pericope (31[34Hb],1 – 8), which deals with dreams and the unreal. The vivid and realistic experience of travelling clashes with the deceptive fantasy of dreams. Our pericope consists of two clearly distinguished parts: vv. 9 – 12 and vv. 13 – 17, which are united by the expression τούτων χάριν[18]. Both parts are subdivided, the former consists of vv. 9 – 10 and 11 – 12, and the latter of vv. 13 – 15 and 16 – 17.

---

17 This position contrasts with the negative view of Qoheleth about all that he saw and experienced in the world (e. g. Qoh 1,13 – 14). For a brief treatment of this subject, see WISCHMEYER, Kultur, 96 – 97.

18 We understand τούτων χάριν ("because of these things") to refer to the following verses (13 – 17), which deal with fear-of-God and its effectiveness. Similarly, Smend, Duesberg—Fransen, Alonso Schökel and Morla Asensio. Other authors, however, relate the expression at issue to vv. 9 – 12. According to them, "these things" must be understood as the accumulated experience of the sage (cf. Bretschneider, Fritzsche, Peters, Spicq, Minissale, Di Lella and the interconfessional translation of the Catalan Bible).

Sir 31(34Hb),9–10 present us with the figure of the traveller as a man of experience (πολυπειρός), who knows many things (πολλά), increases his resourcefulness (πληθυνεῖ πανουργίαν), and shares his knowledge with others (ἐκδιηγήσεται σύνεσιν). Only one colon (v. 10a) is devoted to the one who has not been tested (in this context, the one who has not travelled): such a person knows few things (ὀλίγα).

Unexpectedly, the author interrupts this general presentation (in 3rd per. sg.) and starts to speak of personal experience in 1st person singular. It is as if the writer wanted to say, "Listen carefully, this experienced, tested and intelligent traveller ... is me!". For, immediately he discloses to us that he has seen many things (πολλά), that his knowledge goes beyond his words (πλείονα τῶν λόγων) and that all his vicissitudes in the world have brought him more than once (πλεονάκις) to the gates of death. Not everything is advantageous in travelling. A traveller must always reckon with serious and unexpected circumstances that can endanger his life. The main instruction, then, he holds till last (v. 12b and vv. 13–17). He came away safely from all dangers, thanks to the Lord; for the Lord protects the pious person who respects him, puts his or her trust in him and loves him. In other words, all those who fear the Lord need not fear anything, for the Lord watches over their ways. In this pericope about travel (Sir 31[34Hb],9–17), fear-of-God and wisdom come into contact with a cultural phenomenon typical of Hellenistic culture and their meeting point is the experience of trial[19].

Although travels are a source of wisdom and experience, they also entail many sacrifices and hard trials. And so Ben Sira speaks of the traveller who has to deal with thirst (Sir 26,12), with storms at sea (Sir 36[33Hb],2), with unpleasant fellow travellers (Sir 42,3), with dangers that lurk on desert roads and in lonely places (Sir 8,16). On land or at sea, on foot or mounted, travelling is a continuous trial and therefore a great learning opportunity for those who seek wisdom.

5 Trial of Abraham (Sir 44,19–21)

Just as trial is a constant reality in life for the one who is searching for wisdom, so also the help of the Lord is never lacking for the one who fears him. In trial, the righteous reckons with the protection and help of the Lord (cf. 1 Kgs 5,18 and Job 5,19). This is what the sage affirms in Sir 36(33Hb),1: "no evil can harm the

---

19 Cf. Philo, Ebr. 158; Abr. 65; Migr. 216–218; Pseudo-Isocrates, Demon. 18.

one who fears the Lord; in trial, he will deliver him again and again". This general affirmation finds its application in an instructive example from tradition: Sir 44,19 – 21.

From the glorious past of Israel one person stands out: the figure of the patriarch Abraham, father of a multitude of nations, unblemished in his glory (Sir 44,19). Taking his inspiration from the narrative material of the book of Genesis, Ben Sira describes Abraham as a pious man who kept the Law of the Most High, who made a covenant with him, putting it as a seal on his flesh (circumcision), and who remained faithful in trial. It should be noted that he concludes the characterization of the patriarch by exalting his unbreakable fidelity, even in the moment of the decisive trial: ובניסוי נמצא נאמן, "and in trial he was found faithful" (Sir 44,20).

Jewish tradition holds that Abraham was tested ten times during his life: in Ur of the Chaldeans, when leaving Haran, with Sara and Hagar, with King Abimelek, in making the covenant and cutting sacrificial animals, in circumcision, and with his sons Ismael and Isaac. He prevailed in all ten trials[20]. Although our text does not specify one particular trial Abraham underwent, tradition suggests that the sacrifice of his son Isaac was the ultimate trial (Gen 22,1 – 19)[21]. God demands of Abraham the greatest sacrifice that could be asked of a father with the sole purpose of probing the soundness of his faith. Abraham does not waver. He is determined to obey the Lord's command. Abraham triumphed in the most severe trial of his life and became a model for future generations (cf. Jdt 8,25 – 27; 1 Macc 2,52; Job 15,17 – 18; Wis 10,5). In answer to his unconditional loyalty and obedience, the Lord promises Abraham that he will bless the nations through his descendants, multiply his offspring as the dust of the earth, exalt his house as the stars and give him as an inheritance the land that stretched from one sea to another (Sir 44,21).

The teaching of the sage is not just the fruit of his observation, reflection and personal experience. It builds upon a long tradition that proclaims tirelessly the infinite mercy of the Lord. That is to say, the example of the ancestors, in this instance the patriarch Abraham, enforces the sage's teaching: when the Lord puts human beings to the test, he also helps them to overcome the trial.

---

20 Cf. 'Abot R. Nat. 33,11(A) and 36,3(B); Pirqe R. El. 26 – 31; 'Abot 5,3 – 4; Jub. 17,7; 19,8. In these trials, Korn perceives an allusion to the Hellenistic tradition of the "12 works" of Hercules (KORN, Πειρασμός, 55 – 56).
21 SWETNAM, Jesus and Isaac, esp. 23 – 80. For abundant bibliography on this passage, see WESTERMANN, Genesis, 429 – 430; MURRAY, Trauma, 96 – 104; WILLI-PLEIN, Versuchung, 100 – 108.

6 Ben Sira's Trial (Sir 51,1–12)

The emblematic example of Israel's far past finds present-day expression in the experience of the sage. The story of Father Abraham now gives way to that of his heir, Ben Sira. In the teaching of the sage, the example of tradition and personal testimony complement each other. For the disciples, the authority of their ancestors must be recognized along with that of those who labor to transmit the tradition to the next generation. Conscious of his responsibility, Ben Sira reinforces his teaching offering illustrations from his own life. Such a testimony undoubtedly impresses his disciples, for whom their own sage is much nearer and more convincing than a glorious figure from the past.

At the end of his book, Ben Sira intones a thanksgiving psalm to the Lord (Sir 51,1–12)[22]. He thanks the Lord for a plethora of blessings: he was saved from death, from destruction, from Sheol, from calumny, from deceit, from lies, from lurking enemies, from a narrow circle of flames, from consuming fire, from the deepest abyss, from lying and insincere lips and from the arrows of a treacherous tongue (vv. 2–6). This multitude of dangers (מרבות צרות) is in fact a concatenation of images, all of which express the frightening experience of a person exposed to a deadly trial: slander from enemies[23]. Full of gratitude, the sage recalls the desperate appeal to God in those terrible moments when he was on the verge of being overcome in the battle between life and death: אל תרפני ביום צרה ביום שואה ומשואה, "do not abandon me on the day of tribulation, on the day of terror and affliction" (v. 10); he remembers the merciful intervention of the Lord on his behalf: ויפדני מכל רע וימלטני ביום צרה, "He saved me from every evil (Gk: from perdition) and he liberated me on the day of affliction (Gk: of the bad moment)" (v. 12).

This personal testimony of the sage (for I believe the prayer is autobiographical) is fully in line with the teaching about the necessity of enduring trials which began in 2,1 ("My son, if you want to serve the Lord, prepare yourself for testing") and which has been developed throughout the book. We can now affirm that the experience of Ben Sira is a vivid example of actively enduring trials. When placed alongside Old Testament tradition, such an example dissipates any possible doubt about the intervention of the Lord on behalf of the righteous person who fears the Lord and loves wisdom (cf. Ps 34,20; 37,39). In the sage's own words: "the Lord saves those who take refuge in him and rescues them from all evil" (51,8cd).

---

22 GILBERT, Action de grâce, 231–242.

23 ALONSO SCHÖKEL, Eclesiástico, 327: "La situación es el peligro de muerte visto como una síntesis de todos los males y como suceso humanamente irremediable".

7 Conclusion

Speaking about the principal themes of the Book of Ben Sira, one usually refers to the famous triptych: wisdom, fear-of-God and the Law, to which one may add, for instance, cult, creation, prayer, history, death and social life, among others. Trial is not normally mentioned in such a list[24].

We have sought to fill this omission by showing that overcoming trials is a repeated theme in the work of Ben Sira. The reason that Ben Sira wanted to underline the presence of trial in human life is that he is concerned mainly with wisdom as a power to do well in life that can only be attained through patient endurance. Trial has the capacity to make a person grow and mature. This educational principle is well appreciated by Ben Sira and so he imparted it to his disciples throughout his teaching.

The systematic treatment of trial in the theme introduced in Sir 2,1 is worked out in various ways and contexts throughout the book. In each instance trial is associated strictly with the search for Wisdom. The quest entails a long and arduous road. It is long, because it lasts for the whole of life, including the moment of death (6,18; 51,13–15). It is arduous, because it demands constant effort in order to grow wiser (6,19; 51,26). The stages of this road to Wisdom constitute a true learning experience, in which trial serves an educational function. In her school, Wisdom subjects the disciples to all sorts of trials. Only after overcoming all of the trials of life will the disciple attain Wisdom and enjoy her company (6,18–22; 14,22–25). The process of journeying on Wisdom's road can be found in the glorious past of Israel, in the figure of Abraham, the faithful Israelite who overcame even the hardest trial sent by the Lord (44,19–21). It can also be found in the daily life of heirs of the tradition, especially in the figure of their teacher Ben Sira, who overcame various mortal dangers in his life (31[34Hb],9–13; 51,1–12).

In all these texts, the Lord and Wisdom put the disciple to the test not to satisfy a simple whim, not to justify themselves as teachers nor to demonstrate the efficiency of their method. The Lord and Wisdom are motivated by love, so they pursue a positive aim: purification and strengthening of the heart of the disciple who wants to serve the Lord (2,1–6). Far from being a destructive reality with negative connotations, enduring trial dignifies the human person. Ben Sira has demonstrated this to us.

---

24 E.g. Minissale, Siracide; Gilbert, Enseignement, 308–318.

Fear of the Powerful or Respect for Authority in Sirach[1]

Already in the first pages of his book, viz. in the parenesis of chapter two, Ben Sira alludes in a very subtle way to a controversial social situation. Expressions like "in the time of calamity", "in the time of tribulation", "the furnace of humiliation" in combination with the terminology of "trial" and "testing" point to a perturbing and alarming reality. It is true that the aforementioned expressions can refer to a personal experience of the disciple, of either psychological, moral, or religious nature, but studies on the *Sitz im Leben* of the book indicate a hidden conflict in the society of the era. This conflict comes to the surface on various occasions, and, in a very particular way—not always easily detectable—it emerges when Ben Sira broaches the question of authority.

The object of our study consists in analysing the teaching of Ben Sira on authority. What attitude is one to assume before the legitimate representatives of authority? How to behave before kings, rulers, governors, magistrates, judges, nobility and other powerful figures in society?[2]. The answer covers a wide range of possibilities that oscillate between fear, refusal, distance, aloofness, or precaution on the one hand, and submission, obedience, and respect on the other.

1 A Hidden Conflict

According to information furnished by the prologue, Ben Sira unfolds his didactic and literary activity between 200 BC and 180 BC, in a Jerusalem which was then under Seleucid control after one century of Ptolemaic hegemony[3]. Palestine expectantly embraced the new political course hoping for a less burdened economy and better conditions of life for the people. In fact, the Seleucid king Antiochus III the Great (223–187 BC) not only favoured the Jewish population

---

1 The title is inspired by the comment of Tcherikover on Sir 4,7: "Yet in several places in his book we feel that behind his humility lies a feeling of fear for the powerful rather than respect for authority" (TCHERIKOVER Civilization, 148). The article was translated from the Spanish original by Jan Liesen.

2 On the theme of power and the powerful in Ben Sira, see PETRAGLIO, Potere, 40–61, esp. 41–54, and MARBÖCK, Macht und Mächtige, 185–194.

3 Cf. TCHERIKOVER, Civilization, 142–151; HENGEL, Judaism and Hellenism, vol. 1, 131–153; SKEHAN—DI LELLA, Wisdom, 8–16.

https://doi.org/10.1515/9783110492316-007

with a reduction of taxes, but also promoted a policy of respect and tolerance with regard to religion. After his death he was succeeded by his son Seleucus IV Filopator (187–175 BC), who in theory was faithful to the policy initiated by his father. In reality, however, he was corrupted by an unbridled ambition (2 Macc 3,4–40) and proved utterly unsuccessful in the task of ruling the nation. The rise to power of his junior brother Antiochus IV Epiphanes (175–163 BC) made an abrupt end to the climate of peaceful living together that had characterised the two preceding governments. Keen on the Hellenistic culture, Antiochus wanted to hellenize Palestine at all costs. Two of the more powerful families of the local aristocracy played a decisive role in this ambitious project, viz. the Tobiads and the Oniads[4], who were both involved in the struggle for power. Antiochus profaned the Temple of Jerusalem and unleashed a bloody persecution against the Jews. This dramatic situation resulted in the revolution of the people under the leadership of the Maccabean brothers (167 BC).

Even though Ben Sira makes no clear allusions to persons or political events mentioned above (he had finished writing when the tension erupted), a close reading of his book gives rise to the suspicion that the crisis provoked by the attempt of enforced hellenization of the Jewish people was already latent during the time of the sage. We may, therefore, affirm that during the first decade of the 2nd century BC the confrontation between Hellenism and the faithfulness to the traditional values of the Jewish religion began to harden. Ben Sira touched on this confrontation indirectly in his work, so that it requires reading in between the lines, and probably allows for considerable space for interpretation. According to the sociological categories which L.G. Perdue applies to the sapiential tradition of Israel, we encounter a society that, even when externally good and institutionally part of the "paradigm of order"[5], harbours in its interior the seed of a conflict that, in spite of being still in a germinal phase, will not delay much in producing its first fruits.

2 The Audience of Ben Sira and the Power of the Word

The theme of authority (government, power, public offices) constitutes an important part in the teaching of the sage. This comes as no surprise if one takes into account that his primary audience consisted of young men who were preparing

---

4 Cf. BÜCHLER, Tobiaden; GOLDSTEIN, Tales, 85–123.
5 Cf. PERDUE, Character, 5–39; ID., Cosmology, 457–478: on p. 477 the author affirms: "Ben Sira represents an *accommodation* to the political order of Ptolemaic and then Seleucid rule" (italics ours).

themselves for holding positions in the government or exercising authority in a not too distant future, either as administrators, scribes, or public officeholders.

Among the many subjects which had to be studied, command of language stood out prominently. Control of language is indispensable in the field of social relations and especially in all what touches upon the duties of government (diplomatic contacts, international relationships), and all of the other bureaucratic, administrative, and judicial affairs undertaken on behalf of the nation.

2.1 The Authorities of the Future

Thanks to the exhortation of Sir 51,23 ("Draw near to me, you who are uneducated, and lodge in my school") we know that Ben Sira directed a school (בית מדרש, "house of study"), probably in his own house, where he imparted classes of wisdom[6]. This house of instruction was frequented by young men (young women received a household type education in domestic circle)[7], belonging to the well-to-do families in Jerusalem, who were the only ones who could economically afford the expenses connected with the education of their sons, especially the salaries of the teachers[8].

In line with the sapiential tradition of the Ancient Near East, the disciples of Ben Sira prepared themselves for occupying the leading positions in various areas of society (cf. Prov 8,15–16; 16,10–15)[9]. Aware of his responsibility as teacher, the sage does not hesitate to remind his disciples that the future of the nation is in their hands. Thus it reads in Sir 36(33Hb),19: "Hear me, you who are great among the people, and you leaders of the congregation, pay heed!"; these words function as a conclusion to a brief autobiographical note by Ben Sira (36[33Hb],16–18) and at the same time initiate a new series of instructions (36[33Hb],20–33).

It is not necessary to inquire, as some have done, after the identity of these managers and leaders. They are no more and no less than the authorities of the future, the new leaders of the Jewish society. By means of figurative language the sage stimulates his disciples to identify themselves with their future mission and

---

6 This is the only time that this expression occurs in the Bible. Gk: οἰκὸς παιδείας corresponds to Syr: *byt ywlpn'* (Hb: בית מוסר). On the school in Israel, cf. LEMAIRE, Sage, 165–181, esp. 166–176, and HEATON, School, 1–23: "A Jerusalem School Inspected".

7 Cf. GASPAR, Ideas, 150–151; DE VAUX, Ancient Israel, 50, and the comments by CRENSHAW in Education, 602 note 5.

8 Cf. GORDIS, Background, 77–118, esp. 83–93; HEATON, School, 14.

9 Cf. CRENSHAW, Sage, 212.

to prepare themselves with determination and dedication in order to be able to accomplish it with responsibility and wisdom[10].

2.2 Wisdom, Word, and Leadership

In his wisdom program Ben Sira dedicates several lectures to the theme of the "tongue" (Sir 5,9 – 6,1: sins ofthe tongue; Sir 19,4 – 17: bad tongues; Sir 23,7 – 15: discipline of the tongue; Sir 27,8 – 28,6: dangers of the tongue) without even taking into account many other references dispersed throughout his work[11].

One aspect of this typical sapiential topic interests us here: the relationship between command of language and authority. By way of example let us consider two wise counsels that Ben Sira gives to his disciples. In chapter 23, after an instruction on the oath and unmannered words (vv. 7 – 15), the sage admonishes: "Remember your father and mother when you sit among the great (μεγιστάνων); lest you be forgetful in their presence, and be deemed a fool (i.e. by speaking unreasonably) on account of your habits; then you will wish that you had never been born, and you will curse the day of your birth" (v. 14). Whether it be these, or "the great" alluded to in the text (Seleucid leaders, Jewish aristocracy...)[12], so much is clear that an adequate training in speech is absolutely essential in meetings of the leadership. The mention of parents transcends the family circle, since here the figures of father and mother evoke the homeland, the religion, the tradition, and all of the other aspects of one's native culture—unassailable values that no good Israelite should betray with base language under any pretence. The temptations to do otherwise could arise from a desire to please the powerful, to avoid conflict with the authorities of the day, or just to drift in the mainstream of culture. In these contexts, correct speech signifies fidelity to one's own identity.

When participating in a banquet (Sir 35[32Hb],1 – 13) the young disciple should be modest in his speech and should also give preference to persons of senior age and higher social rank (cf. Prov 17,27). In this way the sage advises him (v. 9): "Among the elders do not boast (אל תקומם)[13] and with the powerful do not quarrel (אל תרב לטרד)". The Greek text has some changes in which the

---

10 Cf. Skehan—Di Lella, Wisdom, 405; Morla Asensio, Eclesiástico, 166.

11 Cf. Okoye, Speech.

12 Cf. Desečar, Necedad, 264 – 272, esp. 272.

13 One of the meanings of the verb קום (Polel) is "to boast", "to acquire greater confidence", "to inflate oneself". In our verse the context and the Greek version make another translation possible: "to discuss" (cf. Alonso Schökel, Diccionario, 655).

use of words is made more explicit: "In the midst of the great do not pretend to be strong (μὴ ἐξουσιάζου) and among the elders do not speak too much (μὴ πολλὰ ἀδολέσχει)[14]. We shall see, therefore, how in the company of elders and the powerful one needs moderation in speech and modesty in behaviour. These are qualities that a young man has to practise, if ever he wants to become someone whom people listen to and respect. The lesson is clear: authority is not acquired with a presumptuous attitude nor much less with a flood of words (cf. 9,18).

Finally, we present a text in which Ben Sira corroborates and renders more explicit the teaching contained in previous counsels. Sir 9,17 opens a brief but suggestive treaty on leadership (9,17–10,5)[15]. In this case the sage does not restrict himself to giving counsel but also affirms with conviction: "Skilful hands secure justice, an eloquent person (wise in his/ her discourses) rules the people"[16]. Just as there is a manual kind of wisdom (ability, dexterity) which allows workers to practise their various occupations (cf. 38,24–34b), so there is also a verbal kind of wisdom (command of language with regard to content and form) that enables intelligent leaders to exercise authority (cf. 9,18 for the contrast)[17]. Therefore, in order to be a ruler it is necessary to know how to speak with wisdom, i.e. to know how to use the right words, in the right way, in the right time, and with the right measure (cf. 20,27a).

---

14 Cf. Sir 7,14: אל תסוד בעדת שרים ("do not deliberate in the assembly of leaders"). In Greek: μὴ ἀδολέσχει ἐν πλήθει πρεσβυτέρων ("do not speak too much in the assembly of elders"), where the verb ἀδολέσχειν translates the Hebrew סוד ("to deliberate") instead of טרד ("to drip", fig. "to insist"), which is perhaps due to a confusion between תטרד and תסוד (cf. BEENTJES, Jesus Sirach 7.1–17, 251–259).

15 According to Marböck (Macht und Mächtige, 189–191), these verses open a large section (9,17–11,6[9]) on public life (esp. on the powerful, their influence and responsibility) that could be subdivided in two contrasting parts: 9,17–10,18 (negative part) and 10,19–11,6[9] (positive part).

16 The text of MS A is difficult to understand. We read 17b with the first word of 18a (ביטה, feminine denominative noun of the verb בטא/בטה, "to speak"; in Gk it corresponds to λόγος). Skehan substitutes it with בינה (in the sense of skill, dexterity) and translates חכם בינה as "the skilled sage". Cf. SKEHAN–DI LELLA, Wisdom, 222. Barthélemy–Rickenbacher (Konkordanz, 51), perhaps due to the fact that ביטה is a *hapax legomenon*, propose to read the pres. ptc. m. sg. of the quoted verb, i.e. בוטה (cf. 5,13 in MS C; MS A: בוטא).

17 Cf. ALONSO SCHÖKEL, Eclesiástico, 175: "La elocuencia no es puramente formal, sino que incluye un contenido honesto; algo así como el latino *vir bonus dicendi peritus*; la oposición del verso siguiente lo confirma".

3 The Relationship with Authority

Leaving aside, for reasons of lengthiness, the subject of family (Sir 3,1–16: relationship with the parents) and cult (Sir 7,29–31: relationship with priests), we restrict our study to the social and political authorities, without forgetting the strict liaison of the priestly class with the social, political, and economic centre of power of the day[18].

The varied terminology utilised by Ben Sira for designating the important persons in society does not allow us to determine the identity of the distinct figures, nor their respective functions (in reality this was no concern of the sage in his book). In spite of these difficulties, in order to facilitate our disquisition, we will speak of sages and elders, judges and leaders, and the powerful and mighty in general[19].

3.1 Sages and Elders

Sir 8,1–19 is an instruction in the form of negative counsels concerning the dangers that one has to avoid in social relations. According to the sage, erroneous attitudes in most cases consist in the indecent use of words (such as litigating with the powerful, challenging the rich, discussing with boasters, jesting with the foolish, opening one's heart to an irritable person, or trusting a fool). In vv. 8–9 Ben Sira, by way of a parallelism (the discourse of the sages/the stories of the elders), combines two types of authority: the sages and the elders.

Negative counsel:	Do not despise the discourses of the sages;
Positive counsel:	occupy yourself with their riddles/sayings
Motivation:	because herefrom you will learn instruction
	in order to present yourself before rulers[20] (Sir 8,8).

Negative counsel:	Do not despise the stories of the elders;
Explanation:	which they heard from their fathers,

---

18 Cf. WISCHMEYER, Kultur, 49–69 ("Gesellschaft"), 70–74 ("Politik und Staat"), 75–82 ("Recht").

19 Excluding the terminology referring to the sages and the elders, we will take into account the following: in Hb אדון, גדול, מלך, מושל, נדיב, נשיא, ראש, רדים, רוזנים, שד, שלטון, שופט, and in Gk ἄρχων, βασιλεύς, δυνάστης, ἡγούμενος, κριτής, μέγιστάν. Cf. the terminological analysis by MIDDENDORP, Stellung, 140–162: "Die Bezeichnungen für Regierung und Beamte".

20 In Hebrew: להתיצב לפני שרים (Gk: λειτουργῆσαι μεγιστᾶσιν).

Motivation: because from these you will receive prudence
               in order to answer when it is needed (Sir 8,9).

In the same way that the discourses and the sayings of the sages are a source of instruction (לקח, παιδεία) and teach listeners how to be of service to the great, so the stories of elders, orally transmitted, are in turn a source of prudence (שכל, σύνεσις) and teach to respond opportunely.

On the one hand, the relationship with the great, to whom we know the company and the counsel of the experts was pleasing (e. g. Sir 38,3 on the physician), has to be considered as a privilege of the sage (cf. Prov 22,29). His presence at the court or in aristocratic circles allowed him to increase his contacts, to travel abroad, to widen his culture, to enrich his experience, and, definitely, to deepen his knowledge of the human being. On the other hand, the sage was obliged to adopt a lifestyle of extreme vigilance in order to resist the temptation of corruption and bribery (Sir 20,27–29): "The sage is to be respected *for his words*[21], the prudent pleases the powerful. He who cultivates the soil heaps up the harvest, and he who pleases the powerful atones for injustice. Gifts and presents blind the eyes of the wise and as a muzzle they smother reproofs" (cf. Prov 17,8.23; 18,6). Ben Sira knows very well, probably from his own experience, that the person who gives in to pressure of the powerful and falls victim to corruption and bribery, will lose credibility with the people. And what is worse, such a person will lose something more valuable: the freedom of expression which is an indispensable condition for carrying out his or her educational task.

Although the sage's study, prayer, and pedagogical activity are perfectly compatible with civil service (Sir 39,4: "he renders service among the powerful and will be present before rulers", cf. 39,10Gk)[22], his primary and principal task should under no circumstance be made secondary to his involvement in secular affairs. In other words, for professional reasons, the sage has to ward off whatever type of bribery or extortion, whatever type of agreement or political alliance that could endanger and restrict his freedom. We must not forget that the sage does not work for himself alone, but for all who seek wisdom (cf. Sir 24,34; 36[33Hb],18)[23].

---

21 Here we follow the reading of Rahlfs (ἐν λόγοις), against Ziegler who reads ἐν ὀλίγοις.

22 Cf. GAMMIE, Sage, 366. According to this author, Sir 39,4a alludes to the service of jurisprudence that Ben Sira gave in the Ptolemaic tribunals. On this, cf. PRÉAUX, Monde, 277–280, quoted by Gammie.

23 Cf. MARBÖCK, Macht und Mächtige, 191–192.

3.2 Judges and Rulers

Most of the texts that refer to judges rebuke them for their reprehensible behaviour except for Sir 10,24 and 41,18Gk, where the judge is considered as an honourable person and a respectable authority. In fact, Ben Sira shows no restraint in dissuading his disciples from following this profession:

Do not seek to become a judge (משל, κριτής)
lest you will not be able to cease arrogance (זדון, ἀδικία)[24]
lest you be afraid before the powerful (נדיב, δυνάστης)
and sell out for a bribe your integrity (תמים, εὐθύτης)[25] (Sir 7,6).

The negative tone of the advice is indisputable. In the opinion of the sage the duty of administering justice is practically impossible, so that it may seem that the majority of judges succumbed to the arrogance of the powerful and accepted bribes without offering much resistance. One would have to be very strong and valiant, according to Ben Sira, in order to stand up against injustice and to fend off the corruption of the great. Maintaining personal and professional integrity as a judge appears therefore to be something impossible to accomplish in the social context of the sage and his disciples[26].

According to the text, the principal difficulty for performing as a judge derives from the side of the powerful, who, with their enormous influence, are able to corrupt the ministers of justice. It does not say anything about the weak and marginalised of society, whose situation of dependency and inferiority could contribute equally to problems in the administration of justice. In fact, the judge always has to see to it that he is objective and impartial in judgement, without wavering in favour of the powerful, because they are powerful, or in favour of the weak, because they are weak[27].

If the former counsel resounded with a completely negative tone, so does the following one: "Do not enter into judgement against a judge, because the

---

24 This is the only instance in the book where αδικία ("injustice") translates the Hebrew זדון ("arrogance").
25 On תמים, cf. MARGOLIS, Ecclus. 7,6d, 323.
26 According to Hengel, Sir 7,1–7 refers concretely to the high priest Onias III, successor to Simon (HENGEL, Judaism and Hellenism, vol. 1, 133–134).
27 The following comment by a jurist on this verse is interesting: "In fondo l''a ciascuno il suo' comporta certamente di tener conto, laddove però è legittimo il farlo, del destinatario; ma ciò che importa è che la considerazione appunto del destinatario non resti, nel rendere giustizia, un fattore inquinante irrazionale" (PAJARDI, Giurista, 355).

sentence will be in his favour" (Sir 8,14)²⁸. The words of the sage are convincing and need no comment. Their purport is clear: it is better not to engage in any type of conflict with judges, and much less, to frequent them on their own grounds, because the critic will always be at a disadvantage and the outcome will be certain beforehand. It is noteworthy that the Greek translator slightly changes the text emphasising its negative tone: "Do not enter into judgement against a judge, because they will judge in his favour". The use of the plural refers implicitly to the colleagues of the judge in question, who will not hesitate to cover up injustice in order to save one of their profession²⁹. By putting it in this way, the professional class of judges loses all its grounds for respect from the people.

The only judge who escapes from this fierce criticism is the Lord, the impartial judge who will not be bought with gifts and sacrifices: "Do not offer a bribe (to the Lord), because he will not accept it, and do not rely on an unjust sacrifice, for he is the God of justice (Gk: "for he is judge") and does not show partiality" (32[35Hb],11–12)³⁰. Besides being an impartial and incorruptible judge, the Lord demonstrates a special preference for the marginalised of society: the poor and the oppressed, the orphan and the widow (32[35Hb],13–15; cf. 4,7–10). This preference is evident throughout the entire Bible (Exod 22,21–23; Deut 10,18; 24,17; Prov 23,10–11)³¹. The justice of God is what Ben Sira eventually claims for his people, for they had to bear with the injustices of the powerful who wanted to promote a new concept of the world at all cost.

In order to discuss the rulers, we have to go back to Sir 9,7–10,5, a text already mentioned above. First, we considered the relationship "wisdom, word, and leadership", now we envisage another aspect: the fact that authority over the land and its citizens depends ultimately on the Lord, who chooses adequate persons for this mission. Ben Sira affirms:

> In the hands of the Lord rests the rule (ממשלת, ἐξουσία) over the world,
> and over it he raises up the right person for the time.
> In the hands of the Lord rests the rule (ממשלת, εὐοδία) over all people,
> he confers his majesty to the sovereign (Sir 10,4–5).

---

28 Cf. the duplicate of this verse in 4,27cd in MS A: "Do not sit with a wicked judge, because you will judge with him according to his whims".
29 Cf. PETRAGLIO, Potere, 51: "[...] così i giudici fanno fronte comune, impegnandosi nei modi più svariati per difendere la loro posizione anche a scapito della giustizia".
30 Cf. PAJARDI, Giurista, 361.
31 ALONSO SCHÖKEL, Eclesiástico, 270–271: "Si alguna parcialidad siente Dios, es a favor del oprimido e indefenso: en toda la historia de Israel, Dios se pone de parte del oprimido. Parece parcialidad, pero es la suprema justicia, que es victoria y salvación".

Motivated by the flagrant injustices and the continuous abuses of power on the part of the rulers (both foreign kings and local authorities), Ben Sira insists on the supremacy of God in ruling the world. In the end, it is God who directs providentially the course of the nation and makes it possible to maintain the social order[32].

The intention of the sage, according to our opinion, goes far beyond being a simple teaching on the actual providence of the Lord. His words are to be understood as a denunciation of the politics carried out by the leaders of the country. It is as if he declares openly: the only ruler of the world is the Lord and the only glory is the glory of the Lord; all the rest are illegitimate usurpations of the true authority. Once again the hidden conflict, to which we referred to at the beginning, can be guessed, though only from reading between the lines.

Since the theme of leadership is of vital importance for the formation of his students, Ben Sira puts his ideas on it in some practical counsels:

> Do not ask the Lord for power (ממשלת, ἡγεμονία),
> nor the king for a position of honour.
> Do not justify yourself before the Lord (ἔναντι κυρίου, לפני מלך)
> nor play the sage before the king (Sir 7,4–5).

In this way, then, the sage advises his disciples not to aim for the glory, the prestige, and the privileges that normally go with the persons who wield power. The disciples should not give in to the temptation to accept high offices and places of honour. Neither should they pretend to be what they are not, in order to obtain the favour of those who hold a higher status. Asserting one's righteousness before the Lord and playing the wise person before the king are two reprehensible attitudes, because they reveal a false motivation. The purpose of Ben Sira seems evident: to teach young students that authority does not consist in showing off honours and riches, nor in making use of false appearances (pretending righteousness, goodness, wisdom) in order to obtain advantages under false pretexts (cf. Sir 10,14; 11,5–6). The disciples should understand that to exercise authority is a service to the common good which more than anything else requires wisdom, honesty, and responsibility (cf. 10,1–3): three qualities that regrettably appeared not to characterise the rulers of that time.

---

32 Cf. CLEMENTS, Wisdom, 119–122, in chapter four: "Wisdom and Politics", 94–122.

3.3 The Powerful

If we question Ben Sira on what attitude one should assume before the powerful, we do not get a single categorical answer but rather various and nuanced counsels, from which emerges a humble and cautious approach that prefers a prudent distance to a radical opposition[33]. Let us consider some texts. In chapter 4 the positive series of vv. 7–10 begins with the following exhortation: "Make yourself beloved by the assembly and by the leader (לשלטון)[34], incline still more the head"[35]. On the same line of thought is found Sir 4,27, where the sage advises the youth in two ways: on the one hand, he must not let himself be dominated by a fool, and on the other hand he should not confront the powerful: "Do not submit yourself to a fool, do not resist to those who rule (תושלים)"[36]. This attitude of total submission and obedient respect before the powerful becomes much more concrete in Sir 8,1: "Do not litigate with the powerful (גדול), do not turn against his hand (Gk: fall in his hands)"[37]. Here the sage does not restrict himself to giving an advice but also adds the corresponding motivation. It is because of this that we obtain some information about the powerful: they turn out to be dangerous, since falling in their hands represents too high a price to pay for daring to confront them.

In a pericope on companions Ben Sira insists repeatedly on the danger involved in dealing with a powerful person:

> Stay away from the person who holds the power (שליט, ἐξουσίαν) to kill
> and you will not fear the fears of death.
> If you draw near (to him), do not offend him,
> lest he rob you of your life.
> You should know that you walk amidst snares
> and stroll on a net (Sir 9,13).

---

33 Cf. PETRAGLIO, Potere, 52: "Tale comportamento fondamentalmente e intessuto di sfiducia, di diffidenza e di autocontrollo".

34 According to Box—Oesterley (Book, 328), the term has to be understood in plural (thus in Syr and some Greek MSS), for it cannot refer to an individual but rather to the "gerousia" or assembly of elders. For the opposite opinion, see SKEHAN—DI LELLA, Wisdom, 167.

35 Rüger, on the basis of Syr ("before the princes of the town"), reads עיר instead of עיד and translates "before the leader of the town" (cf. RÜGER, Text, 102). Gk speaks only of μεγιστᾶνι.

36 Gk is much more explicit: μὴ λάβῃς πρόσωπον δυνάστου ("do not show partiality to the powerful").

37 Cf. the doublet of MS A (= Syr): "Do not fight with a man much stronger than you, lest you fall into his hands".

Whatever the identity of the person be to whom Ben Sira alludes, the message of the text leaves no room for doubt: it is better to keep away from the powerful than to seek his company, since approaching him involves a danger of death[38]. The sage illustrates his message of prudence with the use of images. Walking amidst snares and strolling on a net are metaphors that express in poetical form the danger which the proximity of the powerful represents: the snares are the pits that provoke the fall of a traveller and the net is the wall with battlements from where the enemy is constantly watched. In such a situation all precaution means little and the greater the distance between the adversaries, the better it is.

And when speaking of precaution, we may not ignore the instruction of Ben Sira in 13,8–13, a pericope which deals with a very influential social group, the nobility or aristocracy (cf. vv. 1–7, on the rich):

8 Be careful not to be presumptuous,
  do not be as those devoid of judgement.
9 If you approach a noble man (נדיב), keep your distance,
  so that he insists that you come closer.
10 Do not come too close, lest he sends you away,
  do not keep too much distance, lest he hates you.
11 Do not believe that you can feel secure with him,
  and do not put your trust in his speaking,
  for with his many words he will put you to the test
  and, laughing at you, he will scrutinise you.
12 With cruelty he will lord it over you
  and he will not spare you the chains[39].
13 Be careful and stay alert
  do not walk with violent men (אנשי חמס).

---

38 According to Di Lella, Ben Sira alludes to the intrigues of the courts of the Ptolemaic and Seleucid kings that easily lead to situations that might cost people their lives (SKEHAN–DI LELLA, Wisdom, 220). Morla Asensio, on the contrary, thinks of a typological situation in which the "person capable of killing" is the one who leads others unto their destruction (cf. MORLA ASENSIO, Eclesiástico, 59).

39 The Hebrew text of MS A is corrupt. The Greek reads: ἀνελεήμων ὁ μὴ συντηρῶν λόγους καὶ οὐ μὴ φείσηται περὶ κακώσεως καὶ δεσμῶν ("he is a heartless person who does not keep his word and who will not spare you beating and chains"). As far as the first colon is concerned, cf. the Origenic recension: ἀνελεημόνως δὲ συντηρήσει λόγον σου ("without compassion he will keep you to your word") and the Lat: *immitis animus illius conservabit verba tua.*

Leaving aside the well known parallelism between our text and the Instruction of Phibis (P.Insinger 10,12–11,23)[40], we concentrate on the teaching of Ben Sira. The inclusion between Sir 13,8 (השמר, "be careful") and 13,13 (השמר והיה זהיר, "be careful and stay alert") defines the tone of the text and warns the hearer or reader. In the presence of an aristocrat one should be careful, pay attention, be watchful, stay alert, or, what is the same, keep the right distance. The wise do not stay too far away nor come to close to the powerful because going to either extreme could antagonize them and, without warning, cause the sage to fall into a trap. The aristocrat has no scruples and is capable of tricking someone with his smooth and sarcastic talk. The aristocrat does not respect the freedom of the other, for it is his goal to dominate at any cost, making use of cruelty and violence[41]. With regard to such a person the sage advises acting with common sense, i.e. with caution and precaution, since otherwise one could lose one's life. Many similar ideas, but less forcefully expressed, are found in 'Abot 2,3: "Be cautious with (those in) authority, for they do not let a man approach them but for their own purposes; and they appear like friends when it is to their advantage, and stand not by a man in the hour of his need"[42].

4 Conclusion

With the data obtained in our study we now want to answer the initial question: Is Ben Sira primarily motived by fear of the powerful or by respect for authority? Faced with the choice between these alternatives our answer—in keeping with the pedagogy of the sage—will be neither single nor categorical. We intend to approach the question under consideration from the point of view of experience, without pretending to impose a solution or to distort the data.

On the one hand, there is no denying that Ben Sira presents a rather negative image of the authorities, though a faithful representation of the hard reality of that time. The texts on the judge, the aristocrat, the ruler, or the powerful person expose the dark side of the persons, i.e. their faults (partiality, corruption, abuse of power, intimidation, violence, and the like). In the face of this reality, instead of demonstrating his disapproval or promoting rebellion, the sage recommends submission (not offering resistance), obedience (bowing one's head), moderation

---

40 Cf. SANDERS, Ethics, 73–106; ID., Egyptian Parallel, 257–258; ID., Demotic Wisdom, 85.92–93.

41 According to Di Lella, "the violent men" could be members of the pagan aristocracy of Israel (cf. SKEHAN—DI LELLA, Wisdom, 253).

42 Quoted by BOX—OESTERLEY, Book, 363.

(not speaking too much), and prudence (keeping some distance between the wise person and the powerful). All these are attitudes which maintain the established order and avoid any type of confrontation.

Behind this humble, calm, and prudent attitude we perceive a certain "sensation of fear" which the sage wants to cover up with what Sanders calls an *Ethik der Vorsicht* (ethics of caution). Aware of the grave dangers that beset the Jewish people, Ben Sira prefers to keep a reasonable distance from the powerful rather than to confront the injustice and the corruption of their system openly.

On the other hand, the judicious realism of the sage does not prevent him from recognizing and showing his disciples the values of authentic authority. We should not forget that, although the social-political situation of the country might be very dramatic, Ben Sira is faced with the task of encouraging his audience, the young leaders of the future. Therefore, he speaks without reservation on the supremacy of God in ruling the world and of his initiative when appointing the elect to exercise authority within his realm. Not only in this case, but also on other occasions he considers the authorities (in the familiar, social, and political atmosphere) as persons worthy of honour and respect. When speaking of what one has to be ashamed of, he says: "Be ashamed of immorality before your father and mother, and of lies before rulers and aristocracy (Gk: leaders). Of deceit before masters and matrons[43], and of iniquity before the assembly of the people" (Sir 41,17–18). We should note the fact that rulers and leaders of the history of Israel also belong to the category of the illustrious ancestors, and therefore are equally worthy of eulogy and praise (cf. Sir 44,3–7).

Fear of the powerful? In the end: Yes! Respect for authority? In the end: Yes! What it boils down to, then, is: exercise extreme caution with those in power, and show extreme respect for those who fear the Lord. Honour, riches, nobility, influence and power are values that enjoy high esteem among people, but they can never surpass fear-of-God. Fear-of-the-Lord is the essential attitude of a sage and of all who sincerely seek wisdom: "The leader, the ruler, and the judge are honoured, but no one is greater than he who fears the Lord" (Sir 10,24), since the fullness of wisdom consists in fear-of-the-Lord and in observance of the Law (cf. Sir 19,20).

---

43 While the Hebrew text (MSS A and Mas) speaks of "master and matron" (מאדון וגברת), the Greek version prefers "judge and magistrate" (ἀπὸ κρίτου [= מדין] καὶ ἄρχοντος [= מגביר]). Cf. MINISSALE, Versione greca, 107 note 126, where the author underlines the fact that the Hb and Gk represent a different sociological context: the service of the aristocratic Jews at the court of foreign kings and queens (Smend) and the duty of citizens before the authority of the judge (Segal).

"Cut Her Away from Your Flesh": Divorce in Ben Sira

The Book of Ben Sira is known for its decidedly misogynist outlook, a feature that it shares with other Wisdom books (cf. Proverbs) and other Jewish authors of the Greco-Roman era (cf. Flavius Josephus). Whether this hostile attitude to women simply reflects the patriarchal society of the time (Gilbert, Di Lella, Camp)[1], or a personal obsession of the sage (Trenchard)[2], or faithfulness to tradition for pedagogical purposes (Wischmeyer)[3], or an attempt at the construction of an ideal androcentric reality (Schroer)[4] is debated by authors of all tendencies, not just feminists.

Nevertheless, Ben Sira always portrays Lady Wisdom in a positive light, despite the negative attitude of the sage towards women in general. This contrast certainly is astonishing and provokes very different reactions among readers (cf. e. g. McKinlay, Bergant, and Strotmann)[5].

1 Women in the Book of Ben Sira

The Book of Ben Sira pays a great deal of attention to women[6]. About 100 verses speak of them, either directly or through expressions like "the mother's womb" (1,14; 40,1; 46,13Hb; 49,7; 50,22) or "born from a woman" (10,18). Some verses are part of a larger literary unit: 3,1–16 (respect for the father and mother); 7,18–28 (family relations, vv. 24–26: daughters and spouse); 9,1–9 (dangerous women); 23,16–27 (sexual passions, vv. 22–27: the adulteress); 25,13–26 (the evil spouse); 26,1–18 (the good and the evil spouse) and 41,14–42,8 (true and false shame, vv. 22–24: the married woman, the prostitute and the maidservant). Some verses are part of a smaller literary unit: 7,27–28 (parents), 22,3–5 (daughters), 33(36Hb),21–26 (the wife) and 42,9–14 (daughters). To this list can be added a series of verses scattered throughout the book, in which mention is also made

---

1 GILBERT, Femme, 426–442; SKEHAN—DI LELLA, Wisdom; ARCHER, Price; CAMP, Understanding Patriarchy, 1–39.
2 TRENCHARD, View on Women.
3 WISCHMEYER, Kultur.
4 SHROER, Weisheit.
5 MCKINLAY, Gendering Wisdom, 160–178; BERGANT, Israel's Wisdom; STROTMANN, Buch, 428–440.
6 For a general presentation, cf. CALDUCH-BENAGES, Mujeres, 37–44.

https://doi.org/10.1515/9783110492316-008

of widows, virgins, Lady Wisdom, and, of course, women in general: 4,10; 7,19; 15,2; 19,2.11; 20,4; 23,14; 25,1.8; 28,15; 30,20; 31(34Hb),5; 32(35Hb),14; 36(33Hb),20; 37,11; 40,19.23; 42,6; 47,6Hb.19.

In the book, therefore, mothers, spouses, widows, daughters, virgins, maid-servants, popular singers, courtesans and prostitutes always appear in relationship to a man whose role determines the nature of the relationship (son, husband, father, eunuch, master or victim/customer). Moreover, all these women are described from a masculine point of view: that of the Jewish sage, who, faithful to the tradition of the ancients, writes his book thinking only and exclusively of his young disciples in whom he wants to inculcate a rigorous doctrine/discipline regarding women.

Married women receive special attention. The sage divides them into two basic ethical categories: good spouses and bad spouses (cf. especially Sir 25,13–26,18[7] and 36Hb,21–26 [33Gk,26–31). This division, made from a completely androcentric perspective, is exclusively concerned with the happiness, desires, convenience and authority of the husband. In other words, with regard to the wife, goodness or wickedness are to be judged from the perspective of the husband.

2 The Syriac Version and Women

The Syriac version of the Book of Ben Sira[8] probably was written by a Jew (3rd–4th century AD) and revised by a Christian before the 5th century AD. Compared with the Hebrew and Greek text this version is characterized by a series of significant theological changes regarding belief in eternal life, the creation of wisdom, the authority of the Jewish "fathers", the practice of poverty and especially regarding the attitude towards women. With regard to women the Syriac version is more benevolent and more condescending, or at least more respectful, in some aspects.

On the theme of women the Syriac version basically coincides with the Hebrew/Greek text, but there are some exceptions to this general rule. There are inexplicable changes (modifications, additions and omissions) that do not fall under the category of linguistic errors due to a mistaken or excessively subjective interpretation of the Hebrew text. Other changes, of course, seem to have been

---

7 GkII and Syr contain an addition of 9 verses (26,19–27) missing in Hb and GkI. According to P.W. Skehan, "The presumption is that the verses were composed in Hb, though they are not extant in that language" (SKEHAN–Di LELLA, Wisdom, 346).

8 Cf. CALDUCH-BENAGES–FERRER–LIESEN, Wisdom of the Scribe, 13–58.

inserted deliberately into the text for reasons of a different kind. Moreover, the translator perhaps decided not to translate some verses of the Hebrew text, either because he did not agree with the content or perhaps they offended his sensibility.

I mention five texts that are significant regarding women: in the first two the translator diverges from the original text, introducing some changes that favour women (Sir 37,11 and 40,1)[9]; in the other three he prefers to remain silent and not to translate a series of expressions in bad taste, some of which (esp. Sir 42,14a: "The wickedness of a man is better than the goodness of a woman") have become classical examples of a misogynist attitude often quoted by authors (cf. Sir 41,22–24; 42,6).

3 Ben Sira and Divorce

Our objective is not to take up the whole theme of Ben Sira and women, which would certainly go beyond the limits of this essay, but we want to zoom in on one particular question of this theme: divorce. Divorce is a topic that touches upon the whole institution of the family, starting with the two spouses, the husband and the wife[10]. For this topic, we take into consideration those texts of Ben Sira that mention divorce either explicitly or allude to it indirectly. As far as we know, apart from the monograph by Warren C. Trenchard (1982)[11], which till today is the only one dedicated to women in Ben Sira, these texts have not been the object of a specific study; we are speaking of Sir 7,26 (cf. 42,9); 25,26 and 28,15.

---

9 Sir 37,11aGk/Hb: "Do not consult with a woman concerning her rival"; Syr: "With a woman, do not commit adultery". Sir 40,1Gk/Hb: "A heavy destiny was assigned (Hb: has been assigned by God) to every person, a heavy yoke is upon the sons of Adam, from the day they went forth from their mother's womb till the day they return to the mother of all (Hb adds: 'the living')"; Syr: "Great things God has created and many labours for human beings, from when they went forth from their mother's womb and till they rest in the land of life".
10 On divorce in Ben Sira, cf. COLLINS, Jewish Wisdom, 65–66. On divorce in second temple Judaism, cf. ARCHER, Price, 217–220; COLLINS, Marriage, 115–121; INSTONE-BREWER, Divorce, 59–84.
11 [cf., also, Balla, Family (2010) and Ellis, Gender (2013)].

3.1 Your Spouse and Divorce (Sir 7,26)

The second part of Sir 7[12] (vv. 17–36) contains some advice concerning family life (vv. 18–28), divine cult (vv. 29–31) and service to one's neighbour (vv. 32–35) culminating in v. 36: "In all that you do think of the end and thus you will not commit sins". In 7,18–28 the sage gives the disciple pieces of advice on domestic life (vv. 18–21), then on the possessions of the husband (vv. 22–26), and finally, on relationships with one's father and mother (vv. 27–28)[13].

Characteristic of Sir 7,22–26 is the quadruple repetition of the possessive pronoun לך referring to livestock, to sons, to daughters, and, in the last place, to the wife. The text is in line with the tradition of the Decalogue which groups together in the last commandment house, woman, servants and livestock (Exod 20,17; cf. Deut 5,21 where the woman is mentioned first, followed by house, fields, servants and livestock). The advice of the sage concerning livestock and sons follows the same linguistic pattern (impv. + impv.) and is formulated positively; the same applies to the advice concerning daughters except for v. 24b ("do not show yourself too indulgent with them"). However, when it comes to the spouse (v. 26), Ben Sira not only changes the pattern, introducing an antithetical proposition, but also expresses himself exclusively in the negative mode: אשה לך אל תתעבה ושנואה אל תמאן בה ("If you have a spouse, do not abhor her, but if she is hateful, do not trust her").

3.1.1 First colon (Sir 7,26a)
In 7,26a the use of the verb תעב is surprising. It is not frequent in the Old Testament and in the Piel it means: "regard as an abomination", "abhor", or "cause to be an abomination", "make abominable"[14]. In Deut 7,26 it refers to idols, and in Deut 23,8; Job 19,19 and 30,10 to persons. In the last two instances, it expresses the repugnance which the friends of Job feel when confronted with his festering wounds. Apart from 7,26 Ben Sira also uses תעב in 11,2b (MSS A and B): "Do not abhor a man for his looks", which the Gk translates with βδελύσσω (cf. 16,8;

---

12 On the thematic and literary unity of Sir 7, cf. GRANADOS, Humildad, 155–169.
13 These verses exist in Gk and Syr but are missing in Hb (MS A), probably because of homoiarcton. Cf. HASPECKER, Gottesfurcht, 298 note 39. According to Hart, "the verses (27–28) complete the scale of duties ascending from cattle to God" (HART [ed.], Ecclesiasticus, 110–111).
14 Cf. the two possible translations in Skehan–Di Lella's commentary: "If you have a wife, let not seem odious to you/abhor her not" (SKEHAN–DI LELLA, Wisdom, 205 and 206).

20,8). In 7,26a the sage offers no explanation for אל תתעבה[15], nor does he add reasons or specify concrete situations, but he only limits himself to saying: "Do not abhor your wife". It is therefore understood that one should not abhor her in any case or circumstances. Although the text does not explicitly mention divorce, various authors detect here an allusion to it[16]. Yaron, e. g. considers תעב in this case to be synonymous with שׂנא (meaning "to divorce") and thinks that the sage uses it in order to avoid repetition of the expression in the same verse. Hence his translation: "Hast thou a wife divorce her not, and trust not a divorcee"[17]. However, the use of תעב instead of גרשׁ, the technical expression for divorce (ἐκβάλλω in the LXX)[18], attested in the Old Testament (cf. Num 30,10; Lev 21,7.14; 22,13; Ezek 44,22) and also in Qumran (4Q159 2–4, 10; CD XIII, 17; 11Q19 LIX, 4) should put us on our guard against Yaron's interpretation[19].

Let us now turn to the Greek version: γυνή σοί ἐστιν κατὰ ψυχήν; μὴ ἐκβάλῃς αὐτήν ("If you have a wife that pleases you, do not cast her out"). With the addition of κατὰ ψυχήν (lit. "according to [your] soul")[20] the translator breaks away from the parallelism which is characteristic of 7,22a (κτήνη σοί ἐστιν), 7,23a (τέκνα σοί ἐστιν) and 7,24a (θυγατέρες σοί ἐστιν) and makes a clear concession to the husband, appealing to his personal taste. If the spouse is pleasing to the husband, then Ben Sira advises not casting her out. With the verb ἐκβάλλω

---

15 The verb תעב leads us to the noun תועבה ("abomination"), a strong expression that normally refers to the sins of idolatry (esp. in Deut and the later prophets) and, in some cases, to matters of a sexual nature (Lev 18,22.26.27.29; 20,13; Deut 22,5; 23,18). Mopsik (Sagesse, 111) quotes these texts in order to justify his translation of אל תתעבה in 7,26a ("qu'elle ne te répugne pas" [that she doesn't disgust you]) and his surprising explanation: "Il est donc probable que l'aversion ou la répugnance dont il est question dans ce verset [...] se rapporte à la sexualité feminine" (It is therefore likely that the aversion or repugnance referred to in this verse [...] relates to female sexuality).

16 Among others, Ryssel, Smend, Box—Oesterley, Spicq, Snaith, Morla Asensio in their respective commentaries. GASPAR (Social Ideas, 35) and MINISSALE (Siracide, 65) also see an allusion to divorce in 7,19a. Thus, Minissale proposes to translate אל תמאס ("do not despise") with "do not send away".

17 YARON, Divorce, 118. See also COLLINS, Jewish Wisdom, 66: "Ben Sira is most probably advising against trusting a divorced woman, probably on the realistic ground that 'hell hath no fury like a woman scorned'".

18 Other technical expressions are שלח, הוציא, עזב, and the disputed שׂנא to which we will return later. Cf. YARON, Divorce, 117–121.

19 The translation by Kaiser (Weisheit, 23) is extremely favourable to wives and eliminates all possible allusions to divorce: "Hast du eine Frau, so bleibe ihr zugetan".

20 VL: secundum animam tuam (= Syh: ʾyk npšk, "according to your soul"). Minissale (Versione greca, 254) understands this as "un'aggiunta esplicativa" (an explanatory addition).

("repudiate, send away")[21] the translator passes from cause to effect[22], leaving open for the husband the possibility of divorce, a possibility that was certainly not foreseen in the Hebrew text. In ancient law, the verb ἐκβάλλω (together with ἀποπέμπω and ἐκπέμπω) was used as the technical expression for a husband taking the initiative to separate from his wife[23]. Thus, e.g. Demosthenes (4th century BC) tells us how Phrastor, an Athenian of Aegilia put away (ἐκβάλλει) his woman after living with her for about a year (Neaer. 51), and Andocides (5th–4th century BC) tells us of the scandal caused by Callias, son of Hipponicus (Myst. 125). After having married a young woman, Callias took as wife her mother also, i.e. his mother-in-law. The three of them lived together in the same house, until the young woman, on the verge of suicide, made her escape. Shortly afterwards Callias grew tired of his mother-in-law also and sent her off (ἐξέβαλε)[24].

3.1.2 Second colon (Sir 7,26b)

In 7,26b Hb and Gk coincide. Both texts present a man married to a "hateful/hated" wife שנואה (Gk: μισουμένη; VL: odibili)[25]. In this case, the sage advises the husband not to trust her, because, understandably, the "hateful/hated" woman represents a serious danger to the husband. According to Trenchard, "This line is merely a corrective, added to line a [7,26a] to dampen the effect of what could be taken as an unconditional injunction against abhorring one's wife"[26]. It is evident that the problem here is the interpretation of שנואה, a f. pass. ptc. from שנא, which has the same meaning in all West Semitic languages: "to hate", "to feel aversion toward someone or something".

(1) The expression can refer to, and this is how we understand it, a woman that a man has to put up with, because—we do not know the reasons—she makes herself hateful, horrible and detestable to the man. In other words, this woman is at the opposite pole of the woman "that pleases you" of the Greek version. Consequently, it is most probable—although the text does not state it—that the husband ends up by sending her off. This is the case in Prov 30,23a. Among all the things that make the earth tremble, there is the "woman שנואה (Gk: μισητή) who

---

21 Syr: *l' tšbqyh* ("do not send her away"). VL: *Non proicias illam.*

22 MINISSALE, Versione greca, 190.

23 HARRISON, Law, 40.

24 Charondas, the giver of laws of the Thurians, said: "If a man sends his wife away (ἐκβάλη) he may not marry a woman younger than the wife whom he had sent away (ἐκβληθείσης)" (DIODORUS SICULUS, Bib. hist. 12,18).

25 Syr: *w'n 'wl'* ("and if she is wicked").

26 TRENCHARD, View on Women, 91.

finds a husband". Some think of a spinster of a certain age, unbearable and without any redeeming features. On the basis of the context we prefer to think that it refers to a hateful, horrible or undesirable wife who in the end is sent off by the husband. The characters in Prov 30,21–23[27] either find themselves in a situation for the first time that previously they were envious of, or in a situation in which they have suffered humiliation, or confronted by a situation that they have gone through before they become resentful. This is the case with the servant who becomes king, with the fool who, thanks to a stroke of fortune, fills up with bread, with the maidservant who takes the place of her mistress, and with the wife who, after having been rejected/sent off by her husband, succeeds in getting married again. Of this last one, Alonso Schökel comments: "when in the end she finds a husband, her resentment bursts free and she becomes unbearable"[28].

It seems that Ben Sira employs the verb שנא also in Sir 42,9d referring to a married daughter. In spite of the bad condition of MSS B (ובבתוליה פן [....]) and Mas (ובֹ[..]יה פן [....])[29] and notwithstanding their differences we can, with the help of the versions[30], attempt to reconstruct the Hebrew text: ובעלה פן תשנא ("and when married, lest she be hated"). That is to say: the father suffers because of his daughter, who, if married, is hated and then sent away by the husband. If this were the case, the daughter would return to the house of her father, and then he would again have to take care of her, at least until she could find a new husband. And the worst of it is that the honour of the father would suffer a hard blow[31]. Mopsik, on the other hand, basing himself on b. Sanh. 100b, understands that the father suffers on account of his married daughter not bearing children[32], since a barren woman ran the risk of being sent away by the husband (cf. y. Yebam. 64a).

(2) The participle שנואה could also be taken as the neglected spouse, the one not loved, the one not preferred, which would presuppose a polygamous

---

27 On this numerical proverb, cf. VAN LEEUWEN, Proverbs 30:21–23, 599–610.

28 ALONSO SCHÖKEL—VÍLCHEZ LÍNDEZ, Proverbios, 519: "Cuando por fin encuentra marido, desfoga su resentimiento y se vuelve insoportable".

29 BEENTJES, Book, 167. Cf. the reconstruction by Yadin: ובימיה פן תן[נש]ה ("and in her heyday lest she be [forgotten]") (YADIN, Ben Sira Scroll, 182, 218 and 219); and E. QIMRON, Notes on the Reading, 229.

30 Gk: καὶ συνῳκηκυῖα, μήποτε μισηθῇ ("and if married, lest she be hated"); Syr: "and (staying) with her husband, lest she be rejected" (dl' tstn').

31 CAMP, Understanding Patriarchy, 37: "As his property, he [the father] is honor-bound to prevent encroachment on them [his daughters]".

32 MOPSIK, Sagesse, 253. Cf. GREENFIELD, Ben Sira 42.9–10, 167–173.

marriage, or at least a bigamous marriage[33] (cf. the situation of Rachel and Leah in Gen 29,31.33 or the legislation of Deut 21,15–17 which deals with the case of a husband with two wives, one preferred [אהובה] and the other hated [שנואה]). This is the position of Sauer who, following Ginzberg and Kuhn, translates שנואה with "Nebenbuhlerin", i.e. rival, intruder, or competitor of the spouse (cf. Sir 25,14 [disputed text]; 26,6; 37,11)[34]. We do not know much about the practice of polygamy at the time of Ben Sira. In any case, most authors think that though polygamy was permitted in the second temple period (it was declared illegal for Jews by emperor Theodosius I in 393 AD), monogamous marriage was the general rule[35]. This commonly-held view has been challenged by the Babatha archive from Naḥal Ḥever near the Dead Sea (early 2nd century AD). A Greek papyrus dated the 9th July 131 AD contains the conflicting claims of the two wives (Babatha and Miriam) of Yehuda. This case shows that polygamy, or at least bigamy, was not such an exceptional practice among the Jews of the Tannaitic period[36].

(3) We also have to take in consideration the use of the verb שׂנא in the Judeo-Aramaic marital contracts from the colony of Elephantine in Upper Egypt (5th century BC)[37]. While in these juridical documents the verb גרשׁ does not appear, the Aramaic תרך does and, in most cases, it is accompanied by the noun בית in the expression "drive [him/her] from the house" (AP 15,30; BMAP 7,30; BMAP 6,16).

On the basis of a study of the only three contracts preserved in good condition (AP 15; BMAP 2; BMAP 7), H. Nutkowicz recently has demonstrated that the verb שׂנא in this specific matrimonial context does not mean "to divorce"—as is usually held—but rather "to break a covenant". The expression under consideration is part of the formalities of separation of spouses, which go through various stages: the declaration of hate, the acquiring of the right to be divorced and the actual leaving of the house. In other words, שׂנא introduces the separation, marks the rupture but not the dissolving of the marriage[38]. Taking into account the fact that the matrimonial contracts from Elephantine employ a juridical language that is not proper to Ben Sira, we believe that what has been said

---

33 Cf. EGGER-WENZEL, Polygamie, 57–64.

34 SAUER, Jesus Sirach, 90 note 113. Cf. also PETERS, Buch, 73; DUESBERG—FRANSEN, Ecclesiastico, 124; ALONSO SCHÖKEL, Eclesiástico, 168.

35 COLLINS, Jewish Wisdom, 65; ID., Marriage, 121–122.128–130; INSTONE-BREWER, Divorce, 59–65. Polygamy was prohibited in Qumran (cf. CD IV, 20–V, 2; 11Q19 LVII, 15–19).

36 LEWIS (ed.), Greek Papiry, 113–115; see also 22–24.

37 Cf. the following expressions: כסף שנואה, "the money of hate" (AP 15,23; BMAP 2,8.9; 7,22.25) and דין שנואה, "the law or judgement of hate" (AP 18,1; BMAP 7,34.39).

38 Cf. NUTKOWICZ, Verbe, 169.172.

about the verb שׂנא also applies to Sir 7,26b. Here, instead of affirming explicitly the divorce as the versions do, the participle שׂנואה rather denotes a strong disagreement between husband and wife[39] that weakens the affective ties between the spouses and can become the beginning of a definite separation.

It is noteworthy that while in the text of Ben Sira the initiative for the separation/divorce comes from the husband (cf. the Talmudic law), in the Elephantine contracts the wives too have the freedom to decide to separate from their spouse[40]. Thus we read in AP 15,23: "Tomorrow or another day (if) Miphtahiah should stand up in the congregation and say, I hate (שׂנאת) Azor my husband", and in AP 9,8–9: "If tomorrow or another day you lay out this land and then my daughter hates you (תשׂנאנך), and goes away from you". This juridical practice reflects the free condition of women and at the same time testifies to a mental openness and broadness of vision that do not seem typical of the time[41].

The papyri of Elephantine are not the only ones to attest the freedom of women to divorce their husbands. Among the documents found by Yigael Yadin in Naḥal Ṣe'elim, just south of Naḥal Ḥever, there is a divorce bill sent by a wife to her husband in 135 AD. Shelamzion, daughter of Joseph Qesbshan, says to her husband Eleazar, son of Hananniah: "This is from me to you a bill of divorce and release (גט שבקין ותרכנין)" (P.Ṣe'elim 13)[42].

3.2 The Evil Wife and Divorce (Sir 25,26)

In Sir 25,13–26,18 Ben Sira offers four instructions on the married woman, in which the two aforementioned ethical categories alternate: wickedness and goodness. The evil wives of Sir 25,13–26 and 26,5–12 are set in contrast with the good wives of Sir 26,1–4 and 26,13–18. The contrast between both figures is disproportionate, given the fact that the evil wives receive greater attention than the good ones. Moreover, the merits of the good wives are narrowed down to attitudes and actions that are in favour of their husbands.

After the fatal affirmation of Sir 25,24 ("From a woman sin had its beginning and because of her we all die") the sage concludes his first instruction on the evil

---

39 SKEHAN–DI LELLA, Wisdom, 203: "where there is ill feeling".
40 Whether this is due to an Egyptian influence or rather the fruit of an ancient West Semitic tradition attested since the 19th century BC is a matter of debate among scholars. Cf. LIPIŃSKI, Marriage, 63–71.
41 Cf. NUTKOWICZ, Verbe, 173.
42 Cf. ILAN, Notes, 195–202.

wife with two verses, which, though missing in Hebrew, have been preserved in the versions. The Greek text runs like this:

μὴ δῷς ὕδατι διέξοδον μηδὲ γυναικὶ πονηρᾷ παρρησίαν·
εἰ μὴ πορεύεται κατὰ χεῖράς σου, ἀπὸ τῶν σαρκῶν σου ἀπότεμε αὐτήν.

Do not give water an outlet, nor boldness of speech to an evil wife;
if she does not walk by your hand, cut her off from your flesh (Sir 25,25–26).

Let us analyse v. 26 in greater detail, which in the words of Cohen, contains a "pithy phrase or sentence" that can be considered as the crystallization of the concept of divorce[43].

3.2.1 First colon (Sir 25,26a)

In 25,26a Ben Sira presents the motive[44] (the only one!) that can bring a husband to separate himself from an evil spouse. The expression "if she does not walk by your hand" (reconstructed Hebrew: אם לא תלך על ידך) is so generic as to embrace all possibilities in favour of the husband, and can be understood as a broad interpretation of the legislation on divorce in Deut 24,1–4. Instead of the controversial expression ערות דבר (lit. "nakedness of a matter"), "some indecency" (Deut 24,1), which seems to restrict the supposed fault of the woman to the sexual sphere, in Sir 25,26a the sage uses an image that denotes total submission to the husband. A wife who "does not walk by the hand" of the husband is an independent spouse who does not want to be governed, directed or controlled in any circumstance or situation of life[45]. Snaith remarks in a very acute way: "Ben Sira seems remarkably liberal—perhaps because of his prejudice!"[46]

In fact, the advice of the sage is in line with the later legislation according to which any motive alleged by the husband was valid in order to justify divorce. According to the school of Hillel, [he may divorce his wife] "even if she spoiled his dish" and R. Akiba adds "even if he found someone more beautiful than her" (m. Giṭ. 9,10)[47]. Flavius Josephus is of the same mind when he writes: "At this

---

43 COHEN, Law, 387.
44 VL adds: [25,35b]*et confundet te in conspectu inimicorum* (cf. 42,11).
45 Some translations that have been proposed: if she does not behave according to your wishes/if she does not do what you want/if she does not want to submit to you/if she does not obey you punctually/if she go not as you would have her/if she refuses to walk by your side/ if she does not accept your control.
46 SNAITH, Ecclesiasticus, 131.
47 Conversely, according to the school of Shammai, "a man should divorce his wife only because he has found grounds for it in unchastity" (m. Giṭ. 9,10).

time I also divorced/sent away my wife [his second wife], being displeased at her behaviour" (Vita, 426) or also: "One who wishes for whatever reason [...] to be divorced from a woman who is living with him" (A.J. 4,253; cf. Matt 19,3–9). The same goes for Philo of Alexandria in Spec. 3,30, where he presents the case from the perspective of the woman[48].

3.2.2 Second colon (Sir 25,26b)
In the case of an evil and rebellious wife Ben Sira does not hesitate to recommend a divorce. His wording is powerful: "cut her from your flesh" (reconstructed Hebrew: מבשרך גזר/כרת אותה). This original metaphor can be understood as a correlative of the text in which here man and woman are said to become "one flesh" (cf. Gen 2,23–24)[49]. It is also a kind of *formula contraria* that preceded the document of divorce and that indicated the separation of the spouses (cf. Hos 2,4: "She is not my wife and I am not her husband")[50]. In this respect, it is worth mentioning a Babylonian marriage contract from ca. 625–623 BC which uses a slight variation of the same metaphor that Ben Sira employs. Here the metaphor does not refer to divorce but to the commitment to be established between the two future spouses. It is a curious case in which it is the bride who contracts her marriage (the groom's request for the bride was most often addressed to the bride's father, brother or mother). The son of Nadinu says to his fiancée Qunnabatu: "Cut yourself off from any other man. Be a wife", and the text continues: "Qunnabatu consented (to this proposal) and she will cut herself off from any other man"[51].

MS 248 completes the colon by adding to it: δίδου καὶ ἀπόλυσον (give and send [her]). Still more explicit is Syr: *hb lh wšdyh mn bytk* ("give to her[52] and dismiss her from your house")[53]. These two texts seem to suppose the presentation by the husband of a document of divorce, the ספר כריתות (Deut 24,1.3; Isa 50,1; Jer 3,8)[54], which literally means, "document of cutting", "deed of cutting asunder".

---

48 Cf. NEUDECKER, Ehescheidungsgesetzt, 350–387, esp. 356–360.
49 CAMP, Understanding Patriarchy, 29: "But 'one flesh' also implies, specifically, an exclusive sexual relationship. Thus, the particular way in which the wife has not walked by her husband's side is also suggested".
50 FALK, Hebrew Law, 151. For other interpretations, cf. TRENCHARD, View on Women, 84.
51 Cf. ROTH, Babylonian Marriage, 39–40.
52 It can refer to the divorce document, or, according to Smend, to the dowry or to the material goods in the case of a rich wife (cf. SMEND, Weisheit, 233).
53 VL adds: [25,36b]*ne semper te abutatur* (cf. 26,10).
54 Gk: τὸν βιβλίον τοῦ ἀποστασίου; VL: *libellus repudii*.

This expression probably harks back to the ceremony that accompanied the divorce. In an Old Assyrian document of divorce (ca. 1400 BC) the husband says: "I have cut off the fringe of her garment" (*sí-is-sí-ik-ta-sha ab-ta-táq*)[55]. It is not surprising, therefore, that from this ancient ritual the document of divorce took its name of "document of cutting".

With the addition "dismiss her from your house", the Syriac version signals the conclusion of the process ending in divorce. The same expression is found in Deut 24,1–2 where the action of the husband (ושלחה מביתו, "he sent her away from his house") corresponds to that of the wife (ויצאה מביתו, "and she left his house")[56]. Given that cohabitation is the essential element of a marriage, the wife leaving the house marks the effective dissolution of the matrimonial bond.

3.2.3 The Babylonian Talmud

The Babylonian Talmud contains 31 verses from the Book of Ben Sira, 12 of which deal with women[57]. Not all verses are authentic quotations: there are also close renderings, which we will consider below. In b. Sanh. 100b we read:

"An evil woman is a plague to her husband (אשה רעה צרעת לבעלה). What is the solution? (מאי תקנתיה) Let him banish [divorce] her from his house (יגרשנה מביתו) and be healed from his plague (ויתרפא מצרעת)".

While the first phrase reminds us of Sir 26,7 ("An evil wife is an ox yoke which chafes; taking hold of her is like grasping a scorpion"), the last one certainly is inspired by the extended form of Sir 25,26 as found in Syr and the Greek MS 248[58]. Like Ben Sira, the rabbis recommended that the husband divorce an "evil wife", because she is considered as on par with a disease (lit.: "leprosy"), which if not dealt with in time, could destroy the health of the husband. Metaphors change but the ideas are the same.

---

55 For this and other legislative Sumerian texts that contain the same expression, cf. KOSCHAKER, Rechtsurkunden, 24.

56 The terminology for divorce is very similar in Roman law: *discidium* ("a cutting asunder"), *dimittere* ("to send away"), *domo expellere* ("to drive out of the house"), *baete foras* ("go out"). On divorce in both legislations, cf. COHEN, Law, 377–408.

57 Cf. ILAN, Integrating, 155–174: "Ben Sira's Misogyny and its Reception by the Babylonian Talmud". For other perspectives on this theme, LEVENE, Theology, 305–320, esp. 309–311.

58 Cf. WRIGHT III, B. Sanhedrin 100b, 48.

3.3 The Valiant Wife and Divorce (Sir 28,15)

Sir 28,15 is part of a passage dedicated to the abuses of the tongue (28,13–26), in which the sage warns about gossip, lies and, in a special way, about slander. The first section focuses on the destructive force of slander (28,13–18) and the second praises piety as a remedy for it (28,19–26).

Slander (lit. "the third tongue") causes various disasters: it leads many into exile, destroys strongholds and overturns the house of the nobility (28,14). Even entire families fall victim to its devastating power; it is an irresistible power that destroys peace and sows discord among its members. In 28,15 the sage affirms:

γλῶσσα τρίτη γυναῖκας ἀνδρείας ἐξέβαλεν
καὶ ἐστέρεσεν αὐτὰς τῶν πόνων αὐτῶν.

The third tongue has driven away [from their houses] valiant women
and deprived them of the fruit of their work[59].

Besides the context, also the use of the verb ἐκβάλλω (Hb: גרשׁ) also indicates that Ben Sira is referring to divorces caused by slander. "The third tongue" became the standard formula in the Rabbinic writings for a slanderer. Thus, in b. 'Arak. 15b: "The third tongue (לישׁון תליתאי) kills three, viz. the slander, the slandered, and he who believes the slander" (cf. Midr. Rab. Lev. 26 and y. Pe'ah 16a). In our text the third tongue refers to a "third person", who interferes maliciously with the life of a couple in order to disrupt the harmony between husband and wife[60]. The instruction is imparted in a general way, and therefore it is difficult to find allusions to concrete situations or persons. Most authors, including Di Lella[61], understand 28,15 to be about a husband who, confiding in false accusations that reached him from a third person, decides to send away his wife. According to Vaccari[62], the situation described in 28,15 corresponds rather to a bigamist marriage in which the jealousy between the two wives is the cause of the divorce. In support of this reading he notes the case of Abraham with his two spouses, Sarah and Hagar, in Gen 21,10.14.

---

59 In Hb the entire passage is missing. Curiously, in 28,15, Syr does not mention the wives: "An intriguer has brought many into captivity and he has separated them from their riches". Cf. VL: [28,19]lingua tertia mulieres viritas eiecit et privavit illas laboribus suis.

60 MacKenzie notes: "Iago, villain of Shakespeare's tragedy Othello, would be a prime example" (MACKENZIE, Sirach, 113).

61 SKEHAN–DI LELLA, Wisdom, 365.

62 VACCARI, Libri poetici, 370. Similarly, TRENCHARD, View on Women, 262 note 311.

Breaking up the marriage and causing the wife to be sent away slander deprives her of the fruit of her work and toil. Behind the Greek τῶν πόνων αὐτῶν we can suppose the Hebrew יגיע that, like πόνος, can mean the "work" or the "fruit of the work"[63]. In his commentary Vella inclines towards a third meaning of the Hebrew word, viz. "offspring", since in his opinion, this is more appropriate in the context[64]. We do not know on what he bases his choice, because we could not find any text at all in which יגיע means offspring.

In 7,26 the sage gave advice about divorcing one's wife (Gk: "the wife who pleases you"), in 25,26 about the divorce of the evil and rebellious wife, and finally, in 28,15 about the divorce of the valiant spouse. In the latter, the Greek text speaks of γυναῖκας ἀνδρείας, i.e. wives who are valiant, courageous, strong, capable and excellent. The adjective ἀνδρεία applied to a woman also appears in 26,2a ("a valiant wife rejoices her husband") and in Prov 31,13a ("a valiant woman, who will find her?") as a translation for חיל. In Sir 28,15 the cause of the divorce has nothing at all to do with the woman, but has everything to do with a terrible weapon, the lethal power of which supersedes that of a sword to such an extent that it is more preferable to die than to live under its iron yoke (28,20 – 21).

In conclusion, in Sir 28,15 both husband and wife fall victim to sneaky slander. She will be sent away unjustly and he, if we understand 28,16 as referring to the husband, will never have rest nor live in peace. That will be his punishment for having given credit to the third tongue.

4 Conclusion

The Book of Ben Sira is a wisdom book written with an eminently pedagogical intention. Its author did not mean to write an account of his time but to instruct his young disciples in the way of life that leads to true wisdom. For this reason his interest in social, economic or political themes, is marked by a decidedly pedagogical orientation. The book contains little information and few historically documented facts. This thwarts any attempt to reconstruct in an accurate way the society of that time with all its institutions, customs and tensions. This difficulty has made itself felt in our study on divorce. The Qumran documents were also not of great help, since they rarely speak of divorce (11Q19 LIV, 4 – 5; 11Q19

---

63 Thus SMEND, Weisheit, 253 and VELLA, Eclesiástico, 110. Segal (ספר, 175) prefers חיל; Kahana (בן־סירא, 56) and Hartom (בן־סירא, 101) read מעל.
64 VELLA, Eclesiástico, 110.

LXVI, 8–11; CD XIII, 15–17) and some of the references are difficult to understand (CD IV, 20—V, 2; 11Q19 LVII, 15–19)[65].

The second difficulty for the present study is tied up with the complicated
textual evolution of the Book which remains till today a major challenge for
scholars. Of the three texts studied here, only one (Sir 7,26) occurs in the Hebrew
MSS A and B, both of which are badly preserved as far as this particular verse is
concerned, and this one text differs considerably from the Greek, Syriac and
Latin versions. For the other texts, we had to make use of the versions in
order to reconstruct a hypothetical Hebrew original.

As far as 7,26 is concerned, the Hebrew text is ambiguous. It does not speak
clearly of divorce, although the use of the verb שׂנא probably has to be understood as a breakdown of marriage (cf. the matrimonial contracts from the Elephantine colony). By contrast, the Greek version (followed by Syr and VL) is
more concrete and leaves open the possibility of divorce for the husband who
is displeased with his wife.

In Sir 25,26, with extremely harsh language, Ben Sira recommends divorce to
the husband of an evil and rebellious wife. The content of GkI is further elabo-
rated in GkII and Syr, where there is an unmistakable allusion to the document of
divorce. Here the thought of the sage is in harmony with the later rabbinic tradition as recorded in the Talmud (cf. b. Sanh. 100b), according to which only
the husband can initiate divorce. One has to wait for the Herodian period to
find women (Salome, Herod's sister, and Herodias, Agrippa's daughter) who
take the initiative to divorce their husbands (cf. A.J. 15,11; 18,17).

Finally, 28,15 justifies concluding that divorce was a relatively frequent practice at the time of Ben Sira. If nothing else, the sage alludes to some cases marriages that ended in divorce because of the third tongue, or slander. His discourse is, however, so general that no further conclusions can be gleaned
from it. Without going into possible reasons, Flavius Josephus also refers to divorce as a common practice in the society of his day (cf. A.J. 4,253).

In spite of the scarcity of information (there is e. g. no mention of the consequences for the spouses or for the children of divorced parents), all indications
seem to confirm that Ben Sira defended divorce whenever the husband took the
initiative. The wife appears to be completely dependent on the husband, having
no choice but to accept his will for her (cf. by contrast, the texts of Elephantine
and P.Ṣe'elim 13). This position of the sage need not surprise us, for it is in line
with his negative attitude towards women in general.

---

65 See INSTONE-BREWER, Divorce, 65–72 and COLLINS, Marriage, 128–130.

Animal Imagery in the Hebrew Text of Ben Sira

Animals play an important role in Ancient Near Eastern literature and in the Bible, especially in the prophetic and wisdom writings[1]. Among the latter, Proverbs and Sirach, two wisdom books with an essentially didactic aim and framework, stand out. Their authors use countless ways to capture and retain the attention of their disciples and, most importantly, to leave their teachings fixed in the hearts of the young. One of these means consists in incorporating animal imagery in their wide-ranging repertory of literary patterns (prohibitions, comparative sayings, pieces of advice, rhetorical questions, instructions, numerical sayings...), with the aim of illustrating different aspects of human life as well as different forms of human behavior.

The images of animals in Proverbs were recently studied by Tova L. Forti, in an excellent monograph that has shed light on various aspects of our investigation[2]. Our obviously much more modest work could serve as a starting point for further investigations on the subject. Here, the intention is to analyze the animal images in some selected passages of the Hebrew text of Ben Sirach, according to the following classification: animal imagery and reprehensible behavior (Sir 4,30; 36[33Hb],6; 42,13)[3], animal imagery and social categories (Sir 13,17–19; 36[33Hb],25), a new wisdom paradigm (Sir 11,3), and a controversial image (Sir 25,8ab).

1 Animal Imagery and Reprehensible Behavior

Unlike the Book of Proverbs, where animal images appear as models to be imitated (cf. Prov 6,6–8; 30,25, about the ant)[4], Ben Sira often uses them to illustrate reprehensible forms of human behavior in family and social circles.

---

1 Cf. RIMBACH, Animal Imagery; FELIKS, Nature; SCHOCHET, Animal Life; EATON, Circle; RIEDE, Spiegel; COLLINS (ed.), History; WATANABE, Animal Symbolism; STRAWN, Stronger.
2 FORTI, Animal Imagery. Cf. also DELL, Use, 275–291 (as for the wisdom literature, she only deals with Proverbs, Job and Qoheleth).
3 Cf. also Sir 25,17 in MS C and in Gk, where a person (Hb: "the husband of a wicked woman"; Gk: "the wicked woman") is compared to a bear.
4 FORTI, Animal Imagery, 31–34.

https://doi.org/10.1515/9783110492316-009

1.1 The Lion (Sir 4,30)

Sir 4,30 belongs to a series of negative precepts beginning in 4,20 with the vocative בני ("my son")[5] and ending with 6,4[6]. These precepts are constructed according to the following arrangement: prohibitive particle (אל) + verb in imperfect (with value of imperative) + motivation (missing in some cases). This negative series begins with an instruction about shame and arrogance (4,20 – 31); its final strophe (4,29 – 31) constitutes the immediate context of our verse. The text appears in MSS A (4,29 – 31)[7] and C (4,30 – 31)[8]:

v. 29 MS A	אל תהי גבהן בלשוניך	ורפי ורשיש במלאכתך:
v. 30 MS C	אל תהי כאריה בביתך	ומתפחז בעבודתך
v. 31 MS C	אל תהי ידך מושטת לשאת	ובעת השב קפודה

29 Do not be presumptuous with your tongue,
and sluggish and lax in your deeds.
30 Do not be like a lion[9] in your home,
nor mistrusting[10] with your servants.
31 Let not your hand be extended to take[11],
and withdrawn when it is time to repay[12].

---

5 For a different opinion, cf. SKEHAN–DI LELLA, Wisdom, 181. According to Di Lella, Sir 4,20 – 31 and 5,1– 6,4 are two separate units.
6 For a comparison of the Hebrew text with the Greek version of Sir 4,20 – 6,4, cf. MINISSALE, Versione greca, 33 – 55.
7 The reading of MS A is followed by Syr: "Do not be boastful with your tongue and slack and weak in your works. Do not be a dog (*klb*) in your house and terrible and fearful in your works. Let your hand not be extended to receive and let it (not) be withdrawn to give".
8 The Greek translation of Sir 4,30 – 31 follows MS C: ³⁰μὴ ἴσθι ὡς λέων ἐν τῷ οἴκῳ σου καὶ φαντασιοκοπῶν ἐν τοῖς οἰκέταις σου. ³¹μὴ ἔστω ἡ χείρ σου ἐκτεταμένη εἰς τὸ λαβεῖν καὶ ἐν τῷ ἀποδιδόναι συνεσταλμένη. Cf. also 4,35ᴸᵃᵗ *noli esse sicut leo in domo tua evertens domesticos tuos [et opprimens subiectos tibi]* and 4,36ᴸᵃᵗ *non sit porrecta manus tua ad accipiendum et ad reddendum collecta.*
9 MS A: כבלב ("like a dog"). Reading preferred by PETERS, Buch, 50; VELLA, Eclesiástico, 25; SAUER, Jesus Sirach, 73. On the origin of these two readings, cf. DI LELLA, Hebrew Text, 23 – 24; RÜGER, Text, 34; PENAR, Philology, 18.
10 With Rüger (Text, 34) and Minissale (Versione greca, 39), we believe that ומתפחז in MS C (Hitphael of פחז, "to behave insolently") is probably the *Vorlage* for Gk φαντασιοκοπῶν (ptc. of φαντασιοκοπέω, "to strecht one's imagination", "to indulge in fantasies"), which could mean here: having unfounded misgivings about the servants or bluffing with them. Cf. also SEGAL, ספר, 29. For φαντασιοκοπῶν, cf. WAGNER, Septuaginta-Hapaxlegomena, 321– 322.
11 MS A: פתוחה לקחת ("open to receive").
12 MS A: וקפוצה בתוך מתן ("and closed in middle of the gift"), referring to the gift you make to another person.

In this instruction, the sage advises against a series of actions arising from great cowardice: speaking much and doing little[13], intimidating one's family and mistrusting the servants, and finally "keeping one's hand open to receive and closed when it comes to giving" (cf. Deut 15,7–8; Acts 20,35)[14]. From a literary point of view, the three negative precepts in Sir 4,29–31 are accentuated by the double anaphora at the beginning of each verse (אל תהי, "do not be"), the use of parallelismus (גבהון, "presumptuous" / ורפי ורשיש, "sluggish and lax"; בלשוניך, "with your tongue" / במלאכתך, "in your deeds"; כאריה, "as a lion" / ומתפחז, "mistrusting"; בביתך, "in your home" / בעבודתך, "with your servants"; מושטת, "extended" / קפודה, "withdrawn"; לשאת, "to take" / ובעת השב, "when it is time to repay") and the absence of any statement about motivations (cf., in contrast, 4,21.24.27d).

The expression "like a lion", placed in the very center of 4,29–31, receives special emphasis. Instead of this expression, Ben Sira could have used an adjective (cf. 4,29) like "authoritarian", "imperious", or "dominating" but he preferred to use the image of an animal, i. e. the lion. His roar and his ferocity characterize the king of the beasts[15], and these qualities make him a very fearsome animal, although less dangerous—according to Ben Sira—than a wicked woman (!). Of her, Ben Sira says, "It is better to live with lion and dragons than with a wicked woman" (25,16Gk). In 21,2Gk, it is said that "the snake with lion's teeth destroys people's lives" (cf. Joel 1,6). In 27,10Gk, the lion lying in ambush for a prey is compared to sin that stalks workers of iniquity and, in 27,28Gk, to vengeance waiting for the insolent. Finally, in 28,23Gk we read that death, like a lion, shall be sent to those who abandon the Lord. So, the lion appears like a ferocious animal stalking, attacking and devouring its prey[16].

Ben Sira's admonition in 4,30a ("Do not be like a lion in your home") could be understood to mean: do not impose yourself forcefully on your family, since the home is not the appropriate place for such behavior[17]. The man acting in

---

13 'Abot 1,16: "Rabbi Shammai said, 'Make thy Thorah an ordinance; say little and do much; and receive everyman with a pleasant expression of countenance'".
14 In Did. 4,5; Barn. 19,9 and Apos. Con. 7,12,1, there is an adaptation of this verse: "Do not be like those who reach out their hands to take, but draw them back when the time comes for giving".
15 Cf. STRAWN, Stronger, 34–36.
16 Cf. Ahiqar 9: "The lion catches the scent of the stag in (its) hidden den, and he ... and sheds its blood and eats its flesh. Just so is the meeting of [people]". Here, however, the lion's catching its prey and devouring it is compared to the predatory character of human relations; cf. LINDENBERGER, Aramaic Proverbs, 60.
17 Cf. b. Giṭ. 6b: "R. Hisda (and R. Abbahu) said: A man should never terrorize his household [...] Rab Judah said in the name of Rab: If a man terrorizes his household, he will eventually commit the three sins of unchastity, blood-shedding and desecration of the Sabbath". According

such a way will only be feared by the people closest to him, and thereby create an atmosphere of tension and hostility.

In sum, with relation to close family members, the sage advises against authoritarian conduct, and with servants he advises against distrustfulness (or insolence/boasting). Both attitudes hamper human relations by creating distance and fear between people

1.2 The Horse (Sir 36[33Hb],6)

This "strange"[18] verse belongs to 36(33Hb),1–6, a pericope placed between 35(32Hb),14–24 (on the fear-of-the-Lord) and 36(33Hb),7–15 (on polarities in creation). This pericope is composed of six apparently unrelated proverbs that highlight the opposition between the attitude of the sage (i.e. the one who fears the Lord) and that of the fool.

Sir 36(33Hb),6 appears in MS E (damaged in the beginning of the first cola) and in MS F. Both manuscripts contain the entire passage with the exception of 36(33Hb),3[19]. Sir 36(33Hb),5–6 closes the pericope with two strong images.

ואופן חוזר מחשבותיו	גלגל קל לב נבל	v. 5 MS F
תחת כל אוהב יצהל	כסוס מוכן אוהב שונא	v. 6 MS F

5 (Like) a cart-wheel[20] is the mind of a fool,
   and his thoughts (like) a turning axle.
6 Like a horse prepared (for battle)[21] is an insolent friend[22],
   he neighs under every rider[23].

---

to Epstein, the reason for the blood-shedding sin is the following: "Because the members of his household run away from him and meet with fatal accidents" (EPSTEIN [ed.], Talmud, 21 note 2).
18 We borrow the expression from Smend (Weisheit, 297): "Während v. 5 deutlich hierher passt, erscheint v. 6 zunächst als etwas fremdartig".
19 MS B only has 36(33Hb),1–3.
20 The first two words are missing in MS E.
21 The first two words are missing in MS E. In contrast to MS F (מוכן, "prepared") and Syr (ḥtyr', "prepared [for battle]"), Gk reads εἰς ὀχείαν ("in heat"), creating a more powerful image (Lat: admissarius). According to Minissale (Versione greca, 83) and others the expression probably derives from מְיֻזָּן (ptc. Pual of יזן, "to be in heat", cf. Jer 5,8), of which מוכן would be a corruption.
22 Instead of שונא ("who hates"), "surely secondary" according to Skehan (cf. SKEHAN–DI LELLA, Wisdom, 396), we prefer to read לץ ("insolent, unscrupulous"), which corresponds to reading of Gk μωκός ("mocking, crafty"), Lat: subsannator. Differently, SAUER, Jesus Sirach, 230: "[Wie ein geiler Hengst] ist ein Freund, der da haßt", and MOPSIK, Sagesse, 197: "un ami haineux".

While in 36(33Hb),5 Ben Sira compares the mind of the fool with the unproductive movement of a wheel or an axle that constantly goes around in circles, in 36(33Hb),6 he uses an image from the animal world: he compares the insolent friend with the abrupt and unpredictable movement of a horse prepared (perhaps saddled) for battle[24].

As to the literary structure of the verses, the first proverb has a synonymic parallelism ("cart-wheel" corresponds to "turning axle", and "mind of the fool" to "his thoughts"). The second proverb, on the other hand, is expressed in the form of an explicative parallelism, i.e. the second colon explains the content of the previous one. In other words, in Sir 36(33Hb),6a the sage establishes a comparison between two syntagmas ("horse prepared for battle" and "insolent friend") using the particle -כְ (missing in v. 5), and in 36(33Hb),6b explains it by developing the image previously used. Just as the horse prepared for battle neighs under every rider, the insolent friend speaks and behaves uncontrollably and impulsively with all those who approach him, without discernment[25]. Moved by strong impulses, the horse prepared for battle tries to jolt off anyone who mounts it or tries to restrain it. The same is true of the insolent friend, who is unable to tolerate any "saddle", i.e. any advice or instruction (cf. 6,20–21). This kind of behavior reveals his incapacity for self-control, discernment and learning, in other words, his lack of wisdom[26].

1.3 The Moth (Sir 42,13)

In the much debated pericope about daughters or more precisely about the worries which daughters cause to their father (Sir 42,9–14)[27], Ben Sira includes, among other teachings, two pieces of advice concerning how daughters should relate to other people (men and women) outside the family circle.

---

23 Missing in MS E. Instead of אוהב (repetition of 36[33Hb],6a, also present in Syr), we read רוכב ("rider"), which corresponds to Gk ἐπικαθημένου and fits better into the context; cf. MINISSALE, Versione greca, 83; CORLEY, Friendship, 171 note 131 and 220 note 9.
24 SAUER, Jesus Sirach, 231: "Auch für die Kriegsführung gewann das Pferd, seit der Zeit der Hyksos (17. Jh. v.Ch.) im Vorderen Orient bekannt, immer größere Bedeutung".
25 SKEHAN–DI LELLA, Wisdom, 399: "Considerations of time or place, of courtesy or confidence, mean nothing to him".
26 In Sir 30,8 Ben Sira compares an untamed horse with a spoiled son. Cf. ALONSO SCHÖKEL, Notas, 305–307.
27 Cf. the very detailed study by PIWOWAR, Vergogna, 369–422. Surprisingly in 42,9–14 Ben Sira does not mention the mother! Cf. Sir 7,24–25; 22,4–5; 26,10.

The text appears in MSS B and Mas, but the second cola in the latter are badly preserved.

ובית נשים אל תסתויד   לכל זכר אל תבן תאר   v. 12 MS B

ומאשה רעת אשה   כי מבגד יצא עש   v. 13 MS B

12   Let her not exhibit[28] her beauty (lit. "aspect") before any man[29],
       and let her not speak confidently in the midst[30] of women (i.e. "married women")[31];
13   for from garments comes the moth[32],
       and from a woman [comes] a woman's wickedness[33].

These two preventive recommendations are indirectly addressed to the father[34], since he is responsible for the influences his daughter is exposed to. One of his main duties is to protect the daughter from some dangers, especially before marriage. The dangers could come from questionable relationships, e.g. from men seduced by feminine beauty (cf. 33[36Hb],22), but also from excessive acquaintance with married women who might disillusion a young girl with their cynicism.

Both recommendations are formulated as negative precepts. The formula אל + impf. with imperative value (42,12ab) is followed by a double motivation in two parallel parts (42,13ab). In the first part (42,13a), the mention of the moth appears within its normal context, i.e. related to garments, and in the second part (42,13b) it is metaphorically applied to womanly behavior. The resulting parallelism is the following: "garments" corresponds to "women", the verb "come from" is inferred in 42,13b, and "moth" corresponds to "woman's wickedness" (רעת אשה)[35].

---

28 תבן, Hiphil from the verb בין with the meaning "to expose", "to show", "to reveal" (cf. Dan 8,16). This reading is preferable to MS B: תתן, Qal from the verb נתן ("to give"), cf. YADIN, Ben Sira Scroll, 25 (1ˢᵗ ed. 1965). In contrast, Skehan, following Strugnell, reconstructs תפן, Hiphil from the verb פנה ("to turn") that he translates with "reveal" (cf. SKEHAN—DI LELLA, Wisdom, 480).

29 MS Bmg erroneously reads תזכר from the verb זכר ("to recall").

30 בית is a dittographic mistake in the place of בין ("between"), confirmed by Gk and Syr.

31 The colon is missing in MS Mas.

32 MS Mas reads the synonym סס ("moth"). In Ahiqar 184 and 186, we find the expression ססא נפלת ("the moth fell"). According to Lindenberger, it is impossible to reconstruct the text from the fragment; it was probably an animal saying (LINDENBERGER, Aramaic Proverbs, 183–184).

33 This colon is partly damaged in MS Mas.

34 Note the verbs in 3ʳᵈ per. f. sg. (תבן and תסתויד). Gk and Syr, on the other hand, read the 2ⁿᵈ per. sg.

35 MOPSIK, Sagesse, 255: "Le mot *ra'at ichah* signifie ici 'le malheur d'une femme', l'image de la teigne est éloquente à cet égard: cette moisissure détériore le tissu, cause sa perte, elle ne le rend

The moth (in Hebrew סָס or עָשׁ)[36] is a small nocturnal butterfly, the larva of which eats wool and makes a kind of cocoon with the material (wool, cloth, skins, etc.), effectively destroying the garment to make a nest. Therefore, as the sage rightly states in 42,13a, the moth comes out of the clothing. The correlation between the garment and the moth is indeed the most significant aspect of the image. Most authors who comment on this verse ignore the fact that the moth does not come out of new garments but of old ones. This small but very significant detail is, according to us, the key to understand the meaning of 42,13: Just as out of the (old) garment comes the moth that damages another garment (which is presumably new), likewise from a woman (who is older and who has experienced the difficulties of marriage) comes the wickedness that corrupts another woman (who is younger and who has not yet been married)[37].

2 Animal Imagery and Social Categories

In some texts Ben Sira uses animal images to refer to social (and sometimes moral)[38] categories present in human societies. The sage incorporates these images into his instructions in order to encourage the disciple/reader to further his or her reflection on the chosen topics (relation between the rich and the poor, how to treat the servants) and to draw his or her own conclusions.

2.1 Contrasting Pairs of Animals and Persons (Sir 13,17–19)

Sir 13,17–19 are part of a teaching on social classes (13,15–24), introduced by four general statements (13,15–16). In these verses, it is said that every living being loves its own kind and that humans similarly love those who are like them. The instruction begins, therefore, with a definition of a human being

---

pas 'méchant'!". Instead of "a woman's wickedness", Lat reads "a man's wickedness" (*iniquitas viri*) influenced perhaps by 42,13.

36 The first term (סס) is only found in Isa 51,8, where it symbolizes the destruction that shall strike those who revile the people of the Lord. For this *hapax legomenon*, see COHEN, Hapax, 114 note 21. The second term (עש) is more common and symbolizes either the destruction of a person (Isa 50,9; 51,8; Ps 39,12; Job 13,28; Hos 5,12) or human frailty (Job 4,19; 27,18).

37 Cf. EGGER-WENZEL, Knechtschaft, 27.

38 Cf. Sir 11,29–30 (a very corrupted text) where the figure of the wicked (presented as slanderer, arrogant, talebearer, grumbler) is compared to a predatory bird, a wolf, a dog and a bear! Skehan refers to the expansion of 11,30 in MS A as "an astonishing zoo!" (SKEHAN–DI LELLA, Wisdom, 244).

that likens him or her to animals: by nature, a human being loves his or her as-sociates[39]. Yet, human beings create divisions between those who belong to the same species. These divisions, unlike those in the animal world (cf., in contrast, Isa 11,6 – 7), are not natural but have a social and religious character.

Here are our verses according to MS A:

כד רשע לצדיק	מה יחובר זאב אל כבש v. 17ab
	וכן עשיר אל איש נאצל v. 17c
מאין שלום עשיר אל רש	מאיש שלום צבוע אל כלב v. 18
בן מרעית עשיר דלים	מאכל ארי פראי מדבר v. 19

17   What fellowship has a wolf with a lamb?
      So it is with the sinner and the just[40],
      and so the rich joins the poor[41].
18   Can there be[42] peace between a hyena[43] and a dog?
      Can there be peace between the rich and the poor?
19   Wild asses in the wilderness are the prey of lions;
      so the poor are pasture for the rich.

Combining rhetorical questions and comparative sentences[44], Ben Sira compares the animal world to human society. The protagonists appear grouped in

---

39 This idea is echoed in the following proverbs: *Similis simile gaudet*, "ogni simile ama il suo simile", "cada cual ama a su igual", "le semblable aime le semblable", "birds of a feather flock together", "gleich und gleich gesellt sich gern", "soort zoekt soort".
40 Although preserved Gk and Syr, according to Mopsik, v. 17b does not fit into the context (cf. MOPSIK, Sagesse, 148).
41 Missing in Gk and Syr. According to Skehan, 13,17c is a supplementary colon that does not make sense: "and so for the rich man keeping close to the (poor) man", where נאצל is pf. Niphal of אצל II ("to join") and "poor" (רש) is a conjecture for איש (SKEHAN—DI LELLA, Wisdom, 251). Conversely, we translate נאצל as ptc. Niphal of אצל I ("to separate, remove, withdraw"), cf. ZORELL (ed.), Lexicon, 76: *spoliatus, pauper*. Sauer (Jesus Sirach, 121) offers a different transla-tion: "Und so auch mit einem Reichen in bezug auf einen Mann, dem (Gut) versagt blieb".
42 מאיש can be understood as מא/ה יש, "what is?" (cf. SMEND, Weisheit, 127) or better as מאין, "there is not" (cf. SAUER, Jesus Sirach, 121).
43 The adjective צבוע means "coloured, variegated", cf. Jer 12,9: עיט צבוע (a variegated bird of prey). In the LXX, however, this expression is rendered by σπήλαιον ὑαίνης ("a hyena's cave"). The hyena is also present in Sir 13,18Gk and in Syr. Lat differs from all the versions and reads *sancto homini*.
44 The rhetorical question in 13,17 is immediately followed by two applicative clauses intro-duced by the particles כָּךְ and כֵּן ("thus", "so"); here the first element of the comparison is in-ferred. In 13,18, however, both rhetorical questions are followed by a comparative sentence com-posed of two clauses. In the first one the particle כְּ ("as") is missing while the second one is introduced by כֵּן. In such a way, the applicative clauses are emphasized.

contrasting pairs, the components of which have nothing in common. In fact, some of them are even natural enemies as the hyena and the dog, for example. While the hyena attacks the flock, the dog defends it. Therefore, any kind of association (חבר) or peaceful relationship (שלום) between them is inconceivable. Indeed, it goes against nature.

On one side, the wolf, the hyena and the lion, dangerous and ferocious animals, are identified with the rich person; and, on the other side, the lamb, the dog and wild asses, much weaker and more peaceful animals[45], represent the poor person. In this way, Ben Sira not only asserts the complete incompatibility between rich and poor (between the hyena and the dog, cf. Jer 12,9) but also the great distance between sinners and the just (between the wolf and the lamb, cf. Isa 11,6)[46]. The sage also attributes moral values to these pairs, distinguishing the good ones (just and poor) from the bad ones (sinners and rich). Therefore, in this context the initial statements in 13,15–16 do not refer to just any human being but to one of the same social class who shares the same scale of values or has the same religious spirit.

The climax of the instruction is reached in 13,19, with the mention of the wild ass and the lion (cf. Job 24,4–5 and Ps 35,17; 58,7)[47]. The striking analogy between מאכל ארי (lit. "prey of the lion") and מרעית עשיר ("pasture for the rich") adds a dramatic aspect to the comparison: the poor are devoured by the rich, i.e. they become the victims of their oppressors.

In this instruction Ben Sira used the comparison with the animal world to denounce and condemn the hostility between the rich and the poor. According to Alonso Schökel, such hostility is provoked by the one who holds the upper position; it consists in a permanent attitude of hate that may lead to aggression[48].

2.2 The Donkey and the Servant (Sir 36[33Hb],25)

In Sir 36(33Hb),25–33, Ben Sira presents his teaching about servants (cf. 7,20–21). In the culture of that time servants were considered, just like herds of cattle, to be personal property of the owner (cf. Exod 10,17; Job 1,2, where they are mentioned together with cattle).

---

45 Yet wild asses are notoriously untamable.
46 The sinners and the just do not resemble each other in any way nor have anything in common (cf. Prov 29,27).
47 Cf. Aesop's fable "The wild ass and the lion", the moral of which is "might makes right".
48 ALONSO SCHÖKEL, Eclesiástico, 189.

Here is the beginning of the unit according to MS E:

מספוא ושוט ומשא לחמור v. 25a   Fodder and a stick and burdens for a donkey;

ומרדות מלאכה לע[בד] v. 25b   [bread][49] and discipline[50] and work for a servant.

Inappropriate as it sounds in our ears, this proverb was nevertheless intended to favorably draw the attention of the reader/listener[51]. Without any introductory remark on the subject Ben Sira compares the servant with the donkey, an animal noted for its stubbornness (cf. the Balaam pericope in Num 22,21–30). Due to its initial position this comparison becomes the key for interpreting the following verses (33Hb,25–30). In fact, although the term חמור does not reappear in the instruction, the mention of the yoke and thong that bend the servant's neck in 33Hb,27a[52] reminds the reader/listener of the donkey (cf. Prov 29,19 and Sir 42,5c). Ben Sira seems to have forgotten that in spite of his stubbornness the donkey was indispensable for the farmer and represented the main means of transport for people and merchandise[53].

Both cola are composed of two nominal phrases shaped according to the typology of similarity patterns. The comparison functions without the help of any particle. The fodder, a stick and the burdens for the donkey correspond to the bread, discipline and work for the servant. The implicit teaching in this proverb does not leave any room for doubt: the master of the house must treat the servant as he treats the donkey, i.e. severely, because as it is stated in the book of Proverbs "the servant pampered during his childhood, will be in the end ungrateful" (Prov 29,21). This is also what a popular Spanish proverb says: "Al mozo nuevo, pan y huevo, y andando el año, pan y palo" (to a new lad, [give] bread and eggs and, in the course of the year, [give him] bread and the stick).

---

49 A word seems to be missing (probably לחם, very similar to לחמור), to make the parallel between the cola complete. In fact, this word appears in Gk (ἄρτος καὶ παιδεία καὶ ἔργον, "bread and discipline and work") followed by Lat (*panis et disciplina et opus*) and in Syr in a different position ("and correction and bread and work").

50 The noun מְרְדוּת (from מרד) means "rebellion". Yet here, coinciding with its homonym in Syr (*mardutō'*), it is better to understand it as discipline (cf. ZORELL [ed.], Lexicon, 471) or corporal punishment (SKEHAN—DI LELLA, Wisdom, 403–404).

51 Cf. Ahiqar 5: "A bow for a serving-boy, a rebuke for a slave-girl, and for all your servants discipline (אלפנא)" and P.Insinger, 14,11: "If the stick is far from the master, the servant/slave does not listen to him".

52 According to Gk: ζυγὸς καὶ ἱμὰς τράχηλον κάμψουσιν, since MS E is corrupt: [.......]חוטר תומכר ("the stick of its wielder" [?]). Following the Gk only in the first half of the colon, Segal reconstructs על ועבות חטר ומכות ("yoke and rope, stick and blows"), cf. SEGAL, ספר, 215.

53 Cf. BOROWSKI, Living Thing, 90–99; DEIST, Material Culture, 159.

3 A New Wisdom Paradigm

Sometimes Ben Sira reveals himself to be a sage inventor. It is a matter of fact that in his teaching he makes use of traditional imagery in a free and original way. By inserting an old image into a new context fashioned after wisdom models, he also changes its former meaning and connotations. In such a way, a new wisdom paradigm may come to life[54]. Sir 11,3 is a good example. This verse is part of a small unit (11,2–6), in which the sage advises against judging on the basis of appearances.

Here is his first teaching (conserved in MSS A and B):

אל תהלל אדם בתארו   ואל תתעב אדם מכ[...] במראהו: v. 2 MS A
אליל בעוף דברה   וראש תנובות פריה: v. 3 MS A

2   Do not praise a person for his or her [good] looks,
    nor loathe a person because of his or her [unpleasant][55] appearance.
3   Insignificant[56] among flying creatures is the bee,
    but her product is the first/best of [her] fruits.

The image of the bee is used to explain the two previous prohibitions, which stand out because of their antithetic parallelism (do not praise/do not loathe; beauty/ugliness). Ben Sira asserts that a person's physical appearance is a bad criterion that can be misleading, and the example of the bee corroborates this assertion. Its physical weakness, in comparison to other flying creatures, contrasts with the excellence of the honey it produces[57] (cf. Prov 16,24; 24,13; 25,6.27)[58].

It should be noted that in this piece of advice there is no grammatical link between the negative precepts (11,2ab) and the following example (11,3ab). As in

---

54 The author of the Book of Proverbs did the same thing with the locust (Prov 30,27). Cf. FORTI, Animal Imagery, 62.
55 MSS A and B add an explicative gloss after אדם, probably מכוער, "deformed" (ptc. Pual of כער). MS Bmg reads: מכוע[.] and B מעזב (?).
56 According to Segal, אליל should be understood as "divine, revered like a god" (cf. SEGAL, ספר, 67). MS B presents a repetition of the verse with only one change (קטנה, "small", instead of אליל, "worthless"), which seems secondary (cf. SKEHAN–DI LELLA, Wisdom, 229). Syr has a different reading: šyt' ("despised").
57 Cf. P.Insinger 25,2: "The little bee brings the honey". The theme of slighting small things becomes a topos in Hellenistic times, cf. also Syr. Men. 172 and Sent. Sextus 9–10 quoted in LICHTHEIM, Wisdom Literature, 163.
58 Cf. FORTI, Bee's Honey, 327–341.

other similar cases one would expect the presence of some particle (כְּ or כֵּן for instance) indicating the kind of relation between 11,2 and 11,3. Its absence leaves the decision up to the reader/listener who will have to draw his or her own conclusions.

On the one hand, this positive characterization of the bee is in keeping with the Septuagint's expanded version of the Ant Parable (Prov 6,8a–c), where the bee, while being physically weak, is presented as a model of diligence and industry[59]. On the other hand, this image certainly breaks with the former tradition, according to which our protagonist is an insidious and dangerous insect, especially when it moves and attacks in a swarm. In Deut 1,44, the Amorites chase the Israelites like bees; in Ps 118,12, the psalmist complains that the gentiles surround him like bees; and in Isa 7,18–19, YHWH himself calls the flies of Egypt[60] and the bees of Assyria to invade the kingdom of Judah: "They will all come and settle in the steep ravines, and in the clefts of the rocks, and on all the thorn bushes, and on all the pastures" (Isa 7,19)[61].

Thus, in Ben Sira's view, the image of the bee has become a new wisdom paradigm transmitting a positive teaching: smallness is not incompatible with excellence.

4 A Controversial Image

Sir 25,8ab is a much debated verse. Its difficulty lies in the expression "plow as an ox with a donkey" which can be interpreted literally or in a figurative way.

Before entering into the discussion of this problem, let us remember that the complete reconstruction of the text of MS C was possible thanks to the discovery made by A. Scheiber in 1982. In addition to the sixth Hebrew manuscript of Ben Sira (MS F), this Hungarian scholar discovered two fragments, one of which is the corner of page V (*recto*), containing the missing portions in 25,8[62].

Here is the reconstructed text of MS C:

---

59 Cf. FORTI, Animal Imagery, 107.
60 According to Borowski, it would have been more appropriate to apply the image of the bee to Egypt than to Assyria, since bee-keeping and honey production are not attested in Mesopotamia while they are in Egypt (cf. BOROWSKI, Living Thing, 161).
61 According to some scholars, the denigration of the bee is a reaction of biblical authors to the importance that this animal had among the Philistines. Cf. MARGULIES, Rätsel, 56–76; DEIST, Material Culture, 133–134; BOROWSKI, Animals, 297.
62 SCHEIBER, Leaf, 185; DI LELLA, Sixth Manuscript, 237–238. The other fragment contains the words missing in 25,20–21 on the *verso* of page V.

ולו עבד נקלה ממנו   אשרי שלא נפל בלשון   v. 8cd
ולא חורש כשור עם חמור   אשרי בעל אשה משכלת   v. 8ab

8cd   Happy he who does not fall/sin with the tongue
       and [he who] does not serve an inferior to him.
8ab   Happy the husband of an intelligent[63] wife,
       and [he who] does not plow as an ox (yoked) with a donkey.

Sir 25,8 is part of a numerical poem consisting of ten beatitudes (placed in five parallel pairs), culminating in the praise of the fear-of-the-Lord (25,7–11). Our verse contains four beatitudes, the only ones that exist in Hebrew[64]. For the rest of the text, it is necessary to use the translations.

Except for the last two beatitudes (they call happy he who does the same sort of thing, i.e. "to find wisdom" and "to fear the Lord"), the rest of them juxtapose two unrelated feelings or actions. For instance, to rejoice in one's own children and to live to see the downfall of one's foes (25,7cd), not to fall with the tongue and not to serve an inferior (25,8cd), to find a friend and to speak to attentive listeners (25,9ab). Many authors think that it is also the case for Sir 25,8ab. In our opinion, however, the second beatitude (8b) sheds light on the first (8a). Apparently unrelated, both refer to the same thing, i.e. matrimonial life.

From a literary point of view, it is noteworthy that three times in the poem the formulation of the beatitude is completely positive (25,7cd; 9ab; 10ab) while in 25,8cd is completely negative. Only in 25,8ab Ben Sira combines both. By doing so he creates a link by means of opposition between 25,8a and 25,8b and at the same time puts the accent in the first beatitude, the one formulated in positive terms.

Let's us see the original (and obviously implicit) relationship the sage establishes between the two apparently unrelated cola. While 25,8a evokes a matrimonial context (husband and intelligent wife, cf. 26,1–4; 40,23), 25,8b is associated to the agricultural world (farmer and labor animals) by means of an allusion to Deut 22,10 (cf. Lev 19,19). It is our contention that Ben Sira slightly modified this biblical text to give space to a figurative interpretation[65]. The Deuteronomic prescription, which prohibits working in the field with two different species of ani-

---

63 Cf. SPATAFORA, Sensible Woman, 267–281.
64 Syr has the complete text and the right order (25,8abcd). Gk (and Lat) only has 25,8acd (b is lacking).
65 SMEND, Weisheit, 227: "Der Satz hat hier natürlich bildlichen Sinn [...] Glücklich, wer keine reiche Frau geheiratet hat und somit nicht der Esel neben den Ochsen (כשור) ist (vgl. v. 22.23)".

mals: "You shall not plow with an ox and an ass together" (לֹא־תַחֲרֹשׁ בְּשׁוֹר־וּבַחֲמֹר יַחְדָּו)[66] has been adapted by the Syriac translation of Ben Sira: "(Happy) he who has not yoked the plough with ox and with ass together" (25,8b)[67]. This translation suggests, especially in view of 25,8a, the image of a marriage in which the two wives of the husband (the ox and the ass) do not live at peace with one another because of their incompatible temperament. Consequently, the normal life in the household becomes unbearable (cf. 37,11a; 26,6; 25,14?)[68].

Now, the Hebrew text of Sir 25,8b does not say: "(Happy) he who does not plow with ox and with ass together" but rather "(happy) he who does not plow as an ox with an ass". In this case, the figurative meaning of the sentence changes: the ox and the ass are not the two rival wives in a polygamous marriage but the ox is the husband (supposedly intelligent and strong) and the ass is his wife (supposedly stupid and stubborn)[69]. In other words, the deuteronomic expression is probably intended to evoke "an undesirable marriage"[70] because of the incompatibility between the partners. As Minissale puts it: "The husband is happy when there is no disparity of intelligence with his wife"[71].

In short, Ben Sira has interpreted an ancient agricultural prescription, which discouraged trying to plow with an ox and an ass together, by applying it in a metaphorical sense to a failed marriage[72].

---

66 The same expression is found in 4Q418 103 ii 7–8. According to Rey (4QInstruction, 113), "En 4QInstruction, la mention de celui qui laboure avec un bœuf et un âne ensemble, et de celui qui sème deux semences différentes, vient illustrer l'interdiction de mélanger son commerce avec celui de son prochain".

67 Many modern translations follow Syr. Cf., for example, MINISSALE, Siracide, 131; SKEHAN–DI LELLA, Wisdom, 339; KAISER, Weisheit, 60. Diversely, ALONSO SCHÖKEL, Eclesiástico, 234; SAUER, Jesus Sirach, 189.

68 Smend and Mopsik observe that the reading בשור ("with an ox") instead of כשור ("as an ox") could refer to a polygamous marriage (cf. SMEND, Weisheit, 227 and MOPSIK, Sagesse, 171 note 2). On polygamy in Ben Sira, cf. EGGER-WENZEL, Polygamie, 57–64.

69 According to Mopsik, even the verb "to plow" is to be understood in a figurative way as to get married, to take a woman in marriage (cf. MOPSIK, Sagesse, 171 note 2).

70 SKEHAN–DI LELLA, Wisdom, 342.

71 MINISSALE, Siracide, 131: "L'uomo è felice se non c'è disparità d'intelligenza con la moglie". In view of 25,10ab, Spatafora contends that if the happiest man is the one who finds wisdom and fears the Lord, his wife should be "an intelligent woman who shares in that faith, who shares the same attitude before God" (SPATAFORA, Sensible Woman, 280).

72 MOPSIK, Sagesse, 171–172 note 2.

5 Conclusion

The metaphorical instances of animal imagery in the Book of Ben Sira are, as we have seen, inserted in a broad range of literary forms. Except for one (the bee), all the instances are distinguished by their negative connotations. Far from examples to be imitated, animal images exemplify objectionable and unpleasant aspects of human conduct. While in the fable (cf. Aesop's fables) some human attributes are applied to animals, here some animal attributes (mainly negative ones) are applied to human beings[73].

The first group of images expresses reprehensible types of human conduct: the authoritarian behavior of the *pater familias* in the home (Sir 4,30), the uncontrolled and impulsive reaction of the insolent friend (Sir 36[33Hb],6) or the cynicism of the married woman who corrupts girls without marital experience (Sir 42,13).

In the second group, the animal images have a social perspective: their intention is to denounce the hostility between rich and poor (Sir 13,17–19) and to advise stern treatment of servants (Sir 36[33Hb],25).

In Sir 11,3, the sage creates a new wisdom paradigm contrasting with the former biblical tradition: the bee seen from a positive point of view as a model of human behavior; and, in Sir 25,8ab, he interprets an ancient law metaphorically by slightly changing an expression familiar to the reader in order to apply it to a matrimonial context.

In conclusion, Ben Sira's teaching not only draws on ancestral examples, on his intimate relationship with the Lord or his personal experience but also on an empirical knowledge of nature, especially of the animal world. This knowledge allows him to use animal symbolism as a didactical and rhetorical means for investigating the nature of human behavior, especially its more obscure sides. In this way, his teaching becomes more attractive for his disciples and, at the same time, more convincing.

---

73 FORTI, Animal Images, 50.

The Absence of Named Women from Ben Sira's Praise of the Ancestors

The Book of Ben Sira is without a doubt the wisdom writing that dedicates the greatest amount of space to women[1]. According to Warren C. Trenchard, author of the only monograph on this subject up until now, "of the 1390 verses in Sirach, 105, or about 7 per cent, deal with women"[2]. Its favorite protagonists are daughters (Sir 42,9–14), wives (25,13–26,18; 33[36Hb],21–26) and dangerous women (9,1–9; 23,22–26). However, all of them are anonymous and presented with reference to a man and from a masculine point of view.

In the "Praise of the Ancestors" (Sir 44–50), a parade of illustrious figures from Israel's history, not one woman is named. Whereas, for example, the silence of Ben Sira about Ezra has raised the interest of scholars[3], the same can hardly be said for his silence about Israel's heroines. Contemporary authors generally limit themselves to noting this silence[4] or explaining it away as the sage's "gender bias"[5].

In the present study, I propose to investigate this omission, which, as Jeremy Corley observes, represents a "distasteful aspect for modern readers"[6] as well as a challenge for scholars. We will therefore consider Hellenistic encomiastic literature, then the encomia and the lists of personages in the biblical texts of the Hellenistic period, and lastly some significant verses within Sirach 44–50 in so far as these refer to women.

1 Hellenistic Encomiastic Literature

Without proposing to enter into the discussion about the literary genre of Sirach 44–50[7], scholars often recognize in this composition a series of traits

---

1 For the basic bibliography, see CALDUCH-BENAGES, Cut Her Away, 81.

2 TRENCHARD, View on Women, 1. [cf., also, BALLA, Family (2010) and ELLIS, Gender (2013)].

3 HÖFFKEN, Warum schwieg; BEGG, Non-mention; DUGGAN, Ezra.

4 PETRAGLIO, Libro, 18; JÜNGLING, Vatermetaphorik, 85; DI LELLA, Praise, 167; CORLEY, Sirach 44:1–15, 161 note 38.

5 BERGANT, Wisdom Literature, 184; SCHROER, Wisdom, 85.

6 CORLEY, Sirach 44:1–15, 161 note 38.

7 LEE, Studies, esp. 81–103; cf. MACK, Wisdom, 128–137; DI LELLA, Praise, 151–152. See also GILBERT, Review, 319–334.

https://doi.org/10.1515/9783110492316-010

characteristic of the Greek encomium[8]. Hence, we intend to review, although only briefly, the encomiastic literature of the Hellenistic period in search of feminine protagonists.

Three representative authors of Hellenistic poetry are Theocritus of Syracuse (ca. 310–ca. 260 BC), Callimachus of Cyrene (ca. 315–ca. 240 BC) and Apollonius of Rhodes (ca. 295–ca. 215 BC). Although their works are full of both historical and mythical women[9], none of these authors, as far as we know, ever wrote an encomium about a woman. In fact, the two encomia of Theocritus[10] are dedicated to King Ptolemy II Philadelphus (Id. 17, which includes a great eulogy of the king's mother, Berenice I) and to Hiero II of Syracuse (Id. 16), although the latter is not so much an encomium strictly speaking as a kind of self-recommendation on behalf of the poet in his attempt to obtain the king's patronage. To these poems must be added Hymn. 4 by a certain Isidorus, discovered in 1935 in an Egyptian temple at Medinet Madi, in the southernmost part of Fayum. This hymn, dating at the latest from the 1st century BC, is dedicated to Porramenres (Pharaoh Marres), one of the many names under which Amenemhet III, Pharaoh of the 12th dynasty and probable founder of the temple, was known[11].

Surprisingly the only personages praised are illustrious sovereigns of the epoch, since the Hellenistic queens, far from remaining in silence and in the shadow of their husbands, became influential and autonomous women in the administration of their immense wealth and promoters of culture and religion[12]. Prominent among them is the sister of Ptolemy II, Arsinoë II, whom the demotic papyri call "the female pharaoh"[13]; in Alexandria, she sponsored the festival of Adonis that Theocritus describes in his Id. 15[14]. Another important queen is Berenice II, who married her cousin Ptolemy III Euergetes. Callimachus dedicated two poems to her: The *Song of Victory for Berenice,* a eulogy celebrating her victory in the races at Nemea (Carm. ep. frag. 383) and a composition known as *The Lock of Berenice* (Aet. 4 frag. 110). The queen promised to give a lock of her hair to the gods in order to ensure the safe return of her husband from the war in

---

8 Cf. SCHMITT, Enkomien.

9 POMEROY, Women, xii and 72–82.

10 Cf. VOX, Carmi. On the encomia by Theocritus and Callimachus see LEE, Studies, 158–163.

11 VANDERLIP, Hymns, 67. Cf. also frag. 3 in Theocritus' *Idylls,* where it is not certain whether the protagonist, divinized in this case, is Berenice I or Berenice II.

12 Cf. POMEROY, Women, 3–40.

13 POMEROY, Women, 23.

14 She is also mentioned by Callimachus in *The Apotheosis of Arsinoë* (Lyr. frag. 228), which says that she was abducted by the Dioscuri and that in her honor an altar was erected and a sacred enclosure established near Emporium.

Syria. The lock disappeared and the astrologer Conon converted it into a constellation of stars, as Catullus evokes in his Carm. 66 (*Coma Berenices*). Yet, in spite of their historical relevance, none of these sovereigns was chosen to be the protagonist of an encomium[15].

2 Encomia and Lists of Personages in the Bible

The encomiastic genre is also present in the Bible, especially in the writings from the Hellenistic period. In addition to the "Praise of the Ancestors", the Book of Ben Sira has transmitted to us the eulogy of personified Wisdom or Lady Wisdom (Sir 24,1–22; cf. Wis 7,22–8,1). In the First Book of Maccabees we encounter the eulogy of Judas Maccabeus, who directly after the death of his father, the priest Mattathias, occupied the post of leader of the Jews from 166 to 160 BC (1 Macc 3,3–9), and the eulogy of his brother Simon, high priest and ethnarch of the Jews from 143 to 134 BC (1 Macc 14,4–15). Lastly, some passages of the Book of Judith praise its protagonist: in Jdt 13,18–20 Judith is acclaimed by Uzziah, in Jdt 14,7 by Achior the Ammonite, and in Jdt 15,8–10 by the high priest Joakim, the senate of Israel and the inhabitants of Jerusalem. Accordingly, Judith is the only woman extolled in these writings[16].

Alongside the encomia, the lists of famous personages should be mentioned. One of them figures in the testament that Mattathias leaves to his sons before he dies. Evoking the "Praise of the Ancestors" in Sirach 44–50, the author of 1 Maccabees recalls "the deeds of the fathers" (τὰ ἔργα τῶν πατέρων), naming in the following order Abraham, Joseph, Phinehas, Joshua, Caleb, David, Elijah, Hananiah, Azariah and Mishael, and Daniel (1 Macc 2,52–60). Another list appears in the Book of Wisdom. The author tells of Wisdom's intervention in history through a series of famous personages, from Adam to Moses, who receive her support and protection. This is a very atypical list since the author refers to the protagonists without ever mentioning their names. He does this by alluding to stories that his readers know well. In this way, implicitly he presents Adam, Cain, Noah, Abraham, Isaac, Lot, Jacob, Joseph, and Moses (Wis 10,1–11,3).

---

15 We have to go back as far as the pre-classical and classical epoch in order to find some examples, such as the elegies the poetess Sappho dedicated to her female companions, or the *Elegies of Helen* (Hel.) by Gorgias (ca. 483–376 BC) and Isocrates (436–338 BC) dedicated to Helen of Troy (Hel. Enc. [Or. 10]). Cf. LEE, Studies, 126–128 and 135–136.

16 The poem, from the Persian period, dedicated to the (anonymous) capable woman in Prov 31,10–31 should also be noted. Cf. YODER, Wisdom; BROCKMÖLLER, Frau.

No woman appears here either. Furthermore, the same may also be said about the lists in Psalms 78, 105, and 106.

Let us add some other examples taken from the pseudepigrapha and the literature from Qumran[17]. The mother of the Maccabees exhorts her sons to endure all their trials by citing the examples of Abraham, Isaac, Daniel, Hananiah, Azariah and Mishael (4 Macc 16,20–23) and reminds them of how their father read to them the stories of their ancestors: Abel, Cain, Isaac, Joseph, Phinehas, Hananiah, Azariah, Mishael and Daniel, Isaiah, David, Solomon, Ezekiel, and Moses (4 Macc 18,11–19). Finally, in a meditation on history, the author of the Damascus Document mentions Noah, Abraham, Isaac and Jacob, and implicitly Moses (CD II, 17–III, 12).

In these biblical and pseudepigraphic texts, the female figures do not appear among the famous personages of Israel's history, not even the matriarchs (Sarah, Rebecca, Rachel, and Leah)[18] on whom the realization of the promise made to Israel depends. So Ben Sira is not alone in avoiding naming female characters in his "Praise of the Ancestors".

3 The Feminine Presence in Sirach 44–50

The sparse feminine presence in the "Praise of the Ancestors" can be reduced to two categories: anonymous women (47,6Hb and 47,19) and female images (46,13Hb; 48,19 and 49,7). We will dedicate the following sections to them.

3.1 Anonymous Women

The only women mentioned in the "Praise of the Ancestors" are the girls who acclaim David for his victory over ten thousand (47,6Hb) and the women with whom Solomon dallied and who led to his downfall (47,19). All are anonymous and appear in the text without personal identity, that is, as members of a generic

---

17 For a table comparing such Jewish hero lists, see EISENBAUM, Heroes, 230–231.
18 Similarly, "the matriarchs of Genesis 12–50 have been skipped" in the genealogies in 1 Chronicles 1–9; so BEENTJES, Tradition, 19. These matriarchs are rarely mentioned in Qumran literature except in retellings of Genesis; thus, Sarah appears in the Genesis Apocryphon (e. g. 1QapGen XX, 9) and Leah in 4Q Reworked Pentateuch[b] (4Q364 4b, 1–9). To be sure, Sarah is mentioned in Isa 51,2; Rom 4,19; 9,9; Heb 11,11; 1 Pet 3,6; Rebecca in Rom 9,10–12; Rachel in Ruth 4,11; 1 Sam 10,2; Jer 31,11–21; Matt 2,18; and Leah in Ruth 4,11.

group. The first are connected with music (and dancing) and the second with sexual pleasure.

3.1.1 Sir 47,6Hb

Practically ignoring Saul and after a brief mention of the prophet Nathan (47,1), Ben Sira concentrates on the figure of David (47,2–11)[19]. The introductory verse compares his divine election to the separation of the fat from the sacrificial victims (47,2), thus giving the passage a cultic tenor. In his selection of the material concerning David, the sage emphasizes his military merits, paying special attention to his combat against Goliath (47,3–7)[20] and his cultic activities, notably those related to music (47,8–10). Finally, Ben Sira passes in silence over the dark side of the monarch's life by using a generic expression and a condescending tone, "the Lord forgave his sins" (47,11), and mentions the theme of the royal covenant (47,11Gk), thus establishing a connection with 45,25.

Now let us take a closer look at 47,6, according to MS B[21]:

על כן ענו לו בנות Therefore the daughters/girls sang praises to him
ויכנוהו ברבבה and ascribed to him tens of thousands.

Whereas in Syr "the women" are the ones who praise David, the Greek translator omits the subject of the verbs: οὕτως ἐν μυριάσιν ἐδόξασαν αὐτὸν καὶ ἤνεσαν αὐτὸν ἐν εὐλογίαις κυρίου ("So they glorified him for ten thousand and praised him with the blessings of the Lord"). The same omission occurs in the Vetus Latina.

Since ancient times the "victory over ten thousand" has been a part of the popular epic about David. When David returns after having killed Goliath, women from all the cities of Israel come out to meet Saul, singing and dancing

---

19 Cf. MARBÖCK, Erbe; KLEER, Sänger, 131–177; XERAVITS, Figure; WRIGHT, Use, 201–205; BEENTJES, Portrayals, 167–169.

20 These verses constitute "David's 'prehistory'" according to Xeravits (Figure, 29).

21 For the Hebrew text, we will use the edition of Beentjes (BEENTJES, Book). According to Kleer, Ben Sira consciously used the suffixed preposition לו in an ambiguous way: it can be understood in reference to David or to God. In the latter case, "die Töchter singen Gott zu Ehren, weil *er* durch David Zehntausend erschlagen hat" (KLEER, Sänger, 154). In 47,6 note the surprising masculine form of the verb (ויכנוהו), in view of the feminine subject (בנות), though "daughters" is also construed with a masculine plural verb in Jdg 21,21, while 1 Sam 29,5 has a verb in the masculine form (יענו) despite an implied feminine subject.

to the sound of drums and lutes[22]. While dancing, the women sing: "Saul has killed his thousands, and David his tens of thousands" (1 Sam 18,7). The same song
reappears in 1 Sam 21,12 and 29,5, although these texts do not mention the
women, dancing, or musical instruments. Ben Sira also excludes these elements.
On the other hand, like the first Book of Samuel, he uses the verb ענה ("intone,
sing") and the noun רבבה ("ten thousand"), changes women (נשׁים) into daugh-
ters/girls (בנות), and introduces the theme of praise or honorable mention (כנה).
In Ben Sira's text, the reason for the singing by the daughters/girls appears in
47,5, which says that David succeeded in defeating the giant and re-establishing
the honor (lit. "raising the horn") of his people thanks to his confidence in God
(cf. 1 Sam 17,45). Although Sir 47,5 states that David "called to God Most High", it
must be noticed that in the source narrative (1 Sam 17) there is no record of David
praying. In 1 Sam 18,7–11 the praises sung to David provoke Saul's jealousy. This
is not the case in our text, where Saul's rivalry with David is rigorously passed
over in silence.

Ben Sira has consequently omitted an aspect that Israel's tradition has always considered as characteristic of women (although not exclusively so). We
are referring to their connection with music and dancing. The Israelites expected
that, after a military victory, women gifted in the art of music would welcome the
soldiers coming home from battle[23]. Their performances were always public and
in the presence of the leaders of the people, and so we can suppose that they
were not improvised but the result of their technical preparation and group re-
hearsals. According to Carol Meyers, "Artifacts and texts together establish the
existence of a women's performance genre of drum-dance-song"[24].

3.1.2 Sir 47,19

The passage dedicated to Solomon, "a wise son, who lived in peace", opens with
an introductory verse that confirms the succession based on God's promise and
on the loyalty of David, his father (47,12). This is followed by the description of
his merits (the construction of the temple and his great wisdom, 47,13 – 18b),
which strongly contrasts with his weaknesses—his avidity for wealth and his passion for women—that lead to the division of the kingdom (47,18c–21). The promise of a "remnant" (47,22Gk) and the implicit reference to his successors

---

22 See Exod 15,21 where Miriam, drum in hand, accompanies all the women, who follow her,
dancing and with drums, and leads them in singing (ותען) the canticle of the sea. Cf. MEYERS,
Miriam.
23 On the significance of drumming in the victory song, see PAZ, Drums, 90 – 94.
24 MEYERS, Miriam, 225.

(Jeroboam and Rehoboam), who caused the exile and corrupted the people (47,23–24), conclude this pericope[25] and prepare for the appearance of the prophet Elijah.

Here we are particularly interested in 47,19, according to MS B:

> ותתן לנשים כסליך   And you gave your loins to women
> ותמשילם בגויתך   and let them[26] have dominion over your body.

The Greek version weakens the evocative force of the Hebrew text and freely translates the second line: παρανέκλινας τὰς λαγόνας σου γυναιξὶν καὶ ἐνεξου-σιάσθης ἐν τῷ σώματί σου ("you rested your loins[27] beside women and you were brought into subjection in your body"). Some modern translations have chosen to soften the language. So we read, for example, "you abandoned/sur-rendered yourself to women and gave them domination over your body" (NAB, Skehan—Di Lella), "you brought in women to lie at your side and let them usurp your authority" (REB), "entregaste tu cuerpo a las mujeres y te dejaste dominar por ellas" (BJ). Instead of "your loins", Syr has "your strength", using a term that in 44,6a (MSS B and Mas) translates the Hebrew חיל ("force, wealth, energy"). This noun also occurs in Prov 31,3, a text very similar to our verse: "Do not give your strength to women, and your thighs[28] to those who de-stroy kings". Here, the two parallel terms חילך (your strength) and ירכיך (lit. "your thighs") clearly have a sexual connotation: they allude to the man's sexual vigor.

In contrast to his discourse about David, Ben Sira makes no attempt to hide Solomon's defects, since they were well known to the people. In any case, he cynically softened the tone[29]. While the author of 1 Kgs 11,1–13 accuses Solomon of apostasy (his many women, being foreigners, led his heart away from the Lord and brought him to worship other gods), Ben Sira "only" criticizes him for his unrestrained sexuality (the plural נשים suggests his relations with many "women"). This seems to be his main sin[30]. This rereading of the tradition is in perfect harmony with the sage's ideas about women: although they are a source

---

25 Cf. on this poem BEENTJES, Countries; PETERCA, Porträt.

26 We note that the masculine suffix is used even in reference to women here, as in 7,24 in MS A. Cf. LÉVI, Ecclésiastique, 9.

27 MS 248 reads: τὰ σπλάγχνα σου ("your entrails") and the VL: *femora tua* ("your thighs").

28 Instead of MT's דרכיך ("your ways"), we are following the suggestion of BHS in reading וירכיך ("and your thighs"). On the textual problems of Prov 31,3, see WALTKE, Book, 504 notes 17–20.

29 Cf. MORLA ASENSIO, Eclesiástico, 228.

30 SNAITH, Ecclesiasticus, 236: "Lack of self-control with women seems to be Solomon's chief sin!" So also TRENCHARD, View on Women, 89–91, esp. 90; BALLA, Attitudes, 216–222, esp. 222; BEENTJES, Countries, 9.

of happiness and pleasure, for a man they are a constant danger of which one must always be wary (cf. Sir 9,1–9; 25,13–26; 26,5–12; 42,13–14). Quite definitely, a man cannot let himself be dominated by any woman, not even by his own wife (cf. Sir 36[33Hb],20; 9,2 in MS A[31]). Moreover, he must keep control in all situations, including in his marital relations. As Claudia Camp puts it, "A good wife may provide a proper outlet for one's lust, but even here the danger lurks"[32].

3.2 Female Images

To these briefly presented texts must be added three verses in which the sage alludes to woman indirectly with typically female images like those related to motherhood ("the breast/the mother's womb") or childbirth ("the pains of childbirth").

3.2.1 Sir 46,13Hb

After a bland reference to the Judges (46,11–12), Ben Sira centers his attention on Samuel, judge, prophet, and priest (46,13–20)[33]. The praise mentions the deeds Samuel accomplished during his life (46,13–16), the firm answer to prayer he received from the Lord (46,17–18), the testimony he made before dying (46,19), and his prophetic activity from the tomb (46,20).

Let us take a closer look at Sir 46,13ab, according to MS B:

אוהב עמו ורצוי עושהו   Beloved of his people and acceptable to his Maker,
המשואל מבטן אמו   he was dedicated[34] from his mother's womb[35].

---

31 In Gk, 9,2 can also be understood as referring to the women mentioned in the following verses.
32 CAMP, Understanding Patriarchy, 31.
33 PETRAGLIO, Siracide; CORLEY, Portrait. On 46,19 see BEENTJES, Quotations, 506–507.
34 The unusual Hebrew word is a pun on the name Samuel (שמואל), like that on the name Joshua (יהושע) and "salvation" (תשועה) in 46,1. Cf. SKEHAN–DI LELLA, Wisdom, 517–518; BEENTJES, Prophets, 140.
35 While Syr comes closer to Hb, Gk presents a very different text, in which the allusions to Hannah's vow and the birth of Samuel completely disappear: Ἠγαπημένος ὑπὸ κυρίου αὐτοῦ Σαμουηλ προφήτης κυρίου κατέστησεν βασιλείαν καὶ ἔχρισεν ἄρχοντας ἐπὶ τὸν λαὸν αὐτοῦ ("Samuel was loved by his Lord; as prophet of the Lord, he established the monarchy and anointed princes over his people"). It should be noted that the translator reduced the Hebrew text (46,13a–f) to half the content, i.e. only three lines (hence 46,13c in Gk = 46,13f in Hb).

The expression "his mother's womb" (or "his mother's breast") appears five times in the Book of Ben Sira. This is the first of two occurrences in the "Praise of the Ancestors" (cf. 49,7 discussed below). The other three occurrences are Sir 1,14; 40,1 and 50,22. In 1,14, Wisdom accompanies (lit. "was created with") the faithful in their mother's womb (ἐν μήτρᾳ). In 40,1, the forebodings of death trouble the sons of Adam from the day they leave their mother's womb (MS B: מרחם אמו and Gk: ἐκ γαστρὸς μητρὸς αὐτῶν). Lastly, in 50,22, the sage invites his hearers to bless the Lord who fosters the growth of human beings from their mother's womb (MS B: מרחם)[36]. In all of these texts, the expression mentioned highlights the idea of a person's origin and birth. In our text, on the other hand, it acquires a much more concrete meaning, since it evokes the vow Hannah, the mother of Samuel, made in the sanctuary of Shiloh: "O YHWH Sabaoth, if only you will look on the misery of your servant, and remember me, and not forget your servant, but will give to your servant a male child, then I will give him to YHWH for all the days of his life and no razor shall touch his head" (1 Sam 1,11). The prayer of this woman, whose womb had previously been closed by the Lord (1 Sam 1,5), was soon answered. Hannah conceived and gave birth to Samuel (1 Sam 1,20).

3.2.2 Sir 48,19

After mentioning the deportation of the northern kingdom (48,15cd), Ben Sira dedicates 48,15e–25 to the southern kingdom, and more precisely to Hezekiah and Isaiah, two close collaborators[37]. The mention of Judah and its kings (48,15e–16) is followed by the description of the improvements Hezekiah made in Jerusalem (48,17) and the attack made by Sennacherib (48,18–19). Thereafter, the prayer of the people, the Lord's powerful answer (48,20–21), and the recompense Hezekiah receives for his righteous action (48,22–23) are emphasized. The passage ends with a reference to Isaiah, who sees the future and consoles Israel (48,24–25). Now, let us look at Sir 48,19 according to MS B:

[אז נ]מוגו בגאון לבם [Then th]ey trembled with fear in the arrogance of their hearts[38]
ויחילו כיולדה and were contorted like a woman in childbirth.

---

36 Gk is different here: "Now, bless the Lord... who exalts our days from the womb" (ἐκ μήτρας).
37 On Sir 48,15–25 see HILDESHEIM, Prophet, 125–168; BEENTJES, Hezekiah; HÖFFKEN, Darstellung; MARBÖCK, Jesaja.
38 The expression בגאון לבם ("in the arrogance of their hearts") seems strange in this context, since this sentiment does not easily fit with the situation of the Israelites, unless the phrase alludes to the description of Hezekiah in 2 Chr 32,25: "his heart was haughty" (גבה לבו). Hence,

This verse describes the reaction of the people in face of the threats of the lord chamberlain sent by the king of Assyria. Even when in 2 Kgs 18,36 the people keep quiet before these threats, the message Hezekiah sends to the prophet Isaiah describes a hopeless situation, which perfectly fits in with the content and the pictures in our text: "Today is a day of anguish, punishment, and shame! The children have come to the mouth of the uterus, but there is no strength to give birth to them" (וכח אין ללדה) (2 Kgs 19,3; Isa 37,3).

In the second line, Ben Sira uses the verbs חיל / ὠδίνω ("suffer birth pains") and ילד / τίκτω ("give birth") in a figurative way in order to express the tremendous affliction of the people in face of Sennacherib's imminent attack. The same combination is also found in Sir 19,11 (missing in Hb), where the image of the woman in childbirth serves to illustrate the behavior of the fool who, as soon as he hears a bit of news, begins to suffer[39]. In 31(34Hb),5 (also missing in Hb and Syr), divinations, omens, and dreams are compared with the fantasies of a "woman in labor" (ὠδινούσης), and in 43,17a the verb ὠδίνω is applied to the land that quakes at the voice of thunder (MS Bmg: יחיל). As to the verb ילד, in 8,18b, it refers to what can be born (MS A: מה ילד; Gk: τί τέξεται) from the encounter with a stranger, and in 10,18 it is used in the expression "for those born of women" (MS A: לילוד אשה; Gk: γεννήμασιν γυναικῶν).

In Sir 48,19, Ben Sira has used an image that frequently appears in the ancient Near East, in the Hebrew Bible and in post-biblical literature: the metaphor of birth. The prophets, and above all Jeremiah, show special interest in it. This metaphor usually appears in texts that describe a crisis, in most cases, on a local level[40]. In our text, the pangs, the fear, the anxiety, and the weakness experienced

---

Lévi (Ecclésiastique, 141) suggests: ביגון לבם ("in the sorrow of their hearts"). Some authors translate "despite the arrogance of their hearts", but that does not solve the problem (PETERS, Buch, 415; HILDESHEIM, Prophet, 127 and 145). Gk reads: τότε ἐσαλεύθησαν καρδίαι καὶ χεῖρες αὐτῶν ("then their hearts and hands trembled"), while Syr omits the verse. Alonso Schökel (Eclesiástico, 319) suggests a translation that, although it is free, attempts to decipher Hb: "Entonces los que confiaban se acobardaron" (then, those who were confident became fearful); in other words, the Israelites, who before Sennacherib's arrival were self-assured (this would be their arrogance), let themselves be dominated by fear.

39 In Syr the comparison is much more explicit: "Through a word the fool is in pains of childbirth, as a woman giving birth who is in pain from her (newborn) baby".

40 Cf. Jer 6,22–24; 13,12–13; 22,20–23; 30,4–7; 48,40–41; 49,20–27; 50,41–43; Isa 23,1–7; 37,3; Hos 13,12–13; Mic 4,9–10; Nah 2,6–13. According to Bergmann, the birth metaphor "describes a kind of crisis that is potentially deadly and affects entire groups of individuals. Although this crisis can encompass cities or even countries, it does not have universal ramifications" (BERGMANN, Childbirth, 82).

by the woman before giving birth are meant to reflect the dramatic situation of the Israelites who are facing the threat of being attacked by Sennacherib.

3.2.3 Sir 49,7

After 48,17–25 (on Hezekiah and Isaiah), Ben Sira dedicates a section to Josiah[41], to the kings of Judah, and to Jeremiah (49,1–7)[42]. He begins with warm praise of King Josiah (49,1–3), and then evokes the Davidic dynasty that ruled in Jerusalem until the city was conquered by the Babylonians (49,4–6), so as to conclude with the recollection of Jeremiah, the prophet who witnessed the catastrophe (49,7).

Here is Sir 49,7, the only verse dedicated to Jeremiah, according to MS B:

ביד ירמיהו כי ענוה   As Jeremiah had announced[43], when they mistreated him[44];

והוא מרחם נוצר נביא   for he had been formed a prophet even in the womb,

לנתוש ולנתוץ ולהאביד להרס   to root out, pull down, and destroy[45],

וכן לבנת לנטע ולה[עז]   and then to build, to plant, and to st[rengthen][46].

If in 46,13b the expression "dedicated from his mother's womb" refers to 1 Sam 1,11, here the phrase "he had been formed a prophet even in the womb" recalls Jer 1,5: "Before I formed you in the womb I knew you (בטרם אצורך בבטן ידעתיך), and before you left the womb (ובטרם תצא מרחם) I consecrated you; I appointed you a prophet (נביא) to the nations. It must be noted that the three terms רחם ("womb"), נביא ("prophet"), and יצר ("to form") appear in both texts. Once again Ben Sira's rigorous choice of the material for the praise of these personages is striking. In the present case he wants to emphasize above all the vocation of the prophet. With this intention he reduces the text to its essential elements. He does so by using Jer 1,5 (Sir 49,7b) and Jer 1,10 (Sir 49,7cd) and omitting

---

41 BEENTJES, Memory; TOLONI, Riforma.

42 HILDESHEIM, Prophet, 168–206; URBANZ, Jeremia. See also EGGER-WENZEL, Josiah, 231–256.

43 Lit. "through the hand of Jeremiah".

44 This phrase ends the preceding sentence. Cf. Gk: "By the hand of Jeremiah, for they mistreated him, and he in the womb was consecrated as a prophet, to uproot and to mistreat and to destroy, similarly to build and to plant". Syr omits 49,7cd.

45 In our translation we do not include the infinitive להרס ("to demolish"), which is an addition to this verse, taken from Jer 1,10. Cf. SKEHAN–DI LELLA, Wisdom, 541.

46 We follow the reconstruction by Peters (Buch, 419) and Skehan (in SKEHAN–DI LELLA, Wisdom, 541). The verb ולהשיב ("[and] to restore"; cf. 46,7; 48,10) is read by others, e.g. Smend (Weisheit, 470), Hildesheim (Prophet, 187–188.200), and Beentjes (Book, 88).

Jeremiah's objection, the answer and the sign from the Lord (Jer 1,7–9) as well as the relation of the prophet with the people (Jer 1,10a).

In conclusion, we may say that the female images in Sirach 44–50 are "merely conventional literary figures"[47] that Ben Sira uses not only to express some ideas poetically, such as origin, birth, pain and fear, but also and above all to establish relations and connections with well-known texts from the tradition.

4 Conclusion

The recapitulation of Israel's history in Sirach 44–50 is certainly androcentric[48]. Even the title that appears in MS B before the start of Sir 44 is significant: שֶׁבַח אֲבוֹת עוֹלָם ("Praise of the Fathers of always/of eternity") that Gk transforms into πατέρων ὕμνος ("Hymn of the Fathers"). In other words, the praise is of the eternal fathers, that is, of those fathers who, although ancient, were contemporaries in Ben Sira's time and continue being present today. The sage refers to Israel's ancestors, only men, as the introduction to the poem (44,1–15) corroborates. In 44,1, he mentions the addressees of the praise: godly/glorious men (אַנְשֵׁי חֶסֶד / ἄνδρας ἐνδόξους), our fathers in their generations (אֲבוֹתֵינוּ בְּדוֹרוֹתָם / τοὺς πατέρας ἡμῶν τῇ γενέσει), who reappear in 44,10 as godly/merciful men (אַנְשֵׁי חֶסֶד / ἄνδρες ἐλέους), along with their male descendants (sons and grandsons). Among those who are praised, there are men famous (אַנְשֵׁי שֵׁם / ἄνδρες ὀνομαστοί, 44,3) for their courage as well as skillful, rich and powerful men (אַנְשֵׁי חַיִל / ἄνδρας πλούσιοι, 44,6). We have seen that, in accordance with what was announced in 44,1–15, no woman has been named in the praise. Ben Sira could very well have included the Genesis matriarchs, Miriam, the sister of Moses and Aaron, and Deborah, among others; but he chose to pass over them in silence, thus also passing over their histories and their memory in silence. To be sure, we do not know what reasons led him to make this choice, but in any case, we will attempt to answer the question even if only hypothetically.

Our answer has to do with the topic of collective memory, which is arousing much interest among those who study the origins of Christianity[49]. Thanks to the studies by Maurice Halbwachs (1877–1945), remembering is no longer conceived as a purely individual act, that is, the product of an isolated mind, but as a social

---

47 TRENCHARD, View on Women, 52.
48 Cf. JÜNGLING, Vatermetaphorik, 85.
49 For this paragraph, cf. KIRK, Memory, 2–3.

phenomenon. In other words, memory is inseparable from the social world in which the remembrance arises. Paolo Jedlowski defines the collective memory as "the ensemble of the representations of the past that a group produces, conserves, elaborates and transmits through the interaction of its members"[50]. Consequently, this concerns a common elaboration that coincides with the identity of a group at a given moment in time. The collective memory is constituted by a series of *social frameworks* (such as space, time, social institutions, and communicative practices) that give coherence and readability to memories or else favor their omission. Each social group selects, from the experience of its members, its personal and historical recollections, its particular account of the past. In this way, it distinguishes itself from other groups that claim a different memory and underpins its collective identity. The collective memory moreover creates a close connection between the past and the present. The selection, modification and interpretation of the memories are determined by the current situation. Lastly, when the recollection of the past is realized publicly, the group acquires greater cohesion and its identity is guaranteed.

Was Ben Sira the only representative of the wisdom that he promotes in his book, or was he a part of some group, community or school of thought? Although there is no explicit mention in this respect either in the book or outside of it, it is logical to suppose that Ben Sira was not the only Jewish sage—nor an isolated thinker—in 2nd-century BC Jerusalem, and that there were most likely other teachers and groups with different or even contradictory ideas (such as the Enochic circles)[51]. Ben Sira represents a collectivity (a school of wisdom) that takes a determined position vis-à-vis the progress of Hellenism and attempts to transmit its teachings (its love for the law and for the tradition) to the new generations. Its aim is that the young disciples recognize themselves in the shared past and assume it as a part of their identity.

In his collective memory, however, there is no trace of women, or rather, there are a few generic signs that mention, in passing or with a negative tone, their historical existence and at the same time their minor importance. The recollection of women is insignificant. This is why there are no female names in the "Praise of the Ancestors", just as there are none in the other biblical and extrabiblical praises we mentioned previously. Praising a particular woman would mean showing admiration for her, recognizing her qualities and considering her as a person worthy of being imitated, and this does not fit in with the pre-

---

50 JEDLOWSKI, Sociología, 125: "el conjunto de las representaciones del pasado que un grupo produce, conserva, elabora y transmite a través de la interacción de sus miembros".
51 See BOCCACCINI, Ben Sira.

dominant androcentric prejudice in the ancient Mediterranean societies, where principally masculine names are recalled[52]. The absence of female names in Sirach 44–50 must not be attributed simply to Ben Sira's personal misogyny; rather, its roots go deep into the memory and collective identity of one of the influential groups in the society of that time, a group of which the sage is the greatest representative.

52 Cf. ILAN, Distribution of Women's Names, 186–200.

Polygamy in Ben Sira?

In 1966, Hilaire Duesberg and Irénée Fransen collaborated in writing a commentary on the book of Ben Sira (Ecclesiasticus) in the "The Holy Bible" series, which Monsignor Salvatore Garofalo edited[1]. These monks of the Benedictine abbey of Maredsous (Belgium) had also written *Les scribes inspirés*, a well-known introduction to the wisdom books of the Bible[2]. In the introductory portion of their commentary, Duesberg and Fransen devote a section to the "personal experiences of Ben Sira", in which they state:

> We know that Ben Sira was married because he had a grandson. Celibacy was not a common form of asceticism among the Jews in his day and would have been an anomaly.
> He gained experience as a family head, and his thoughts, principles and advice are in no way speculative. However, aside from the picturesque tone, their originality is not excessive. He has access to the considerations dear to the sages from Ptahhotep until the book of Proverbs, and he does not bring any innovation. Family law remains the same throughout the ages. The most that can be observed is that, though he admits Mosaic divorce (25,26), rejected by the Gospel, he does not speak about a sole wife, as do the books of Tobit, Proverbs, etc. Polygamy is nothing more than a memory suppressed by the customs[3].

However, I wish to point out that the text of Ben Sira calls into question the last statement on polygamy. Though the evidence is limited and ambiguous, a detailed analysis indicates that polygamy, or better polygyny (a husband with multiple wives) was not a thing of the past, but rather an actual practice of limited frequency at the time when the sage taught in Jerusalem[4]. The issue was studied, somewhat imprecisely, by Warren C. Trenchard in his monograph on women in Ben Sira, published in 1982[5], reconsidered in a short article by Renate Egger-Wenzel in 1996[6], and recently detailed by Ibolya Balla in her doctoral thesis on family, gender and sexuality in Ben Sira, published in April 2011[7].

Our contribution aims to examine, firstly, Sir 26,6 and 37,11a, two texts which explicitly mention the rivalry between the wives in a marriage that is likely

---

1 Duesberg–Fransen, Ecclesiastico.
2 Duesberg–Fransen, Scribes.
3 Duesberg–Fransen, Ecclesiastico, 50.
4 On polygamy in the Judaism of the second temple, cf. Collins, Marriage, 104–162, esp. 121–122; Instone-Brewer, Divorce, 59–65; Campbell (ed.), Marriage, 217–219.
5 Trenchard, View on Women.
6 Egger-Wenzel, Polygamie, 57–64. Cf. also Collins, Jewish Wisdom, 65–66.
7 Balla, Family, esp. 102–107.

https://doi.org/10.1515/9783110492316-011

bigamous; and secondly, Sir 7,26; 25,8b; 25,14; 28,15, passages whose interpretations remain under scholarly discussion.

1 Rivalry between Wives (Sir 26,6; 37,11a)

Although these two texts are very different in the translation of Ben Sira's grandson, both use the noun ἀντίζελος, "rival" (from ἀντί, "opposite to" + ζελόω, "to emulate, admire, envy"), in reference to a woman who is supposedly married. In addition to these two occurrences, this term appears only once elsewhere in the LXX, in Lev 18,18, where the context is blatantly sexual; there, it renders the Hebrew verb צרר II ("to show rivalry")[8]. In fact, chapter 18 is entirely devoted to standards for sexual relations. As far as our verse is concerned, the legislation forbids the husband to marry his sister: "you shall not take a woman as a rival wife to her sister, uncovering her nakedness while her sister is yet alive". At this point we cannot help but remember the story of Laban's two daughters, Leah and Rachel, whom Jacob married seven years apart because of the strategy hatched by the father! Although Jacob only loved Rachel, he had to marry her older sister. This is the origin of the drama, the struggle and the pain between the two sisters, wives of the same husband. Leah suffers because she realizes that the favorite bride is Rachel, and Rachel suffers because, unlike her sister, she cannot have children (cf. Gen 29–30).

1.1 Sir 26,5 – 6

Sir 26,5 – 6 is part of a long section of the book dedicated to wives (25,13 – 26,27). It begins with a series of three numerical proverbs (25,1– 11) and the sage introducing the topic of "family" at the first verse: "My soul takes pleasure in three things, and they are beautiful in the sight of the Lord and of humans; agreement between brothers, friendship between neighbors, and a wife and a husband who live in harmony" (25,1). Marital harmony is the topic of our text, which is given below in the Greek version[9]:

5a   Ἀπὸ τριῶν εὐλαβήθη ἡ καρδία μου,
5b   καὶ ἐπὶ τῷ τετάρτῳ προσώπῳ ἐδεήθην·
5c   διαβολὴν πόλεως, καὶ ἐκκλησίαν ὄχλου,

---

8 In addition, some Lucianic witnesses have the Greek noun in 1 Sam 1,6.
9 The Hebrew has not been conserved, and vv. 5d and 6a are lacking in Syr.

5d καὶ καταψευσμόν, ὑπὲρ θάνατον πάντα μοχθηρά.
6a ἄλγος καρδίας καὶ πένθος γυνὴ ἀντίζηλος ἐπὶ γυναικὶ[10]
6b καὶ μάστιξ γλώσσης πᾶσιν ἐπικοινωνοῦσα.

5a My heart fears three things,
5b and a fourth one frightened me:
5c a riot in the city, an assembly of the people,
5d and a false accusation, are things worse than death;
6a a woman jealous of another woman is but heartache and grief,
6b and the scourging tongue affects everyone.

It has already been noted that this numerical proverb exhibits unusual composition, i.e. after listing three things "worse than death" (the worst one could imagine in a negative sense), it ends with something much less terrifying, viz. "heartache and grief". Thus, the sequence, which should be ascending (in this case, going from bad to worse), is in fact descending, thereby weakening the power of what should have been the climax of the proverb. Moreover, the ambiguity of the last clause (25,6b), as we shall see later, makes it difficult to interpret the whole proverb[11].

Be that as it may, one thing is certain: driven by the context, Ben Sira wanted to place the woman in this proverb, and he did so by introducing at its climax the figure of one woman jealous of another, as if to say that her tongue makes her more dangerous than the other three calamities. Although the sage does not describe a family scene (there is no mention of her husband, the marriage or the home), the choice of the term ἀντίζηλος is crucial for understanding that the text is probably referring to the rivalry between two wives in a bigamous marriage. This reading is confirmed by the aforementioned passage of Lev 18,18, as well as by 1 Sam 1,6, the only text in the Hebrew Bible to use the feminine noun צָרָה, "rival" (from the root צרר II), in reference to Elkanah's second wife Peninnah. Unlike her, Hannah, the favorite wife, was barren; it was precisely this condition that made her unhappy of heart and provoked the humiliation that she suffered from Peninnah.

In the text of Ben Sira "heartache and grief" (ἄλγος καρδίας καὶ πένθος) are the consequences of the rivalry between the wives but the reader does not receive any other information about the situation. What is the cause of this jealousy? How does it occur? Who suffers more: her husband, both wives, or just one? A

---

10 According to Smend and Peters, ἐπὶ γυναικί was probably added by the translator, who thus made the clause longer; cf. SMEND, Weisheit, 235; PETERS, Buch, 216.
11 Cf. the remark by ALONSO SCHÖKEL, Eclesiástico, 237 and the lengthy discussion in TRENCHARD, View on Women, 58–62.

look at the ancient stories can be helpful. Both Jacob and Elkanah have a favorite wife, and this preference is presumed to be the main reason for discord and jealousy between the two wives in each case. We can assume that the rivalry between the wives had to do with matters of a sexual nature[12]. Rachel and Hannah, the wives whom their husbands preferred, are initially unable to produce descendants, unlike their rivals Leah and Peninnah. By contrast, in the home of Abraham, he is the one disappointed by Sarah's decision to banish Hagar and her son from the family (Gen 21,11).

As we have already said, the last clause presents an ambiguous text that allows different interpretations. "The scourge of the tongue" (μάστιξ γλώσσης), which probably translates שׁוֹט לשׁוֹן (cf. Job 5,21; Sir 51,2d in MS B)[13], can be understood as the common element (πᾶσιν ἐπικοινωνοῦσα) to the four things that frighten the sage: a riot in the city, an assembly of the people, a false accusation, a woman who is the rival of another woman. So, the first possible translation would be: "...and the scourging tongue is like all (the previous four things)". This is the choice made by the Syriac translator too: "...and a wound (caused by) the tongue (is what) all (these things) together (are)"[14]. Another possibility is to understand v. 6b in reference to the three cases listed in v. 5cd: "...and the scourging tongue is like the other three (things mentioned)". In this case, the scourging tongue is supposed to be that of a woman who is jealous of another woman[15]. Finally, the language of this caustic woman can have devastating effects beyond the privacy of the family home because it affects the husband's honor "[A]nd the scourge of (her) tongue reaches / touches / affects / involves everyone", or, as Trenchard proposes: "And a tongue-lashing shares it with everyone"[16]. In this case, the verb ἐπικοινωνέω is understood to mean "to communicate, participate, share something with somebody" and πᾶσιν refers not to the previously mentioned things (neut. pl. adj.), but to all people without distinction (m. pl. adj.). Consequently, the conjugal misfortunes (in this case of a bigamous marriage) enter into the public domain. The Latin version is along the same lines: *in muliere infideli (zelotypa, zelotypa et infideli) flagellum linguae omnibus communicans*. In conclusion, the comparisons in verses 5a and 5cd, joined by the

---

12 Cf. Balla, Ben Sira, 383; Ead., Family, 104.
13 This is also the reconstruction of Segal, ספר, 161.
14 Cf. Smend, Weisheit, 235; Box–Oesterley, Book, 403; Alonso Schökel, Eclesiástico, 237; Zapff, Jesus Sirach, 151.
15 Skehan–Di Lella, Wisdom, 344: "and a scourging tongue like the other three"; and Kaiser, Weisheit, 62: "und die Geißel *ihrer* Zunge übertrifft alle drei" (italics ours).
16 Trenchard, View on Women, 57.

expression πᾶσιν ἐπικοινωνοῦσα, have enriched the "private" danger of feminine jealousy with unexpected "public" connotations.

1.2 Sir 37,11a

After the communal prayer of Israel (33[36Hb],1–17), the sage begins a long instruction on the theme of discernment applied to food, the wife, friends and advisors (33[36Hb],18–37,31). Our verse belongs to the section on advisors, which is the longest one (37,7–15). After an initial premise (see v. 7a), the sage points out advisors that one should avoid: those who, motivated only by self-interest, always recommend what suits them (vv. 7b–9); those who either envy you or are your enemies[17] (v. 10) and, finally, those who have a contrary predisposition even to the person who consults with them or to whom they go for advice (v. 11). The section ends with a positive series in which the sage moves from the familial and social setting to the religious milieu (vv. 12–15). If the negative series does not offer any concrete information on inadequate advisors, in the positive series the description becomes much more explicit. Ben Sira describes the good advisor as a person who fears God, keeps his commandments, shares the same feeling with the man or woman who seeks advice, and is ready to help when he sees someone stumbling (see v. 12abcd). Let us concentrate our attention on v. 11a, found in two Hebrew manuscripts, MS B (+ Bmg) and MS D, which we quote here together with the Greek version:

11a   צרתה אל אשה עם [תועץ אל 10a]
11a   [Do not[18] take advice] from a woman with respect to her rival[19]

11a   [10a μὴ βουλεύου] μετὰ γυναικὸς περὶ τῆς ἀντιζήλου αὐτῆς
11a   [Do not take advice] from a woman about her rival

This line is, hence, the first of a series of nine recommendations, formulated in parallel (to someone about someone or something), which ultimately depend on v. 10 ("do not take advice from…"). In our case, the sage's advise is not to consult a woman about her rival, although it is unclear whether this is a future rival wife whom her husband is about to marry or his second legitimate wife. However, this

---

17 According Gk and Syr. MS D reads "father-in-law". MS B is damaged.

18 Both MS B and Bmg read עַל instead of אל.

19 Latin reads *et cum muliere de ea quae aemulatur*, while Syr introduces a new idea: "Do not commit adultery with a woman (with her)".

is the only situation where the consultation involves two people[20]. The other consultations pertain to a subject and an activity (with a coward about war, with a merchant about trade, and with a buyer about the sale; with a lazy man about any work; with a laborer at the end of the harvest; with a lazy slave about an important job)[21] or a virtue (with a miser about generosity; with a ruthless person about benevolence). In short, to quote Kearns, "interested parties make poor counselors"[22].

The admonition is wanting, both in details about the woman and also in reasons for her unreliability. (Such rhetorical brevity extends throughout the verse.). Now, why is Ben Sira so direct? It seems obvious to me that the sage ironically lists some emblematic cases taken from daily life to convey his teaching in a manner that makes his disciple smile. There is no need to offer a complete portrait of the characters, to place them in a specific context, to tell all about their actions and even to explain the reasons for their unreliability. He who has ears, let him hear. So, the wise disciple (i.e. listener, reader) is placed in a position to sense the unspoken, to reconstruct a missing scene in the text, to give face and voice to a series of characters presented as types, and even to imagine concrete situations that fit the advice of the sage.

In Sir 37,11 it is hard not to think of a case of polygyny, of the awkward living situation of two wives of the same husband, with or without children; their rivalry becomes apparent in different ways within the home and very probably beyond. Here Ben Sira teaches that asking one of the wives about the other is totally derisory, because it assumes that tension undermines their relationship; indeed, the term צָרָה already indicates that one is the rival of the other. Now, the stories that we presented at the beginning, i.e. those of Sarah and Hagar, of Rachel and Leah, and of Hannah and Peninnah, confirm the sage's teaching.

2 Some Other Disputed Texts

In relation to Sir 26,6 and 37,11, scholars discuss other texts, notably Sir 7,26; 28,15; 25,8b and 25,14. In fact, the technical term צָרָה—or its corresponding Greek ἀντίζελος—does not appear in any of them. However, some authors perceive between the lines a hidden situation of polygamy. Next we present briefly the different interpretations.

---

20 TRENCHARD, View on Women, 92; MINISSALE, Siracide, 174.
21 According to Gk. Missing in Hb.
22 Quoted in TRENCHARD, View on Women, 92.

2.1 Divorce or Polygamy? (Sir 7,26; 28,15)

We begin with Sir 7,26: "If you have a wife, do not abhor her; but if she is hateful, do not trust her"[23]. Here we encounter two problematic terms: the verb תעב in Piel ("to abhor") and the pass. ptc. שנואה ("hated", "hateful").

Even if תעב per se has nothing to do with divorce, in this case, some authors (e. g. Ryssel, Smend, Box—Oesterley, Spicq, Snaith, Morla Asensio, Yaron)[24] consider it synonymous with שנא ("to divorce") because of the context. On the other hand, it is noteworthy that the Greek version uses ἐκβάλλω, the technical term for divorce. Regarding שנואה, rendered in Greek by μισουμένη (Lat: *odibili*), some scholars understand it as referring to the "neglected" wife, i. e. the wife who is not the husband's favorite, and therefore much less loved. This presupposes a polygamous or at least bigamous marriage. This is the position of Sauer in his commentary of 2001, where he translates שנואה with "Nebenbuhler-in", i. e. rival, intruder, the wife's competitor"[25].

Let us now turn to Sir 28,15, which is lacking in the Hebrew text: "The third tongue (= slander) has driven away (from their house) courageous women, and deprived them of the fruit of their toil". The use of the verb ἐκβάλλω (see above) indicates that Ben Sira intends to talk about divorce. In fact, the sage refers generically to divorces caused by slander without any other details. However, for Vaccari and others, the situation described in this verse is that of a bigamous marriage, where the jealousy between the two wives is the cause of divorce[26]. But who is the slanderer? Certainly, the text does not answer this question. Usually one thinks of a third person, outside the marriage, with his or her malicious comments that can undermine the marital harmony. But this is not the only possibility. According to Balla, "one of the situations that might be supposed behind this verse is a polygamous marriage, where one wife is rival of the other, and she is the slanderer"[27].

2.2 Enemies or Rival Wives? (Sir 25,14)

The Greek text of Sir 25,14, which is missing in the Hebrew, says: "Any affliction, except that of the adversaries; any revenge, except that of the enemies". The

---

23 For a complete discussion, cf. CALDUCH-BENAGES, Cut Her Away, 84–89.
24 Cf. CALDUCH-BENAGES, Cut Her Away, 85 note 15.
25 SAUER, Jesus Sirach, 90. Cf. CALDUCH-BENAGES, Cut Her Away, 87–88 note 33.
26 Cf. CALDUCH-BENAGES, Cut Her Away, 93.
27 BALLA, Family, 105.

Syriac version is very similar: "All the afflictions (hurt), but not as the enemy's, and all vengeances (hurt), but not as the revenge of the adversary". Already in 1906 Smend had noticed that this verse does not fit well within the passage, which focuses on the bad wife from the beginning to the end of the section (25,13–26). In his attempt to solve the problem, this author suggested that the scribe made a translation error, reading (ים)שנא, "opponents/haters" instead of שנואה, "hated/divorced" (cf. 7,26b) and (ים)צר, "enemies" instead of צרה, "rival" (cf. 37,11a)[28]. In his view, the text was referring to the rivalry between the many wives of one husband. Significant authors, explicitly or implicitly, have adhered to this proposed solution[29]. Even Trenchard, who opposes this interpretation, ends his long discussion with these thoughts: "But as we saw in v. 13, Ben Sira has arranged this material in this particular context to leave the impression that all these topics are dependent on and enlargements of the theme of the wife's wickedness in v. 13b. Thus, for him the haters and enemies of v. 14 stand for bad wives".

2.3 "Ox and ass": husband and wife or two contending wives? (Sir 25,8b)

The difficulty of Sir 25,8b[30] is how to interpret the following Hebrew expression חורש כורש עם חמור ("plowing like an ox with an ass"). The clause is a clear allusion to Deut 22,10, which prohibits one from tilling a field with two different species of animals: "You shall not plow with an ox and an ass yoked together" (cf. Lev 19,19).

Now let us read Sir 25,8ab in MS C (v. 8b is missing in the Greek): "Happy the husband of an intelligent woman, and (one who) does not plow like an ox (yoked) with an ass". Apparently, there is no connection between the two lines. While 25,8 evokes a context of marriage (husband and intelligent wife, cf. 26,1–4; 40,23), 25,8b is associated with the world of agriculture (peasants and pack animals). However, as we shall see, Ben Sira is able to establish an unprecedented relationship between them, even if it remains hidden.

---

28 SMEND, Weisheit, 229.
29 For example, ALONSO SCHÖKEL, Eclesiástico, 235; MINISSALE, Siracide, 132; SKEHAN–DI LELLA, Wisdom, 347; MORLA ASENSIO, Eclesiástico, 134; COLLINS, Jewish Wisdom, 66; ZAPFF, Jesus Sirach, 145.
30 On this verse, cf. CALDUCH-BENAGES, Animal Imagery, 68–70.

Several authors[31] adopt the Syriac version, because it is allegedly preferable to the Hebrew text. If nothing else, it is certainly closer to the Deuteronomic prescription: "(Happy) he who has not yoked the plow with the ox and the ass together". This translation suggests, in light of the first clause, the image of a bigamous marriage in which the two wives (the ox and the ass) of one husband cannot live in peace because of their incompatible personalities.

Let us return, however, to the Hebrew text. It does not say "(Happy) the man who does not plow with an ox and an ass together" but rather "(happy) the one who does not plow like an ox with an ass". In this case, the metaphorical meaning of the sentence changes: the ox and the donkey are not the two rival wives in a polygamous marriage, but the ox is the husband (supposedly intelligent and strong) and the ass is his wife (supposedly foolish and stubborn)[32]. In other words, the Deuteronomic expression is used to evoke "an undesirable marriage"[33] due to the incompatibility between husband and wife[34].

3 Conclusion

The scant information on polygamy found in the sage's work forces us to limit ourselves to hypothesis. However, the two verses on the rivalry between the wives (Sir 26,6; 37,11a) and some allusions in the texts here discussed suggest the existence of bigamous marriages (one husband with two wives) and the conflicts they generate in marriage and family. Although we cannot know with certainty whether or not such marriages were common, we believe it is more likely that polygyny was an exception to the rule, reserved for wealthy families. In fact, Flavius Josephus, in the 1st century AD, mentions a few cases of polygamy, mainly bigamy, in the royal house (A.J. 14,300; B.J. 1,477) and among the priestly families (Vita 75). Furthermore, documents found in Naḥal Ḥever, in the Babatha archive, near the Dead Sea, attest to the existence of bigamous marriages in the 2nd century AD. For instance, in a Greek papyrus there is a description of disputes between Babatha and Miriam, the two wives of Yehuda, after his death. The

---

31 Cf., for example, SMEND, Weisheit, 227; MINISSALE, Siracide, 131; SKEHAN – DI LELLA, Wisdom, 339; KAISER, Weisheit, 60.

32 Cf. MOPSIK, Sagesse, 171 note 2. According to this author, the verb "plow" is to be understood metaphorically, i.e. "to marry a woman".

33 SKEHAN—DI LELLA, Wisdom, 342.

34 This is also Minissale's understanding: "L'uomo è felice se non c'è disparità d'intelligenza con la moglie" (Siracide, 131).

information contained in the text seems to indicate that this was a wealthy family. But here we are in the Tannaitic period.

In conclusion, Ben Sira seems to warn the young disciples about the dangers of a bigamous marriage. The few texts that evoke this matter, or better allude to this particular family situation, merely highlight the points of conflict without ever mentioning any attendant advantage or gratification. If, on the one hand, in the 2nd century BC polygamy had not yet disappeared from Jewish society, on the other, one of the authoritative representatives advises against it, even if he does so implicitly.

Good and Bad Wives in the Book of Ben Sira: A Harmless Classification?

The book of Ben Sira (also known as Sirach or Ecclesiasticus) was written between 200 and 180 BC in Jerusalem, where its author, a professional scribe, headed some sort of school or academy of wisdom.

The crisis provoked by the attempted hellenisation of the Jewish people under the Seleucid king Antiochus IV Epiphanes (175 – 163 BC) was already latent in the time of Ben Sira. In the first decades of the 2nd century BC, the confrontation between the new Hellenistic ideas and the traditional religious values of the Jews had already begun. Nevertheless, Ben Sira wrote his book not to oppose Hellenism or defend his tradition against foreign views but rather to strengthen the faith and confidence of his people. In other words, his main purpose was to encourage the Jews to stay connected to the religion, wisdom, and traditions of their ancestors[1].

1 Ben Sira and Women

The book of Ben Sira devotes more verses to women than Proverbs, Job, Qoheleth, or the Wisdom of Solomon. In fact, 10 percent of this sage's teachings from Jerusalem refer to particular women or, from time to time, present typically feminine images such as those relating to motherhood ("the maternal bosom/ womb", 1,14; 40,1; 46,13Hb; 49,7; 50,22) or to birth ("born of woman", 10,18). Mothers, wives, widows, daughters, virgins, maids, singers, courtesans, prostitutes, and adulteresses always appear in relation to men: son, husband, father, a eunuch, master, or client. Moreover, they all move in the shadows of anonymity, without an identity, faceless members of a generic and undefined group. Even in the "Praise of the Ancestors" (Sir 44 – 50), a real parade of famous personalities in Israel's history, no woman is named. On that occasion, Ben Sira could well have included the matriarchs or the heroines of his people, among others, but he chose to remain silent about them, thus silencing their stories and memories[2].

---

1 For a good introduction to the book, see COGGINS, Sirach.
2 CALDUCH-BENAGES, Absence, 301 – 317.

https://doi.org/10.1515/9783110492316-012

To make a general survey of women in the book of Ben Sira[3] would exceed the scope of this essay, which will focus on just one category of women: wives and their classification into "good" and "bad" on the basis of the Hebrew text (not always available) and the Greek version[4]. What does this classification correspond to? What are its criteria? For what purpose does the sage use it? What are its implications? None of these questions were addressed by A. B. Davidson, the author of the first article on Ben Sira and women, written in the late 19th century.

> The judgment of Jesus-ben-Sira … regarding women is popularly supposed to be very damnatory. This opinion is scarcely justified. Sirach believes that there are bad women and good women, and if the badness of a bad woman be something as bad as can be, the goodness of a good woman is something superlatively good. … They pretty well balance one another[5].

I will delve into this supposed balance between good and evil to discover the meaning of this classification, its role in the sage's teaching, and the ideological assumptions that support it. My general approach will focus on the literary dimension of the selected texts, paying special attention to the communicative strategies used by the author as well as to the influence of the sociohistorical context on his work and teaching.

Ben Sira is the heir of an ancient wisdom tradition, in which women (mothers, wives, adulteresses, or prostitutes) constitute one of the main topics. Its authors tend to separate them into "good" and "bad", and they often refer to them ironically or even satirically. Some notable examples are the demotic Instruction of Ankhsheshonqy (Ankhsh. 24–25)[6], Papyrus Insinger (P.Insinger 9)[7], the

---

3 See especially the following monographs: TRENCHARD, View on Women; BALLA, Family. See also MCKINLAY, Gendering Wisdom, 160–178; STROTMANN, Sirach, 539–554; and CALDUCH-BENAGES, Mujeres, 37–44. For the Syriac version, see CALDUCH-BENAGES, ¿Sesgos de género?, 686–693.

4 The evolution of the text of Ben Sira is undoubtedly the most complicated of all the books of the Old Testament. Ben Sira wrote in Hebrew (Hb), but his work was mainly preserved in Greek (Gk), Syriac (Syr), and Latin (Lat). Since 1896 the Hebrew text has been gradually recovered, and we now have about two-thirds of it. Notwithstanding many unresolved problems, most scholars now agree on the existence of two text forms, a shorter and a longer one, both in the Hebrew (HbI and HbII) and Greek textual tradition (GkI and GkII). On this question, see SKEHAN–DI LELLA, Wisdom, 51–62; GILBERT, Siracide, 1390–1402; and CALDUCH-BENAGES, Crisol, 113–121.

5 DAVIDSON, Judgment, 402.

6 LICHTHEIM, Wisdom Literature, 88–90.

7 LICHTHEIM, Wisdom Literature, 203–205.

Anthology or Florilegium of Stobaeus (Flor. 22–23)[8] as an example of the gnomic Hellenistic wisdom, or the monostichs of the playwright Menander (Mon. 83–87)[9]. In this sense, then, the texts of Sirach presented below pursue a line of thought that persists in the time of the sage.

2 Two Main Categories of Wives

Along with daughters (7,24–25; 22,3–5; 42,9–14) and dangerously seductive women (9,1–9; 23,22–26), wives receive special attention from Ben Sira. As already indicated, the sage places them in the two basic ethical categories of good and evil, the same categories he also uses to refer to people in general. Among these, the servants stand out as the only ones who, like wives, are explicitly characterized as good/wise/intelligent (7,20–21; 10,25) or bad (36[33Hb],27; 42,5)[10]. We must not forget that, at the time, wives and servants, as well as sons, daughters, and cattle, were considered to be the property of the paterfamilias (see 7,18–28).

The most significant texts on wives are concentrated in chapters 25–26, immediately after the self-praise of Lady Wisdom. If, in chapter 24, the protagonist was the mysterious figure of personified Wisdom, now concrete and real women from everyday life occupy center stage. If the first is distinguished by the excellence of her speech, the latter seem to be voiceless. They do not utter a single word, but are constantly the subject of discussion. They are subject to the sage's teaching. The instructions on the wives alternate in the following order: 25,13–26 (bad wives)[11]; 26,1–4 (good wives); 26,5–12 (bad wives); 26,13–18 (good wives)[12]. To these passages we must add 36Hb,21–26 (33Gk,26–31) on the good wife, situated inside a section on discernment (33[36Hb],18–37,31). Finally, many verses scattered throughout the book complete the portrait of the

---

8 WACHSMUTH–HENSE (eds.), Anthologium, 494–499 (chs. 22–23 = chs. 67–74 in the edition by A. Meinecke). See specifically the *Poem on Women* (Iamb. frag. 7) by Semonides of Amorgos (ch. 22,193, pp. 561–566), the first misogynist work of Western literature (6th century BC).

9 LICHTHEIM, Wisdom Literature, 50.

10 Woman and servant appear together in the Instruction of Ankhsheshonqy: "Do not open your heart to your wife or to your servant" (Ankhsh. 13,17) (LICHTHEIM, Wisdom Literature, 78).

11 On this passage, see EGGER-WENZEL, Knechtschaft, 23–49.

12 The next passage (26,19–27) only exists in Syr and in the long form of the Greek version (GkII); consequently, it does not seem to come originally from Ben Sira (*pace* SKEHAN–DI LELLA, Wisdom, 351). Verses 19–21 talk about the choice of the spouse, and vv. 22–27 give both positive and negative maxims about women and marriage. See on this subject BALLA, Family, 107–110.

good wife (7,19.26a; 9,1; 25,1.8; 28,15; 40,19.23) and of the bad wife (7,26b; 9,2; 36[33Hb],20ab; 37,11a; 42,6; 47,19).

All these texts presuppose a male audience, and especially young men who attended Ben Sira's school in Jerusalem. They belonged to wealthy families of the city and were preparing themselves to occupy positions of responsibility in the future. The sage directed his teachings about the wives specifically to them. Consequently, all the advice reflects the mentality and perspective of a husband—everything in the book suggests that Ben Sira was married—who wants to instruct the future husbands about the virtues they should look for in a wife and about the dangers they must avoid. Hence, the division between good and bad wives, emerging from a totally male-centered perspective, contemplates only the husband's happiness, desire, convenience, honor, and authority. For this reason, some of the sage's statements about marital harmony, in which husband and wife are placed on the same level, are truly surprising; he says, for example, "With three things I am delighted, for they are pleasing to the Lord and to men: Harmony among brethren, friendship among neighbors, and the mutual love of husband and wife [συμπεριφερόμενοι]"[13] (Sir 25,1); or "Friend and companion are encountered at the right time, but especially the woman with the husband" (Sir 40,23Gk)[14]. In these verses, we should note the order in which the spouses are cited: husband and wife, wife and husband, as well as the absence of possessive adjectives to indicate the relationship between them.

2.1 Bad Wives

In texts on bad wives, the Hebrew expression רע[ת] אשה, "a woman's evil", appears three times (25,13.17.19), and the Greek one, γυνὴ πονηρά, "the bad/ evil woman", is repeated four times (25,6.25; 26,7; 42,6)[15]. At first glance, it is unclear what this feminine evil is, since both the noun and the adjective are used in a rather broad sense. Only in the light of context, and in some cases with the help of the different versions, is it possible to discover meanings, nuances, and specific allusions. It is, however, clear that the women's wickedness is worse than any other evil (25,13.19a), and so the evil woman deserves the fate of the sinner (25,19b), that is, to marry a sinner and not a just man, so that

---

13 On this term, see BALLA, Family, 58–60.
14 See, on the contrary, the Hebrew text of MS B in the second colon (the first one is damaged): "but better than both is a sensible woman [אשה משכלת]".
15 See MS Bmg: טפשה, "crazy".

she will serve as punishment for her husband[16]. The same view, although without explicit mention of sin and punishment, is shared by Hesiod in his *Works and Days:* "For a man … there is nothing else more chilling than an evil one [wife], a meal-ambusher who scorches her husband without a firebrand, even though he be strong, and gives him over to raw old age" (Op. 695)[17]. Similarly, Euripides writes: "Terrible is the violence of the ocean waves, terrible the impetuosity of rivers and burning breath of fire, terrible poverty and a thousand other things, but of all calamities the worst is a bad woman" (Frag. 1059)[18]. Much later, the midrash on Ps 59 points out: "If she [a woman] is a bad wife, there is no end to her badness" (Midr. Ps. 59,2)[19].

2.1.1 Communicative Strategies

As a skilled master and teacher, Ben Sira employs various communicative strategies to convey his teachings and to convince the audience. In the two longer passages on bad wives, 25,13 – 26 and 26,5 – 12, two strategies are worth mentioning: the ingenious use of grammatical persons and the concentration of images (the latter will be discussed in the next section).

Both passages abound in general as well as specific judgments, expressed in the third person in a marked proverbial style: "Worst of all wounds is that of the heart, worst of all evils is that of a woman" (25,13); "A bad wife is a chafing yoke; he who marries her seizes a scorpion" (26,7). Among the sayings, there are interspersed pieces of advice given directly to the disciple in the second person, and formulated negatively: "Stumble not upon woman's beauty, nor be greedy for her wealth" (25,21); "Allow water no outlet, and do not trust an evil woman" (25,25)[20]; and positively, "Keep a strict watch over an unruly daughter/wife" (26,10); "Follow close if her eyes are bold" (26,11). One of these pieces of advice is the climax of the first composition, in which Ben Sira unhesitatingly recommends divorce to the husband if his wife refuses to submit to his will: "If she walks not according to your wishes [lit. "if she does not walk according to your hand"], cut her away from you (25,26)"[21].

---

16 COLLINS, Jewish Wisdom, 67; MOPSIK, Sagesse, 173 note 2.
17 WEST (ed.), Hesiod, 129.
18 NAUCK, Tragicorum, 695.
19 BRAUDE (trans.), Midrash, vol. 1, 509. See also P.Insinger 8,10 (LICHTHEIM, Wisdom Literature, 204).
20 Other examples are found in 7,26; 9,2; 36(33Hb),20ab; 37,11a.
21 CALDUCH-BENAGES, Cut Her Away, 90 – 92.

In my view, however, the rhetorical power lies in the use of the first-person singular: "With a dragon or a lion I would rather dwell than live with an evil woman" (25,16). With this rhetorical device, which frequently appears in the book[22], the sage not only expresses his opinion (which appears muted at 25,19b) but also imposes himself as an authority on his disciples, for whom the master's words take on special meaning. His teaching is based not only on the legacy of tradition or wisdom but also on personal experience. This is the special way in which he adds credibility to his words. Moreover, in 25,24, this time using the first-person plural, Ben Sira speaks as an authorized teacher and also apparently as spokesman for all husbands. Now, if we accept the interpretation proposed by Jack Levison, instead of seeing in the text a reference to Eve's sin (see Gen 3,6), this is to be understood in direct relation to the context: "From the woman [implying "wicked"] [is] the beginning of sin, and because of it we all [implying husbands] die"[23].

2.1.2 Description of the Bad Wife

In 25,13–26 and 26,5–12, Ben Sira attributes to the "bad" wife other epithets that render a more detailed portrait of our protagonist. She is described as talkative (25,20: אשת לשון, γλωσσώδης), jealous of other women (26,6: ἀντίζηλος ἐπὶ γυναικί), a drunkard (26,8: μέθυσος), sensual/an adulteress (26,9: πορνεία γυναικός), stubborn (26,10: ἐπὶ θυγατρὶ ἀδιατρέπτῳ)[24], and shameless (26,11: ἀναιδοῦς ὀφθαλμοῦ). These qualifiers, with the exception of the first one, are in the sexual sphere or are related to it by the context. For example, jealousy between wives may be motivated by sex; drunkenness is associated with indecent conduct and illicit relationships (26,8b; cf. 9,9; 19,2); and the wife's stubbornness is related to an offense of a sexual nature against the husband (see 26,11a). This is how Alonso Schökel understands 26,10 when he translates: "Keep a close eye on the shameless [rather than stubborn] girl [i.e. wife], so that she does not take the opportunity to fornicate"[25]. Finally, the evil wife is the one who provides for her husband (25,22) and does not make him happy (25,23). In this category we also find the "hated" or "hateful" (שנואה, μισουμένη) wife, that is, the less beloved wife, possibly in a bigamous marriage, or the abhorrent and undesirable

22 See LIESEN, Self-references, 63–74.
23 LEVISON, Eve, 617–623. For a different view, see ELLIS, Eve, 723–742.
24 Although the Greek text speaks about the daughter, according to Semitic custom (see Gen 30,13; Prov 31,29), this designation can also refer to the wife; see MINISSALE, Siracide, 135.
25 ALONSO SCHÖKEL, Eclesiástico, 238: "Vigila bien a la moza impúdica, para que no aproveche la ocasión de fornicar".

wife who ends up being divorced by her husband. In any case, the sage's advice to the husband is blunt: "Do not trust her" (7,26)[26].

As previously indicated, the use of images is characteristic of the text. Ben Sira employs them to make an impact on his young audience and prepare them for when the time comes to choose a wife. There is a notable abundance of images taken from the animal world[27]. Except for the ox, the animals mentioned in connection with the bad wife are all extremely dangerous: serpent, lion, dragon, bear, and scorpion[28]. In two daring hyperboles, Ben Sira compares the snake's venom with the hatred of women (25,15) and confesses that he would prefer to live with lions and dragons rather than with a wicked woman (25,16)[29]. This last text reminds us of the aphorisms, certainly more gentle, in Prov 21,9.19 and Prov 25,24. Although "living in a desert" (Prov 21,19) or "on a corner of a roof" (Prov 21,9; 25,24) is tiring but feasible, the comparison used in Sir 25,16 states that the time spent with an evil woman is absolutely intolerable. The image of the bear, associated with its proverbial ferocity (see 1 Sam 17,34; 2 Sam 17,8), is reflected in the somber face of the evil woman (25,17). Later, in 26,7, the maladjusted (chafing) yoke of oxen seems to evoke 25,8, which refers to incompatibility between the spouses. Here, however, the difficulty lies only in the woman, who is a constant source of irritation for the husband. Wanting to control an evil woman is like trying to catch a scorpion. It is an arduous and risky enterprise, because this little animal is constantly moving and its sting contains a deadly poison (cf. Deut 8,15).

Other metaphors refer to the human body. A woman's wickedness not only appears in her countenance (25,17) but also affects the husband's health: his drooping hands make him incapable of working, and his quaking knees prevent him from moving with agility and security (25,23). Due to a wicked wife, his life is painful, like walking on shaky ground ("Like a sandy hill to aged feet", 25,20), in other words, he has not got a leg to stand[30] and his prospects for the future will always be dependent on circumstances beyond his control.

The sage's instruction in 26,12 concludes with a series of images of immoderate sexual appetite of the wicked wife; these images are reminiscent of Jerusalem's promiscuous behavior in Ezek 16,25. Like the whoring city, the bad wife

---

26 On this verse, see Calduch-Benages, Cut Her Away, 86–88.

27 Cf. the Instruction of Ankhsheshonqy: "When a man smells of myrrh his wife is a monkey before him. When a man is suffering, his wife is a lion before him" (Ankhsh. 15,11–12) (Lichtheim, Wisdom Literature, 80).

28 See also 26,25, only in Syr and GkII: "A shameless woman is regarded as a dog".

29 See Egger-Wenzel, Knechtschaft, 29–30.

30 Morla Asensio, Eclesiástico, 134.

offers herself to any man who comes along: "As a thirsty traveler with eager mouth drinks from any water that he finds, so she settles down before every tent peg and opens her quiver for every arrow" (26,12).

2.1.3 The Husband of the Bad Wife

The evil woman's husband is always present. Indeed, his presence in the text is constant, and even overwhelming in the text. He is everywhere, either explicitly ("her husband", 3x; "peaceful husband", 1x) or implicitly. Let us recall that the instructions are given by a husband (I, we) and directed to other men, who are already married or are preparing to choose a wife (you).

Ben Sira emphasizes the physical and psychological consequences that living with a wicked wife has for her husband: his strength fails and sadness fills his heart when he is with his friends (25,18.23Hb and Gk). By her irritating behavior and sharp tongue (25,20; 26,6–7), the wife takes away his happiness. Hence, the sage recommends avoiding infatuation with an evil woman, especially if she is beautiful or rich (25,21)[31], since in this case the husband sees his honor sullied when he is forced to rely on her support and endure her abuse (25,22)[32]. Such a situation was inconceivable for the mentality of the time, so that the sage sees it as "hard bondage"[33] and "great shame". The husband's honor will also be seriously threatened if his wife falls into the vice of drunkenness (26,8) or, even worse, maintains illicit relations with other men to satisfy her sexual desire (26,9–12).

Clearly, then, the husband should keep the evil woman in check. Just remember what happened to Solomon and the shame that came over him for having succumbed to women, losing his authority over them and, worst of all, being controlled by them (47,19). In other words, the sage describes "a man 'unmanned' by women"[34]. To prevent this shameful history from repeating itself, Ben Sira gives husbands the following recommendations: Do not trust an evil woman (25,25; 7,26; 9,2), do not give her power (36[33Hb],20ab), mistrust her (42,6), or, in extreme situations, give her a certificate of divorce (25,26). For Judith E. McKinlay, divorce is the only alternative for the husband who wants "to

---

31 SMEND, Weisheit, 231: "Die reiche Frau ist Lockspeise und Falle zugleich".

32 See CAMP, Understanding Patriarchy, 29.

33 Possibly an allusion to the oppression suffered by the Israelites in Egypt (Exod 1,14; 6,9; Deut 26,6).

34 BALLA, Family, 150.

remain in control, and presumably to be seen to be in control for the sake of his honor and reputation"[35].

2.2 Good Wives

In the passages about good wives, the Hebrew expression אשה טובה, "good wife", appears twice (26,1.3), corresponding to the Greek γυνὴ ἀγαθή (26,1.3.16[36]; 7,19[37]). The goodness of such a wife, as noted by Burkard Zapff in his commentary, is not so much a moral quality but rather "the idea that the woman will turn out to support the life of her husband"[38]. Ben Sira is certainly not the first to point out how beneficial the good wife is to her husband (see Prov 31,11–12.23). The same idea is found in the demotic Instruction of Ankhsheshonqy: "A good woman of noble character is food that comes in time of hunger" (Ankhsh. 24,21)[39]; in Hesiod's *Works and Days:* "For a man carries off nothing better than a good wife" (Op. 702)[40]; and in the Elegies of Theognis of Megara collected by Stobaeus in his Anthology or Florilegium: "Nothing, Cyrnus, is more delightful than a good wife" (Flor. 4,22,5)[41].

2.2.1 Communicative Strategies

The communicative strategies that stand out in the texts about the good wives are the presence of a macarism, or beatitude, in 26,1–4; the exclusive use of the third person; and the novelty of some images in 26,13–18 and 36Hb,21–26 (33Gk,26–31) (See the following section).

It is surprising that, in a poem dedicated to the good wife, the first verse contains a statement referring to the happiness of her husband[42]. Instead of "Happy is the husband of a good woman" (the usual translation of 26,1Gk; cf. 25,8c), one would expect something like: "Blessed is the good woman because ..." Thus, the

---

35 McKinlay, Gendering Wisdom, 171.
36 MS C: א[שה] יפה, "a beautiful wife".
37 Gk: γυναικὸς σοφῆς καὶ ἀγαθῆς; MS A: אשה משכלת, "a prudent wife" (also in 25,8; 40,23).
38 Zapff, Jesus Sirach, 150: "Die Vorstellung, dass sich die Frau als lebensförderlich für ihren Ehemann erweist".
39 Lichtheim, Wisdom Literature, 89.
40 West (ed.), Hesiod, 129.
41 West (ed.), Archilochus, 233, line 1225.
42 For Claudia V. Camp, on the other hand, "the point is not that he feels internally happy but that he has attained an honor worthy of social notice" (Camp, Understanding Patriarchy, 24).

accent would fall on the alleged protagonist and not on her husband. We need to note that the Hebrew text of MS C (also Syr) adopts an emphatic position: "Good wife, happy husband". Be that as it may, the important thing is that this initial macarism sets the tone of 26,1–4, which after being interrupted by comments on the bad wife in 26,5–12, is taken up again at 26,13–18.

We have seen that the texts on bad wives are characterized by the alternate use of grammatical persons, in particular, the presence of the "I" (we) of the sage. This is not so in the passages about good wives, since most are formulated in an impersonal style based on statements in the third person with a rhetorical question, for example, in 36Hb,26 (33Gk,31). The only exceptions are the recommendations given directly to the husband/disciple in 7,19: "Do not dismiss a sensible wife" (Hb); "do not separate yourself from a wise and good woman" (Gk); and 9,1: "Do not be jealous of the wife of your bosom" (Hb and Gk). In other words, the personal tone and highly incisive insistence with respect to the bad wife has disappeared and left room for a reflection of a proverbial character, which is more objective and therefore less striking for the audience. Here, too, we would have liked to hear the sage's voice directly. However, for whatever reason, he chose to express himself indirectly and impassively.

2.2.2 The Description of the Good Wife

In 26,1–4.13–18 and 36Hb,21–26 (33Gk,26–31), other adjectives are attributed to the good wife: "strong, brave" (26,2: אשה חיל, γυνὴ ἀνδρεία)[43], "charming/graceful" (26,13: אשה [חן], χάρις γυναικός), "prudent" (26,13b: שכלה, ἡ ἐπιστήμη αὐτῆς), "silent" (26,14: γυνὴ σιγηρά), "beautiful" (26,15: אשה יפה; cf. "beauty of a woman", תואר אשה, in 36Hb,22 (33Gk,27), "beautiful face", κάλλος προσώπου, in 26,17, and "beautiful feet/legs", πόδες ὡραῖοι, in 26,18), "modest" (26,15: γυνὴ αἰσχυντηρά), "chaste soul" or "capable of self-control" (ἐγκρατοῦς ψυχῆς), "of soothing speech" (36Hb,23 [33Gk,28]: מרפא לשון, ἐπὶ γλώσσης αὐτῆς ἔλεος καὶ πραΰτης). If we take into consideration the rest of the book, the good wife is also described as "sensible" (25,8: γυναικὶ συνετῇ; 40,23: אשה משכלת), "wise" (7,19: γυναικὶ σοφῆς), "devoted" (40,19: אשה נחשקת), and "irreproachable/without fault or defect" (40,19: γυνὴ ἄμωμος).

This brief review of the vocabulary renders it obvious that beauty is the quality most appreciated in the good wife. In 36Hb,21–26 (33Gk,26–31), for example, beauty not only is the first of the qualities listed but also is described with a superlative ("it surpasses everything desirable"). If, in these texts, Ben Sira exclu-

---

43 Also in 28,15 (in plural).

sively presents the positive side of female beauty (see also 7,19), on other occasions he also warns of its dangers (9,8; 25,21; 42,12). Of course, in both cases this is always seen from the perspective of the man/husband. Along with beauty, the virtue of silence, traditionally praised by the sages, deserves special attention. Surprisingly, this is the only quality that is accompanied by explicit mention of the Lord: "A silent woman is a gift from the Lord" (26,14; cf. 26,3). For Syriac Menander, the control of the tongue is a decisive criterion for the choice of wife: "And if you want to take a wife, make first inquiries about her tongue, and take her [only] then. For a talkative woman is a hell and ... a bad man a deadly plague" (Syr. Men. 118 – 122)[44]; and a monostich of Menander, the foremost representative of the New Comedy, says: "Silence is any woman's ornament" (Mon. 83)[45].

In addition to specific words, images give much information about the good wife. Inspired by Prov 19,14 ("House and estate are an inheritance from parents, but a sensible woman is granted by the Lord"), Ben Sira equates the good wife with a "generous gift" (good lot or portion) that the Lord bestows on the man who fears him, that is, a good and pious husband (26,3). A very different aspect is the image of the "sealed mouth" found in 26,15. In fact, this is an ambivalent image that can refer either to the control of the tongue or to the chastity of the wife, who should not exercise her sexuality outside of marriage[46]. The latter meaning can be glimpsed in the Greek version that replaces this image with the expression "self-controlled person or character", which refers to the "modest woman" of the first colon. The good and beautiful wife is so attractive that, in 26,15a, she is compared to the glorious spectacle of the sun when it rises to the heights[47].

However, the most innovative images are, without doubt, those that appear in 26,17 – 18. As C. Mopsik puts it: "The comparison of the beauty and grace of the wife *of one who fears God* with the sacred objects of the Jerusalem temple is quite exceptional in ancient Hebrew literature"[48]. Let us consider the text in the Greek version.

---

44 BAARDA, Sentences, 595.

45 LICHTHEIM, Wisdom Literature, 50.

46 According to Di Lella, "(restricted, shut up of) mouth" is a euphemism for "closed vagina" (SKEHAN–DI LELLA, Wisdom, 350). This opinion is shared by Mopsik (Sagesse, 175).

47 In the second colon, the Hebrew text and the Greek notably differ. See on this matter BALLA, Family, 66 – 67.

48 MOPSIK, Sagesse, 176: "La comparaison de la beauté et de la grâce de l'épouse *de celui qui craint Dieu* avec les objets sacrés du temple de Jérusalem est tout à fait exceptionnelle dans la littérature hébraïque de l'Antiquité" (italics ours).

λύχνός ἐκλάμπων ἐπὶ λυχνίας ἁγίας	v. 17a	A lamp shining upon a holy candlestick
καὶ κάλλος προσώπου ἐπὶ ἡλικίᾳ στασίμῃ·	v. 17b	face upon[49] a slender body.
στῦλοι χρύσεοι ἐπὶ βάσεως ἀργυρᾶς	v. 18a	Golden columns on silver pedestals
καὶ πόδες ὡραῖοι ἐπὶ πτέρνοις εὐστάθμοις.	v. 18b	are [her] pretty legs on firm heels[50].

In the previous verse, the sage has compared the good wife to the noblest and most luminous star of nature (26,16; cf. 43,1–5), and now he compares her to the noblest and brightest elements of the cult. Thus, from the cosmic order we pass to the religious and cultic order. The wife's beautiful face, sustained by a well-formed body, shines like a lamp on the holy lampstand, and her pretty legs are supported by firm heels that evoke the majestic columns of gold and silver plinths of the temple. These comparisons raise many questions; for example: Is there, then, "something sacred" about the figure of the good wife described in 26,17–18?[51] Is she able to give dignity to "the liturgy of the home"?[52] Why so much emphasis on physical beauty? Or where are the wife's human, moral, and religious values (cf. Prov 31,10–31)? Are these verses a real compliment to the woman, or do they transmit another, less flattering message?[53]

In my view, the close relationship established between women and liturgical sacred space refers to the discourse of Lady Wisdom, more precisely in 24,10–11. 15, where by means of a series of very suggestive expressions and images the sage describes the liturgical function of the protagonist[54]. In 24,10 she declares her active participation in the worship service: "I officiated in the holy tent before Him, and so I settled in Zion". However, as Judith E. McKinlay rightly indicates in reference to 26,17–18, "this is a static picture; in these verses the wife is very much an object that is being evaluated, in contrast to the picture of Wisdom and Simon actively taking part in liturgical services"[55]. In fact, what Ben Sira exalts is the beauty of the bride, her face, her body, and therefore her sex appeal. Reading between the lines, we can see something that the sage does not say openly: the more beautiful the wife is, the more her husband wants her (see 36Hb,22 in MS B: "The beauty of a woman lights up the face and surpasses any human desire [lit. "eye"]".

Finally, in 36Hb,24–25 (33Gk,29–30), the sage describes the good wife with two images of married life, referencing the urban world and the rural world: as a

---

49 MS C reads: "the splendor of a face".
50 All of v. 18 is missing in MS C.
51 Alonso Schökel, Eclesiástico, 238.
52 Morla Asensio, Eclesiástico, 136: "la liturgia del hogar".
53 Skehan—Di Lella, Wisdom, 351.
54 See Calduch-Benages, Aromas, 15–30.
55 McKinlay, Gendering Wisdom, 172.

column (vertical dimension) and a fence (horizontal dimension), respectively. If, on the one hand, the image of the column suggests the idea of support (foundation, rest), on the other hand, the fence suggests the notion of protection (safety, surveillance)[56]. It is difficult to say what specifically constitutes this support or protection, as the author does not offer any details. In any case, since the main objective of 36Hb,21–26 (33Gk,26–31) is to provide criteria for choosing a wife, we can understand that those pictures are simply intended to highlight the crucial importance of the woman in a man's life. The rabbis taught: "He who has no wife dwells without good, without help, without joy, without blessing, and without atonement" (Midr. Gen. 2,18)[57].

2.2.3 Her Relationship with Her Husband

An attentive reader soon realizes that the good wife is praised not for her intrinsic value as a person but in relation to what she is, does, and means for her husband. As in the texts about the bad wife, here the husband's presence is strongly felt, either explicitly ("[her] husband" four times; "man" twice) or implicitly by means of masculine pronouns and adjectives.

In fact, the central theme of the texts studied here is not so much the good wife but rather the benefits her husband receives from her. Not all men are worthy of her; therefore, the Lord gives her to the husband who fears him (26,3.14). She is a priceless gift, more precious than coral and gold (7,19; 26,14–15; cf. Prov 31,10). She is a blessing that brings a long, peaceful, and joyful life (26,1–2). The wife's goodness is a value that transcends the economic status of the husband, whether he is rich or poor, with positive effects for his body and soul: she causes joy to fill his heart, which in turn lights up his face (26,2.4; 36Hb,22 [33Gk,27]). In a different order, the good wife delights her husband with her physical charms (or kindness) and makes him prosper economically with her prudence or skill (26,13; cf. 40,19cd). It is impossible not to recall the poem of the strong woman in Prov 31, especially verses 11–12: "The heart of her husband trusts in her, and he will have no lack of gain. She does him good, and not harm, all the days of her life".

Dazzled by her beauty, her modesty, her sweet and friendly talk[58] or silence, the husband becomes an exceptional being, unlike other mortals, a kind of angel

---

56 MORLA ASENSIO, Eclesiástico, 180.
57 FREEDMANN–SIMON (eds.), Midrash Rabbah, vol. 1, 132.
58 According to Alonso Schökel, the good wife is a woman who "caresses as she speaks" (ALONSO SCHÖKEL, Eclesiástico, 274).

on earth (36Hb,23 [33Gk,28]). Thus, Ben Sira formulates the sentence: "He who acquires a wife [presumably a good one] gets his best possession, a helper fit for him and a pillar of support" (36Hb,24 [33Gk,29]). A man needs to build a home, a family, have offspring; but above all, he needs social recognition, because as Gilbert rightly noted, the wife is the "principle of social integration"[59]. The husband of the strong woman of Proverbs certainly received social recognition through her. The text says about him, "he is respected in the town square when he sits among the elders of the city" (Prov 31,23). The sage describes the other side of the coin in Sir 36Hb,25–26Hb (33Gk,30–31), three verses that could be summarized as follows: Who will trust a vagabond, without a wife, without a family, and without a home? As the proverb says, a word to the wise is sufficient, and the young disciple, presumably, has gotten the message.

3 Conclusion

A brief comparison between the passages on the bad wife and the good wife leads to the following results. In my opinion, Ben Sira seems to be more interested in the bad wife than in the good one. Indeed, he gives her not only a special place in his instruction (the first of the series, see 25,13–26) but also far more attention (see the number of verses dedicated to each). Moreover, the sage speaks about her in a very personal, vivid, and incisive style. The same is true for the advice and recommendations he gives to the disciples about her, which contrasts sharply with the impersonal and dispassionate tone used to describe the good wife. Is the sage speaking from experience? Does his wife belong to the category of "bad wives"? Of course, we do not know, but the texts may seem to indicate this.

On the other hand, the sage presents both good and bad wives in the same way, that is, in terms of physical appearance, control of language, and behavior in the sexual sphere (more pronounced in the case of the bad wife), as these three aspects affect, positively or negatively, the personal and social life of her husband. Hence, the reference point of all the texts is not, as we might expect, the figure of the wife, whether good or bad, but her husband in his role as paterfamilias for all intents and purposes. The classification proposed by Ben Sira works then as follows: the wife is good when she is good for her husband, and she is bad when she is bad for her husband. This same androcentric perspective is perceptible in the introduction to the commentary of Hilaire Duesberg and

---

59 GILBERT, Femme, 438.

Irénée Fransen: "It would be good to know whether Ben Sira was happy in his family or not". And immediately they add: "He told us about both cases with almost the same vivacity. From his eloquence, it is not possible to make any conclusion in one sense or in the other"[60]—which incidentally is not entirely accurate. The two cases to which the authors refer are, of course, the happily married husband and the unhappy one.

Ben Sira stresses the patriarchal control of women, especially of the wife. Described with attributes that most cultures relate to women (beauty, modesty, silence, and sweetness), the good wife is called to obey meekly the authority of the husband, to please him in everything, and above all not to compromise his honor by her words, gestures, or behavior. In other words, she is regarded as an effective aide who, however, must be kept under control. The one who is in control has the power.

How can the sage's ideas and teaching about wives be judged? How is their apparently harmless classification as "good and bad wives" to be assessed? In my opinion, the answer should not be sought solely in the sage's exacerbated misogyny, possibly associated with his own unhappy marriage, or in the mentality and customs of a society and a culture in which women had almost no rights and were completely subordinated to men, or in the influence that ancient wisdom exercised in his work[61]. Could it be that Ben Sira was interested in maintaining this position and therefore instilled this attitude in his young disciples? In the end, they would be responsible for transmitting it to new generations, that is, perpetuating it among their people. Ben Sira was not the only Jewish sage in 2nd-century-BC Jerusalem. In fact, he represents a collective, a group or school of wisdom that was confronted with others who advocated different and even contradictory ideas, such as the Enochic circles. He was also confronted with the progress of Hellenism and proposed an alternative[62]. As I mentioned in the introduction, Ben Sira did not adopt a polemical approach against Hellenistic culture and philosophy but a conciliatory one. From the beginning to the end of his book, he maintains an impressive balance through the use of pondered expressions, opportune omissions, implicit allusions, and fine sense of irony. His main aim is to transmit the true wisdom (fear-of-the-Lord, love for the law, and the tradition) to the new generations in such a way that the young disciples recognize themselves in the shared past and make it part of their identity. With respect to women (wives), the sage does not make any concession. A change,

---

60 Duesberg—Fransen, Ecclesiastico, 50.
61 See Schroer, Wisdom, 85–86.
62 Calduch-Benages, Absence, 312–313.

however small, in favor of women would have shaken the patriarchal system that protected him, and that would have been too dangerous. One who loses control loses power.

Garment Imagery in the Book of Ben Sira

Although little studied by authors, clothing is an important theme in the Bible[1]. In fact, almost all the books speak of it whether in a literal or in a figurative sense, the only exception, as far as the Old Testament is concerned, being the little book of the prophet Habakkuk. Generally speaking, clothing serves, naturally, as a protection from inclement weather and to safeguard the dignity and the privacy of the person, but it can also be used as a means of seduction or as a declaration of power and of social standing. Not only that, but in many texts it acquires a symbolic significance (anthropological and even theological) which opens up new dimensions of reflection and research.

In the book of Ben Sira, the vocabulary relating to clothing (we include here also some ornaments) is concentrated in Sir 6,18–37 and 45,6–25. The first is a poem on the search for Wisdom to which we shall be devoting special attention in this study. The second is the remembrance of Aaron, which is striking both for its length and for the pleasure with which it describes the complex and imposing vesture of the high priest: ephod, turban or mitre, breastplate, breeches, tunic, crown or diadem, and mantle[2]. The materials (gold, twisted byssus and very fine linen) and the colours of the fabrics (violet, purple and scarlet), employed by the embroiderers in the making of the clothes confer on the one who wears them a regal air that is truly fascinating. By displaying great aesthetic sensibility, Ben Sira succeeds in creating an atmosphere of light, colour and pleasant sounds which envelop the majestic figure of Aaron. The high priest thus appears splendidly clothed and crowned in such a way as to become a true delight for the eyes. In other words, the sage of Jerusalem makes use of liturgical vestments to transmit to his disciples love and respect for the priesthood (cf. also the portrait of the high priest, Simon in Sir 50,1–21, esp. v. 11).

However, our contribution is not intended to be concerned with liturgical vestments[3] or with the terms relating to clothing made use of in the book. Instead, we intend to make a detailed study only of the metaphorical use of this kind of vocabulary which puts us in a more direct relationship with the sapiential genre in general. To this end, we have marked out some categories which will help us in our analysis.

---

1 The two most complete studies in this connection are HAULOTTE, Symbolique; CRASS, Symbolique. Cf., also, some sections in DA SILVA, Rêves.
2 Cf. CALDUCH-BENAGES, Ornamenti, 1319–1330.
3 For liturgical imagery in Sirach, cf. CORLEY, Similes, 104–106.

https://doi.org/10.1515/9783110492316-013

1 Garments as Symbols of Theological and Spiritual Realities

Under this subtitle, we are grouping those texts where some elements relating to clothing are attributed to realities of a theological and spiritual character such as Wisdom (crown, garment and cord/thread of violet purple), the fear-of-the-Lord (crown), and justice/righteousness (robe). We present them in their order of appearance in the book.

1.1 Sir 1,11 and Sir 1,18

Here, we are in the introduction or portico to the entire book (1,1–2,18). From a didactic point of view, the first two chapters can be considered as a programmatic exposition of the sage's teaching: the divine origin of Wisdom (1,1–10), its close relation to the fear-of-the-Lord (1,11–21) and the conditions for attaining it (1,22–30). The most important of these is undoubtedly the fear-of-the-Lord (2,1–18).

Sir 1,11 and Sir 1,18, therefore, are situated within an "elegantly crafted poem" (1,11–30) in which Ben Sira expounds his basic thesis[4]. According to the structure proposed by Alexander A. Di Lella, our two verses form part of the first (1,11–13) and the fourth strophe (1,18–19) respectively[5]. Since the Hebrew text is not available here, we follow the Greek version according to Ziegler's edition[6], accompanied by some notes on the text and my translation.

11   Φόβος κυρίου δόξα καὶ καύχημα
       καὶ εὐφροσύνη[7] καὶ στέφανος ἀγαλλιάματος.
12   Φόβος κυρίου τέρψει καρδίαν
       καὶ δώσει εὐφροσύνην καὶ χαρὰν καὶ μακροημέρευσιν[8].
13   τῷ φοβουμένῳ τὸν κύριον εὖ ἔσται ἐπ᾽ ἐσχάτων,
       καὶ ἐν ἡμέρᾳ τελευτῆς αὐτοῦ εὐλογηθήσεται.

---

4 Di Lella, Fear, 114.
5 Di Lella, Fear, 115–116.
6 Ziegler, Sapientia. For the Syriac version, cf. Calduch-Benages—Ferrer—Liesen, Wisdom of the Scribe.
7 Instead of "joy", Syr reads: "greatness", cf. Sauer, Jesus Sirach, 46; Schreiner, Jesus Sirach, 19.
8 GkII (O [sub ※ Syh] 493–672–743 679) adds: φόβος κυρίου δόσις παρὰ κυρίου, καὶ γὰρ ἐπ᾽ ἀγαπήσεως τρίβους καθίστησιν ("the fear-of-the-Lord is the gift of the Lord, and it leads one in the paths of love"). Instead of "length of days", Syr reads "eternal life" (= 1,20). Note that in the gloss of 12 verses inserted between 1,20 and 1,27, the expressions "eternal crown", "eternal victory" (*3ab) and "eternal reward" (*8b) are also employed.

11 The fear of the Lord is glory and honour,
    and joy and a crown of gladness.
12 The fear of the Lord gladdens the heart,
    and gives joy, gladness and length of days.
13 For the one who fears the Lord it will go well at the end,
    and in the day of his death he will be blessed.

Marked by a decidedly positive tone, the first strophe is completely devoted to the fear-of-the-Lord. Insistence on this theme is expressed by the threefold mention of the fear-of-the-Lord at the beginning of the three verses (11a.12a.13a) and by the grammatical function of the expressions φόβος κυρίου (the subject in vv. 11 and 12) and τῷ φοβουμένῳ τὸν κύριον (indirect object in v. 13). In a crescendo, which passes gradually from the abstract concept (the fear-of-the-Lord) to the concrete one (the one who fears the Lord), the author succeeds in offering a lively exhortation to fear the Lord[9], although without employing the characteristic verbal form of paraenetic passages, that is, the imperative. The positive effects of the fear-of-the-Lord cover the entire gamut of human existence. They make themselves felt in the time which a person passes in this life (honour, joy, long life) and also in the moment of his or her passing (serene death).

Constructed according to the norms of parallelism, synonymous in this case, the first verse establishes a neat correspondence between the nominal predicates of the fear-of-the-Lord: δόξα καὶ καύχημα (11a), on the one hand, and εὐφροσύνη καὶ στέφανος ἀγαλλιάματος (11b), on the other. As far as the two last blessings are concerned, a detail should be noted. Instead of εὐφροσύνη καὶ ἀγαλλίαμα, a combination fairly frequent in LXX-Isaiah[10], the author has made use of εὐφροσύνη καὶ στέφανος ἀγαλλιάματος, a wholly original expression which does not occur in any other book of the LXX. He will use it again in Sir 15,6, with reference, not to the fear-of-the-Lord this time, but to the disciple who seeks wisdom: "He will inherit joy and a crown of gladness and an everlasting name"[11].

But how is the expression "crown" to be understood in our passage? In his commentary, Peters has recourse to the Latin version (corona exultationis) in order to indicate two possible interpretations. It could be alluding to the triumphal crown which we find in Sir 6,31 and Wis 4,2, or to the festive crown, woven

---

9 For Alonso Schökel, Sir 1,11–13 are "a summary of goods" (ALONSO SCHÖKEL, Eclesiástico, 146: "una síntesis de bienes"). Di Lella considers these verses "a pragmatic motivation to fear the Lord" (DI LELLA, Fear, 121) and Marböck is situated along the same lines when he speaks of "Impuls zu ihrer Einübung" (MARBÖCK, Jesus Sirach, 57).
10 Isa 16,10; 22,13; 35,10; 51,3.11; 60,15 (with a variant); 65,18.
11 MSS A and B do not mention the crown but only the term שמחה ("rejoicing").

with flowers, to which Samaria is compared in Isa 28,1.4 (cf., also, Wis 2,7)[12]. In our opinion, two elements are fundamental in establishing the significance of "crown of gladness", i.e. the context and the position which it occupies in the verse. In Sir 1,11, the author offers a "pedagogic" description of the fear-of-the-Lord, that is, instead of focusing on its content, he indicates in an implicit way the benefits/blessings involved in the practice of it. In other words, we are in a religious-pedagogic context very far from the scenario depicted in chapter 28 of Isaiah (an oracle of judgement against the drunken guides of Samaria and Jerusalem) or from the *carpe diem* of Wis 2,6 – 9. According to the text, the first blessing of the fear-of-the-Lord is dignity (glory and honour) followed by joy (rejoicing, jubilation or gladness), something developed further in the following verse. Placed at the end of the second colon, the "crown of gladness" seems —the play on words is important—"to crown" the description of the fear-of-the-Lord. The person who allows himself or herself to be transformed by this religious attitude acquires the greatest joy, namely the fullness of life. This idea of fullness or completeness is also highlighted by Marböck, according to whom "the picture of the festive wreath depicts the fulfilment of mankind"[13].

18 στέφανος σοφίας[14] φόβος κυρίου
ἀναθάλλων εἰρήνην καὶ ὑγίειαν ἰάσεως[15].
19 ἐπιστήμην καὶ γνῶσιν συνέσεως ἐξώμβρησεν
καὶ δόξαν κρατούντων αὐτῆς ἀνύψωσεν[16].

18 The fear of the Lord is a crown[17] of wisdom,
its fruits are (lit. causing to flower) peace and good health[18].

---

12 PETERS, Buch, 13.
13 MARBÖCK, Jesus Sirach, 57: "Das Bild vom Jubelkranz stellt die Vollendung des Menschens dar".
14 Syr reads "beginning of wisdom" (= 1,14.16).
15 GkII (O [sub ⁎ Syh]) adds: ἀμφότερα δέ ἐστιν δῶρα θεοῦ εἰς εἰρήνην, πλατύνει δὲ καύχησις τοῖς ἀγαπῶσιν αὐτόν ("both, indeed, are gifts of God for peace, boasting increases for those who love him").
16 With O 248–694 785 and some Latin MSS, we are omitting 19a: καὶ εἶδεν καὶ ἐξηρίθμησεν αὐτήν (= 1,9b). According to Smend, 19a is an erroneous repetition of v. 9 (SMEND, Weisheit, 12). Syr reads the whole verse differently: "She is a staff of strength and a mansion which sustains glory, and eternal honour for everyone who follows her".
17 Sauer cites Kuhn's proposal to read "young plant" (נצר) instead of "crown" (נזר). He supposes a confusion between two Hebrew terms (SAUER, Jesus Sirach, 47).
18 On its own, the colon turns out to be ambiguous: both wisdom and the fear-of-the-Lord (cf. Syr) can be the subject of the verb. Origen's recension resolves the ambiguity by changing the phrase: ἀναθάλλει δὲ ἐν αὐτοῖς κύριος εἰρήνην μεστήν ("the Lord causes perfect peace to flower in them").

19   It pours down (lit. makes to rain) knowledge and intelligent awareness
      and exalts the glory of those who possess it.

By contrast with vv. 11–13, the presence of wisdom is a constant in vv. 14–20. Just like a *ritornello*, every two verses, exactly at the beginning of the first colon, the fear-of-the-Lord is described in close connection with wisdom, even as intimately united to her: the fear-of-the-Lord is the "beginning", ἀρχή (14a), "fullness", πλησμονή (16a), "crown", στέφανος (18a) and "root", ῥίζα (20a) of wisdom. All these expressions indicate the importance of the fear-of-the-Lord in the process which leads to the acquisition of wisdom.

The expression στέφανος σοφίας, which does not occur elsewhere in the LXX, confers on the verse a strongly expressive charge[19] because it includes within itself various semantic connotations. Since the crown is the most important item of the regalia of the prince (Lat *princeps*, the first), our expression reveals the idea of the "beginning" (Lat *principium*, Gk ἀρχή). This is not a temporal beginning, however (cf. Prov 1,7; 9,10; Ps 111,10), but a beginning or preeminence of dignity. The crown can also be understood as a metaphor for the foliage of a tree, that is, its most leafy part, with the densest branches and leaves and, therefore, in this case, the crown of wisdom would be expressing the idea of fullness or completeness (πλησμονή) or even, according to Alonso Schökel, would suggest vitality and dynamism[20]. In fact, the vegetable metaphor continues in verses 18b and 19a with the verbs ἀναθάλλω, "flower, cause to flower", and ἐξομβρέω, "cause to rain", respectively and, finally, in v. 20 with the expression "root of wisdom", ῥίζα σοφίας and the reference to "its branches", οἱ κλάδοι αὐτῆς (cf. Sir 24,10 – 17)[21].

1.2 Sir 6,29–31

The third poem on Wisdom in the book of Ben Sira (Sir 6,18–37) describes the disciple's desire and passionate search for Wisdom. The poem abounds in images, especially in the first two strophes. While, in the first (6,18–22), images taken from the world of agriculture predominate, in the second (6,23–31), they move between three different areas (slavery, hunting and the amorous relationship) and their boundaries are not easy to establish. In our opinion, the

---

19 SMEND, Weisheit, 12: "stark rhetorisch".
20 ALONSO SCHÖKEL, Eclesiástico, 147. For Di Lella, on the other hand "Presumably, wisdom's crown is made of leaves (see 1 Cor 9,25)" (DI LELLA, Fear, 124).
21 For the vegetable metaphor, cf. FOURNIER-BIDOZ, Arbre, 1–10.

author has intended a deliberate overlapping of metaphors. So much so that in vv. 29–31 they constitute precisely the climax of the strophe: the heavy effort of the search presented to the disciple becomes, in the end, the source of innumerable benefits. The Hebrew text of Sir 6,29–31 is found only in MS A, a text which we shall record in the following, and in a very fragmentary way in 2Q18[22]:

והיתה לך רשתה	v. 29a	Her nets[23] will be a strong bulwark for you[24]
מכון עז וחבלתה בגדי כתם:	v. 29b	and her cords garments of gold.
עלי זהב עולה ומוסרתיה	v. 30a	An ornament of gold[25] will be her yoke
פתיל תכלת:	v. 30b	and her bonds will be a cord of violet[26].
בגדי כבוד תלבשנה	v. 31a	(As) a garment of glory, you [sg.] will put her on
ועטרת תפארת תעטרנה:	v. 31b	and (as) a crown of splendour[27] you will put her on.

Sir 6,29–31 takes up the same images as vv. 24–25, where Wisdom is presented as a hunting net and a heavy yoke to which the disciple has to submit himself as well as accepting her cords. However, in our text, these images are not being used to shed light on the "dark side" of Wisdom's apprentice but to show how this laborious search reaches a happy conclusion. We are present, therefore, before an original and suggestive transformation of the images: nets, cords, a yoke and bonds become, respectively, a bulwark, golden garments, an ornament of gold and a purple cord. And, finally, by way of conclusion, Wisdom herself becomes the clothing for the disciple in the form of a "garment of glory" and a "crown of splendour".

The images related to clothing concentrated in these verses refer to two environments very typical of the period of Ben Sira, namely that of the royal court and that of the cult. If we accept the reading of Smend, Skehan and Mopsik, who interpret the strong bulwark (מכון עז) of 29a as a royal throne, with more reason, then, the garments of gold (בגדי כתם)[28], that is, woven out of gold thread (cf.

---

22 Only the two last words of 29b (בגדי כתם), the two last letters of the final word of 30b (לת) and the following fragment of 31b (ת תפארת תעטרנה) can be read.

23 Instead of "(hunting) net", Gk reads: "fetters", αἱ πέδαι (cf. v. 24).

24 In the light of Ps 89,15, Smend translates: "herrlicher Standort" (SMEND, Weisheit, 60), Skehan: "a throne of majesty" (SKEHAN–DI LELLA, Wisdom, 191) and Mopsik: "un trône majestueux" (MOPSIK, Sagesse, 99).

25 Following Gk (κόσμος), we read עֲדִי (cf. 43,9 in MS B). Cf. MINISSALE, Versione greca, 51; SAUER, Jesus Sirach, 84; SCHREINER, Jesus Sirach, 46; MARBÖCK, Jesus Sirach, 117. Instead of "ornament of gold", Lévi and Mopsik translate: "feuilles d'or" (LÉVI, Ecclésiastique, vol. 2, 37; MOPSIK, Sagesse, 100).

26 This verse is lacking in Syr.

27 Gk reads: στέφανον ἀγαλλιάματος ("crown of gladness"), cf. 1,11; 15,6.

28 Gk reads: στολὴν δόξης, "robe of glory".

Ps 45,10), together with the ornament of gold (עדי זהב) (cf. Gen 41,42) of 29b and 30a²⁹, allow us to glimpse the figure of the sage as a powerful king, with all the authority, greatness, and nobility which belong to him (cf. Prov 4,9 and Ps 89,15). Mopsik's commentary is interesting in this respect: "But the sage was also invested with great authority in ancient society, and he was able to assume the functions of a scribe, a political adviser, a notary, a magistrate, a controller of public finance, and, above all, of course, the functions of a well-known and respected teacher"³⁰.

The cord or thread of violet purple (פתיל תכלת) refers to Num 15,38 (cf. also Exod 28,28.37; 39,21.31). The first text is a ritual prescription concerning the vesture of all the Israelites. In the fringe of each corner of the mantle, there must be inserted a "cord of violet purple" (coloured with a substance extracted from a particular mollusc) which serves as a reminder to perform all the precepts of the Law. The other texts from the book of Exodus, however, are concerned exclusively with the clothes of the high priest. In this case, the cord serves to bind the breastplate with its rings to the rings of the *ephod*, so that the breastplate does not separate from the *ephod*, or to attach the gold plate on which were inscribed the words "Holy to Yhwh" to the front of the turban³¹.

In addition to these ritual evocations, often underlined by authors and especially the last one³², in our text, the violet purple cord seems to acquire a dimension of a spiritual character connected with the school of Wisdom. The bonds (ומוסרתיה) which at first prevented the disciple from progressing in his search, now permit him to go deeper in obedience to the precepts of the Law and in the religious practices associated with them. In other words, the violet purple cord symbolises the interiorisation and assimilation of the religious teachings received from Wisdom. As Mopsik rightly notes, it is possible that Ben Sira is playing on the double sense of the word מוסר, which can be vocalised as מוֹסֵר "bond", "fetter", "chain" (from the verb אסר, "to bind with ropes or chains")

---

29 Cf. Sir 21,21: "(As) an ornament of gold is discipline for the sage and (as) a bracelet on the right wrist".
30 MOPSIK, Sagesse, 99: "Mais le sage était investi aussi d'une grande autorité dans la société antique, et il pouvait assumer des fonctions de scribe, de conseiller politique, de notaire, de magistrat, de contrôleur des finances publiques, et surtout bien sûr d'enseignant réputé et estimé". Cf. SKEHAN–DI LELLA, Wisdom, 194.
31 Note that purple was the colour used for the clothes of the king, the princes and the nobles (Esth 8,5; Dan 5,7.16.29; 1 Macc 10,20.62) and was, therefore, a symbol of power and royalty.
32 For example, STADELMANN, Schriftgelehrter, 50–51; SCHRADER, Leiden, 174.

or as מוּסָר, "instruction", "lesson", "reproof" (from the verb יסר, "educate", "instruct", "punish", "correct")[33].

Finally, in v. 31, the rhetorical weight of the images becomes more intense thanks to the presence of the verbs "clothe" (לבש) and "put on" (עטר) formulated in the 2nd person singular. Having become a garment and a crown, that is, complete clothing from head to foot, Wisdom will be put on by the disciple after he has overcome all his tests (nets, yoke, cords and bonds). But what does the sage intend to say with the expressions "garment of glory" (בגדי כבוד) and "crown of splendour" (עטרת תפארת)?

The "garment of glory" refers once more to the cultic sphere. In fact, both the Hebrew expression בגדי כבוד and the Greek στολὴν δόξης occur (in addition to our text) only in Sir 50,11 referring to the vestments put on by the high priest, Simon II, a contemporary of Ben Sira, while he was officiating in the temple of Jerusalem. Two similar expressions ([34]בגדי עוז / περιστολὴν δόξης and בגדי קדש / στολῇ ἁγία) are employed in the description of Aaron's sacerdotal garments (cf. 45,7.10) to which we referred at the beginning of this article.

By contrast with the first expression, the "crown of splendour" is not exclusive to Ben Sira. It occurs in some prophetic texts, among which Isa 62,3 catches the eye. Here, Jerusalem becomes a crown, sign of the royalty of the Lord[35]. Another two occurrences are found in the book of Proverbs (Prov 4,9; 16,31). We should note that Prov 4,9 closes the fifth instruction (Prov 4,1–9) precisely with an aesthetic reference to the decoration whose beauty derives from Wisdom. As in Sir 6,31, here too, the ornament (the crown) reveals the close connection between Wisdom and the son/disciple.

The crown, made of gold (2 Sam 12,30) or of silver (Zech 6,11.14), is worn by kings (Cant 3,11; Jer 13,18), queens (Esth 8,15) and high priests (Sir 45,12) and is, therefore, a sign of honour and nobility. So, then, in Sir 6,31, the pairing of "crown of splendour" and "robe of glory" presents us with the sage as a noble person, of great dignity, authoritative, and influential in society to the extent of being close to the political and religious leaders of the period[36]. This

---

33 Cf. Mopsik, Sagesse, 99; Calduch-Benages, Wordplay, 13–26.
34 According to MS B: ו[..]ב עוז. For Skehan, "bĕkābôd wāʿōz is more easily understood as a corruption from a text containing bigdê" (Skehan–Di Lella, Wisdom, 509).
35 Cf. Jer 13,18; Ezek 16,12; 23,42.
36 Skehan–Di Lella, Wisdom, 195: "The wise, in other words, because of their fidelity to the Law will enjoy the splendour of royalty and the glory of the high priesthood". Cf. Schreiner, Jesus Sirach, 47; Marböck, Jesus Sirach, 121.

reading, however, is not the only one possible[37]. Alonso Schökel, for example, while conceding that the nuptial metaphor is not present in vv. 29 – 31, mentions that the robe and the crown could be an allusion to the wedding feast (cf. Isa 60,10; Cant 3,10)[38]. In the light of the context, we understand the above-mentioned images as an expression of the intimate relationship which unites Wisdom and the disciple/sage, that is to say, a kind of spiritual symbiosis. The relationship is so deep that the disciple "clothes himself" with and "puts on" Wisdom, becoming one with her. It could be said that, in a certain way, he is identified with Wisdom. The robe of glory and the crown of splendour, therefore, can be understood also as a sign of communication, relationship, and even of spiritual harmony.

1.3 Sir 25,6

This verse forms part of Sir 25,1– 11, a series of numerical proverbs that are well delimited and structured[39]. Between the three proverbs (vv. 1.2.7– 10), there is inserted a small unit of four sentences on old age (vv. 3 – 6). According to Di Lella, this could be autobiographical in nature, "for Ben Sira was well 'on in his years' (v. 4b) when he published the book"[40]. This is the text:

3   Ἐν νεότητι οὐ συναγείοχας,
    καὶ πῶς ἂν εὕροις ἐν τῷ γήρᾳ σου;
4   ὡς ὡραῖον πολιαῖς κρίσις
    καὶ πρεσβυτέροις ἐπιγνῶναι βουλήν.
5   ὡς ὡραία γερόντων[41] σοφία
    καὶ δεδοξασμένοις διανόημα καὶ βουλή.
6   στέφανος[42] γερόντων πολυπειρία[43],
    καὶ τὸ καύχημα αὐτῶν φόβος κυρίου.

3   If you have not gathered in your youth,
    what do you think to find in your old age?

---

37 For Ueberschaer, on the other hand, "der Siegeskranz war die Auszeichnung des erfolgreichen Athleten, der sich im Gymnasium trainiert und dann im Wettkampf bewiesen hat" (UEBERSCHAER, Weisheit, 202).

38 ALONSO SCHÖKEL, Símbolos, 270. For the nuptial metaphor in Trito-Isaiah, cf. TAIT, Jesus, 157– 164.

39 Cf. REITERER, Freundschaft, 155 – 162.

40 SKEHAN–DI LELLA, Wisdom, 341; REITERER, Freundschaft, 155 note 34.

41 Instead of "the aged", Syr reads: "chiefs/princes".

42 Instead of "crown", Syr reads: "honour".

43 Instead of "great experience", Syr reads: "much deliberation".

4   How fitting is judgement for white hairs
      and for the aged to give good advice!
5   How fitting is wisdom for the aged,
      discernment and counsel for the venerable!
6   The crown of the elderly is their great experience
      and their boast is the fear of the Lord.

These remarks on old age are meant as a reply to the proverb in 25,2 which exposes the lust of the old man: "My soul has hated three kinds of persons and their conduct have I detested: a proud pauper, a rich dissembler, the old man who is lustful through lack of good sense". This unpleasant description of what an old man ought not to be (cf. Dan 13,5–27) is followed by a much longer passage where, after an initial rhetorical question (25,3), there are listed those qualities which, according to Ben Sira, old persons[44] should have: judgement (κρίσις), the ability to give advice (ἐπιγνῶναι βουλήν), wisdom (σοφία), reflection (διανόημα) and prudence (βουλή).

This list culminates in 25,6 where the two final qualities are mentioned, that is, great experience (πολυπειρία)[45] and, above all, the fear-of-the-Lord, the concept with which the series closes, anticipating at the same time the theme of vv. 7–11[46]. Great experience is said to be the crown of the aged[47], and the fear-of-the-Lord to be their boast. If the "crown" (στέφανος) refers in this context to 1,18 (the fear-of-the-Lord is the crown of wisdom), the "boast" (καύχημα), in its turn, refers to 1,11 (the fear-of-the-Lord is glory and boasting). In other words, wisdom and the fear-of-the- Lord are the characteristics of the exemplary old man, who, given the average age span of the time, was considered to be a privileged person as well as worthy of the greatest respect as the guarantor and transmitter of tradition to the new generations (cf. 8,9).

1.4 Sir 27,8

Our verse forms part of Sir 26,28–27,21, a series of sentences which are intended to illustrate a sound criterion of discernment: the tree is known by its fruits. Human beings should, therefore, be assessed on the basis of their daily behaviour: on their relation with money, in their conversation, in their relation with

---

44 We should note the variety of terms used to describe this group of people: πολιαῖς, πρεσβυτέροις, γερόντων, δεδοξασμένοις.
45 Cf. Sir 21,22; 31(34Hb),9; 36,20, where πολυπειρός stands for the sage.
46 Cf., in this respect, HASPECKER, Gottesfurcht, 52 note 7.
47 Cf. Prov 16,31 (20,29b) and 17,6.

their equals. Within this section, we can distinguish a small unit which focuses on justice and sin (27,8–10).

8   Ἐὰν διώκῃς τὸ δίκαιον⁴⁸, καταλήμψῃ
       καὶ ἐνδύσῃ αὐτὸ ὡς ποδήρη δόξης⁴⁹.
9   πετεινὰ πρὸς τὰ ὅμοια αὐτοῖς καταλύσει,
       καὶ ἀλήθεια⁵⁰ πρὸς τοὺς ἐργαζομένους αὐτὴν ἐπανήξει.
10   λέων θήραν ἐνεδρεύει,
       οὕτως ἁμαρτία ἐγραζομένους ἄδικα.

8   If you pursue what is just, you will attain [it]
      and clothe yourself in it as with a robe of glory.
9   Birds flock together with their own kind,
      and truth returns to those who practise it.
10   The lion lies in wait for its prey,
      so does sin for those who act unjustly.

The teaching, formulated by means of a hypothetical period (protasis: if you pursue what is just + apodosis: you will attain [it]), is illustrated in what follows by two contrasting examples taken from the animal world (birds/their own kind versus lion/prey) which have their equivalents in the human world (truth/those who practise it versus sin/those who act unjustly).

We are especially interested in v. 8 on account of the expression ποδήρη δόξης (robe of glory) which echoes Sir 45,8, where ποδήρη (Hb מעיל) is mentioned in the description of Aaron's vesture. The substantive ποδήρης (ποδ + the root ἀρ) signifies length down to the feet and thus is referring to the cassock-like robe of the high priest which, in the LXX, is properly called χιτῶν ("tunic")⁵¹. According to Wis 18,24, the long robe is a sign of the whole world, perhaps because of its size: the reaching down to the feet represented the link between heaven and earth, and so the entire universe⁵².

---

48 Syr reads: "truth" (= Hb אמת). This is the reading of ALONSO SCHÖKEL, Eclesiástico, 241. Cf. SMEND, Weisheit, 244–245.
49 Lat adds: *et inhabitabis cum ea et proteget te in sempiternum et in die agnitionis invenies firmamentum.*
50 DUESBERG–FRANSEN, Ecclesiastico, 212, read: "justice" (cf. 4,28Hb: צדקה; Gk: ἀλήθεια).
51 Cf. CALDUCH-BENAGES, Ornamenti, 1324.
52 Cf. PHILO, Mos. 2,117–118; Spec. 1,84–85; JOSEPHUS, A.J. 3,179–180. ATHENAEUS NAUCRATIS, Deipn. 5,12,535–536: "His riding cloak had a lustrous dark-grey colour, and the universe with its golden stars and the twelve signs of the Zodiac were woven in it". With these words, Athenaeus is referring to the clothing of Demetrius Poliorcetes, son of the Macedonian general, Antigonus I Monophthalmus (382–301 BC).

Moreover, the image of justice as a splendid long robe is found also in Isa 61,10, where the prophet proclaims that the Lord has clothed him with the robe of salvation and wrapped him in the mantle of justice/righteousness (מעיל צדקה) as a bridegroom puts on[53] the diadem and as a bride adorns herself with jewels. We should note that two of the terms used, mantle (מעיל) and diadem (פאר), are also used in the description of priestly garb (Exod 39,22.28). However, the closest text to Sir 27,8, and, in a particular way, to the second colon, is, without any shadow of doubt, Sir 6,31. In fact, the same image which was applied there to wisdom is being applied here to justice. In 6,31, during the period of his apprenticeship and after having overcome his initial difficulties, the pupil has attained the stage of being able to put on the garb and the crown of his master, that is, of Wisdom. Similarly, in 27,8, the pupil is employed in the search for things that are just, not only so that he may attain them but also so that he can put on the mantle of justice. So then, to be clothed with justice means to identify oneself with justice, which in practice is conveyed in thinking, feeling, and acting justly.

2 The Crown as a Social Reward

With the Greek institution of the *symposion*[54] as his background, Ben Sira concludes his instruction on banquets (Sir 34[31Hb],12–35[32Hb],13) with a passage which gathers together various practical counsels on how to conduct oneself at these social events (35[32Hb],1–13). The first two pieces of advice are addressed to the master of the feast. The Hebrew text of the whole pericope is found with some lacunae in MSS B and F.

ראש סמוך אל תותר	1a	MS F	They have put you at the head[55]. Do not be puffed up
ובראש עשירים אל תסתורה והיה[56]	1b	MS F	and do not grab your seat[57] at the head of the rich;
היה להם כאחד מהם:	1c	MS B	be for them as[58] one of them.
דאג להם ואחד תסוב	1d	MS B	Look after them, and then make yourself comfortable,

---

53 We are translating the Hebrew יכין (a reading proposed by BHS), but the MT reads יכהן ("officiates").

54 KIEWELER, Benehmen, 208.

55 That is, at the head of your fellow guests.

56 לך כאחד מהם are written above תסתורה והיה in a smaller script.

57 Lit. "do not throw yourself". Lacking in MS B and Gk but not in Syr, this colon is a gloss that does not fit in the context (cf. MINISSALE, Versione greca, 70).

58 להם כ is lacking in MS F.

הכין צרכם ואחר תרבץ 1e MS B provide[59] for their needs and then[60], yourself, recline,
למען תשמח בכבודם 2a B, F so that they gladden you with their praise,
ועל מוסר תשא שכל: 2b B, F and, in return for [your] manners, you will earn favour.

Surprisingly, however, the text of the Greek version is the only one which mentions an item of clothing, in this case, once again, the crown[61]:

1a Ἡγούμενόν σε κατέστησαν; μὴ ἐπαίρου·
    They have made you master[62], do not exalt yourself,
1b γίνου ἐν αὐτοῖς ὡς εἷς ἐξ αὐτῶν,
    be among them as one of them,
1c φρόντισον αὐτῶν καὶ οὕτω κάθισον·
    look after them first and then be seated.
2a καὶ πᾶσαν τὴν χρείαν σου ποιήσας ἀνάπεσε,
    And [once you have] fulfilled your task, settle down
2b ἵνα εὐφρανθῇς δι'αὐτοὺς
    to enjoy yourself with them
2c καὶ εὐκοσμίας χάριν λάβῃς στέφανον[63].
    and receive the crown for [your] courtesy.

For Ben Sira, the presidency over the banquet is not just a question of honour. In fact, the master of the feast has to carry out a series of duties so that the feast goes well and the guests are satisfied[64]. If, at the end, he has succeeded in his role, he will receive the compliments of his fellow guests. According to the Hebrew text, he will earn their [65]שכל ("judgement", "reason", "prudence", "ability"), which here, however, has to be understood in the sense of sympathy or benevolence (cf. Prov 3,4). In the Greek text, however, the courtesy or good behaviour (perhaps also the good organization, εὐκοσμίας) of the master of the feast is rewarded with a "crown". But what is the crown in question? Taking into account the festive context of these verses, one could think of a floral wreath, perhaps of rosebuds (cf. Wis 2,8), a practice very popular with the

---

59 MS F reads: הבו (emphatic imperative of יהב, "to give").
60 MS F reads: ובכן (= Gk καὶ οὕτω).
61 For a comparative study of the Hebrew texts and the Greek version, cf. MINISSALE, Versione greca, 66–77.
62 That is, master of the feast.
63 Syr: "and you will receive glory at the table".
64 Cf. SPICQ, Ecclésiastique, 723.
65 Following Syr, Smend proposes reading כבוד (SMEND, Weisheit, 286; SKEHAN—DI LELLA, Wisdom, 387). For Peters, the original reading was כליל (PETERS, Buch, 263), while Spicq and Segal suppose that the Greek has exchanged שכל for כליל (SPICQ, Ecclésiastique, 723; SEGAL, ספר, 202).

Greeks[66] and sometimes adopted, apparently, in Palestine. In the light of the Hebrew text, however, we advocate a symbolic use for the term "crown", that is, the host who has carried out his duty with efficiency and care will be rewarded with the approbation and acknowledgement of the guests. This is the understanding of the Latin version: *et dignationem consequaris conrogationis* (35[32Hb],3c).

3 Two Significant Comparisons

In this last section, we present two texts in which clothing forms part of a comparison, explicitly in Sir 14,17, implicitly in Sir 42,13. In the first case, the comparison is indicated with the preposition כְּ, while, in the second, it is suggested by the synonymous parallelism between the two cola. In both texts, moreover, the clothing is related to the long robe, implicitly in 14,17, explicitly in 42,13. It should also be noted that, while the comparison of 14,17 is well anchored in the prophetic and sapiential tradition, that of 42,13, by contrast, reveals the literary creativity of the author in that it is wholly original.

3.1 Sir 14,17

Because all end up in Sheol, where there is no place for joy, Ben Sira advises enjoying the goods which one possesses in the present. This idea reminiscent of Qoheleth is what underlies Sir 14,11–19, an instruction on the just enjoyment of riches. It concludes with a poetic reflection on human frailty and the way to confront death (vv. 17–19). This is our verse according to MS A:

כל הבש / כבגד יבלה	v. 17a	All flesh wears out[67] moth-eaten like a garment[68]
וחוק עולם גוע יגויו:	v. 17b	and the eternal decree[69] is: "they[70] all shall surely die"[71].

---

66 Cf., for example, ARISTOPHANES, Eq. 221 and 965.
67 Gk: παλαιοῦται, "grows old" (= Lat: *veterascet*).
68 Gk: ὡς ἱμάτιον, "like a garment, mantle, material" (cf. Sir 11,4; 29,21; 39,26; 42,13). Lat: *sicut foenum*, "like grass" (cf. Ps 103,15; Isa 40,6; 51,12).
69 Gk: ἡ γὰρ διαθήκη ἀπ' αἰῶνος, "because the covenant is for ever" or "because this covenant is in force for ever". In Lat: *testamentum enim huius mundi*, is anticipated in v. 12.
70 Gk uses the 2nd per. sg.: Θανάτῳ ἀποθανῇ, "you must die".
71 Another possible translation: "and the decree from eternity is that we shall surely die". Syr reads: "Because all the human beings of the world wear out with age and the generations of the world die".

The statement of the first colon derives from the careful observing of reality: with the passage of time, clothes grow old and are ruined by moths. Similarly, human beings grow old with the years and their bodies wear out with the labour, toil, pain, and diseases which eat up their strength. Ben Sira was not the first to employ the image of the worn-out and moth-eaten garment in his book. We find it also in Isaiah and Job. The prophet takes it up to depict the destruction of the enemy: "Behold, like a garment (כבגד), they will all be worn out (יבלו), the moth will eat them up" (Isa 50,9) and Job to describe his illness: "Meanwhile, man is consumed (יבלה) like wood eaten by woodworm or like a garment (כבגד) spoiled by moths" (Job 13,28). Moreover, in Isa 51,6 and Ps 102,27, the same image is applied, respectively, to the earth and to the heavens.

By contrast with the texts just mentioned, Sir 14,17 is eye-catching for its universal significance, indicated with the expression כל הבשר, "all flesh" (cf. כל מעשיו, "all its [the human being's] works" in v. 19 with which it forms an inclusion) and reinforced in the second colon by means of the verbal construction with emphatic or asseverative value גוע יגועו (inf. abs.—impf. indic.)[72], "they all shall surely die", referring to the eternal decree. This decree is the decree of Sheol, which remains unknown to all because it has not been revealed to anyone (v. 12). No one knows when his or her descent into Sheol will happen, that is to say, no one knows the moment of his or her own death. In this context, therefore, the worn-out or moth-eaten garment represents the frailty of human life, an idea which will be developed further with another image in the following verse. This time, it will be the leaves of the tree which evoke the vital process of the human generations: "As the leaves grow on the flourishing tree, one falls and another sprouts, so it is with the generations of flesh and blood: one dies, another is born" (v. 18)[73].

In his commentary, Di Lella adds a humorous note to the sage's profound and serene reflections here on the human destiny. He cites a witty remark by Richard Chenevix Trench (1807–1886), famous philologist, writer and poet, and one-time Anglican Archbishop of Dublin: "The Italians have a proverb in which they express their sense of the tardiness of the despatch of all business in Spain, and the infinite delays which are sure to attend it—*May my death*

---

72 SMEND, Weisheit, 135–136: "גוע יגועו ist in Anführungszeichen zu denken". Th. van Peursen suggests comparing the above expression with מות תמות (Gen 2,17), which has the same significance (VAN PEURSEN, Verbal System, 280 note 20).

73 A very similar image is found in Homer's Iliad: "Just as are the generations of leaves, such are those also of men. As for the leaves, the wind scatters some on the earth, but the luxuriant forest sprouts others when the season of spring has come; so of men one generation springs up and another passes away" (HOMER, Il. 6,146–149).

come to me from Spain, for so it will come late or not at all"[74]. As a Spaniard who has lived in Italy for thirty years, I would like to offer another version of this proverb: *May my death come to me from Italy.*

3.2 Sir 42,13[75]

In the much debated pericope about daughters or, more precisely, about the worries which daughters cause their fathers (42,9 – 14)[76], Ben Sira includes, among other teachings, two pieces of advice concerning how daughters should relate to other people (men and women) outside the family circle.

The text appears in MSS B and Mas, but 12b and 13b in the latter are badly preserved.

v. 12 MS B לכל זכר אל תבן תאר   ובית נשים אל תסתויד

v. 13 MS B כי מבגד יצא עש   ומאשה רעת אשה

12 Let her not exhibit[77] her beauty (lit. aspect) before any man[78],
    and let her not speak confidently in the midst[79] of women (i.e. "married women")[80];
13 for from garments comes the moth[81],
    and from a woman comes a woman's wickedness[82].

---

74 Trench, Proverbs, 53 note 1 (Lecture III: "Proverbs of Different Nations Compared"). Cited in Skehan–Di Lella, Wisdom, 260, where the phrase, treated in *On the Lessons in Proverbs* (1853), is presented in an abbreviated form.

75 For this text, cf. Calduch-Benages, Animal Imagery, 60 – 62.

76 Cf. Piwowar, Vergogna, 369 – 422. Surprisingly, in 42,9 – 14, Ben Sira does not mention the mother! Cf. Sir 7,24 – 25; 22,4 – 5; 26,10.

77 תבן, Hiphil from the verb בין with the meaning to expose, to show, to reveal (cf. Dan 8,16). This reading is preferable to MS B: תתן, Qal from the verb נתן ("to give"), cf. Yadin, Ben Sira Scroll, 25 (1st ed. 1965). By contrast, Skehan, following Strugnell, reconstructs תפן Hiphil from the verb פנה ("to turn") which he translates with "reveal" (cf. Skehan–Di Lella, Wisdom, 480).

78 MS Bmg erroneously reads תזכר from the verb זכר ("to recall").

79 בית is a dittographic mistake in place of בין ("between"), confirmed by Gk and Syr.

80 The line is missing in MS Mas.

81 MS Mas reads the synonym סס ("moth"). In Ahiqar 184 and 186, we find the expression ססא נפלת ("the moth fell"). According to Lindenberger, it is impossible to reconstruct the text from the fragment; it was probably an animal saying (Lindenberger, Aramaic Proverbs, 183 – 184).

82 This line is partly damaged in MS Mas and reconstructed according to MS B.

These two exhortations are indirectly addressed to the father[83], since he is responsible for the influences his daughter is exposed to. One of his main duties is to protect her from certain dangers, especially before marriage. The dangers could come from questionable relationships, e.g. from men seduced by feminine beauty (cf. 33[36Hb],22), but also from excessive acquaintance with married women who might disillusion a young girl with their experience.

Both exhortations are formulated as negative precepts. The formula אל + impf. with imperative value (42,12ab) is followed by a double motivation in two parallel parts (42,13ab). In the first part (13a), the mention of the moth appears within its normal context, i.e. related to garments, and, in the second part (13b), it is metaphorically applied to women's behaviour. The following parallelism results: "garments" corresponds to "women", the verb "come from" is implied in 13b, and "moth" corresponds to "woman's wickedness" (רעת אשה)[84].

The moth (in Hebrew סָס or עָשׁ)[85] is a small nocturnal butterfly, the larva of which eats wool and makes a kind of cocoon with the material (wool, cloth, skins, etc.) effectively destroying a garment in order to make a nest. Therefore, as the sage rightly states in 42,13a, the moth comes out of the garments. The correlation between the garment and the moth is indeed the most significant aspect of the image. Usually ignored by authors when commenting on this verse, the moth does not come out of new garments but old ones. This small but very significant detail is, in our opinion, the key to understanding the meaning of 42,13. Just as out of the (old) garment comes the moth that damages another garment (which is supposedly new), likewise from a woman (who is an elderly, married and, therefore, experienced woman) comes the wickedness that corrupts another woman (who is supposedly young and does not have the experience of marriage)[86].

---

83 Note the verbs in 3rd per. f. sg. (תבן and תסתויד). Gk and Syr, on the other hand, use the 2nd per. sg.

84 MOPSIK, Sagesse, 255: "Le mot *ra'at ichah* signifie ici 'le malheur d'une femme', l'image de la teigne est éloquente à cet égard: cette moisissure détériore le tissu, cause sa perte, elle ne le rend pas 'méchant'!". Instead of "a woman's wickedness", Lat reads "a man's wickedness" (*iniquitas viri*), influenced perhaps by 42,13.

85 The first term (סָס) is found only in Isa 51,8, where it symbolizes the destruction that will strike those who revile the people of the Lord. For this *hapax legomenon*, see COHEN, Hapax, 114 note 21. The second term (עָשׁ) is more common and symbolises either the destruction of a person (Isa 50,9; 51,8; Ps 39,12; Job 13,28; Hos 5,12) or human fragility (Job 4,19; 27,18).

86 Cf. EGGER-WENZEL, Knechtschaft, 27.

4 Conclusion

According to Minissale, "In the most ancient sapiential tradition, the metaphorical use of words which indicate the most concrete objects of daily observation is based on a global perception of reality in which analogies between natural events and the various situations of human existence are established"[87]. Our study of the images relating to clothing in the book of Sirach has shown how our sage succeeds in making a comparison between quite different categories. However, very similar phenomena are to be found in these categories, and it is precisely for this reason that they can be related to one another in the same text. Thus, we have seen how different elements of clothing are treated in relation to realities of a theological and spiritual character (1,11.18; 6,29 – 31; 25,6; 27,8), to social behaviour (35[32Hb],2; 42,13), and to the reality of death (14,17).

In the first group of texts, the most numerous, by means of the image of the crown, Ben Sira succeeds in expressing the close correspondence between wisdom and the fear-of-the-Lord (1,11.18; 25,6). The two realities, indeed, are involved with each other from the fact that one is the condition of the other and *vice versa*. To grow in the fear-of-the-Lord involves growing in wisdom just as the maturing of wisdom develops the sense of the fear-of-the-Lord. Moreover, robe and crown reveal the identity and the psychology of the one who puts them on, in this case the pupil, and also disclose his rank and even his profession (6,29 – 30), if we think of the figure of the sage. Erasmus said that "clothing is the body's body" and that "it gives an idea of the dispositions of the spirit"[88]. Thus, then, for Ben Sira, to be clothed with wisdom or with justice (6,31; 27,8) means being identified totally with these values both in the spirit and in the works which derive from them. Finally, in the last two texts, he makes use, on the one hand, of an image well known to the tradition (the moth-eaten garment as the symbol of the transitory nature of human life, 14,17) and, on the other hand, he demonstrates his literary genius with an unusual comparison between the effects of the moth on a new garment and the bad influence which women with a long experience of marriage exercise on young women who are still unmarried (43,12).

In conclusion, as a good teacher, Ben Sira knows how to exploit to the maximum the symbolism of clothing, highlighting its social, anthropological and

---

87 MINISSALE, Radici, 79: "Infatti nella tradizione sapienziale più arcaica l'uso metaforico delle parole che indicano gli oggetti più concreti dell'osservazione quotidiana, si basa su di una percezione globale della realtà nella quale si stabiliscono delle analogie tra gli avvenimenti della natura e le varie situazioni dell'esistenza umana".
88 Cited in CRAS, Symbolique, 149 note 2.

theological-spiritual dimensions in order that his teaching, anchored in the reality of life, is able to encourage his disciples in their search for the highest good, namely the wisdom that comes from God.

The Exodus Traditions in the Book of Ben Sira

Ben Sira's interest in the history of Israel is well attested in the final section of the book, the "Praise of the Ancestors" (Sir 44–50). In these chapters, inspired by the ancient biblical accounts, the author presents a gallery of famous characters in chronological order, beginning with Enoch and ending up with his own contemporary, the high priest Simon. From the period of the covenants with the patriarchs, we pass through the time of the prophets and kings, ending up with the reconstruction of Jerusalem and the temple[1].

The attentive reader immediately notices that the construction of this historical survey lacks some important, indeed fundamental, building blocks which are passed over in silence. Notably surprising, for example, is the fact that there is no mention of the departure of the Israelites from Egypt (Exodus 14–15). By contrast with Wisdom 10–19, a Hellenistic re-reading of the Exodus, Sirach 44–50 neglects the foundational event of the constitution of Israel[2]. The same thing happens in Sir 16,6–11ab, a sapiential reflection on the history of the people, and in Sir 16,26–17,14, which passes from the creation to the covenant at Sinai without any interval[3]. No hint, therefore, of the pursuit by the Egyptians, the miracle of the Red Sea, the drowning of Pharaoh's army with his chariots and his horses...

On the other hand, many passages of Ben Sira take their inspiration from the books of Exodus[4], Numbers and Deuteronomy[5] and refer to the Exodus traditions (the miracles, the plagues, Pharaoh, the rebellion of the people, the gift of the Law). These are the kinds of passages in which we are especially interested. However, since we cannot be exhaustive and must make a choice, we shall confine ourselves here to the following texts: Sir 44,23fg–45,5; 45,18–19 and 38,5.

1 The Praise of Moses (Sir 44,23fg–45,5)

Moses, the son of Amram and Jochebed, is a central character in the history of Israel. The references to his person and his deeds are concentrated chiefly in the Pentateuch and particularly in the Exodus traditions. In fact, outside the

---

1 Cf. Ska, Éloge, 181–193.
2 For a comparison betwen Sir 44–50 and Wisd 10–19, cf. Gilbert, Review, 319–334.
3 Cf. Wénin, Création, 147–158.
4 Reiterer, Influence, 100–117.
5 Veijola, Law, 144–164; Beentjes, Deuteronomistic Heritage, 275–296.

https://doi.org/10.1515/9783110492316-014

Pentateuch, the references to Moses are rather scanty (cf. Ps 105,26; 106,16.23.32; Jer 15,1; Mic 6,4; Neh 9,14...). Even so, there was abundant material at his disposal and Ben Sira had to make a choice. What was he to say about Moses and what was he to keep quiet about? What aspects to emphasise and what just to pass over lightly? As Benjamin G. Wright correctly observes, "most of Ben Sira's praise of Moses focuses on the Exodus events and the giving of the Law, although he shapes them to fit his own agenda and themes"[6]. In fact, it takes only five verses for Ben Sira to give his encomium on one of the great leaders and masters of Israel, much loved in late Judaism.

According to Otto Kaiser, "the verses devoted to Moses are highly emphatic, bringing out in extremely terse phrases his exceptional position amongst all mankind and his special gifts from God, which culminate in his transmitting the divine law of life to Israel in 45,5"[7]. Kaiser's observation is completely correct. However, in our opinion, the sketch of Moses is not without irony. Some speak even of cynicism[8], but that seems to be going too far. The irony emerges, in the first place, in the comparison of the brief space which Ben Sira dedicates to Moses (9 bicola) with the 40 bicola devoted to the high priests Aaron and Phinehas, of the tribe of Levi, who where thought to be the ancestors of the Zadokites (cf., also, Sir 50,1–21). Moreover, it is surely ironic to pretend to "forget" Moses' mission as liberator of his people, an essential element of Old Testament theology.

Here is the translation of the Hebrew text according to MS B (when the MS is defective we follow Gk). For a detailed analysis of the textual questions, we refer to the studies by Friedrich V. Reiterer, Patrick W. Skehan and Markus Witte[9].

44,23fg	He brought forth[10] from him (i.e. Jacob / Israel) a man, who found favour in the sight of all the living.
45,1	Beloved[11] of God and humans, Moses, whose memory is blessed.
45,2	He made him glorious like the angels/holy ones[12]

---

6 WRIGHT, Use, 191.

7 KAISER, Covenant, 242.

8 MORLA ASENSIO, Eclesiástico, 217.

9 REITERER, Urtext, 117–142; SKEHAN—DI LELLA, Wisdom, 509–510; WITTE, Mose, 164–166.

10 It is ironic that exactly the same Hebrew verbal form is used to narrate the exodus event in Ps 136,11.

11 According to Gk (= Syr and Lat).

12 According to Antonino Minissale, the LXX translates "holy ones" (ἁγίων) in the sense of angels, after Exod 7,1[LXX] which is how it translates the Hebrew אלהים ("I will make of you *a god* for Pharaoh") on account of a theological scruple (MINISSALE, Siracide, 213). See, also, WRIGHT,

	and strengthened him with/in fearful things.[13]
45,3	By his word he wrought swift miracles[14]
	and sustained him in the king's presence.
	He gave him commandments for his people[15]
	and revealed to him his glory.
45,4	For his faithfulness and meekness
	he chose him out of all flesh.
45,5	He permitted him to hear his voice
	and let him draw near into the dark cloud.
	He placed in his hand the commandment,
	the law of life and understanding,
	that he might teach to Jacob his statutes,
	and his decrees and ordinances to Israel.

After the reference to the patriarch Jacob/Israel ("from him", 44,23f)[16], Ben Sira begins his panegyric of Moses without, however, mentioning his name yet (the same for Solomon in 47,12). In this way, the reader's expectations are heightened with regard to this extraordinary man "who found favour in the sight of all the living" (44,23g). The expression "to find favour in the eyes of" (מצא חן בעיני), frequently found in the Exodus narrative, is to be understood as the favour of his people, of Pharaoh's daughter (Exod 2,5–10), of the priest of Midian and his daughters (Exod 2,15–22), of Pharaoh's servants as well as the favour of the Egyptian people (Exod 11,3)[17]. Of undisputed prestige and blessed memory, Moses was loved both by God and human beings (45,1). Up to this point, we have a characterisation of Moses that is very general and does not leave room for any details.

Beginning with 45,2 until the end of the passage, Ben Sira composes, according to the expression of M. Witte, "a functional biography that fits within salvation history" (*eine funktionale heilsgeschichtliche Biographie*)[18], where he collects the most important actions and accomplishments of the life of Moses. We should note that all these actions and accomplishments are presented as gifts and

---

Use, 192. Cf. Witte's reconstruction of the Hebrew text: ו[יכנהו איש א[להים, "und [er gab ihm den Namen G]ottes" (WITTE, Mose, 165).

13 According to MS Bmg (= Gk, Syr and Lat).

14 According to Gk.

15 According to Gk and Syr. Cf. Segal's recostruction of the Hebrew text: ויצוהו [א]ל [ומע] (SEGAL, ספר, 307).

16 The absence of Joseph, apart from a brief mention in 49,15, is surprising.

17 SKEHAN – DI LELLA, Wisdom, 510.

18 WITTE, Mose, 170.

favours which come from God[19]. Venerated in a superhuman way, Moses was able to perform "fearful things" (במוראים, 45,2b) and "swift signs" (אותות מהר, 45,3a) in the presence of the king (45,3b), that is, the Pharaoh. The two expressions we have singled out probably refer to the account of the ten plagues which afflicted Egypt before the Exodus (Exod 7,1– 11,10)[20], even if the plagues are never described as "fearful" in the book of Exodus. In this connection, B.G. Wright suggests that the reading of Exodus 9, and in particular of verses 20 and 30, would have induced Ben Sira to link the "fearful things" with "the fear-of-God", a theme very dear to him[21].

As for the Pharaoh of Egypt, he is mentioned only once as such in Sirach, that is in 16,15. This verse, like the following one, is attested in HbII (MS A), GrII and Syr (absent, however in GkI and Lat) and both represent a late expansion of the text. Verses 15 and 16, in fact, are not only too long but also interrupt the author's argument. This opinion is shared by Marco Rossetti and, more recently, by Severino Bussino, authors who have studied the addition in some depth[22].

We record the translation of the Hebrew text of v. 15 according to MS A:

The Lord hardened the heart of Pharaoh, who did not recognize him,
in order to manifest his deeds under heaven.

With the mention of Pharaoh's hardened heart (cf. Exod 7,3; 9,12; 10,27; 11,10; 14,4.8), the verse is linked to the historical exposition of Sir 16,6 – 11ab and offers a concrete example of what is stated in 16,14b: "everyone will receive according to his deeds". In Rossetti's words, "The king of Egypt is for everybody the example of someone who remains unconcerned and unrepentant in the face of God's action, and precisely for this reason, the Lord will harden his heart still further preventing him from reaching the truth"[23].

---

19 Cf. PETRAGLIO, Libro, 101: "Ben Sirac, presentando Mosè, compone il suo testo mostrando Dio come unico soggetto".

20 Cf. Deut 4,34; 26,8; 34,11– 12.

21 WRIGHT, Use, 192.

22 ROSSETTI, Aggiunte, 607– 648; BUSSINO, Additions, 176 – 189.

23 ROSSETTI, Aggiunte, 639: "Il re di Egitto è per tutti l'esempio di chiunque rimanga impassibile ed impenitente di fronte all'agire di Dio, ed il Signore, proprio per questo, gli renderà il cuore ancora più duro impedendogli di raggiungere la verità".

Now let us return to the praise of Moses. Without making any mention of the Exodus from Egypt[24], beginning with 45,3c, Ben Sira concentrates on the Sinai experience and, in particular, on the gift of the Law. Several words of a legislative character (מוצה, "commandment"; תורה, "law"; חקים, "statutes"; עדות, "decrees"; and משפטים, "ordinances") are concentrated at the end of the passage (45,5cdef) and are placed to indicate the central role of the Law in the sage's thought and work. We do not know if the sentence in 45,3c (cf. the verb צוה, "to command") refers to the giving of the Decalogue or not, but, in the light of the context, it is very probable that this is the case (cf. 45,5c). In 45,3d, the revelation of the glory of God echoes some Exodus passages such as Exod 24,15 – 17; 33,18 – 23; 34,5 – 8. We should note that, in Sir 45,4, the portrait of Moses acquires more concrete traits than those mentioned at the beginning (cf. 44,23g–45,1). Like Abraham, who was found faithful in trial (44,20), Moses is described as a faithful and humble man (cf. Num 12,3.7). It is precisely because of "his faithfulness and humility" that he was chosen by God. In 45,5abcd, Ben Sira seems to have been inspired by various texts from Exodus, Numbers and Deuteronomy where there is mention of the voice of God (Exod 33,11; Num 12,8; Deut 5,22; 34,10), the entry of Moses into the cloud (Exod 20,21; 24,28; Deut 5,22) and the handing over of the commandments (Exod 32,15; Deut 9,15).

The passage reaches its climax in 45,5ef, where we learn of the mission which God entrusted to Moses. It is a question of communicating and teaching the "Law of life and understanding" (תורת חיים ותבונה) to his people Israel. As Burkard M. Zapff puts it, in Sir 45,5ef, Moses is presented as "the paradigm of the Legislator, who is the link between the Law and wisdom as well as the ancestor of all wisdom teaching"[25].

2 Aaron and Korah's Rebellion (Sir 45,18 – 19)

The High Priest Aaron is certainly one of Ben Sira's favourite characters. As we have already mentioned, his memorial is three times longer than that of his brother, Moses (Sir 45,6 – 22). For the most part, this greater length is the result

---

24 REITERER, Pentateuch, 176: "Wenn auch der Auszug aus Ägypten nicht ausdrücklich erwähnt wird, bedeutet doch jene Rettungstat den geistigen Hintergrund". Cf., also, ZAPFF, Jesus Sirach, 326.

25 ZAPFF, Jesus Sirach, 327: "5e.f sieht in Mose das Paradigma des Gesetzeslehrers, der aufgrund der Verbindung von Gesetz und Weisheit zugleich der Urahn jeglicher Weisheitslehre ist". Cf. REITERER, Pentateuch, 177.

of the laudatory and vivid description of his imposing liturgical vesture[26]. In his praise of Aaron, our sage reveals his enthusiasm for the legitimate cult which he will take up again in Sir 50,1–21, a passage entirely devoted to the High Priest Simon.

Without entering into a discussion over the structure of the pericope[27], we now turn our attention to Sir 45,18–19. These two verses form a tiny unit which interrupts the praise of Aaron with an historical account describing in harsh tones an event in which the High Priest was involved during the journey in the desert. We are speaking of the rebellion of Korah, Dathan and Abiram recounted in Num 16,1–17,15, of which Ben Sira here offers us a much shorter version with some very interesting details. Here we use the translation of the Hebrew text according to MS B:

> 45,18   Strangers burned with anger against him (i.e. Aaron)
> and were jealous of him in the wilderness.
> The men of Dathan and Abiram
> and the band of Korah in their vehement anger.
> 45,19   The Lord saw it and became angry
> and destroyed them in his burning anger.
> He brought a miracle against them
> and consumed them in his flaming fire.

The beginning of the unit is very emphatic. The first information about the conspirators which the reader receives is not their names (cf. Num 16,1) but a somewhat pejorative description. They are זרים ("foreigners", "strangers"). But how is this term to be understood in the context? It could mean people who do not belong to the family of Aaron and so are not authorised to perform priestly functions[28] or else, as F.V. Reiterer has recently suggested, behind this provocative and hostile "outsiders" there could be hidden an allusion to Ben Sira's contemporary opponents[29]. The second piece of information concerns the object of the conspiracy. While, in the Numbers account, Korah, Dathan and Abiram rebel against Moses and Aaron (Num 16,3), in Ben Sira's text, Aaron becomes the only target of the protest. In this way, all the attention is placed on him. The third piece of information is the reason for the rebellion. The fact that Korah, Dathan and Abiram were contesting the authority of the two brothers as recounted

---

26 CALDUCH-BENAGES, Vesti di Aronne, 69–81.
27 Cf., in this connection, REITERER, Aaron's Polyvalent Role, 27–30.
28 Cf. SKEHAN–DI LELLA, Wisdom, 513 and MOPSIK, Sagesse, 286: "étrangers à la prêtrise" (strangers to the priesthood).
29 REITERER, Aaron's Polyvalent Role, 51.

in Numbers, is avoided. In Ben Sira's judgement, the single stimulus for the conspiracy is jealousy with regard to Aaron. He is the principal character, and the whole focus is on him.

Ben Sira does not hide his antipathy towards the conspirators, whom he also describes as a wrathful and angry band (lit. בעזוז אפם, "in the violence of their anger", 45,18d)[30]. We should note the play of words on the term "anger" (אף). The anger of Korah, Dathan and Abiram directed against Aaron finds its response in the following verse (19ab) where, on seeing them, God is angered (ויתאנף) and in his wrath (lit. בחרון אפו, "in the heat of his anger") strikes them a mortal blow. Finally, in 19cd, God's punishment is presented as a wonderful, extraordinary action, that is, a miracle (אות). It is easy to see here an allusion to Num 16,30 – 35, where there is an account of a miracle performed by God against the rebels: first, the earth opened wide its mouth and swallowed up Dathan and Abiram alive, and then a fire came forth from God and devoured the band of Korah (cf. Ps 106,17 – 18). This would be the miracle spoken of in our text[31].

Now we have to ask ourselves, why did Ben Sira want to recount this episode? Couldn't he have done without it? What message lies hidden behind this dramatic evocation of the past? If we read between the lines, we can discover some allusions to the situation of the priesthood in Ben Sira's day. The priesthood was a basic institution in ancient Jewish society and it is logical to suppose that it aroused the admiration of some (our author included) and gave raise to rejection and attacks by others (the opponents)[32]. The record of the conspiracy recounted in Numbers and in particular the punishment which God inflicts on the rebels could be understood, bearing in mind Ben Sira's predilection for the priestly class, as "a warning to any potential 'usurper' of the priesthood"[33].

Let us add a final observation. In addition to Sir 45,18 – 19, Ben Sira alludes to the rebels' conspiracy in 16,6, even if in this text he does not mention anyone by name: "Against a sinful band fire is enkindled; upon a godless people wrath flames forth" (cf. Wis 18,20). It is precisely with this verse that he begins a historical demonstration of the punitive intervention of God (Wis 16,6 – 11ab), which forms part of Wis 15,11 – 18,14, a long passage devoted to the subject of

---

30 According to Roland De Vaux, the adherents of the Korah clan were "full of intrigue, battling their way forward, first as doorkeepers, then as singers and finally even usurping priestly functions" (DE VAUX, Ancient Israel, 393).

31 SKEHAN—DI LELLA, Wisdom, 513; ZAPFF, Jesus Sirach, 332; WRIGHT, Use, 200.

32 In Sir 45,19ab, F.V. Reiterer glimpses the priests contemporaries with Ben Sira desiring that the glory of God strike their enemies (cf. REITERER, Aaron's Polyvalent Role, 51).

33 WRIGHT, Use, 200.

theodicy[34]. Through some examples drawn from the history of Israel, our sage teaches that God punishes the wicked for their sin of pride: Korah, Dathan and Abiram (v. 6; cf. Num 16,1–30), the giants of antiquity (v. 7; cf. Gen 6,1–7), the inhabitants of Sodom (v. 8; cf. Gen 19,1–29), the Canaanites who dwelt in Palestine (v. 9; cf. Josh 11,16–20), the Israelites who came out of Egypt (v. 10; cf. Exod 12,37) and rebelled against God several times with their murmuring and perished in the desert (cf. Sir 46,6; Num 11,21; 14,20–23) and, finally, by way of summary, the "stiff-necked" people (v. 11ab; cf. Exod 32,9; 33,5; 34,6–7). The pole position which Ben Sira grants to Korah, Dathan and Abiram in this rogues' gallery speaks for itself.

3 The Doctor and the Miracle of the Sweetening of the Waters (Sir 38,5)

The final text (Sir 38,5) we wish to consider is in 38,1–15, a passage commonly described as the "praise of the doctor"[35]. This passage reveals how Ben Sira understands the medical profession and the medicine practised in his day. We have to remember that, in ancient Judaea of the 2nd century BC, the confrontation between Hellenistic novelty and the tradition of the fathers was beginning to come alive. This disagreement was broad and deep, beginning with the distinction between what constitutes health and sickness. While the Old Testament looked on doctors with evident suspicion (Job 13,4; Isa 3,7; Jer 8,22; 46,11; 51,8), in the Hellenistic world, by contrast, they enjoyed a good name and high esteem. In the Old Testament illness was understood as caused by sin (Num 12,9–10) while healing was seen as the effect of God's forgiveness (2 Chr 16,2), while in the Hellenistic environment illness was diagnosed and treated as a natural event that could be understood by reason and treated medically.

In 38,1–15, Ben Sira in a masterly way successfully integrates the Jewish faith with the scientific progress of his time in the matter of pharmacology and medicine[36]. In the words of Silvana Fasce, the sage of Jerusalem "moves

---

34 Cf., among others, Prato, Problema della teodicea, 209–299; Gilbert, God, 118–135; Beentjes, Theodicy, 509–524.

35 Among the numerous studies on this pericope, I cite only some of the most recent: McConvery, Physician, 62–86; Wainwright, Gendering Healing, 257–272; Fasce, Medico; Zapff, Sir 38,1–15, 347–367.

36 We should recall the great founding doctors of the Alexandrian school: Erasistratus of Ceos (ca. 304–250 BC) and Herophilos of Chalcedon (ca. 335–280 BC). Their teaching and methodology had a decisive influence in the following centuries. Cf. Fasce, Medico, 35–38.

naturally between the old and the new, not so much by introducing novelties but by integrating them with the Jewish tradition, which provides a background for the elements and dynamics that came from Alexandrian Greek sources: in fact the praise of the doctor begins with the praise for his service [the reference is to the Greek text][37], but is immediately set in a religious perspective which proclaims that the doctor and his science are divinely created gifts"[38].

The "praise of the doctor" can be divided into two large sections: 38,1–8 (advice on how to behave towards the doctor) and 38,9–15 (advice on how to deal with illness). Verse 1a acts as introduction to the whole passage and v. 15 encloses the conclusion in the form of a warning. We shall focus on the first part because it is that which is of interest to our subject. It is made up of two strophes: vv. 1–3 and vv. 4–8. The first strophe emphasises the importance of the doctor. The respect due to him and to the practice of medicine has a religious motivation: his profession and his wisdom (understood as the art of healing) come from God. It is precisely this that justifies ranking the doctor among the great. Since the doctor was generally a court official, he received his salary from the king[39] and respect from those who exercised authority. In brief, having received his wisdom from God, the doctor becomes his close collaborator in the healing process.

Verse 4 sees the beginning of the second strophe where attention is shifted from the doctor to the remedies (תרופות, φάρμακα) which he employs in his treatment. Also created by God, these medications are natural substances drawn from the earth. Despite their horrible taste, the sensible person should never disregard them[40]. In the following verse, Ben Sira unexpectedly interrupts his exposition with a rhetorical question which provokes the reader's curiosity:

---

37 Sir 38,1Gk: "Honour the doctor for his service". The Hebrew text is distinguished by its utilitarian tone: "Make friends with the doctor before you need him" (MS B); "Make friends with the doctor because of his usefulness" (MSS Bmg and D).

38 FASCE, Medico, 31–32: "Ben Sira [...] si muove con naturalezza fra l'antico e il nuovo, non tanto per introdurre il nuovo, quanto per consolidare la tradizione giudaica, entro cui agiscono istanze e correnti culturali di provenienza greco-alessandrina: infatti la lode del medico parte con l'ossequioso riconoscimento delle sue prestazioni, ma subito si inquadra in una prospettiva religiosa, proclamando che il medico e la sua scienza sono doni della creazione divina".

39 The following Spanish proverb seems to have been inspired by Sir 38,2: "Dios es quien sana y el médico se lleva la plata" (God heals and the doctor receives the fee).

40 Cf. Jer 8,22; P.Insinger 32,12: "He [God] created remedies to end illness, wine to end affliction" and 24,2: "Do not slight a small illness for which there is a remedy; use the remedy" (LICHTHEIM, Wisdom Literature, 230.222).

> 38,5 MS B   Was not the water sweetened by a twig
> so that all might learn his power?

The question evokes a well-known episode recounted in the book of Exodus[41]. After three days of journeying in the desert without finding water, the Israelites reached Mara, an oasis of bitter water (in Hebrew מרה signifies "bitter") and thus undrinkable. They murmur against Moses, asking him to solve the problem, and he, without delay, turns to God to find a solution. The Lord showed Moses a piece of wood (עץ) which, when immersed in the water, rendered it sweet (Exod 15,23–25)[42].

What message did Ben Sira intend to transmit with this biblical allusion? Do we have here, as some maintain, a simple proof from Scripture to give authority to his teaching? In answering these questions, I can do no less than take up and amplify the observations made in this connection by F.V. Reiterer in his essay on the influence of the book of Exodus on Ben Sira[43]. First, Ben Sira does not evoke the miraculous character of the episode but the natural properties and the therapeutic benefits of the wood which, in the final instance, come from God. This idea is shared by S. Fasce: "Behind a gesture which could appear magical and behind a phenomenon which could be understood as the effect of a thaumaturgical action, Ben Sira discerns a natural power, a property of the plant, and, therefore, again, an aspect of the divine creation for the benefit of humanity"[44]. In our opinion, Ben Sira is also implicitly promoting the study of plants and their healing properties. Second, in the face of the people who are desperate through the lack of drinking water, Moses seeks the Lord's help. It is no human power that renders the bitter water drinkable but Moses' supplication to the Lord[45]. Third, Moses is presented indirectly as the prototype of the doctor even if he never practised this profession himself. Just like Moses, the doctor receives his vocation and authority from God, maintains a close relationship with him

---

41 In Sir 2,10 too, for example, the sage makes use of rhetorical questions to ask about Israel's past. Cf., in this connection, CALDUCH-BENAGES, Crisol, 123–148.

42 Water is rendered drinkable also in 2 Kgs 2,19–22 and Ezek 47,8–11.

43 REITERER, Influence, 100–117.

44 FASCE, Medico, 49: "Alla base di un gesto che potrebbe apparire magico e alla base di un fenomeno che potrebbe essere inteso effetto di un'azione taumaturgica, Ben Sira scorge un potere naturale, una proprietà della pianta, quindi ancora un aspetto della creazione divina, per l'utilità dell'uomo".

45 Philo's account describes the immediate help which God grants in reply to Moses' supplications (cf. PHILO, Mos. 1,181–185 and, also, JOSEPHUS, A.J. 3,6–7).

through prayer, and is appointed to perform a task on behalf of the people. In sum, like Moses, the doctor is truly an instrument of divine salvation[46].

4 Conclusion

This study has allowed us to grasp, if not completely, at least in some aspects, how Ben Sira employs the Exodus traditions. He selects only a few aspects of the Exodus traditions which coincide with what he wants to teach and how he wants to teach it. In the words of B.G. Wright, the sage "had his own interests, agendas and ideological commitments"[47]. Ben Sira is not interested in citing the Bible in order to give authority to his words (even if, at times, he employs it also with this aim, cf. 2,10), but mainly in the service of his teaching. In other words, our sage expects not only that his disciple knows the ancient Scriptures but that he is also able to understand the purpose of the biblical quotation/ allusion and its meaning in the present context. Knowledge and interpretation of ancient texts thus become pedagogical tools employed by Ben Sira with great creativity.

In the praise of Moses, for example, the use of the Exodus traditions is wholly oriented towards the gift of the Law. As a result, Moses is presented not as the liberator of the people (as one gathers from the account in Numbers), but as the interpreter and master of the Law *par excellence* (cf. 45,17 concerning Aaron). Not by chance, the Law, together with wisdom and the fear-of-the-Lord, is at the base of Ben Sira's theological teaching (cf. 19,20). The reference to the rebellion of Dathan, Abiram and Korah in the praise of Aaron seems to be aimed at turning the attention of his disciples to the priestly class and particularly to its detractors. Finally, the reference to the episode of the waters of Marah in the passage on the doctor reveals, on the one hand, Ben Sira's interest in medicine as a science (openness to the Hellenistic world) and, on the other, his concept of the doctor as a collaborator in creation and instrument of the salvation of God (faithfulness to Jewish tradition and faith). Moreover, the context of sickness and healing in which this passage is inserted recalls the theology of trial to which both Israel in the desert and the disciple in his search for wisdom are subjected (cf. 2,1–6). In the work of our sage, the crossing of the desert with all its trials

---

46 Cf. ZAPFF, Sir 38,1–15, 361: "Wie Mose, so ist auch der Arzt demnach nichts anderes als Vollzugsorgan des heilenden Jhwh, hat also in Mose [...], eine Art Paradigma".
47 WRIGHT, Use, 206.

becomes the paradigm for the long and troubled way through which the disciple must pass to reach the wisdom he desires[48].

In conclusion, Ben Sira has recourse to the Exodus traditions with a predominantly pedagogical purpose (the same goes for the other biblical texts he uses). The selection of passages, the manipulation of the language and the new context where they are inserted reveal the main centres of interest of his teaching on which his disciples have to reflect. At the same time, however, as Wright claims, his use of Scripture "opens a window also into the broader concerns of Jews, or at least a particular segment of elite Jews, in the early second century BCE"[49].

---

48 Cf. CALDUCH-BENAGES, Crisol, 88–94; Trial Motif, 135–151.
49 WRIGHT, Use, 207.

Part III. **Essays on Specific Passages**

Amid Trials: Ben Sira 2,1 and James 1,2

The Book of Ben Sira (Ecclesiasticus) enjoyed great popularity during the first centuries of Christianity, as is well demonstrated in its notable impact on the New Testament writings and the works of the Church Fathers[1]. Although there is not a single explicit quotation from Ben Sira to be found in the New Testament—neither the author nor the book is mentioned—certain terminological and thematic analogies cannot be denied[2]. This article proposes a comparison between Sir 2,1 and Jas 1,2, which are two texts that belong to different eras but are similar in form and content and in the response they seek from hearers or readers.

1 Previous Research on the Book of Ben Sira and the New Testament

At the end of the 18th century Eichhorn remarked that the New Testament authors employed some expressions in common with the work of Ben Sira[3]. Some years later Bretschneider included in his commentary on Ben Sira (1806) an excursus on the use of this book for interpreting the New Testament (*De usu huius libri in interpretando N. T.*), in which he compiled a list of many parallels between Ben Sira and the New Testament[4]. At the end of the 19th century Edersheim maintained that there are passages in various parts of the New Testament where the meaning or the expression recalls Ben Sira[5]. Nevertheless, he did not share the opinion of his predecessors regarding the list of parallel texts. He found the catalogue compiled by Eichhorn incomplete and the one by Bretschneider "altogether fanciful". Starting from the popularity of Ben Sira in Jewish and Hellenistic circles, especially in Alexandria, Edersheim preferred to concentrate his analysis on two works that reflect a certain familiarity with Ben Sira

---

1 See VATTIONI, Ecclesiastico, xxxii–lx; GILBERT, Introduction, 41–47; CALDUCH-BENAGES, Padres, 199–215.

2 Cf. the index of allusions to extracanonical literature in the New Testament compiled by SUNDBERG, Old Testament, 54–55, and the list of literary connections between Ben Sira and the New Testament in DUESBERG–FRANSEN, Ecclesiastico, 18.

3 Cf. EICHHORN, Einleitung, 75–76. For this section, cf. CALDUCH-BENAGES, Nuevo Testamento, 305–316, esp. 306–307.

4 Cf. BRETSCHNEIDER, Liber, 709–722 (Excursus II). In his selection of parallels the author includes many texts from the Pauline letters. Cf. however ELLIS, Paul's Use, 76.

5 EDERSHEIM, Ecclesiasticus, 22–23.

https://doi.org/10.1515/9783110492316-015

even without containing any explicit reference to it. He dealt with the Letter to the Hebrews, representing a Hellenic form of Christianity and the Letter of James, representing a more Jewish form.

From the early 20th century until today, the relationship between Ben Sira and the New Testament has not roused much interest among exegetes. Notable exceptions are Box—Oesterley, as well as Spicq. Box—Oesterley recognize the influence of Ben Sira on the Gospels of Matthew and Luke[6], while Spicq also finds resonances in the Pauline corpus and the Gospel of John, especially in the prologue[7]. Fortunately, in the last fifteen years some studies have appeared that revive the question and offer new insights. We refer to the dissertation by van Broekhoven and the articles by Petraglio, Kurz, Calduch-Benages, Wischmeyer and Dumoulin[8], without taking into account the more specific studies on the relationship between Ben Sira and James, which we will consider below.

2 Ben Sira 2,1–18 and James 1,2–12: Two Exhortations in Times of Crisis

The Letter of James is undoubtedly the NT writing that comes closest to the Book of Ben Sira[9]. Although it would be an exaggeration to speak of literary dependence, there are numerous points of contact that merit closer study. Prominent among these is the literary, thematic and contextual affinity between Sir 2,1–18 and Jas 1,2–12. Both are exhortations belonging to the same biblical tradition, as Frankemölle has demonstrated[10]. In both texts, various trials (sent by the Lord) may serve, even for a faithful and law-abiding person, as a means of interior purification, further growth in faith, and a cause for deep joy (cf. Gen

---

6 Cf. Box—Oesterley, Book, 294–295. Regarding the relation of Ben Sira and Matthew, see Feuillet, Jésus, 161–196, esp. 173–176; Cerfaux, Sources, 331–342, esp. 336–342; Lambert, Joug, 963–969; Rinaldi, Onus, 13–23. Regarding Ben Sira and Luke, see Winter, Observations, 111–121, esp. 114–115 [Sir 48,10 = Luke 1,17].

7 Cf. Spicq, Ecclésiastique, 547; Id., Épîtres, 220–223; Id., Siracide, 183–195.

8 van Broekhoven, Wisdom; Petraglio, Figli e Padri, 489–504; Kurz, Intertextual Use, 308–324; Calduch-Benages, Nuevo Testamento, 305–316; Wischmeyer, Gut und Böse, 120–136; Dumoulin, Parabole, 169–179.

9 Cf. Boon, Dissertatio; and the lists of parallels in Mayor, Epistle, lxxxiii–lxxv, and Chaine, Épître, li–lvii. See also Davids, Tradition, 113–126; Id., Pseudepigrapha, 228–245; Hanson, Use, 526–527; Bauckham, James, 303–317, esp. 306–309.

10 Frankemölle, Thema, 21–47. In contrast with the author, we consider Jas 1,13–18, which deals with the origin of temptation, not of trials, as a transition or bridge between Jas 1,2–12 and 1,19–27.

22,1; Exod 15,25; Deut 8,2; Job 1–2; Tob 12,14; Wis 3,5; Matt 6,13; Luke 11,4)[11]. We do not intend to make a full comparison between Ben Sira and James but will limit ourselves to examining them as witnesses to a society in turmoil.

In Sir 2,1–18 Ben Sira addresses the disciples who are searching for wisdom in a situation of crisis[12] and dedicates a vivid exhortation to patience (2,4, "be patient", μακροθύμησον; 2,14, "endurance", τὴν ὑπομονήν; 2,1 [title in MS 248], "on endurance", περὶ ὑπομονῆς). Sirach 2,1–11 points to a disturbing and alarming reality with such expressions as "in time of adversity" (ἐν καιρῷ ἐπαγωγῆς), "all that befalls you" (πᾶν, ὃ ἐὰν ἐπαχθῇ), "in humiliation" (lit. "in the changes of your humiliation", ἐν ἀλλάγμασιν ταπεινώσεως σου), "in the furnace of humiliation" (ἐν καμίνῳ ταπεινώσεως), "in time of tribulation" (ἐν καιρῷ θλίψεως), together with the terminology of "trial" (πειρασμός) and "purifying" (δοκιμάζω). The same can be said of other, metaphorical expressions such as "cowardly hearts" (καρδίαις δειλαῖς), "slack hands" (χερσὶν παρειμέναις), "a sinner walking on two roads" (ἁμαρτωλῷ ἐπιβαίνοντι ἐπὶ δύο τρίβους), "a feeble heart" (καρδίᾳ παρειμένη), all of which evoke the figure of a Jew who was once a law-abiding person, but who now lets his faith dissolve through immersion in new currents of thought and alien religious practices (2,12–14). Finally, with the exhortation not "to fall into the hands of human beings" (2,18; cf. 2,7), Ben Sira seems to allude to Hellenistic circles and Hellenized Jews who were proliferating in his day. Although it is true that the text nowhere specifies the nature of the trial and that all the above mentioned expressions could be understood as referring to personal experiences of the disciple, be they psychological, moral or religious, it is also true that nothing prevents us from imagining trials caused by the relentless influence of Hellenistic civilization.

Jas 1,2–12 also suggests a crisis that is hard for us to identify in all of its details. In his letter, which seems to be more of a homily, James addresses Christians of Jewish origin living in the Diaspora (lit. "to the twelve tribes of the dispersion", Jas 1,1), i.e. those dispersed in the Greco-Roman world, especially perhaps in the border regions of Syria and Palestine. He exhorts his readers insistently to have joy (cf. 1,2, "perfect joy", πᾶσαν χαράν; 1,9, "let him boast", καυχάσθω; 1,12, "blessed/happy", μακάριος) and patience (1,3.4, "endurance", ὑπομονή; 1,12, "endures", ὑπομένει) in times of trial. This exhortation seems appropriate for a community that has become weak and insufficient because of a lack of wisdom

---

11 Cf. DI LELLA, Belief, 188–204, esp. 196.
12 See DI LELLA, Belief; CALDUCH-BENAGES, Crisol; EAD., Gioiello.

(1,5–6a), a lack of faith (1,6b–8), and a lack of solidarity between the rich and the poor (1,9–11)[13].

One important aspect can be added. After having taught that the gift of wisdom must be sought from the Lord with faith and without wavering, James concludes the lesson with a rapid and incisive description of a person of unstable faith (Jas 1,8). To this end he employs two rare words: δίψυχος ("double-minded")[14], a biblical *hapax*, and ἀκατάστατος ("inconstant, restless")[15], a New Testament *hapax*. In our opinion, this "double-minded man" (ἀνὴρ δίψυχος), who is "inconstant (ἀκατάστατος) in all his ways/actions", symbolizes the conflicts that the Christian communities of the Diaspora experienced (cf. the analogous image in Sir 2,12) because of their continuous internal and external tensions.

A breath of hope concludes both exhortations in the form of implicit praise in the one and of a blessing in the other. With his invitation to let oneself fall into the hands of the Lord, and not into those of human beings, Ben Sira exalts the greatness and mercy of the Lord (2,18), who is compassionate and merciful, forgives sins and saves in times of affliction—as is taught by the ancestral tradition (2,12). James, for his part, takes up the theme of trial again by way of a macarism with a certain eschatological flavor[16] that seems to be associated with the man described in 1,8: "happy the man who endures trial" (μακάριος ἀνὴρ ὃς ὑπομένει πειρασμόν). Once the trial is overcome (lit. "having been proven"), he will receive the crown of life which is a symbol of the recompense of the just and a cause for joy. This is the reward that the Lord has promised to those who love him.

3 Ben Sira 2,1 and James 1,2: Two Promising Openings

The two first verses of the exhortations in question have the following features in common: the use of the vocative, the use of the imperative, and the presence of the noun πειρασμός ("trial" or "testing").

---

13 Cf. FRANKEMÖLLE, Thema, 26.

14 In Jas 4,8, the author again uses the word δίψυχοι, now in synonymic parallelism with ἁμαρτωλοί: "Cleanse your hands, you sinners (ἁμαρτωλοί), and purify your hearts, you double-minded (δίψυχοι)". On this word, see DAVIDS, Epistle, 74–75 (with bibliography).

15 In Jas 3,8 the adjective ἀκατάστατος (cf. Isa 54,11[LXX]) refers to the tongue, which appears as the personification of evil (a "restless" evil). It is noteworthy that Codices C and Ψ read ἀκατάσχετον ("uncontainable"), probably a *lectio facilior* that offers an easier understanding of the text.

16 Cf. the first six of the twelve verses in the Syriac version of Ben Sira that replace 1,22–27 of the Greek text.

Ben Sira 2,1–18 opens with the vocative τέκνον ("child" or "son"), equivalent to the Hebrew word בני ("my son")[17]. This form of address is a very frequent formula in Ben Sira (24x), in the Book of Proverbs (22x), and in the wisdom literature of Egypt, Babylon, and Assyria. Ben Sira employs it to address his young disciples, thereby establishing a family relationship with them (father/son). The vocative τέκνον expresses the authority and at times the affection with which the father/teacher instructs his son/disciple. In twenty-one instances (including our text), this address is found at the beginning of the sentence and indicates the beginning of a theme or a new unit. In Jas 1,2 the vocative ἀσδελφοί μου ("my brothers")[18], immediately after the verb in the second person, mitigates the authoritarian tone of the discourse. This form of address occurs often in the letter: ἀσδελφοί, "brothers" in Jas 4,11; 5,7.9.10; ἀσδελφοί μου, "my brothers" in Jas 1,2; 2,1.14; 3,1.10.12; 5,12.19; ἀσδελφοί μου ἀγαπητοί, "my beloved brothers" in Jas 1,16.19; 2,5. This repetition confers a certain tone of intimacy on the letter, which compensates for the harshness of some texts. This assertion of a familial bond between the sender and recipients continues to puzzle many authors, for whom the formula stands out more on account of its stylistic value than on account of its profound theology concerning Christian fraternity[19].

The conditional clause "son, if you approach to serve the Lord" (Sir 2,1a) expresses the premise upon which Sir 2,1–6 depends. The exhortation continues with a crescendo of imperatives about how to act in times of trial and adversity. The first four concern the interior life of the disciple ("prepare your soul/self", "direct well [straighten] your heart", "remain firm", "do not be anxious", 2,1b–2b), while the last two concern his personal relationship with God ("cling to him", "do not get separated [from him]", 2,3a). To these are added the imperatives in 2,4 ("accept", "be patient") and in 2,6 ("believe in him", "make straight your paths", and "trust in him"). The author of the Letter of James (like the writer of 1 Peter) also begins his instruction with the imperative as the predominant verbal form[20]. The verb ἡγήσασθη (aorist impv. of ἡγέομαι), denoting some sort of mental judgment, could here be translated as "hold, believe, consider". The addressees are called to anticipate, in the present and in the future (aorist impv.), the complete joy that will come from enduring trials or tribulations:

---

17 In Sir 2,7–14 the sage addresses to οἱ φοβούμενοι [τὸν] κύριον ("you who fear the Lord").
18 As L.T. Johnson has noted, the letter resists a completely inclusive translation, especially when the author uses ἀνὴρ ("man" in Jas 1,8.12); cf. however the mention of ἀδελφή ("sister") in Jas 2,15 (JOHNSON, Letter, 176).
19 MARCONI, Lettera, 52.
20 From a total of 1735 words, 43 are imperatives (2.5%), while another 5 are participles that function as imperatives.

"consider [it to be] a perfect joy (πᾶσαν χαρὰν ἡγήσασθη), my brothers, when you are engulfed by all kinds of trials" (Jas 1,2).

Both Ben Sira and James mention the reality of "trial" or "testing" in a vague and imprecise way. The former employs the expression "prepare yourself for trial" (Sir 2,1) with no other specification, while the latter qualifies the noun "trials" (Jas 1,2) with an adjective underlining its general character: πειρασμοῖς ... ποικίλοις can be translated with "various trials" or "trials of every kind" (ποικίλος originally meant "of various colors")[21]. In both texts, however, the context points toward a test of the religious stance of the disciple who wants to serve/ follow the Lord. In Sir 2,1 the instruction "prepare your soul/self" (ἑτοίμασον τὴν ψυχήν σου) is congruent with the statement in Sir 2,17: "Those who fear the Lord (οἱ φοβούμενοι κύριον) ... humble themselves before him (ἐνώπιον αὐτοῦ ταπεινώσουσιν τὰς ψυχὰς αὐτῶν)". A similar message appears in Sir 18,23, where the service of the Lord takes the form of fulfilling a vow: "Before making a vow, prepare yourself" (πρὶν εὔξασθαι ἑτοίμασον σεαυτόν). We are dealing here with the integral preparation of a person to accept and overcome the various trials that inevitably flow from choosing to follow the Lord and that may help to develop a progressive human and religious maturity in the young person. In Jas 1,2–3 the various trials or tribulations of the followers of Jesus should bring them joy because acceptance of such "the testing of your faith" (τὸ δοκίμιον ὑμῶν τῆς πίστεως, 1,3) will purify them. Just as fire is used to separate gold from its impurities, so the Lord cleanses and enriches the faith of his disciples through trials and adversities (cf. 1 Pet 1,7, which uses the same Greek phrase, ἵνα τὸ δοκίμιον ὑμῶν τῆς πίστεως, "so that the genuineness of your faith", to specify the blessings that come to those who stay faithful in times of trial)[22].

4 Conclusion

In accordance with the sapiential tradition of the Old Testament (cf. Prov 3,11–12; Deut 8,5; Wis 3,5; 11,9), Ben Sira sees a God-given trial as a means of education. In Sir 2,1–18 the sage announces from the very beginning the hard reality of trials. A "trial" (πειρασμός) is a kind of adversity that may either build up or tear down the disciple's fear-of-the-Lord. If those who face the crisis react with

---

21 For Johnson, the conjunction ὅταν ("whenever") also contributes to this sense of vagueness and generalization (JOHNSON, Letter, 177).

22 Cf. Sir 2,5: "For gold is tested (δοκιμάζεται) in the fire, and those found acceptable, in the furnace of humiliation".

fear-of-the-Lord and all that is entailed by this attitude, then they will enjoy divine mercy (2,7–11). If, however, they turn away from the fear-of-the-Lord, then they will collapse (2,12–14). Wisdom's disciples have to know that their determination to gain Wisdom (which is in fact a decision for the Lord) entails a series of difficulties that can only be overcome with the help of divine mercy.

As an heir of this sapiential tradition[23], the author of the Letter of James constructs a variation on the theme of trial for the catechesis of the primitive Church. Being familiar with this tradition, he uses many of the same terms and much the same style as the sages in order to offer a message of hope to Christian communities in crisis. In Jas 1,2–12 we see not only the author's familiarity with the tradition he has inherited, but also his specific contribution to it: trials become an occasion for joy because the power of faithful endurance cannot be gained in any other way[24].

Both Sir 2,1 and Jas 1,2 contain the authentic wisdom of a teacher who is always ready to help the disciple in times of difficulty. On the one hand, the teacher displays a sense of reality, for following the Lord inevitably brings trials, but on the other hand, counsels hope and optimism. The teacher offers a solemn warning that those who want Wisdom must suffer, but just as solemnly promises that if they remain faithful in times of trial, their patience will bring them great joy.

---

[23] For the multiple connections of James with the biblical wisdom tradition, see JOHNSON, Letter, 33 note 119.
[24] MARCONI, Lettera, 54.

A Wordplay on the Term *mûsar* (Sir 6,22)

In their commentary on the Book of Ben Sira, also known as the Wisdom of Jesus Son of Sirach or Ecclesiasticus, Hilaire Duesberg and Irénée Fransen make the following observation concerning Sir 6,22:

> The verb *sûr* means to separate. It has nothing in common with *mûsar*, "discipline", but its passive participle, *musar*, has a simple homophony that permits this well-made etymological fantasy. *Mûsar*, discipline, rejects *(sûr)* the fool, and benefits the "happy few"[1].

In fact, this "etymological fantasy" has been used by several authors (Bacher, Lévi, Skehan–Di Lella, Minissale, Mopsik) to explain the meaning of a verse that, in our opinion, is essential for understanding the whole poem. There are, however, other suggestions that must be taken into account. Our aim is therefore to investigate this uncertain etymology and its impact on the interpretation of the text. To do this we will proceed as follows: First, we will situate Sir 6,22 in its context; then we will analyze the verse in question; and, finally, we will focus our attention on the wordplay that the author very likely intended on the basis of a popular, non-technical etymology of the term מוסר.

1 The Search for Wisdom (Sir 6,18–37)

Sir 6,18–37, the third poem about Wisdom in order of appearance in the Book of Ben Sira (cf. 1,1–10; 4,11–19; 14,20–15,10; 24; 51,13–30), describes the disciple's desire for, and pursuit of wisdom[2]. The root חכם (in Gk the noun σοφία) opens and closes the pericope, thus forming a long inclusion (v. 18: חכמה and v. 37: יחכמך). The poem, composed of 22 couplets[3] spread over three stanzas and beginning with the vocative בני, τέκνον (vv. 18.23.32), addresses the disciple who wishes to attain wisdom. The disciple's quest and the trials he must endure are touched by all of the joys and sorrows of love.

The most significant element of the poem is the profusion of images used in it. Through them, Ben Sira wants to illustrate the intense process of searching

---

1 DUESBERG–FRANSEN, Ecclesiastico, 118.
2 ARGALL, 1 Enoch, 60–63; DI LELLA, Search, 188–190; CALDUCH-BENAGES, Trial Motif, 143–145; GILBERT, Sages, 172–177; HASPECKER, Gottesfurcht, 130–131; MARBÖCK, Weisheit im Wandel, 113–118; MINISSALE, Siracide, 46–55; RICKENBACHER, Weisheitsperikopen, 55–72; ROGERS, Ploughing, 364–379; SCHRADER, Leiden, 161–177; UEBERSCHAER, Weisheit, 194–202.
3 Note that there are also 22 letters in the Hebrew alphabet.

https://doi.org/10.1515/9783110492316-016

that is to be undertaken by the disciple. In the first stanza there is an abundance of images from the world of agriculture (vv. 19 – 22), while in the second (vv. 23 – 31) they refer to slavery and love. By contrast, in the third stanza (vv. 32 – 37) the images disappear and are replaced by pieces of advice that culminate in the observance of divine precepts[4]. The Lord only comes in at the end (v. 37cd): "He will make your heart capable of understanding and make you wise in your desires" (Gk: "He will strengthen your heart and you will obtain the wisdom you desire").

1.1 The Search for Wisdom is like Plowing (Sir 6,18 – 22)

The poem opens by announcing the theme (the pursuit of wisdom) in the form of an invitation (v. 18)[5]. Ben Sira invites the young disciple to embrace discipline in order to be able to attain wisdom in old age. This invitation includes two important lessons: firstly, the close relationship between discipline (מוסר, παιδεία) and wisdom (חכמה, σοφία), since there can be no knowledge without discipline; and, secondly, the gradual process of learning, for Wisdom is not acquired overnight; on the contrary, it requires a long and arduous journey that begins in the vigor of youth and ends with graying hair.

From v. 19 on, the world of agriculture comes into play. The relationship between the farmer, or the one who plants, and the land he tills is the same as that between the disciple and wisdom. The relationship is based on effort and reward, just as plowing leads to the harvest and hard work produces good fruit. Wisdom is a fertile field that calls forth care, patience and dedication from the young man who seeks understanding. The disciple is attracted by the fruits of wisdom, but must work to obtain them. The great reward to be gained motivates the laborer, just as the farmer planting the fields hopes to enjoy the harvest at the end of the growing season (cf. 24,19 – 21): "The task is hard but not unbear-

---

4 Cf. the slightly different suggestion by SKEHAN–DI LELLA, Wisdom, 192 and DI LELLA, Search, 188: "The poem may be divided into eight stanzas that form naturally into three groups, each with a thematic unity: vv. 18 – 22; 23 – 31; 32 – 37". Rickenbacher, on the other hand, divides the poem into seven stanzas of three couplets: vv. 18 – 19; vv. 20 – 22; vv. 23 – 25; vv. 26 – 28; vv. 29 – 31; vv. 32 – 35 and vv. 36 – 37 (cf. RICKENBACHER, Weisheitsperikopen, 56 – 57 and also SCHRADER, Leiden, 172 – 173).

5 The entire verse is missing in MS A, and MS C has only conserved the last two words: תשיג חכמה ("you will obtain wisdom"), according to BEENTJES, Book, 96. However, the rest of v. 18 has been found in the newly discovered leaves of MS C; cf. ELIZUR, Two New Leaves, 24.

able"[6]. This very positive relationship between the disciple and wisdom contrasts sharply with the attitude of the fool or the uninstructed (vv. 20 – 21). For the latter, wisdom is (a path) "steep/winding" (עקובה; in Gk: τραχεῖα, "hard") that makes it unbearable "like a heavy stone" (כאבן משא; in Gk: ὡς λίθος δοκιμασίας, "like a testing stone"). That is why he soon throws it off. From the standpoint of the disciple, wisdom is characterized by vitality, dynamism and fruitfulness; for the fool, lag between planting and reaping makes wisdom seem inert and sterile, which inspires rejection instead of attentive intimacy.

The conclusion of v. 22, as we shall see, is rather obscure. The lively and striking images disappear and make way for a claim that seems more like a riddle. The next section is dedicated to this.

1.2 The Name of Discipline (Sir 6,22)

The unexpected mention of discipline (המוסר) in 6,22a forms an inclusion with 6,18a (מוסר), thus delimiting the first stanza of the poem. This statement surprises the attentive reader, because from 6,18b on, wisdom has been the main protagonist. Its relationship with the disciple and the fool has been the main focus. Now, however, Ben Sira speaks about discipline, and especially about its name, in a discourse that at first glance is incomprehensible. The disciple (and the reader) really has to strain to grasp the meaning of each couplet and the relationship between them. Let us consider, firstly, the verse in all its textual forms:

כי המוסר כשמה כן הוא	22a MS A[7]	For discipline, like its name, so it (is):
ולא לרבים היא נְכוֹחָה	22b	it is not *accessible*[8] to many.

σοφία γὰρ κατὰ τὸ ὄνομα αὐτῆς ἐστιν	22a Gk[9]	For wisdom is according to its name:
καὶ οὐ πολλοῖς ἐστιν φανερά.	22b	it is not evident/obvious to many.

---

6 MORLA ASENSIO, Eclesiástico, 49.
7 Beentjes erroneously transcribes כמשה instead of כשמה (BEENTJES, Book, 28.133); see his Errata et Corrigenda, 375.377.
8 On the Hebrew word and its translation, see the discussion in the last paragraph.
9 ZIEGLER, Sapientia, 153.

šmh 'yk ywlpnh	22a Syr[10]	Its name (is) like its teaching:
wlskl' l' mtbḥr'	22b	it is not selected/approved by fools.

Sapientia enim doctrinae secundum nomen est eius	23a VL[11]	For wisdom of teaching is according to its name:
et non multis est manifesta;	23b	it is not evident to many;
quibus autem agnita est	23c	for those who recognize her
permanet usque ad conspectum	23d	it remains until God's visitation.

The versions differ, to a lesser or greater degree, from the Hebrew text because their reference point is not discipline but wisdom. Gk substantially coincides with Hb, except for the subject of the sentence: σοφία[12]. As for Syr, in the first colon, wisdom (*šmh*, "its name" refers to *ḥkmt'* of 6,20)[13] is the subject of the sentence and discipline is the predicate; the translator's free rendering of the second colon is difficult to explain. The corrupt reading of 22a in Syr is followed by VL (*sapientia doctrinae*) that expands it with an addition that has an eschatological character, typical of the long text-form in GkII (cf. 15,8; 23,4; 24,32; 31[34Hb],13). According to Kearns, the expression *Dei conspectus* is not to be understood as the beatific vision of God in heaven but as the visitation at the end of time, i.e. Judgment Day[14].

Leaving the versions aside, let us now focus on the Hebrew text of MS A. In the first colon (22a) scholars differ on the vocalization of כשמה. Some put the vocalization in the feminine[15] and others in the masculine[16]. In the first case, either it is supposed that כְּשְׁמָה refers to חכמה (f. sg. noun), or else מוסר is considered to be feminine because of its assimilation to חכמה; in the second case, כְּשְׁמֹה is in agreement with חמוסר (m. sg. noun), the subject of the sentence, to which the author refers with the masculine pronoun הוא. In fact, מוסר is actually treated as feminine also in Prov 4,13: "Hold on to discipline (הַחֲזֵק בַּמּוּסָר), do not let go of it; keep it (נִצְרֶהָ) because it (הִיא) is your life". From a strictly grammatical

---

10 Calduch-Benages—Ferrer—Liesen, Sabiduría, 86: "Her name is as her teaching and by fools she will not be approved".
11 Thiele, Sirach, 294–295.
12 The reading followed by Smend, Weisheit, 58; Box—Oesterley, Sirach, 336; Marböck, Jesus Sirach, 116.
13 With respect to Gk, Rahlfs reads σφόδρα (Rahlfs, Septuaginta, 387), while Ziegler, following Syr and Arm, infers σοφία (Ziegler, Sapientia, 153). VL: *nimium sapientia*. Cf. Smend, Weisheit, 58.
14 Kearns, Expanded Text, 134–136.262.
15 Peters, Liber, 14; Smend, Weisheit, 58; Kahana, שמעון בן־סירא, 24.
16 Peters, Buch, 62; Segal, ספר, 39; Hartom, בן־סירא, 29.

point of view, both the suffix of the verb נצר and the personal pronoun that follows it should be masculine. Interestingly, however, the feminine gender of חכמה
is maintained because this term is somehow considered synonymous with מוסר:
"In these cases [referring to Prov 4,13 and Sir 6,22a in MS A] *mûsar* is equivalent
to wisdom, and the feminine gender of *hokmâ* is maintained in speaking about
mûsar, though that word is formally masculine"[17].

The same problem appears in the second couplet, where מוסר is still spoken
of in the feminine gender: היא נכוחה. In this case, however, we have the help of
2Q18[18], an incomplete Qumran fragment, with only the last two letters of the last
word of v. 22: נ]כח. Since this is a masculine form (the adjective is נָכֹחַ,
"straight"), it would presumably be preceded by the pronoun הוא. Unlike Shekan
and Baillet, Émile Puech[19] proposes the reconstruction הוא נ]כח, which is consis-
tent with the masculin noun of 22a, המוסר.

The unusual vocalization of the word נכוחה may correspond to the opinion of
those who prefer to read נוֹכְחָה (probably a mistake for נִכְחָה or נוֹכְחָה, Niphal ptc.
of יכח, "discuss", "reason", "justify"), instead of the feminine adjective נְבוֹחָה,
"straight", "straightforward", "flat", "easy", "convenient", "viable" (cf. Prov
8,9)[20]. Now, given that the meaning of יכח in the Niphal does not fit the context,
Peters and Smend, following Bacher, gave the participle a specific meaning of
the Hiphil: "appointed" (cf. Gen 24,14.44)[21]. However, in our opinion and that
of the majority of authors[22], the relation of v. 22 with the preceding verses and
the metaphorical system used there favors reading נְבוֹחָה. Note that this adjective
is precisely the antonym of עקובה (v. 20).

2 Proposed Etymologies of the Term מוסר

All authors, to a greater or lesser extent, strive to imagine the etymology of מוסר
used by Ben Sira that would account for his claim that the word for discipline
reveals the nature of discipline. The first scholar who devoted a specific study

---

17 Fox, Proverbs 1–9, 180. See also, Segal, ספר, 41; Skehan–Di Lella, Wisdom, 191, and
Reymond, Wordplay, 42 note 19.
18 Beentjes, Book, 123.133 (read כה instead of כה); see his Errata et Corrigenda, 376.377.
19 Puech, Ben Sira, 81–82.
20 Here, Wisdom asserts that her words "are all straight (נְבֹחִים) to one who understands".
21 Peters, Text, 25; Smend, Weisheit, 58.
22 The same opinion is held, among others, by Lévi, Ecclésiastique, 35; Peters, Text, 25; Id.,
Liber, 14; Smend, Weisheit, 58; Segal, ספר, 39; Skehan–Di Lella, Wisdom, 193; Mopsik, Sagesse, 98; Reymond, Wordplay, 42 note 20.

to this issue was Norbert Peters; in the late 19th century, he proposed a reconstruction of Sir 6,22 based on Gk:

כי החכמה כשם יהיה   For wisdom is like Yhwh's name
ולוא נודע לרבים   and is not known to many[23].

At that time this reconstruction offered a plausible solution to the enigmatic verse. However, after the discovery of MS A and its publication in 1899[24], Peters himself was forced to withdraw his conjecture in favor of another explanation which, as we shall see later, found several followers[25].

Before presenting our proposal, we will consider the four explanations offered by the authors from the early 20th century until today.

2.1 מוסר and the Verb סור

The noun מוסר is not derived from the verb סור ("turn aside", "depart", "withdraw") but from יסר, which will be discussed later (see 2.4). However, the Hophal ptc. of סור ("what is taken away, removed") actually has the same pronunciation as מוסר. This is what led to the "etymological fantasy" mentioned at the beginning of our study. Thus, although מוסר and סור are not related etymologically, some authors use this alleged relationship to explain Sir 6,22. It was first mentioned by Bacher, who was followed by others such as Lévi, Duesberg—Fransen, Skehan—Di Lella, Minissale, and Mopsik[26]. If, for Duesberg—Fransen, discipline "rejects" (סור) the fool, for Minissale and Mopsik the fool is the one who "rejects" (סור) discipline because it is a burden for him. This coincides perfectly with 6,21: "[Wisdom] is like a heavy stone that weighs down [on a fool] (lit. "over him") and he soon shakes it off/gets rid of it". According to Mopsik, for Ben Sira, the word מוסר means "a designation of the path that leads to wisdom, and in his eyes, this term refers to a verb meaning 'to remove', 'to exclude', because of its difficulty and the effort it requires [...] (6,22)"[27].

---

23 PETERS, Rätsel, 98: "Denn die Weisheit ist wie der Name Yahwe's und nicht vielen ist sie bekannt".
24 SCHECHTER—TAYLOR, Wisdom.
25 PETERS, Text, 25.
26 BACHER, Notes, 277; LÉVI, Ecclésiastique, 34; DUESBERG—FRANSEN, Ecclesiastico, 118; SKEHAN—DI LELLA, Wisdom, 193; MINISSALE, Siracide, 50; MOPSIK, Sagesse, 98 note 1.
27 MOPSIK, Sagesse, 344: "une désignation de la voie qui mène à la sagesse et, à ses yeux, ce terme se réfère à un verbe qui signifie 'écarter', 'exclure', à cause de sa difficulté et des efforts

This wordplay is repeated, according to Skehan–Di Lella, in 51,23ab, in a similar context to 6,22. However, this wordplay depends on introducing some modifications in the text of MS B:

פנו אלי סכלים   Draw near to me, you who are untaught,
ולינו בבית מדרשי   and lodge in my house of study (school).

According to Gk and Syr, סורו אלי ("come to me", lit. "depart to me") should be read instead of [28]פנו אלי and בבית מוסר ("in the house of discipline/instruction") rather than בבית מדרשי. In 6,22 Ben Sira insinuated that מוסר is not directly accessible to all and that its name be understood as withdrawn, remote; then, in 51,23, the sage invites the disciples to "depart" (סור) to him and to lodge in the ("remote") house of instruction[29].

This explanation of the noun מוסר fits perfectly with the statements in the second couplet. This leads to the following interpretation of the entire verse: because of its reserved or remote nature, discipline is not accessible to many.

2.2 מוסר and the Noun מֹסֵר

In the Hebrew text of Sir 6,22a Peters (1902) discovered a wordplay between מוסר ("discipline", from the verb יסר) and מֹסֵר ("chain", "bond", "tie", from the verb אסר)[30], which is reinforced by the presence of מוסרתיה ("her chains" in reference to wisdom) in 6,30 and the corresponding Greek τοῖς δεσμοῖς αὐτῆς in 6,25[31] (cf. also 6,24: τὰς πέδας αὐτῆς, "her stocks" and 6,29: αἱ πέδαι). The relationship between discipline and the stocks is explained in 21,19Gk: πέδαι ἐν ποσὶν ἀνοήτου παιδεία ("for a fool discipline is [like] stocks on his feet").

In his commentary of 1913, Peters uses the same explanation and adds a detail. According to him, in that wordplay one might even see an allusion to the author's lineage, since his name סִירָ[אֶ] comes from אסר ("to bind with ropes

---

qu'elle exige [...] (6:22)". The exact form מוּסָר (Hophal ptc. of סור), meaning "removed", occurs in Isa 17,1.

28 MOPSIK, Sagesse, 333 note 4.

29 SKEHAN–DI LELLA, Wisdom, 578. This hypothesis is adopted from SKEHAN, Acrostic Poem, 388.397.

30 PETERS, Text, 25; ID., Buch, 63; HASPECKER, Gottesfurcht, 130 note 20; MARBÖCK, Weisheit im Wandel, 114; ID., Jesus Sirach, 117–118; MINISSALE, Siracide, 61 (he manifests some hesitation over this explanation); SCHRADER, Leiden, 167; SEGER, Utilisation, 90.94.95.

31 Skehan corrects the text of MS A in accordance with Gk and instead of בתחבולתיה ("in her counsels"), reads במוסרתיה ("in her chains"); SKEHAN–DI LELLA, Wisdom, 192.

or chains"). Here is his comment: "בֶּן סִירָא, puts on the ropes or shackles (אֲסוּרִים) of discipline (מוּסָר)"[32]. The same wordplay is found again in 4,19b (MS A) in the mouth of Wisdom who, referring to the disciple who abandons (סור) her, states: ויסרתיהו באסורים ("and I will punish him with chains/cords")[33].

Like the previous explanation, this interpretation of Sir 6,22a also coincides with 6,22b. In the first case, the reserved or remote nature of discipline made it inaccessible to many; in this case, its demands are chains (or bonds) that stand in the way of the disciple who wants to reach wisdom.

2.3 מוסר and the Verb סתר

While acknowledging that the etymological reference of Sir 6,22 "is not clear", L. Alonso Schökel suggests the rapport between מוסר and מוסתר ("hidden")[34], the Hophal ptc. of סתר ("hide", "conceal", "cover")[35]. This form is also found in 41,14a (MS B): חכמה טמונה ואוצר מוסתר ("concealed wisdom and hidden treasure")[36], at the beginning of an instruction about shame. In support of Alonso Schökel's view, we note that 4,18b (MS A) uses the noun מִסְתָּר ("cache" or "secret"), which is derived from the same verb סתר. To the disciple who listens and is attentive, Mistress Wisdom promises many rewards (cf. 4,15–18), the last of which is that "she will reveal her secrets to him" (וגליתי לו מסתרי)[37].

By emphasizing the hidden and enigmatic nature of learning, this proposal connects better with the Greek version of Sir 6,22b ("to many it is not clear/obvious") than with the Hebrew text, in which the image of the road prevails.

---

32 Cf. PETERS, Buch, 63: "בֶּן סִירָא, legt die Seile oder Fesseln (אֲסוּרִים) der Zucht (מוּסָר) an" (cf. also ibid., 46–47). The name in Syr is given as Bar Asira, son of the prisoner.
33 REYMOND, Wordplay, 50–51, esp. note 49. According to this author, the word אסורים can mean "bonds" (אסור) or perhaps "trial, example" (יסור in post-biblical Hebrew, but spelled איסורא in the Targums).
34 ALONSO SCHÖKEL, Eclesiástico, 164; ID., Símbolos, 269; RICKENBACHER, Weisheitperikopen, 59; in his commentary of 1980, Minissale shows some hesitation over this (MINISSALE, Siracide, 61), while some years later (ID., Versione greca, 50) rejects the suggestion outright.
35 Cf. ZORELL, Lexicon, 562.
36 In fact, however, MS Bmg (חכמה טמונה וסימה מסותרת), practically coincides with MS Masada (כמה טמונה ושימה מסותרת[.]). Instead of מוסתר both manuscripts read מסותרת, a Pual ptc., cf. BEENTJES, Book, 72.115.163.
37 On Sir 4,11–19, cf. among others, SARACINO, Sapienza, 257–272; CALDUCH-BENAGES, Prueba, 35–48; EAD., Trial Motif, 141–143.

2.4 מוסר and the Verb יסר

The final explanation of Sir 6,22 refers to the verbal origin of the word מוסר, i.e. the verb יסר ("educate", "instruct", "punish", "correct")[38]. According to its proponents, Ben Sira merely alludes to the true etymology of the term. In other words, discipline (i.e. the learning of wisdom) entails correction or punishment, which of course comes into play only when necessary[39], for example when the disciple, having heard wisdom's words, freely and voluntarily chooses to abandon her (cf. 4,18). For Ueberschaer, in our text the root יסר connotes "chasten" in both a verbal and physical sense (cf. Prov 22,15: "Folly is close to the heart of a child, but the rod of discipline will drive it far from him"). Undoubtedly, the pursuit of wisdom is an arduous task that involves many duties, sacrifices, trials and even punishment. This side of the coin is certainly not attractive (cf. by contrast Sir 6,28–31 and 15,2–6), but Ben Sira, as a good teacher, does not want to ignore it[40].

According to this proposal, the relationship between the two cola of Sir 6,22, although not fully satisfactory in the opinion of some[41], is coherent and tenable. Because the pursuit of wisdom requires testing, correction and, at times, punishment, it is not an easy undertaking.

3 Conclusion

Agreeing with Smend[42], we maintain that Ben Sira had no intention of discussing the etymology of the word מוסר—which we assume did not require great effort from his listeners or readers—but rather wanted to illustrate, through a clever play on words, the difficulty involved in searching for wisdom and learning from her. In fact, the four interpretations of Sir 6,22 that we have presented

---

38 GLÜCK, Paranomasia, 60; SCHREINER, Sirach, 45; UEBERSCHAER, Weisheit, 200.

39 SCHREINER, Sirach, 45.

40 UEBERSCHAER, Weisheit, 200: "Zurechtweisung bedeutet, so Ben Sira, eben das, was der Begriff sagt—und das ist nicht immer angenehm, ist sie doch auch eine Krisis für das eigene Wollen und die eigenen Zielsetzungen".

41 REYMOND, Wordplay, 42.

42 SMEND, Weisheit, 53: "Eine Etymologie des Namens חכמה oder מוסר sucht man hier übrigens mit Unrecht".

emphasize the dark side of that learning by intimating that it is reserved, remote, demanding, hidden, mysterious and sometimes punitive[43].

Ben Sira likes to play on words in his instructions[44], making use of polysemy, antanaclasis and paronomasia. Other cases of wordplay may have come from the transmission of the text: they seem to be the result of scribal errors or deliberate emendations of the text. Alliteration and the repetition of words or roots are key elements in Ben Sira's humor. According to Reymond, puns usually create euphony and emphasize the connection between a particular verb and an etymologically related object. In some cases, the wordplay is more complex because it plays with the meaning of a particular word and other differing terms exhibiting homophony or having a similar pronunciation[45]. In our view, this precisely is the case in Sir 6,22. At first glance, it seems that Ben Sira is referring to the strict etymology of מוּסָר as a form of the verb יסר, but the sound of the word may also have aroused many other associations: מוּסָר (from סור), מֹסֵר (from אסר), and מוּסְתָּר (from סתר). Ben Sira did not stop to diagram the meaning or multiple layers of meaning in his bon mot; he left the task of interpretation to the judgment of his audience. With this pun, Ben Sira exhibits his mastery of language and artistic sensibility as well as his ability to convey an important message about the way of life that he has cultivated and that he hopes others will follow: learning wisdom is an arduous task reserved for the few. The "linguistic enigma" set before the disciple is an example of the point that it makes. To solve the riddle "demonstrates the dedication one must have in order to acquire wisdom"[46].

---

43 Cf. J. Marböck's commentary on our text: "Mit dem Wort von der Weisheit, die nicht vielen offenkundig ist, betont V 22 Gr ihren elitären, forderndern Charakter, der in dieser Perikope deutlich zur Sprache kommt (vgl. auch Sir 4,17; 15,7; 51,26 sowie 2,1–5 von der Furcht des Herrn), vor allem durch die Verbindung von Weisheit und Bildungsprozess bzw. Zucht, so auch 6,32–33. H^A hat (ursprünglich?) diesen Aspekt betont" (Marböck, Jesus Sirach, 119–120).
44 Seger studies Sir 4,11; 6,22.24; 9,4.8; 14,9; 32(35Hb),21ab; 48,17–25 (Seger, Utilisation, 78–129) and Reymond analyzes Sir 51,19ef; 6,22; 13,10; 3,12–13; 4,9; 7,25; 42,2; 35(32Hb),14; 43,19; 4,19; 40,13; 43,8 (Reymond, Wordplay, 41–53).
45 Cf. Reymond, Wordplay, 42.
46 Reymond, Wordplay, 42.

Poetic Imagery in the Book of Ben Sira: A Case Study of Sir 21,1–10

In 2008, at the Theological Faculty of Sicily in Palermo, Antonino Minissale opened his presentation on the metaphor of "falling" in the book of Ben Sira with these words:

> The study of metaphors is useful to us for understanding not only the style but also the thought of an author. If we are concerned with an author of well-defined identity, as is the case with Ben Sira more than in other books of the Old Testament, the systematic study of a metaphor which runs through all his works will help us to fathom the nature of his personality and the particular sensibility in which his thought is soaked[1].

As far as I know, A. Minissale was the first scholar to devote extensive attention to the poetic imagery in Sirach. He called attention to this subject matter in 1988. Other scholars, such as Jeremy Corley[2], came to share this interest. More recently, I began publishing various studies on the topic[3].

Minissale tended to focus on one metaphor in particular, whereas Corley examined various types of metaphors (zoological, botanical, astronomical, and liturgical), and I attended to a single type of metaphor. However, in this essay I shall treat Sir 21,1–10 as a *case study*. I begin by discussing some formal questions related to the text and then examine significant similes and metaphors, which Ben Sira employs for various types of sin in this religious instruction. The sage's handling of such figurative vocabulary ties his work directly to the sapiential literary genre.

1 Text, Delimitation and Structure of Sir 21,1–10

My analysis of Sir 21,1–10 begins with an examination of the text, the delimitation of its boundaries, and the components of its structure. I do not intend to

---

1 MINISSALE, Metaphor, 253. In his little book Siracide. Le radici nella tradizione (pp. 77–79), which he published twenty years earlier, Minissale made a list of words that Ben Sira employed in a figurative sense. He classified these lexemes in various categories (the world of animals, plants, minerals, nature, human activity, words concerning clothing, objects and various products) but did not provide a more detailed analysis.
2 CORLEY, Similes, esp. 94–106.
3 CALDUCH-BENAGES, Animal Imagery, 55–71; EAD., Garment Imagery, 257–278; EAD. Decoding a Metaphor, 57–72.

https://doi.org/10.1515/9783110492316-017

offer a complete textual and literary analysis of the passage; I provide only essential information on these questions with a view to a more detailed study of the poetic imagery.

1.1 Text and Translation

Since the Hebrew text of Sir 21,1–10 is not available[4], my investigation is based on the Greek version according to Ziegler's edition[5]. Here I provide my own translation, with textual notes.

1   Τέκνον, ἥμαρτες, μὴ προσθῇς μηκέτι
    καὶ περὶ τῶν προτέρων σου δεήθητι[6].

2   ὡς ἀπὸ προσώπου ὄφεως[7] φεῦγε ἀπὸ ἁμαρτίας·
    ἐὰν γὰρ προσέλθῃς, δήξεταί σε·
    ὀδόντες λέοντος οἱ ὀδοντες αὐτῆς[8]
    ἀναιροῦντες ψυχὰς ἀνθρώπων.

3   ὡς ῥομφαία δίστομος πᾶσα ἀνομία[9],
    τῇ πληγῇ αὐτῆς οὐκ ἔστιν ἴασις.

4   καταπληγμὸς καὶ ὕβρις ἐρημώσουσιν πλοῦτον·[10]
    οὕτως οἶκος ὑπερηφάνου ἐκριζωθήσεται.[11]

5   δέησις πτωχοῦ ἐκ στόματος ἕως ὠτίων αὐτοῦ,
    καὶ τὸ κρίμα αὐτοῦ κατὰ σπουδὴν ἔρχεται.[12]

6   μισῶν ἐλεγμὸν ἐν ἴχνει ἁμαρτωλοῦ,
    καὶ ὁ φοβούμενος κύριον ἐπιστρέψει ἐν καρδίᾳ.

---

4 Even if not directly relevant to our passage, we should take note of a fairly recent discovery. In 2007, a bifolium of MS C was discovered containing some fragments (vv. 22.23.26) of Sir 21,11–28, the pericope following ours; cf. Elizur, New Fragment; Ead., Two New Leaves; Egger-Wenzel, Sira-Fragment; Rey, Nouveau bifeuillet; Palmisano, Recente scoperta.

5 Ziegler (ed.), Sapientia. For the Syriac version (Syr), cf. Calduch–Ferrer–Liesen, Wisdom of the Scribe, and for the Latin (Lat), cf. Thiele (ed.), Sirach.

6 Verse 1 is missing in Syr. Before δεήθητι, the Lucianic recension (L[-248]) reads ὁλοσχερῶς ἐπιστρέψας ("after you have been converted from everything"), and Lat adds *ut tibi remittatur*.

7 Syr lacks the image of the serpent which, in the variant of Basil the Great (Hom. 21 [PG 31,541]), is set in close relationship with the woman: ἀπὸ προσώπου γυναικὸς ὡς ἀπὸ προσώπου ὄφεως φεῦγε ("flee from the sight of a woman as from the sight of a serpent"); cf. vv. 3–4 in Syr.

8 Syr reads: "Falsehood is as the teeth of a lion".

9 In Syr, from v. 3 to v. 4, the subject of the phrase is the prostitute.

10 According to Smend (Weisheit, 189), "πλοῦτον ist auffallend, man erwartet, 'Palast', 'Burg', oder 'Stadt'".

11 To avoid the repetition of the verb ἐρημόω in 4b (cf. Rahlfs: ἐρημώσουσιν), Ziegler conjectures ἐκριζωθήσεται (= Syr and Lat).

12 Syr: "and rises before the judge of the ages"; cf. Peters, Buch, 170.

7   γνωστὸς μακρόθεν ὁ δυνατὸς ἐν γλώσσῃ,
    ὁ δὲ νοήμων οἶδεν ἐν τῷ ὀλισθάνειν αὐτόν[13].

8   ὁ οἰκοδομῶν τὴν οἰκία αὐτοῦ ἐν χρήμασιν ἀλλοτρίοις
    ὡς συνάγων τοὺς λίθους αὐτοῦ[14] εἰς χῶμα[15].

9   στιππύον συνηγμένον συναγωγὴ ἀνόμων,
    καὶ ἡ συντέλεια αὐτῶν φλὸξ πυρός.

10 ὁδὸς ἁμαρτωλῶν ὡμαλισμένη ἐκ λίθων,
    καὶ ἐπ᾽ἐσχάτων αὐτῆς βόθρος ᾅδου[16].

1   My son, have you sinned? Do so no more,
    and pray ["seek pardon" is understood] for your past [sins].

2   Flee from sin as from the sight of a serpent,
    for if you get near, it will bite you;
    its [sin's] teeth are lion's teeth
    which destroy human lives.

3   All transgression of the Law is like a two-edged sword,
    there is no healing for its wound.

4   Threats[17] and arrogance strip away wealth;
    thus the house of the proud will be destroyed.

5   The prayer of the poor person rises from his mouth to his [the Lord's] ears
    and his judgment comes swiftly.

6   The one who scorns reproof is on the way of the sinner,
    [but] the one who fears the Lord is converted in his heart.

7   From afar, the presumptuous[18] in speech is recognised,
    but the sensible one is aware of his slipping.

8   The one who builds his house with the money of another

---

13 Syr reads: "the wise man recognises the wicked from afar and immediately puts him to the test".

14 Rahlfs: αὐτοῦ τοὺς λίθους. Cf. SMEND, Weisheit, 191: "Vermutlich gehört αὐτοῦ an das Ende; es ist umgestellt, weil es zu εἰς χειμῶνα nicht passte".

15 In contrast to Rahlfs (εἰς χειμῶνα, "for the winter" = Lat), Ziegler reads εἰς χῶμα, "for the grave" (cf. Syr: "heap of stones," "rubble"). His reading corresponds with the variant in *L'* Mal.: εἰς χῶμα ταφῆς αὐτοῦ, "for the mound of his grave".

16 Lat reads: *et in fine illorum inferi et tenebrae et poena.* Verses 9–10 are very different in Syr: "Like a sandy ascent for an old man's feet (= 25,20), so the strength of the wicked is compared to [eternal] fire. The path of the perverse is a hurdle/obstacle for himself because its end is a deep cistern".

17 The abstract καταπληγμός (Lat: *cataplectatio*), a *hapax* in the LXX, represents a type of human behaviour (the same goes for ὕβρις, Lat: *iniuriae*). It refers to the person who instils terror through threatening acts or words, parading his wealth and his power (cf. WAGNER, Hapaxlegomena, 228–229).

18 Lit. "powerful in words". Skehan—Di Lella (Wisdom, 307), translate as "the ready speaker" (one skilled with his tongue), while others think of gossip: "der Beredten" (SMEND, Weisheit, 190); "chi fa sfoggio di parole" (MINISSALE, Siracide, 113); "der Schwätzer" (SCHREINER, Jesus Sirach, 114). In the light of the context, I prefer rather "presumptuous or arrogant".

is like one who heaps up stones for his grave.
9   The assembly of the evil is a heap of tow,
    and their end is a flame of fire.
    10 The path of sinners is cleared of stones,
    but at its end is the pit of Hades.

1.2 Delimitation

The delimitation of Sir 21,1–10 is partially disputed. There are no disagreements about the beginning. The formula τέκνον ("my son"), together with the initial question ἥμαρτες ("have you sinned?") of v. 1, introduces a new subject. While in the previous passage (Sir 20,27–31) Ben Sira is reflecting on the appropriate use of wisdom, his speech from Sir 21,1 onwards takes on an explicitly religious content. He speaks about sin (ἥμαρτες, v. 1; ἁμαρτίας, v. 2; ἁμαρτωλοῦ, v. 6; ἁμαρτωλῶν, v. 10), understood as the transgression of the Law (ἀνομία, v. 3; ἀνόμων, v. 9).

Defining the end of the text, on the other hand, is more controversial. The majority of scholars[19]—myself included—hold that the passage finishes in v. 10, based on a twofold internal evidence: the cognate terms ἥμαρτες and ἁμαρτωλῶν form an inclusion (vv. 1 and 10); and the conclusive character of v. 10 where the tragic fate of the sinner is revealed. Moreover, verses 11 to 28 treat of a new theme, namely, the contrast between the wise and the fool (cf. Sir 20,13–17 and 20,27–31). Note the similarities between Sir 21,11 and Sir 19,20: both verses mention the close relationship between wisdom, fear-of-the-Lord, and the observance of the Law; and verses function as the introduction to a new textual section (21,11–18; cf. 19,20–30).

Alonso Schökel, Snaith, Morla Asensio and Palmisano proffer a different perspective[20]. They view Sir 21,11 as a concluding verse (with the classic summary of wisdom, fear-of-the-Lord, and Law), which also sets the stage for the following section, on the wise and the fool. Haspecker[21] posits yet another delimitation since he extends this *Gottesfurchtperikope* to v. 12. His argument is based, on the one hand, on the thematic relationship between vv. 11 and 12, which form a con-

---

19 For example, Smend (Weisheit, 187); Box–Oesterley (Sirach, 387); Peters (Buch, 170–171); Spicq (Ecclésiastique, 669); Segal (סב, 125); Minissale (Siracide, 112–113); Shekan–Di Lella (Wisdom, 308); Sauer (Jesus Sirach, 160); Kaiser (Weisheit, 49); Schreiner (Jesus Sirach, 113), and Marböck (Jesus Sirach, 254–255) among others.
20 ALONSO SCHÖKEL, Eclesiástico, 216; SNAITH, Ecclesiasticus, 106; MORLA ASENSIO, Eclesiástico, 108; PALMISANO, Siracide, 205.
21 HASPECKER, Gottesfurcht, 161 note 85.

clusion to the whole pericope, and, on the other hand, on the change of style that begins at v. 13 (with the use of comparisons in almost every verse).

1.3 Structure

Scholars tend to express little interest in the structure of the pericope and seldom justify their division of the text. Nevertheless, one may note this feature in the commentaries: while there is diversity in their manner of arranging the first seven verses, there is a general consensus in viewing Sir 21,8 – 10 as the concluding section of the passage[22]. I preclude discussion of these various delineations while proposing the following structure.

I view Sir 21,1-10 as consisting of three units (vv. 1-3, vv. 4-7, and vv. 8-10) each of which is similar in length[23]. Each of the first two units contains 4 bicola (2+2+2+2) and the third only 3 bicola (2+2+2). In all three, there is at least one term derived from the root ἁμαρτ-: the verb ἁμαρτάνω and the substantive ἁμαρτία in the first; the adjective ἁμαρτωλός in the second; and ἁμαρτωλοί in the third. The first and the third units have these factors in common: a word derived from νόμος (ἀνομία and ἀνομοί respectively); an abundance of images in contrast to the central unit where the language is more doctrinal; and, finally, a negative tone in each individual colon. This last aspect contrasts markedly with the alternation between negative and positive which characterises vv. 4-7. Let us look at it in detail: 4a (-), 4b (+), 5a (+), 5b (+), 6a (-), 6b (+), 7a (-), 7b (+). This confirms the following rhythm: negative/negative, positive/positive, negative/positive, negative/positive.

At the level of content, the first unit (vv. 1-3) is a warning against sin because of its terrible consequences; the second unit (vv. 4-7) describes the contrast between the sinner and the wise person who fears the Lord, and the third unit (vv. 8-10) cautions against the fatal destiny that awaits the sinner.

2 Poetic Imagery in Sir 21,1-10

The profusion of images in Sir 21,1-10 extends throughout Sir 21,1-22,18, the entire section which Di Lella entitles "Sin and Folly of Various Kinds". Just as there

---

22 Cf., for example, SMEND, Weisheit, 187; PETERS, Buch, 170-171; DUESBERG–FRANSEN, Ecclesiastico, 182.184; SAUER, Jesus Sirach, 162; MARBÖCK, Jesus Sirach, 255.
23 Cf. SPICQ, Ecclésiastique, 669-671. He follows the same division of the text but without offering any explanation.

is a predominance of *yeš*-proverbs ("There is…") in Sir 19,20–20,26, so our section is distinguished by a series of "sentences with vivid comparisons" (*Sentenzen mit plastischen Vergleichen*)[24] beginning from v. 2 (there are about twenty in total). I now focus on those images of Sir 21,1–10, which are outstanding for their rich texture[25].

2.1 Serpent's Bite, Lion's Teeth (Sir 21,2)

21,2a ὡς ἀπὸ προσώπου ὄφεως φεῦγε ἀπὸ ἁμαρτίας·
21,2b ἐὰν γὰρ προσέλθῃς, δήξεταί σε·
21,2c ὀδόντες λέοντος οἱ ὀδόντες αὐτῆς
21,2d ἀναιροῦντες ψυχὰς ἀνθρώπων.

After the exhortation to avoid sin and to take up the path of conversion (Sir 21,1), Ben Sira describes sin's pernicious power and devastating effects by means of two images from the animal world: the serpent and the lion. The first image is in fact a simile (note the presence of ὡς at the beginning of 21,2a). The sage urges his student to flee from sin, just as one flees from the serpent as soon as one sees it. He goes on to explain the reason (cf. γάρ in 21,2b) for his warning (surely obvious to all his listeners): if one gets near a serpent, one will not be able to escape its bite (δήξεταί σε).

The biblical tradition teaches that the dangerous nature of serpents is due to the way in which they attack, which is wholly without warning (Qoh 10,8), and to their ability to inject lethal poison into a wound (Num 21,6.8.9). In Sir 21,2ab, without mentioning the poison[26], the sage emphasizes the deadly bite, of which even snake charmers were sometimes victims (Ps 58,4; Jer 8,17; Sir 12,13). In various texts, the serpent's bite or poison refers to a range of elements including: the military power of a tribe (Gen 49,17), the wicked state of humanity (Deut 32,33; Ps 140,4), the excesses of wine (Prov 23,32), the day of the Lord (Amos 5,19), and the foreign oppressor (Isa 14,29). This is but a small selection of referents for the serpent figure.

However, the mention of the serpent in Sir 21,2ab points in particular to Gen 3,1–5. Here "the most subtle of all the wild creatures which God had made" (v. 1)

---

24 Haspecker, Gottesfurcht, 162.
25 We shall pass over the images belonging to the second unit of the passage: the "house in ruins" (ἐκριζωθήσεται, v. 4) and the "sliding of the tongue" (ὀλισθάνειν, v. 7).
26 The only text where the sage mentions the serpent's poison is Sir 25,15: "There is no poison worse than that of the serpent and no hatred worse than that of a woman" (Ziegler's edition).

is personified as speaking with the woman and inducing her to sin. Ben Sira makes no direct allusion to the Genesis account, but this is true to his way of using Scripture[27]. Thus, it is highly probable that Gen 3,1– 5 was the principal source of inspiration here. Sauer rightly notes, "There as here, the approach of the serpent brings with it temptation and transgression. There as here, it is a matter of life or death"[28].

The image of the serpent's bite gives way to that of the lion's teeth as the metaphor of sin (Sir 21,2cd). By contrast with 21,2ab, here the sage avoids using any particle: the first colon contains the image "its [sin's] teeth [are] lion's teeth", and the second brings it into focus with a participial phrase: ἀναιροῦντες ψυχὰς ἀνθρώπων ("which destroy human lives"). In addition to its roar, the lion is distinguished for its ferocity, two qualities which classify it among the most dangerous of animals. "The lion roars: who will not fear?" is the threat which the prophet launches against Israel (Amos 3,8); "Save me from the lion's jaws" prays the psalmist in his distress (Ps 22,22a). Instead of the roar, the jaws or the claws, Ben Sira mentions the lion's teeth[29], perhaps to graphically illustrate its dangerous nature which is exceeded only by the wicked woman![30] In Joel 1,6, the teeth of the lion refer to a "a nation powerful and without number", a metaphor which the prophet employs to indicate the devastating plague of locusts (cf. 1,4); and, in Ps 57,5, the psalmist laments that he is lying among lions (understood as his enemies) whose teeth are spears and arrows that destroy, dismember and devour their prey. Returning to the book of Ben Sira, among the eight texts that mention the lion (Sir 4,20; 13,19; 21,2; 25,16; 27,10; 27,28; 28,23; 47,3), Sir 27,10 is only other instance in which sin is compared to the lion (cf. Sir 21,2cd). If, in Sir 21,2cd, the sage focuses attention on the lion's teeth, in 27,10 he presents the lion as lying in wait for his prey (cf. Gen 4,7). In the same way, sin lies in wait for the evildoers (lit. "those who practise injustice")[31].

The serpent and lion imagery provide striking illustrations of the constant threat that sin represents for human beings. Its attack is unexpected and violent,

---

27 Cf. GILBERT, Reader of Genesis, 90.

28 SAUER, Jesus Sirach, 161: "Dort wie hier bewirkt die Nähe der Schlange Versuchung und Vergehen. Dort wie hier geht es um Leben oder Tod".

29 The strong teeth of the lion are made up of three types, which allow them to choke their prey, break its bones and devour its flesh.

30 Cf. Sir 25,15: "I prefer to dwell with the lion and the dragon than to dwell with a treacherous woman".

31 Cf. Sir 27,28: "Ridicule and reproach for the proud, revenge lies in wait for him like a lion".

and its effects are lethal. The conclusion is obvious: the only way of avoiding the danger is to steer clear of it.

2.2 Two-edged Sword, Incurable Wound (Sir 21,3)

21,3a   ὡς ῥομφαία δίστομος πᾶσα ἀνομία,
21,3b   τῇ πληγῇ αὐτῆς οὐκ ἔστιν ἴασις.

Sir 21,3 presents images of a different nature from the preceding ones. With the mention of a two-edged sword and a wound that cannot be healed, we pass from the animal world to the world of war[32]. However, this is not the only change. If the grammatical subject of the phrase in 21,2 was ἁμαρτία ("sin"), it is now replaced by ἀνομία ("iniquity", "transgression or disobedience of the Law")[33]. In view of the context and the parallel arrangement of the text, the two terms may be considered almost synonymous. As in 21,2a, we have a simile. The comparative particle ὡς in the first colon introduces the image of the sword, which is developed further in the second colon with the image of the wound. In both cola, the striking feature is the tone of the discourse, which is almost drastic and which does not contemplate any exception. The adjective πᾶσα before ἀνομία in 21,3a accentuates the contrasting negative formulation of the phrase in 21,3b (τῇ πληγῇ αὐτῆς οὐκ ἔστιν ἴασις). Both elements reveal the grave consequences of acting against the Law.

Ben Sira compares all iniquity to a two-edged sword. This is obviously a military image because the sword—especially, the sharp two-edged variety—is an instrument of warfare for destroying the enemy. However, as Joshua Berman rightly notes, the expression recorded in the text "bears a metaphorical or figurative meaning pertaining to orality"[34].

In Sir 21,3, Segal rightly claims that ῥομφαία δίστομος is probably a translation of the Hebrew חרב פיות ("sword of mouths"). This identical expression occurs in Prov 5,4 and, with slight variations, also in Judg 3,16 (חרב ולו שני פיות, "a sword, which has two mouths") and in Ps 149,6 (חרב פיפיות, "a sword of

---

32 A possible parallel to Sir 21,1–3 might be 1QH[a] XIII, esp. lines 11–13, which connect the three motifs: lions, snakes and swords (cf. QIMRON, Dead Sea Scrolls, vol. 1, 76). I am indebted to Noam Mizrahi for this information.
33 According to Segal (ספר, 125), ἀνομία here is translating פשע as in 41,18 (cf. MSS B and Mas). In 49,2, it translates הבל (cf. MS B), and, in 23,11 and 46,20, texts where the Hebrew is missing, Segal reconstructs שבועה and עון respectively (SEGAL, ספר, 139.321).
34 BERMAN, Sword of Mouths, 299.

mouths")[35]. All these texts employ the expression "sword of mouths" as a word-play in a context related to the power of the word; but in Sir 21,3 the expression appears in a different context, namely in an instruction about sin (cf. Gen 3,24). On the other hand, the oral image is also present in our text. It surfaces first in 21,2 (the bite of the serpent and the teeth of the lion) and continues in 21,3a with the "sword of the mouth". Unfortunately, the "overt oral reference"[36] of this expression is lost when it is translated into our modern languages with the blade replacing the mouth[37]. In his commentary on Prov 5,4, Fox[38] observes, "The blade of a sword is thought of as a 'mouth' that 'eats' its victims"; it is precisely under this image that Ben Sira conceives of sin. In the words of Joshua Berman, the two-edged sword is represented as a "mouth of danger"[39].

Like the bite of the serpent or the lion, the wound (πληγή) of the two-edged sword is incurable (Sir 21,3b) and leads inexorably to death. In chapter 25, Ben Sira twice mentions a wound of the heart (πληγὴ καρδίας). However, in spite of being represented as one of the worst possible injuries (Sir 25,13) and compared to the treacherous woman (Sir 25,23Gk)[40], this mutilation does not exhibit a letal effect equivalent to an injury produced by the two-edged sword. According to Alonso Schökel, the double blade signifies that the sword "wounds the one who tries to wound, i.e. it turns against the one who handles it"[41]. Sauer's comment follows the same line:

"No movement of the sword remains without effect. It works whichever way it is wielded, forward or backward. Consequently, however, the one who wields the sword is taken by surprise at that very moment. If he is not careful, he can be injured slightly by the backward movement"[42].

---

35 The word פיפיות is an intensive plural form of the substantive פה. Cf. BERMAN, Sword of Mouths, 300.

36 BERMAN, Sword of Mouths, 302.

37 German: "ein zweischneidiges Schwert"; Dutch: "ein tweesnijdend zwaard"; French: "un glaive à deux tranchants"; Spanish: "una espada de doble filo"; Italian: "una spada a doppio taglio"; Catalan: "una espasa de doble tall".

38 FOX, Proverbs 1–9, 192.

39 BERMAN, Sword of Mouths, 298.

40 On the other hand, MS C does not mention the "wound of the heart": "Hesitant hands and wobbly knees; [such a] woman will not render her husband happy".

41 ALONSO SCHÖKEL, Eclesiástico, 215: "De dos filos porque hiere al que intenta herir, se vuelve contra el que la emplea".

42 SAUER, Jesus Sirach, 161: "Keine Bewegung des Schwerts bleibt ohne Erfolg. Sowohl beim Vorwärtshauen als auch beim dem Zurückholen enfaltet es seine Wirkung. Davon ist er aber gleichzeichtig auch der betroffen, der dieses Schwert führt. Ist es nicht achtsam, dann wird er sich durch die zurückholende Bewegung selbst leicht verletzen können".

The same "boomerang" effect is brought about by iniquity: it turns against the one who practises it.

2.3 Stones for the Grave (Sir 21,8)

21,8a ὁ οἰκοδομῶν τὴν οἰκία ἀυτοῦ ἐν χρήμασιν ἀλλοτρίοις
21,8b ὡς συνάγων τοὺς λίθους αὐτοῦ εἰς χῶμα.

After the pause in Sir 21,4–7, the comparisons return. From v. 8 to v. 10, images from the world of nature (stones [twice], tow, fire, path, pit), follow one another in a crescendo until they reach a climax with the pit of the abyss. Ben Sira employs these comparisons to illustrate how the behaviour of the wicked person (8a: the unjust rich person; 9a: the lawless; 10a: the sinners) is destined for final ruin. If in the first unit the figurative language depicted sin, now the emphasis is placed on the persons who commit it, that is sinners[43].

As noted above[44], the first image (heaping up stones), presents a textual problem (εἰς χειμῶνα vs. εἰς χῶμα). The housebuilder is someone who enriches himself (cf. Ps 49,17) with money that does not belong to him; he acquired the finances unjustly. He is compared (cf. ὡς in 8b) to one who heaps up stones[45]. Debate surrounds the purpose of this action. Are the stones being heaped up "for winter" or "for the grave"?

Scholars who choose the first reading[46] differ in their interpretation of the image. Some interpret "stones" as synonymous with "wood", which is what is really needed in winter for protection against the cold. In this case, heaping up stones for winter would illustrate foolish and improvident behaviour. "A particularly useless way to prepare for the future", comments Snaith[47]. Others associate the expression "heaping stones" with the construction of a house. But since the winter is not a suitable time to build because of the damp, the resulting structure would be precarious, unstable, and impermanent.

---

43 I thank Benjamin G. Wright for this observation.
44 Cf. note 15.
45 Wilhelm Smits sees in this verse an allusion to the deaths of Achan (Josh 7,26) and Absalom (2 Sam 18,17), cf. SMITS, Ecclesiasticus, 228.
46 KNABENBAUER, Commentarius, 238; SPICQ, Ecclésiastique, 670; MORLA ASENSIO, Eclesiástico, 108.
47 SNAITH, Ecclesiasticus, 106.

The second, more common reading views the text as referring to customary burial mounds for the deceased in antiquity[48]. The internment process consisted of digging a ditch, depositing the corpse in it, and then covering it with earth and stones. In this case, the image communicates a harsh message: to accumulate wealth at the cost of others is equivalent to signing one's death warrant. Di Lella comments that those who behave in this manner "...are building their 'funeral mound' (v. 8), i.e. they shall die prematurely as punishment for their exploitation of the disadvantaged"[49].

Besides these two readings, a few scholars take the passage to mean that the stones are heaped up as rubble. For example, Israel Peri[50] views the ruins (*Schutthaufen*) as the stones that piled up in the wadis of the Negev as a result of the winter rains. The stone heaps remained in the wadis throughout the dry summer months, until the next rainy season. It would be useless, therefore, to gather stones and place them in wadis because, in the end, the force of the water would disassemble them. The same goes for the goods of the unjustly wealthy. Schreiner too translates the Greek text with "for a heap of rubble" (*für einen Schutthaufen*). Here is his commentary[51]:

> This is a graphic statement of the instability and transitory nature of a life plan that is not solidly built, but rests on injustice. Such a house has no durable existence since it is founded on money that one has misappropriated.

All three readings are plausible. However, the second ("for his grave") is preferable since it best suits the context in which sin is linked with death. There is a noteworthy sequence of images in the second cola (8b: stones for his grave; 9b: flame of fire; 10b: pit of the abyss).

---

48 Cf. SMEND, Weisheit, 191; BOX—OESTERLEY, Sirach, 388; PETERS, Buch, 172; SNAITH, Ecclesiasticus, 106; SEGAL, ספר, 125 (like Smend, he supposes the Hebrew גל, "heap"); ALONSO SCHÖKEL, Eclesiástico, 216; SKEHAN—DI LELLA, Weisheit, 304; SAUER, Jesus Sirach, 160; KAISER, Weisheit, 50; MARBÖCK, Jesus Sirach, 249.
49 SKEHAN—DI LELLA, Wisdom, 309.
50 PERI, Steinhaufen, 420–421; cf. DUESBERG—FRANSEN, Ecclesiastico, 182: on the basis of the Syr ("ruins") the authors translate "for his own ruin".
51 SCHREINER, Jesus Sirach, 115: "Bildhaft wird die Unbeständigkeit und Vergänglichkeit eines Lebensentwurfs ausgesagt, der nicht solide gebaut ist, der sich auf Unrechtstaten stützt. Mit Geld, das einem nicht gehört, das man an sich angebracht hat, läßt sich kein dauerhaftes Haus, keine Existenz gründen".

2.4 Heap of Tow, Flame of Fire (Sir 21,9)

21,9a στιππύον συνηγμένον συναγωγὴ ἀνόμων,
21,9b καὶ ἡ συντέλεια αὐτῶν φλὸξ πυρός.

Segal's reconstruction of the Hebrew in Sir 21,9a reflects a fine play on words[52]. Ben Sira compares an assembly of the wicked (συναγωγὴ ἀνόμων, צבור רשעים) with a heap of tow (στιππύον συνηγμένον, נערת צבורה). Tow is a bundle of waste fibres derived from the thrashing of plants like cotton, hemp or linen. Since this harvest refuse has little worth, it is customarily thrown on the fire (cf. Dan 3,46). This processing typifies the destiny of the ἄνομοι ("wicked", "evil", "transgressors", "lawless"). Being insubstantial as a bundle of tow (cf. Judg 16,9), they will end up being consumed by fire. This is the irrevocable judgment of the sage: "[and] their end is a flame of fire" (Sir 21,9b).

The connection between the wicked/sinners and fire is frequent in biblical texts. In Sirach, we find it in 8,10[53], in 11,32Gk[54] and in 16,6. In the first two texts, fire expresses the irresistible and destructive passion that overwhelms the sinner; in 16,6, on the other hand, it becomes an instrument of divine judgement (due to the divine passive voice): "Against an assembly of sinners (בעדת רשעים, ἐν συναγωγῇ ἁμαρτωλῶν) fire is kindled, upon a godless people wrath blazes up". The careful reader discerns here an allusion to Num 16,30–35[55], which recounts God's punishment against the rebels who are revolting against Moses and Aaron: first, the earth swallows alive Dathan, Abiram and their families, and, then, a fire comes forth from God and devours Korah's band. Fire, as an expression of divine judgement, is also found in several prophetic texts, among which we would point to Isa 1,31 on account of its figurative affinity with Sir 21,9. This Isaian text compares the man, who gains power through his trust in idols, with tow in a manner that corresponds with the typifying of evil in our text. Both share the same fate: burning until they are consumed.

Ben Sira's message in Sir 21,9 does not presuppose any divine intervention or contain an eschatological inference; to the contrary, it is situated within the human horizon. One may summarise his point in this way: the wicked are as

---

52 SEGAL, ספר, 125.
53 MSS A and D: "Do not profit through the possessions of the wicked (Gk: kindle not the coals of a sinner), lest you be burned in the flame of his fire".
54 MS A: "A spark of fire kindles many coals and a man of Belial lies in wait (Gk: a sinner plots) to shed blood".
55 Cf., also, Num 11,1–2, where fire is employed by God as a punitive instrument in response to the laments of the people.

unstable and transitory as a bunch of tow in the fire. Di Lella goes further in his commentary: "The images of tow and blazing fire are meant to suggest the impermanence of the wicked in the present life, and not their punishment by fire in the afterlife"[56].

2.5 Path without Stones, Deep Pit (Sir 21,10)

21,10a ὁδὸς ἁμαρτωλῶν ὡμαλισμένη ἐκ λίθων,
21,10b καὶ ἐπ'ἐσχάτων αὐτῆς βόθρος ᾅδου.

We have reached the climax of a passage marked by the contrast of life and death. It is no accident that the instruction proper begins with the verb "sin" (21,1a) and concludes with an image connected with death (21,10b: "the pit of Hades").

In Sir 21,10a, the behaviour of sinners is compared to a path ὡμαλισμένη ἐκ λίθων. This expression is not easy to translate because of the rare combination ὁμαλίζω ("make even") + ἐκ. As Smend noted[57], ἐκ λίθων seems to reflect an error derived from the Hebrew מאבן. I view the Greek expression as referring to a path cleared of stones, and therefore easy to negotiate[58]. Segal understood it in this way in his reconstruction of the Hebrew text: he renders ὡμαλισμένη ἐκ λίθων with מסקלת ("free from stones", Pual ptc. of the verb סקל; cf. Isa 62,10; 5,2)[59]. However, not all authors follow this interpretation. Some[60] view this expression as referring to a paved path, covered with stones. The Latin text reads thus: *via peccantium complanata lapidibus*[61]. Others offer a variant of

56 Skehan–Di Lella, Wisdom, 309.
57 Cf. Smend, Weisheit, 191; Stummer, Via peccantium, 44. Moreover, MS 248 reads ὑπό λίθων and Maximus the Confessor, ἀπό λίθων (Sermo 70 [PG 91,1013]).
58 Cf. Smend, Weisheit, 191: "von Steinen frei gemacht"; Duesberg–Fransen, Ecclesiastico, 184: "levigata di pietre"; Kaiser, Weisheit, 50: "von Steinen befreit"; Sauer, Jesus Sirach, 162: "glatt und ohne Steinen"; Schreiner, Jesus Sirach, 115: "frei von Steinen".
59 Segal, ספר, 125. Cf. Kahana, בן־סירא, שמעון בן־סירא 483: מסקלת מאבן; Hartom, בן סירא, 76: מחלקת מאבנים.
60 Peters, Buch, 170 and Marböck, Jesus Sirach, 249: "mit Steinen gepflastert"; Morla Asensio, Eclesiástico, 108: "bien pavimentado".
61 Cf. Stummer, Via peccantium, 40–44. On the question of the paved roads of the period, cf. Smend, Weisheit, 191; Stummer, Via peccantium, 41; Sauer, Jesus Sirach, 162.

this reading and picture a path made of polished stones[62]. While different in details, the three readings express the same message: the path of sinners is apparently a path without obstacles, and thereby convenient to negotiate.

In Sir 21,10b, the author completes the image by disclosing its negative side. The path is smooth but deceptive because it leads to death. The text seems to have been inspired by Prov 14,12 (=16,25) even if the vocabulary is different: "There is a path that appears to be right, but in the end, it leads to the pathways of death". The link between the life (moral conduct) of a person and the point of arrival of this path (death) associates this text with Sir 21,10b. The same goes for Prov 7,27 (cf. 5,5; 9,18) where the dwelling of the adulterous woman is presented as the abode of the underworld, a place from which there is no return: "Her house is the road of the kingdom of the dead which leads down into the dwellings of death". The expression βόθρος ᾄδου ("the pit of Hades") probably translates שחת שאול ("the pit of Sheol/the abyss")[63]. Thus, Sheol is described in spatially: it is like a pit, a ravine into which one can fall (cf. שוחה עמקה, "deep pit" in Prov 22,14; 23,27). As heir to the Old Testament tradition, Ben Sira conceives Sheol not as a place of retribution (cf. 21,11b[Lat]), but as the abode of the dead[64]. One's existence there is inert and devoid of significance, without even the possibility of praising God (cf. Ps 6,6; 88,5). Such is the life and fate of sinners[65].

3 Conclusion

Themes in Sir 21,1–10—such as sin, repentance, and pardon—are not new (viz., for example, Sir 17,25–32). The outstanding feature of this passage is not its content but its literary form. In these ten verses, after the fashion of a good teacher, Ben Sira magnificently combines the proverbial element with the theological one. In other words, he speaks of sin by using powerful figurative language. Drawn from the worlds of animals, nature and war, the images are familiar to

---

62 Cf. MINISSALE, Ecclesiastico, 115: "di pietre lisce"; ALONSO SCHÖKEL, Eclesiástico, 216: "de piedras lisas"; SKEHAN—DI LELLA, Wisdom, 304: "smooth stones"; PALMISANO, Siracide, 205: "di pietre levigate".
63 Cf. SEGAL, ספר, 125.
64 Differently, MARBÖCK, Jesus Sirach, 256. He discovers in the text, together with 21,9b and 7,17bGk, "ein Blick in eine Welt jenseits des Todes".
65 In Sir 21,9–10 Duesberg—Fransen (Ecclesiastico, 184) glimpse "gli empi 'che hanno abbandonato la Legge dell'Altissimo' (41,8) adottando i costumi ellenici".

his audience[66]. Each of them has a negative value and a distinctive form. Ben Sira's conviction about the danger of sin evokes his desire to persuade his pupils. As Di Lella puts it, with these words he wants to evoke in his readers "a horror of sin"[67].

We share Di Lella's reading in a pedagogic key, while further attending to the use of poetic imagery and its rhetorical functions. In line with the older sapiential tradition (cf. Proverbs), Ben Sira loves to employ verbal images in his teaching. In this way, he establishes analogies between the natural world and the life situations of people. The two orders are mutually distinctive, but paradoxically very close. He may have had numerous reasons for adopting figurative language in his teaching. According to Corley, these would include "indicating structure, making the sayings memorable, intensifying the emotion, provoking thought, expressing ambiguity, and creating beauty"[68]. In our opinion, the images in Sir 21,1–10 confirm all these motives in one way or another.

Together with other criteria, the concentration of images in vv. 2–3 and 8–10 indicate the structure of the pericope. The play on words in v. 9 (heap of tow/assembly [i.e. heap] of the evil) facilitates memorisation of the text. The tremendous force of the images in vv. 2–3 (serpent's bite, lion's teeth, incurable wound) provokes the audience to both fear—in the face of sin—and also reflection. The same holds for vv. 8–10. The recourse to funereal or macabre images (grave, flame of fire, pit of the abyss) instils a profound respect for the dark perspective of death while simultaneously pressing for a serious examination of behaviour. Finally, the image of a path cleared of stones as a metaphor of the sinner's behaviour (21,10a) generates an interpretative ambiguity that is immediately resolved in 21,10b.

In conclusion, the instruction on sin in Sir 21,1–10 is a fine illustration of various didactic resources in Ben Sira, including: direct and personal address, contrast between the wise man and the sinner, proverbial style, variety of syntactical forms. The passage highlights his poetic sensitivity, as evinced in his use of a series of very attractive images. All these elements combine to ensure the sage's success in effectively transmitting his teaching without compromising its literary beauty.

---

66 SAUER, Jesus Sirach, 200: "Es ist nicht verwunderlich daß er auf einem Löwen zu sprechen kommt; den dieser lebte zu seiner Zeit noch in dichten Untergehölz im Jordangraben, war also auch damals noch eine gefürchtete Erscheinung".

67 SKEHAN–DI LELLA, Wisdom, 309.

68 CORLEY, Similes, 94. He is referring to both the similes and the sound patterns.

Emotions in the Prayer of Sir 22,27–23,6

Ben Sira is more interested in prayer than any other wisdom writer. In his book of wisdom, we find several instances of advice on how to pray and some real prayers too, both individual and communal. Sir 22,27–23,6 is a good example of individual prayer. The person who recites the prayer (a disciple, or perhaps Ben Sira himself) asks God for help in avoiding sins of the tongue and unruly passions. After giving a short survey of research and an annotated translation of the Greek text, we will focus on the close relationship between the language of the prayer and the emotions it reveals. We intend to show that Ben Sira uses the emotions expressed in Sir 23,4–6 with a pedagogical intent. In other words, emotions in prayer may also lead to wisdom[1].

1 Survey of Research on Sir 22,27–23,6

The prayer of Sir 22,27–23,6 had been virtually unexplored until 1978. In that year, a programmatic article by Pancratius C. Beentjes appeared in the Dutch journal *Bijdragen*[2]. According to him, this prayer is not an isolated corpus in the book. On the contrary, it is closely related to its context. The prayer consists of two stanzas (22,27–23,1 and 23,2–6) structured in parallel, the themes of which are developed and elucidated in the subsequent verses. The theme of the first stanza (the sins of the tongue) reappears in 23,7–15, and the theme of the second stanza (the sins of passion) continues in 23,16–26. The last verse (23,27) functions as a conclusion not only to the prayer but also to the entire unit (22,27–23,27)[3].

After a long pause of twenty-six years, two well-known scholars again focused their attention on our text. I am referring to Maurice Gilbert and Friedrich V. Reiterer. Their contributions in the first volume of the *Deuterocanonical and Cognate Literature Yearbook* series (DCLY 2004) are worthy of our attention[4]. Gilbert deals with the prayers in Sir 22,27–23,6; 33(36Hb),1–13a.16b–22; 51,1–12, and with some other related texts seeking to emphasize the function

---

1 The subject of emotions has recently attracted significant attention from Old Testament scholars. See for instance: Smith, Heart, 427–436; Krüger, Emotions, 213–228; Schroer–Staubli, Emotionswelten, 44–49; Wagner, Emotionen; Id. (ed.), Aufbrüche; van Wolde, Sentiments, 1–24; Gillmayr-Bucher, Emotion, 279–290; Egger-Wenzel–Corley (eds.), Emotions.
2 Beentjes, Sir 22:27–23:6, 144–151.
3 See Calduch-Benages, Ben Sira 23:27, 186–200.
4 Gilbert, Prayer, 117–135; Reiterer, Gott, 137–170.

https://doi.org/10.1515/9783110492316-018

and the relevance of prayer according to the sage. For Ben Sira, "prayer is first of all a matter of teaching" and "even the three explicit prayers we read in his book are strictly related to the context in which he teaches"[5]. The same idea was expressed in 1995 by James L. Crenshaw, namely, "prayer and instruction go hand by hand"[6], and proposed again by Werner Urbanz in 2009[7]. As far as Sir 22,27 – 23,6 is concerned, Gilbert highlights its universal value and states that because of it "Ben Sira can invite the reader to assume its truth, before hearing his teaching about faults in speaking and misdeeds of uncontrolled sexuality. In any case, the link between prayer and teaching is the main point"[8].

Reiterer concentrates on Sir 22,27 – 23,6, both in the Greek and the Syriac version. His in-depth poetic and stylistic analysis is used as an instrument to shed light on the content of the prayer. In Reiterer's view, the two parallel stanzas of the prayer deal with human instincts, i. e. the impulses or powerful motivations coming from a subconscious source. The powerful impulses to which Ben Sira refers belong to different human domains such as speech (*die Fertigkeiten der Redeanlage*), thought (*die Fähigkeiten des Denkens*) and desire (*die Triebebene*), in particular the desire for food, the sexual drive and the desire for power. Even if the three domains just mentioned are—when not properly controlled—all considered sources of danger for the disciple/human being, they are not equivalent. Reiterer glimpses, in the way they are presented, a crescendo of intensity: starting from the power of the tongue, it passes at a second stage to self-control through fixed ideas and, finally, it concludes with the autonomous force of desire[9].

Furthermore, we should note two contributions by Werner Urbanz. The first is his doctoral dissertation on prayer in the book of Ben Sira (2009)[10]. In chapter 6, on the interaction between praise and lament in Ben Sira's prayer texts, he devotes three pages to Sir 22,27 – 23,6. In his analysis, he highlights two relevant characteristics of this prayer for self-control, i. e. the absence of traditional prayer vocabulary and the various formal and thematic links it shares with other texts related to prayer (that is, explicit prayers and teachings on prayer).

Urbanz's second contribution, published in DCLY 2011, explores human emotions toward God in prayer, as evidenced in Ben Sira's work[11]. In the last

---

5 GILBERT, Prayer, 117.
6 CRENSHAW, Restraint, 216.
7 Cf. URBANZ, Gebet, 247.
8 GILBERT, Prayer, 118.
9 Cf. REITERER, Gott, 158 – 159.
10 See footnote 7.
11 Cf. URBANZ, Emotionen, 150 – 151.

part of his study, the author considers Sir 22,27–23,6, esp. vv. 4–6, from an anthropological perspective, focusing on emotions and their relevance in the search for wisdom.

Lastly, these verses have also been the subject of careful analysis in Ibolya Balla's doctoral dissertation on family, gender and sexuality in Ben Sira (2011). In her analysis, she is mainly concerned with Ben Sira's attitude toward unruly passions and self-control. This is her conclusion: "Sir 23:4–6 does not condemn sexual desire *per se*; on the one hand, it implies that desires should not be excessive [in] controlling one's life, on the other, it warns against having illicit desires"[12].

2 Text, Translation and Textual Notes

Since the Hebrew text of Sir 22,27–23,6 has not survived[13], we shall present the Greek version according to the edition of Ziegler[14] together with our translation accompanied by some textual notes.

22,27 Τίς δώσει ἐπὶ στόμα μου φυλακὴν
      καὶ ἐπὶ τῶν χειλέων μου σφραγῖδα πανοῦργον,
      ἵνα μὴ πέσω ἀπ' αὐτῶν[15]
      καὶ ἡ γλῶσσά μου ἀπολέσῃ με;
23,1 κύριε πάτηρ καὶ δέσποτα ζωῆς μου,
      μὴ ἐγκαταλίπῃς με ἐν βουλῇ αὐτῶν[16],
      καὶ μὴ ἀφῇς με πεσεῖν ἐν αὐτοῖς.

2 τίς ἐπιστήσει ἐπὶ τοῦ διανοήματός μου μάστιγας
      καὶ ἐπὶ τῆς καρδίας μου παιδείαν σοφίας,
      ἵνα ἐπὶ τοῖς ἀγνοήμασίν μου μὴ φείσονται
      καὶ οὐ μὴ παρῇ τὰ ἁμαρτήματα αὐτῶν,

---

12 Balla, Ben Sira, 164–167, esp. 167.
13 A medieval Hebrew rhymed poem based on Sir 22,22cd–23,9b survives in a Cairo Genizah manuscript (MS Adler 3053) housed at the Jewish Theological Seminary of America in New York. It was first published together with Genizah MS E. See Marcus, Hebrew, 223–240.
14 Ziegler, Sapientia, 230–231. The blank space used to indicate the two main stanzas of the text is ours. For a comparison with the Syriac version, see Reiterer, Gott.
15 With codex V, MS 46, Lat and Syr. All the other witnesses read ἀπ' αὐτῆς, referring to "my tongue" in v. 27c (cf. Rahlfs, Septuaginta, 415).
16 With Lat and Syr some authors (Peters, Alonso Schökel, Skehan—Di Lella, Gilbert, Kaiser, Schreiner) read v. 1b after 4a, the result being that all the verses are bicola; cf. esp. Gilbert, Livres, 190; Id., Vetus Latina, 5–6. Others (Smend, Sauer, Minissale, Reiterer), conversely, read the text as it is; cf. esp. Reiterer, Gott, 155.

3   ὅπως μὴ πληθυνθῶσιν αἱ ἄγνοιαί μου
    καὶ αἱ ἁμαρτίαι μου πλεονάσωσιν
    καὶ πεσοῦμαι ἔναντι τῶν ὑπεναντίων
    καὶ ἐπιχαρεῖταί μοι ὁ ἐχθρός μου,
GkII ὧν μακράν ἐστιν ἡ ἐλπὶς τοῦ ἐλέους σου;[17]
4   κύριε πάτερ καὶ θεὲ ζωῆς μου,
    μετεωρισμὸν ὀφθαλμῶν μὴ δῷς μοι
5   καὶ ἐπιθυμίαν ἀπόστρεψον ἀπ' ἐμοῦ·
6   κοιλίας ὄρεξις καὶ συνουσιασμὸς μὴ καταλαβέτωσάν με,
    καὶ ψυχῇ ἀναιδεῖ μὴ παραδῷς με.

22,27 Who will set a guard over my mouth
       and upon my lips a seal of prudence[18],
       so that I may not fall through them
       and my tongue may not destroy me?
23,1   Lord, Father and Ruler of my life,
       do not abandon me to their whim
       and let me not fall because of them.

2   Who will apply lashes to my thoughts
       and to my heart the rod of discipline,
       so that my errors may not be spared,
       nor my[19] sins overlooked;
3   lest my errors be increased
       and my sins multiply;
       and I fall before my adversaries
       and my enemy rejoice over me?
GkII   *For them, the hope of your mercy is distant*[20].
4   Lord, Father and God of my life,
       do not give me a brazen look[21]
5   and remove from me passion.
6   Let neither sensuality nor lust[22] overcome me
       and do not surrender me to shameless appetite.

---

17 Besides this colon, MS 248 and the Lucianic Recension have other expansions. See ZIEGLER's edition, Sapientia, 230 – 231; MARBÖCK, Jesus Sirach, 264 – 265.

18 Lit. "a seal suited to all necessities". Skehan–Di Lella translate "an all-purpose seal" (SKEHAN–DI LELLA, Wisdom, 318).

19 With some authors (Alonso Schökel, Morla Asensio, Gilbert) we change "their" into "my" to fit in the context. See the reading given by Skehan–Di Lella: "the sins of my heart" (SKEHAN–DI LELLA, Wisdom, 318).

20 On this addition, cf. BUSSINO, Additions, 356 – 360.

21 Lit. "a lifting up of the eyes".

22 Lit. "longing of the belly" or "cohabitation".

3 A Prayer for Self-control

Sir 22,27–23,6 is the only individual prayer of petition in the book of Ben Sira (cf. the collective plea for the deliverance of Israel in 33[36Hb],1–22). Apart from the parallel structure of the stanzas, the most striking formal feature of the prayer is the use of the 1st p. sg. (cf. the verbal forms and the occurrences of μου [11x], με [5x], μοι [2x] and ἐμοῦ [1x]). As in the Psalms, the literary "I" helps the readers to identify themselves with the person who recites the prayer, or at least to feel a strong empathy with that person.

But about whom are we speaking? Who is this person? Who is hiding behind this literary "I"? The fact is that we do not have enough information to give a satisfactory answer. Georg Sauer, for instance, in his commentary defends the autobiographical character of the prayer. To put it in his words, "It should be emphasized that this prayer is a very personal prayer, which Ben Sira offers with exactly the same attitude of the psalmists who express their own laments and petitions in a highly personalized manner"[23]. Conversely, Gilbert argues that the content of the prayer, which applies to everyone, "does not allow us to see any autobiographical note relevant to Ben Sira"[24]. Thus, the prayer could have been recited by Ben Sira himself or by one of his disciples. Another possibility, and this is the one we prefer, is to go beyond the discussion on the real identity of the literary "I", focusing instead on the universal dimension of the prayer.

As far as the content of the prayer is concerned, there are two ideas that deserve special attention. First, the idea of self-control or self-discipline in the use of the tongue and in the sexual domain. To illustrate this idea the author makes use of such images as "guard", "seal", "lash" and "rod"[25]. Applied to the mouth, the lips, the mind and the heart, they would prevent the person in trouble from abuses of the tongue and excessive sexual appetite. Second, the idea of sin and the sinner's downfall. The reader notices the variety of terms the author uses to refer to sin: τὰ ἀγνοήματα, αἱ ἄγνοιαι ("deviations", "errors", "mistakes"), and τὰ ἁμαρτήματα, αἱ ἁμαρτίαι ("sins", "faults", "errors")—all concentrated in vv. 2–3[26]. Allusion is made to the sins of the tongue and the sins of the flesh

---

23 SAUER, Jesus Sirach, 171: "Es ist dabei hervorzuheben, daß dieses Gebet ein sehr persönliches Gebet ist, das Ben Sira ganz in der Haltung der Psalmenbeter zeigt, die ihre Klagen und Bitten in persönlicher Weise und in singularischer Form vortragen".
24 GILBERT, Prayer, 118.
25 Some of the imagery here derives from Ps 141,3. Compare also 4QInstruction (4Q412 1.5).
26 Reiterer observes the balanced combination of neuter nouns (ἀγνοήμασιν, ἁμαρτήματα) and feminine nouns (ἄγνοιαι, ἁμαρτίαι) in 23,2 (cf. REITERER, Gott, 154).

through the metaphor of falling[27]. The threefold repetition of the verb πίπτω (to fall) in 22,27; 23,1 and 23,3 should be noted. On all the three occasions, "falling" is to be understood in a metaphorical sense. According to Minissale, in 22,27 and 23,1 "falling" concerns the misuse of the tongue, i.e. the action of speaking unguardedly, not its consequences[28]. Indeed, these are never mentioned in the prayer. In 23,3 "falling"—associated here with disorderly passions—becomes extremely dangerous since it happens in front of the supplicant's enemies who see his downfall and rejoice over it.

In Crenshaw's words, "The prayer's motivation arises from fear of being abandoned to merciless foes or to one's own base inclination"[29]. Having lost the capacity to control both one's tongue and sensual desire, the supplicant decides to turn to God and ask for help. Although the addressee of the prayer is not at first explicitly mentioned, his identity will be soon revealed in 23,1 ("Lord, Father and ruler of my life") and confirmed in 23,4 ("Lord, Father and God of my life"). Did God hear the prayer? Did God answer the afflicted supplicant? Our text does not speak about God's reaction but we know from many passages in the book that Ben Sira considers prayer as a true dialogue between individuals and God[30]. One example will suffice. Ben Sira's prayer of 51,1–12 records his urgent appeal to God for help—he was most probably at the point of death—and the immediate reaction of the only one who could rescue him from such a distressing situation: "I raised my voice from the dust, my plea from the gates of the netherworld. I extolled the Lord, You are my Father! My mighty savior, only you! Do not leave me in this time of crisis, on a day of ruin and desolation! [...] Then the Lord heard my voice; listened to my plea! He redeemed me from evil of every kind and kept me safe in time of crisis" (vv. 9 – 10.11cd.12ab)[31].

4 The Language of Emotion

As do many other Old Testament prayers and Psalms, Sir 22,27 – 23,6 describes the supplicant's inner experience with the language of emotion. Such a language, as W. Urbanz has rightly noted[32], is concentrated in the last verses of the second stanza, i.e. vv. 4 – 6. In these verses, the author depicts unruly

---

27 See MINISSALE, Metaphor, 253 – 275, esp. 255 – 256.
28 Cf. MINISSALE, Metaphor, 256.
29 CRENSHAW, Restraint, 219.
30 Cf. URBANZ, Emotionen, 153.
31 The translation is taken from SKEHAN–DI LELLA, Wisdom, 561.
32 Cf. URBANZ, Emotionen, 150.

passions and some of their symptoms by way of the following expressions: μετεωρισμὸν ὀφθαλμῶν, ἐπιθυμίαν, κοιλίας ὄρεξις, συνουσιασμός and ψυχῇ ἀναιδεῖ.
This is not the first time that Ben Sira warns against uncontrolled passions. He
has done so in Sir 6Hb,1–3 (6Gk,2–4) in a rather general way and, more specifically, in Sir 18,30–19,3. Let us now consider the five expressions mentioned in
Sir 23,4–6.

4.1 Μετεωρισμὸν ὀφθαλμῶν

That the eyes reflect the feelings of the heart is well illustrated in the expression
μετεωρισμὸν ὀφθαλμῶν (lit. "a raising up of the eyes"), usually translated as
"haughty eyes". Although arrogance, pride or haughtiness is its usual meaning
(cf. Isa 2,11; 5,15; Ps 131,1 and Prov 21,4), in our text μετεωρισμὸν ὀφθαλμῶν
should be interpreted differently, i.e. with a sexual connotation[33]. This is supported by the context of the prayer (23,2–6 and 23,16–26) and the vocabulary
of the last verses. Hence "haughty eyes" refers to the brazen eyes that fuel the
fire of lust in the heart[34]. For instance, in 26,9 the same expression concerns
the sensual woman who arouses men's desire with her enticing eyes and (probably decorated) eyelids[35]. The connection between eyes and desire is also attested, among others, in Prov 6,25 and in 4Q184/4QWiles[36]. In Prov 6,25 the youth is
warned to avoid being seduced by the beauty and by the staring look of the adulteress: "Do not desire her beauty in your heart, or let her take you in with her
glances (lit. "eyelids")". In 4Q184/4QWiles, the wicked woman, just by looking
at him with a seductive gaze, captivates her victim: "Her eyes glance keenly hith-
er and thither, and she wantonly raises her eyelids to seek out a righteous man
and lead him astray and … to make him stumble" (1,13–14)[37].

---

33 Cf. SMEND, Weisheit, 204: "Der Uebermut ist der Anfang aller Sünde (Ps. 18,28. Pr. 6,17),
namentlich auch der Unzucht" (Arrogance is the beginning of all sins [Ps 18,28; Prov 6,17], especially fornication).
34 Cf. SKEHAN–DI LELLA, Wisdom, 322.
35 Cf. BALLA, Ben Sira, 52.222.
36 Cf. BALLA, Ben Sira, 52.
37 On 4Q184/4QWiles; cf. the recent study by LESLEY, Wiles, 107–142.

4.2 Ἐπιθυμίαν

In the Septuagint ἐπιθυμία (and also ἐπιθυμέω) usually has a neutral meaning, i.e. desire, passion, or appetite. Only in certain cases does it acquire moral or sexual overtones as, for instance, in Num 11,34; Prov 6,25, or in the story of Susanna[38]. In the book of Ben Sira ἐπιθυμία occurs nine times, most of them in the first part of the book (3,29; 5,2; 6,37; 14,14; 18,30.31; 20,4 and 23,5). In our view, only on four occasions (5,2 and 33[36Hb],27 are not clear enough) is the term used with a sexual meaning: in 18,30.31 (warnings against lustful appetites), in 20,4 (the example of a eunuch lusting for intimacy with a maiden) and in 23,5. As far as our text is concerned, the addition by Clement of Alexandria confirms what we have just said: "Remove always from your servant vain hopes (ἐλπίδας κενάς), and indecent desires (ἐπιθυμίας ἀπρεπεῖς) turn aside from me, and sustain always him who wishes to serve you"[39]. Perhaps the Alexandrian author considered that ἐπιθυμία denoted a notion too general and decided to add the adjective ἀπρεπής ("improper", "indecent", "unseemly") to render it more specific and thus unequivocal. The short annotation by Rudolf Smend in his commentary seems to take the same line: "[ἐπιθυμίαν] ist ungenügend"[40].

4.3 Κοιλίας ὄρεξις

The expression κοιλίας ὄρεξις, which literally means "longing of the belly", is generally interpreted in two different ways. Some authors understand it as gluttony, i.e. either the habit of eating or drinking to excess, or the inordinate desire that moves somebody to behave in such a way[41] (cf. the warning in Prov 23,20). Many others, following Syr ("lasciviousness of the flesh") and Lat (*ventris concupiscentias*), interpret the expression as referring to lustful or carnal desires, and translate accordingly[42]. See, for example, the translation by Skehan—Di Lella: "the lustful cravings of the flesh". In the light of the context, the second interpre-

---

38 Cf. Dan[LXX] 13,32.56 and Dan[Th] 13,8.11.14.20.56.
39 See HART, Text, 341. The addition is also found in GkII, but here ἀπρεπεῖς is lacking. See ZIEGLER, Sapientia, 231.
40 SMEND, Weisheit, 205.
41 Alonso Schökel, Sauer, Reiterer, Balla.
42 Peters, Minissale, Skehan—Di Lella, Morla Asensio, Gilbert, Kaiser, Schreiner, Marböck, Urbanz.

tation is in our view to be preferred[43]. Most illuminating is Fox's observation on drunkenness and gluttony when commenting on Prov 23,20: "These two vices may represent dissolute behaviour generally and include sexual wantonness"[44].

4.4 Συνουσιασμός

The noun συνουσιασμός is a *hapax* not only in Ben Sira but also in the Septuagint. Like συνουσία, it derives from the verb σύνειμι ("to be/live with"), its first meaning being "cohabitation". This is, however, a neutral meaning that does not fit in the context of Sir 23,4–6. Should we perhaps consider καὶ συνουσιασμός as a later addition to the text?[45] From a stylistic point of view, it introduces an irregularity in the sentence pattern, i.e. 23,6a is the only colon in which the verb has two objects. Further, the second object makes the colon excessively long compared with the others. In any case, what must be decided is the meaning of the *hapax* in our text. For most authors συνουσιασμός has sexual connotations and, according to Gilbert, it is a euphemism for coitus (cf. ὕπνος in Wis 4,6 and 7,2)[46]. Such an interpretation is supported by the context of the prayer.

Apart from Sir 23,6, συνουσιασμός is also attested in two later pseudepigrapha[47]. In both writings it refers to sexual intercourse. The first attestation is found in 4 Maccabees, a philosophical book on the primacy of reason over the emotions (gluttony, lust, malice, anger, fear and pain). In chapter 2, the author praises the temperate Joseph because through mental effort he overcame sexual desire: "For when he was young and in his prime for intercourse (πρὸς συνουσιασμόν), by his reason he nullified the frenzy of the passions" (4 Macc 2,3). The second attestation belongs to the Aramaic Levi Document[48], traditionally known as the Aramaic Testament of Levi or Aramaic Levi. In chapter 6, devoted to priestly teaching on purity, Levi teaches his son with these words: "First of all, beware my son of all fornication (ἀπὸ παντὸς συνουσιασμοῦ, מן כל פחז) and impurity and of all harlotry".

---

43 Cf. also Sir 18,30: "Do not follow your lusts (τῶν ἐπιθυμιῶν σου), but restrain your desires (τῶν ὀρέξεών σου)".
44 Fox, Proverbs 10–31, 735.
45 So SMEND, Weisheit, 205.
46 GILBERT, Sexualité, 1031.
47 Cf. BALLA, Ben Sira, 166.
48 Cf. GRENFELL—STONE—ESHEL, Levi Document, 74.

4.5 Ψυχῇ ἀναιδεῖ

In this expression, the noun ψυχή acquires a negative connotation due to the adjective ἀναιδής[49] which means "wanting in self-respect and restraint"[50]. This connotation is made evident in the translations. Instead of soul, mind or spirit, scholars tend to use terms such as appetite, passion or desire. In the book of Ben Sira, ἀναιδής occurs 3 times (23,6; 26,11 and 40,30), two of which are in a sexual context. We are referring to 23,6 and 26,11 (cf. Prov 7,13). The latter verse belongs to Sir 26,5 – 12, a passage where the sage combines his instruction on the evil wife with fervent warnings addressed to the young disciple. This is an example: "Be on guard against her bold eye (ἀναιδοῦς ὀφθαλμοῦ), and do not wonder if she betrays you" (v. 11). The bold eye stands for seduction. As far as 23,6 is concerned, it is our contention that, like the terms previously examined, ψυχῇ ἀναιδεῖ also refers to the sexual domain and can be rendered with impudent or shameless appetite. Once more the context of the prayer has proved to be decisive.

5 The Function of Emotions

Two articles on emotions in the Old Testament have proved to be very illuminating in our study of the emotional dimension of Sir 23,4 – 6. Their authors are well-known OT scholars, Mark S. Smith and Paul A. Krüger[51]. Thanks to them, we become acquainted with different social-scientific approaches to emotions and their respective theories, mainly the physiological and cognitive approaches. Some of their insights have been very useful in exploring the role that emotions play in Ben Sira's prayer.

Emotions have a wide range of functions, both in the physiological and the psychological domain. Needless to say, we do not claim to deal with the whole variety of functions. Our attention will be directed at only three of them, that is, those significant for our purpose.

49 Cf. ἀναίδεια, "effrontery", "impudence", "shamelessness" (Sir 25,22): *hapax* in Ben Sira and LXX; see WAGNER, Hapaxlegomena, 149 – 150.
50 MURAOKA, Lexicon, 39.
51 SMITH, Heart, 427 – 436; KRÜGER, Emotions, 213 – 228.

5.1 Emotions and the Physical Body

In recent years, psychologists have become increasingly interested in embodiment based on the assumption that thoughts, feelings and behaviour are grounded in bodily interaction with the environment. The embodiment of feelings has been deeply explored by anthropologist Michelle Z. Rosaldo[52], who placed her study of emotions in the context of cultural analysis. In her view, emotions are not involuntary or irrational reactions that escape our control but are the result of a deliberate and engaged body. Emotions can be explained as "embodied thoughts"[53] in which the thought/affect dichotomy dissolves. In other words, emotions/body goes as an inseparable unit.

This inseparable unit is essential to Israelite anthropology in which there is no difference between the mental and the physical functions since both depend on the body organs. In fact, many texts of the Old Testament attest a close connection between body parts, especially the heart and liver/innards, and the experiencing of emotions.

In Sir 23,4–6[54] the person who recites the prayer mentions the eye (raising of the eyes), the belly (longing of the belly) and the soul (shameless appetite). According to our reading of the text, the three body parts are related to the sphere of emotions, and specifically to sexual drive. In the first expression, sexual desire is connected to sight (the gleam of passion), in the second expression it is placed in the interior of the human body, where emotions are strongly felt (the seat of passion), and in the third, it is considered from a moral perspective.

5.2 Emotions and Communication

Emotions are highly important in interpersonal communication. According to psychologists, "every human interaction, drawing near as well as drawing apart, is emotionally determined"[55]. Recent studies in the field investigate the functions that emotions play in communication. Emotions are not isolated feelings that humans experience in the interior of the heart totally separated from external communication with others. On the contrary, emotions "serve a

---

52 ROSALDO, Anthropology, 137–157.
53 ROSALDO, Anthropology, 143.
54 In Sir 22,27: mouth (στόμα), lips (χειλέων), and tongue (γλῶσσα), and in 23,2: heart (καρδίας).
55 AICHHORN–KRONBERGER, Nature, 515.

communicative purpose by conveying specific emotional intentions to others"[56]. In other words, we communicate with others also through our emotions. In addition, emotions may help people to adapt to a new situation, to cope with environmental challenges and to be ready for an effective response in the face of unexpected changes.

Mark S. Smith applies this new view on emotions to Israelite prayer (esp. the Psalms), reaching the conclusion: "Applied to ancient Israelite cult, emotions expressed in prayer convey the speaker's pain and joy to the community and God. The emotions expressed in the Psalms help those who pray to move to appropriate action. Prayer ultimately enables people who undertake it to move beyond the emotions which they feel and express"[57].

The emotions expressed in Ben Sira's prayer do not communicate pain or joy to the community (the group of disciples) and God, but the fear of falling, i. e. falling into the grip of desire. The supplicant feels in his heart a consuming passion that not only puts at risk his moral integrity but makes him the sport of his enemies as well. Aware of these dangers and not being strong enough to control his impulses alone, he puts all his confidence in God, the ruler of his life, the only one who can prevent him from downfall. Anyone who listens to this prayer will be encouraged to look for a similar solution.

5.3 Emotions and Pedagogy

The articles by Smith and Krüger deal with anthropological, psychological and psychobiological concepts. This reflects the choice of their authors. Thus, it is not surprising that they do not speak of pedagogy at all. Yet we argue that in Israelite prayers, especially in wisdom books, besides the functions above mentioned, emotions serve a pedagogical purpose as well. This concerns in particular the book of Ben Sira, a compendium of wisdom teachings addressed to all who seek to become wise, especially the young disciples who attended his school.

Any disciple can learn a lot from Ben Sira's prayer and from the person who recites it, especially from his emotions, the way in which he expresses them, the way he handles them and the message they convey. When listening to this prayer, the disciple understands that the fear of falling and succumbing to his enemies has determined the supplicant's decision and action. Emotions are thus very

---

56 KRÜGER, Emotions, 216.
57 SMITH, Heart, 436. See also GILLMAYR-BUCHER, Emotion, 279 – 290.

powerful; they cannot be ignored nor underestimated. At the same time, he realizes the fatal consequences of uncontrolled desires, which may lead the person to sin, and—what is still more important—of the incompatibility between sin and wisdom. As Gilbert puts it, "the one who wishes to be wise, either the master or his disciple, will ask the Lord for his help to avoid sin"[58].

In conclusion, emotions in Sir 23,4–6 are a source of teaching. They have an impact on the relation between the supplicant and God, on the relation between the supplicant and the community/disciples, and on the relation of the supplicant with himself. The supplicant learns from his emotional experience and so do the ones who listen to his prayer. It does not matter in which direction the communication goes; it is always emotional. In our text, to be attentive to the emotions, to recognize them and to learn from them is a way to reach wisdom.

---

58 GILBERT, Prayer, 132.

Ben Sira 23,27—A Pivotal Verse

We do not know whether Ben Sira was in a bad mood when he wrote his passage on the adulterous woman (!), as Duesberg—Fransen assert in their commentary[1], but it is a fact that, in Sir 23,22–27, the sage becomes very intransigent and his discourse acquires some very harsh tones. It is sufficient to compare this pericope with the previous one on the adulterer. While in Sir 23,18–21 the emphasis falls on the relationship between the adulterer and God who sees everything and whose attention nothing escapes, in Sir 23,22–27 the offence of the adulterous woman becomes the passage's centre of attention and its consequences are described in every detail. It is obvious that Ben Sira is more severe with the adulterous woman than with the adulterous man.

At any rate, our purpose is neither to make a comparative study of these two texts nor to investigate the different presentation of the two characters. We intend, rather, to focus our attention on Sir 23,22–27, dwelling not on the triple aspect of the offence of adultery nor on the dramatic consequences suffered by the children conceived in adultery, but on the function of the last verse, a question that is usually passed over by scholars. The analysis of Sir 23,27 will be preceded by a brief presentation of previous studies on the entire passage, by our annotated translation of the Greek text and by an investigation into its literary composition. We shall conclude with some observations on 23,28(GkII).

1 Previous Studies on Sir 23,22–27

The first scholar to make a detailed study of Sir 23,22–27 was W. C. Trenchard in his 1982 monograph on Ben Sira's vision of women[2]. The fourth chapter of this work ("Woman as Adulteress and Prostitute") begins precisely with the analysis of our text, with the exception of the last verse. This analysis is preceded by a discussion of the immediate (23,7–27[3]) and remote (23,16–27) context. Sir 23,16–27 is devoted to various sexual misdemeanours and particularly to

---

1 DUESBERG—FRANSEN, Ecclesiastico, 50.
2 TRENCHARD, View on Women, 95–108.
3 For the analysis of this section, he follows faithfully the proposal of HASPECKER, Gottesfurcht, 165–167. It should be noted that in the Greek text the above-mentioned section is entitled παιδεία στόματος, "discipline of the mouth", a title which interrupts the indisputable unit of 22,27–23,27 (the title is absent in codices S, A and O-V, in several minuscules as well as in the Syriac version). Beentjes and Marböck doubt its authenticity (cf. BEENTJES, Sir 22,27–23,6, 144.149–150; Full Wisdom, 89; MARBÖCK, Jesus Sirach, 270).

https://doi.org/10.1515/9783110492316-019

adultery, whether it was committed by a man or a woman. Convinced of Ben Sira's misogyny, Trenchard takes the side of the adulterous woman, looking for a reason to explain and to justify her behaviour. And the result? Contrary to the seductress ("the strange/foreign woman") of Proverbs (cf. Prov 2,16; 5,3; 7,5; 6,24), who supposedly is moved by sexual desire, the adulterous woman is moved by a desire for motherhood. Trenchard presupposes therefore that the adulterous woman did not have any children by her husband. Since the legitimate way had been unsuccessful, the woman tries the illegitimate one. In order to have a child, she does not hesitate to put her own life at risk. In Warren C. Trenchard's words, "the woman's primary motivation for her act or acts was the desire to have children of her own. The prospect of an heir was probably her rationalization, since an heir would be an asset to her husband"[4].

Claudia V. Camp's approach to our text and to the question of women in general in Ben Sira is different. In a well-known study published in 1991, she rereads Sir 23,22 – 27 from the point of view of the "honor-shame complex", a determining element in understanding Mediterranean anthropology. Within this framework, "social identity is construed with particular attention to sexual relationships, such that male 'honor'—the highest, and a highly contested, good—is determined essentially by the control men exercise over women's 'shame', that is her sexuality"[5]. This control by the man, however, is not limited to the sphere of sexuality but embraces also the area of the family economy. It is the husband, and he alone, who has to maintain his house, his wife and his children (cf. Sir 25,21 – 22). As far as our passage is concerned, behind the sage's detailed description, Camp glimpses a rather unusual family situation, "the wives of poor men engage in sexual activity with wealthy patrons in order to help support their families. The issue here not would be the desire of childless women for heirs but the shameful necessity for a man—in order to avoid shame!—to accept as legitimate the fruit of his wife's labor for another"[6].

Finally, we should note the contribution of Ibolya Balla in her doctoral thesis on family, gender and sexuality in Ben Sira (2011). In its fourth chapter, on illicit or inadvisable sexual behaviour, Balla devotes some pages to Sir 23,22 – 27[7]. In her analysis, she makes continual references to the passage on adultery with the aim of showing the differences between both texts, especially with regard to the gravity and consequences of the woman's adultery. In addition to infringing the divine law and introducing an illegitimate heir into the family, the

---

4 TRENCHARD, View on Women, 100.
5 CAMP, Understanding Patriarchy, 2.
6 CAMP, Understanding Patriarchy, 28.
7 BALLA, Family, 134 – 137.

woman's transgression lies in beginning a sexual relationship on her own initiative. In other words, in the situation described she does not perform a passive sexual role, as one would be expect, but an active one. It is not, therefore, the husband who is controlling the sexuality of the woman but *vice versa*. Now clearly, in a patriarchal society such as that of Ben Sira, such sexual freedom on the part of the woman could only be considered a grave offence against the honour of the husband. According to Balla, "it appears that Ben Sira takes a pragmatic approach to the issue of extramarital intercourse, where transgression against the divine law is an important factor, but transgression at communal level resulting in shame, and including the reversal of the normal order of things (female sexual initiative instead of male), seem to be equally important factors, if not more important"[8].

2 Text, Translation and Textual Notes

Since the Hebrew text of Sir 23,22–27 is not available, we go on to record the Greek version according to the edition of Ziegler[9] together with our translation accompanied by some textual notes.

23,22 Οὕτως καὶ γυνὴ καταλιποῦσα τὸν ἄνδρα
καὶ παριστῶσα κληρονόμον ἐξ ἀλλοτρίου.

23 πρῶτον μὲν γὰρ ἐν νόμῳ ὑψίστου ἠπείθησεν,
καὶ δεύτερον εἰς ἄνδρα αὐτῆς ἐπλημμέλησεν,
καὶ τὸ τρίτον ἐν πορνείᾳ ἐμοιχεύθη
καὶ ἐξ ἀλλοτρίου ἀνδρὸς τέκνα παρέστησεν.

24 αὕτη εἰς ἐκκλησίαν ἐξαχθήσεται,
καὶ ἐπὶ τὰ τέκνα αὐτῆς ἐπισκοπὴ ἔσται.

25 οὐ διαδώσουσιν τὰ τέκνα αὐτῆς εἰς ῥίζαν,
καὶ οἱ κλάδοι αὐτῆς οὐκ οἴσουσιν καρπόν.

26 καταλείψει εἰς κατάραν τὸ μνημόσυνον αὐτῆς,
καὶ τὸ ὄνειδος αὐτῆς οὐκ ἐξαλειφθήσεται,

27 καὶ ἐπιγνώσονται οἱ καταλειφθέντες
ὅτι οὐθὲν κρεῖττον φόβου κυρίου
καὶ οὐθὲν γλυκύτερον τοῦ προσέχειν ἐντολαῖς κυρίου.

GkII28 *δόξα μεγάλη ἀκολουθεῖν θεῷ,*
μακρότης δὲ ἡμερῶν τὸ προσληφθῆναί σε ὑπ᾽ αὐτοῦ.

---

8 BALLA, Family, 137.
9 ZIEGLER, Sapientia, 235–236.

22	So too the woman who leaves her husband[10]
	and generates an heir[11] by another (lit. strange) man[12].
23	Firstly, she has disobeyed[13] the law of the Most High[14];
	secondly, she has offended against her husband[15]
	and third, she has committed adultery by prostituting herself[16],
	generating children by another man (lit. strange man)[17].
24	She will be brought into the assembly[18]
	and on her children will fall punishment (lit. there will be a visitation)[19].
25	Her children[20] will not put forth roots[21],
	and her branches will not bear fruit.
26	She will leave behind an accursed (lit. in a curse) memory
	and her disgrace[22] will not be blotted out.
27	And those who have survived will know[23],
	that nothing is better than the fear of the Lord

---

10 Lat reads: *mulier omnis*. Syr makes explicit: "who sins against". After τὸν ἄνδρα, some MSS of the Lucianic recension (*L*) add the possessive αὐτῆς (= Syr and Lat).

11 MS 248 and other MSS of *L* read the noun κληρονομίαν (= Lat *ereditatem*).

12 The Origenic recension (*O*-V) and MS 248 read ἐξ ἄλλου (= Syr), cf. v. 23d. Lat translates freely *ex alieno matrimonio*, a choice which Peters considers "ganz schief" (totally askew) (PETERS, Buch, 192).

13 Syr: "she was unfaithful". The same verse is to be understood in the following phrase (v. 23b). Lat reads: *incredibilis fuit* and so has not understood the meaning of ἠπείθησεν (cf. PETERS, Buch, 192).

14 Syr: "the law of God".

15 Syr translates freely: "[she was unfaithful] to the husband of her youth", cf. Prov 2,17.

16 Syr translates strangely: "[she was unfaithful] in the fornication of adultery".

17 *O*-V and MS 248 read: ἐξ ἄλλου ἀνδρός (cf. v. 22b) (= Lat: *ex alio viro*). Syr instead: "by a stranger".

18 Lat: *in ecclesiam adducetur* (= Gk). Syh: "in the assembly she will be treated with hatred". Syr: "she will be driven out from the assembly".

19 According to Peters, Lat *respicietur* is not a variant but a free translation of ἐπισκοπὴ ἔσται so that "das Zusammentreffen mit der vermutenden Vorlage יִפָּקֵד zufällig ist" (the coincidence with the conjectural *Vorlage* יִפָּקֵד is coincidental) (PETERS, Buch, 193). Syr, more explicitly, anticipates v. 26: "and her sins will be remembered against her children".

20 Smend comments: "Man erwartet des Parallelismus halber eher von 'Sprossen' zu hören" (For the sake of the parallelism, one expects to hear of 'shoots) (SMEND, Weisheit, 214).

21 The preposition εἰς is absent in *L*, Syh, Syr and Lat. Syr adds: "in the land".

22 Syr: "her debts/faults".

23 Syr has two cola: "And all the inhabitants of the earth will know, and all those who have survived in the world will understand", which emphasise the universal dimension of the sage's teaching. According to some authors, for reasons chiefly connected with the rhythm, Syr is to be preferred (cf. SMEND, Weisheit, 214, even if he considers "in the world" an addition of the translator; PETERS, Buch, 190; BOX—OESTERLEY, Sirach, 396; SKEHAN—DI LELLA, Wisdom, 320; SCHREINER, Jesus Sirach, 128).

and nothing sweeter than observing the commandments of the Lord[24].

GkII28 *It is great glory to follow God*
and length of days to be accepted by him[25].

3 Literary Composition

Criteria of both form and content point us to a tripartite division of the passage: the threefold offence of the adulterous woman (23,22–23), the consequences for the children (23,24–26) and the conclusion (23,27), which the glossator of the long form of the Greek version (GkII) completes by adding a further verse (23,28). We should note the presence of the verb καταλείπω (22a.26a.27a) in all three parts of our passage, even if it is employed with a different meaning each time[26].

3.1 Section One: Sir 23,22–23

There is no doubt that the link between our passage and the preceding one is indicated by the adverbial expression οὕτως καί at the beginning of v. 22. There are discordant opinions concerning the interpretation of the said expression. While, for some authors, it represents a relationship of equality between the adulterer and the adulterous woman (both, in fact, have committed the same sin and both have attracted the attention of the narrator)[27], for others, instead, this equality is only apparent since the two characters, having a different importance, are treated in a different way[28]. Moreover, there are those who maintain that the initial expression could be a concrete reference to the punishment

---

24 Instead of κυρίου, 253 *L*-743 *b* 46 Arm read θεοῦ, while MSS 443 and 543 omit it. Syr: "his commandments".

25 This verse is found only in L, in MSS 672 and 743, and in Lat: *et gloria magna est sequi Dominum /longitudo enim dierum adsumetur ab eo.*

26 In 23,22a and in 23,26a, καταλείπω is transitive. In the first case, it is a question of leaving the wife (real sense), while in the second case a leaving behind of an accursed memory (figurative sense). In 23,27a, on the other hand, the verb is intransitive. Cf. *supra.*

27 TRENCHARD, View on Women, 97: "The effect of this [the reference is to οὕτως καί] is to suggest that the man described in vv. 18–21 was also engaged in adultery. But since we are not told whom the man offended by his behavior, we are left to conclude that Ben Sira sees this offense being against the institution of marriage itself..."; cf., also, ibid., 267 note 37. On the same lines, cf. COLLINS, Jewish Wisdom, 68; BALLA, Family, 167.

28 MARBÖCK, Jesus Sirach, 275.

that awaits the adulterer in the public square since this is the last thing mentioned in v. 21²⁹. So, consequently, the same punishment would apply also to the woman committing the same sin.

Several factors contribute to the unity of the first section of our text.

- First, the presence of our protagonist, who without ever being called exactly "adulteress", is described in the first verse with two participial phrases as "the woman who leaves (καταλιποῦσα) her husband and generates (παριστῶσα) an heir by a stranger".
- Second, the inclusions between παριστῶσα (v. 22b) and παρέστησεν (v.23d) and between ἐξ ἀλλοτρίου (v. 22b) and ἐξ ἀλλοτρίου ἀνδρός (v. 23d).
- Third, the triple repetition of the term ἀνήρ, "man/husband" (vv. 22a.23b.23d) and the repetition of ἀλλότριος, "strange" (vv. 22b.23d) both put emphasis on the male figure, whether the woman's husband or her lover.
- Fourth, both the use of a numeric series (πρῶτον, καὶ δεύτερον, καὶ τὸ τρίτον) and of four verbs in the aorist (ἠπείθησεν, ἐπλημμέλησεν, ἐμοιχεύθη, παρέστησεν) to describe the woman's adultery serve to emphasise the gravity of the offence.
- Fifth, the chiastic arrangement which links 22b: καὶ παριστῶσα / κληρονόμον / ἐξ ἀλλοτρίου with 23d: καὶ ἐξ ἀλλοτρίου ἀνδρός / τέκνα / παρέστησεν, highlighting the centrality of the words κληρονόμον and τέκνα, "heir" and "children". Not by chance τέκνα (23d) functions as hookword with the following section by anticipating its chief theme³⁰.

3.2 Section Two: Sir 23,24 – 26

In 23,24 – 26, the presence of the woman makes itself felt by means of the pronoun αὕτη in v. 24a and the possessive adjective αὐτῆς, which is found in all the verses (5x) except the first. However, the author's attention shifts towards the children upon whom the guilt of the mother falls. Notable is the repetition of τὰ τέκνα αὐτῆς (vv. 24b.25a), together with οἱ κλάδοι αὐτῆς, "her branches"

---

29 SKEHAN–DI LELLA, Wisdom, 325.
30 According to Trenchard, the step from the singular ("heir") to the plural ("children") "raises the question of whether this woman mothered more than one illegitimate child in her quest for an heir, or whether the text beginning in v. 23 becomes a discussion of general principle rather than a specific incident" (TRENCHARD, View on Women, 100). In our opinion (and in this we agree with the author), it is impossible to reply to this question which, besides, seems to us to be forced on the text.

(v. 25b), that is, her children in a figurative sense. Placed between two references to the woman (vv. 24a and 26ab), the discourse on the children occupies the central position of this section. While in 23,22–23 the verbs are all in past tense, here they are all in the future because they refer to the punishment, which both the mother and the children will undergo as a result of her adultery. The fact that the two verbs which express the actions of the children are formulated in the negative: οὐ διαδώσουσιν... εἰς ῥίζαν (v. 25a) and οὐκ οἴσουσιν καρπόν (v. 25b), underlines forcefully the dramatic repercussions of the mother's behaviour on her children, already mentioned—albeit in a different way—in v. 24b.

If we also take into consideration the last verse, which we shall be speaking of below, we can already glimpse in the three sections of the text an internal dynamic orientated towards ends which are typically pedagogical. Its route could be described as follows: starting point is the original relationship between the woman and the husband (man) in 23,22–23; it passes in a second moment to the relationship between mother and children in 23,24–26, in order then to come to rest finally in a sphere different from and larger than that of the family, viz. the relationship between people (disciples) and God in 23,27(28).

4 The Last Verse (Sir 23,27)

We intend to concentrate now on the last verse. After a detailed analysis of 23,27, we shall try to establish its function at the formal and thematic level within the passage to which it belongs just as in its immediate and wider context.

4.1 Analysis

Since the bicolon is the most characteristic literary unit of Sirach, it is striking that Sir 23,27 has three cola instead of two. Even if this is not the only case in the book (there are forty or thereabouts), some authors have recourse to the Syriac version to resolve the anomaly[31]. Our preference, however, is to follow the Greek text as it has been handed down to us without altering it. From a syntactic point of view, the verse is composed of a principal statement (v. 27a), governed by a verb of knowing (ἐπιγνώσονται), which rules a subordinate clause introduced by the conjunction ὅτι (v. 27b). In its turn, this subordinate clause

---

31 Cf. note 23.

contains two coordinate nominal phrases (v. 27bc). We turn now to an analysis of the statements one at a time.

There is an unexpected change of subject in v. 27a. If, in the previous verses, with the exception of 23,24 where the children have been introduced, the subject has always been the adulterous woman, now οἱ καταλειφθέντες enter the scene as addressees of the teaching. But to whom is the author referring with this appellation?[32] If we translate the term (part. pass. aorist of καταλείπω) literally, the addressees are "those who remained", that is, those who came later[33] (later than the woman is being understood), the future generations or posterity[34]. The formulation of v. 27a, very similar to 46,10, confers on this colon a tone which some define as "moralising"[35]. However, we find here the pedagogic intention of the sage who avails himself of every opportunity to point to the essential. In the light of what has happened, therefore, those that come after can learn (ἐπι-γινώσκω) something very important from the case of the adulterous woman and her progeny.

But what will they learn? The content of the teaching is made explicit in v. 27bc by means of a "better"-saying. According to Roland E. Murphy[36], the "better"-saying can be described as "a common form of the proverbial sayings scattered in wisdom literature. It is not usually found in clusters, and hence perhaps it stands out more prominently than other sayings". In the book of Ben Sira there are eight "better"-sayings structured according to the formula "better than" (10,27; 16,3cd; 19,24; 20,31; 23,27bc; 29,22; 30,14–17; 42,14). To these texts, we should add the series 40,18–26[37], where, instead of the usual formula, the sage employs the variant "(better) than both". Apart from the use of the said formula, 23,27bc has other points in common with the texts listed above. At the formal level, it shares the position at the end of the unit with 20,31 (conclusion of

---

32 According to Peters, the expression "all those who have remained in the world" (Syr) would be the best interpretation of οἱ καταλειφθέντες (PETERS, Buch, 193). Differently, SAUER, Jesus Sirach, 175 and KAISER, Weisheit, 56 translate: "die sie zurückläßt". In his recent commentary, Marböck translates: "die zurückgelassene werden" and comments: "Die übrig gelassene (27a) Zeugen des Gerichtes über die Ehebrecherin und deren Kinder kommen zu einer sehr grundsätzlichen Erkenntnis" (MARBÖCK, Jesus Sirach, 270.275). Cf., also, ALONSO SCHÖKEL, Eclesiástico, 226: "Los restantes" and FRAGNELLI, Siracide, 1622: "I superstiti".

33 Spicq translates "ceux qui viendront après" and then comments: "Les survivants doivent tirer cet enseigement" (SPICQ, Ecclésiastique, 684).

34 OESTERLEY, Wisdom, 156; MINISSALE, Siracide, 123.

35 Cf. DUESBERG–FRANSEN, Ecclesiastico, 196; COLLINS, Jewish Wisdom, 70; BALLA, Family, 136 speaks of "moral lesson".

36 MURPHY, Proverbial Sayings, 35.

37 REYMOND, Sirach 40,18–27, 84–92.

20,27–31 on the appropriate use of wisdom), with 40,26 (conclusion of 40,18–26 on the better thing) and with 42,14 (conclusion of 42,9–14 on a father's concern for his daughter). On the thematic level, it is close to 40,26 where the fear-of-the-Lord constitutes the climax of the series, and to 19,24 where the fearer, ἔμφοβος (of God) is set in contrast with the one who transgresses the law. Even if the God-fearer is without intelligence and the transgressor of the law is laden with prudence, the first is better than the second in the eyes of the sage. In other words, the one who fears the Lord occupies the first place, independently of his ability.

The "better"-saying of 23,27cd follows the law of parallelism in which the members of the second colon correspond to those of the first, in this case in a synonymous relationship:

ὅτι οὐθὲν κρεῖττον   φόβου κυρίου
καὶ οὐθὲν γλυκύτερον τοῦ προσέχειν ἐντολαῖς κυρίου

The parallelism between fear-of-the-Lord (God) and law (commandments), the focal point of our verse, is frequent in Sirach. It is found also in the following texts: 1,25–26; 9,15–16; 10,19; 15,1; 19,20.24; 21,11; 35(32Hb),15–16; 35(32Hb), 24–36(33Hb),1; 37,12; 39,1. However, the precise expression προσέχειν ἐντολαῖς appears otherwise only in 35(32Hb),24 ("whoever believes in or trusts in the law, observes the commandments")[38]. The Hebrew text, available in three manuscripts, presents a notable difference with respect to the Gk: "whoever observes the law (שמר תורה MS B)/whoever gives heed to the law (נוצר תורה MSS E and F), takes care of himself"[39]. As Antonino Minissale rightly observes, this difference can be understood only if one takes into account the different structure which 35(32Hb),21–24 presents in the two texts[40]. While in the Hebrew text v. 24 opens a new strophe (35[32Hb],24–36[33Hb],3), in the Greek version it concludes the passage starting in v. 18 (35[32Hb],18–24). Therefore, in addition to the expression προσέχειν ἐντολαῖς, Sir 23,27 and 35(32Hb),24 also have another element in common, that is, the concluding function which they perform in their respective passages, even when, as we shall see later, the significance of our verse is much broader.

As to the comparative adjectives, "sweeter" (γλυκύτερον) corresponds to "better" (κρεῖττον). The adjective γλυκύς is also found in a passage on friendship

---

38 Cf., also, 32(35Hb),1: "whoever observes the Law [offers] a communion sacrifice".
39 We should note that in the reading of MS B there is a repetition of the same verb as in 35(32Hb),23b: "because whoever does this observes the commandments (שמר מצוה)".
40 Cf. MINISSALE, Versione greca, 86–87.

with reference to speaking: "the sweet throat multiplies friends and the gracious tongue finds a welcome" (6,5), and, in Wisdom's address to those who desire her: "the remembrance of me is sweeter than honey, my inheritance [is better] than the honeycomb" (24,20). The mention of remembrance or memory (μνημόσυνον) reminds us of the adulterous woman, whose memory is marked with a curse. However, this is not the only reference to our protagonist. In fact, in his description of the adulterous woman, the sage employs the same images which he has already applied to Wisdom in chapter 1 and which he will take up again in chapter 24. I refer to the terms ῥίζα, "root" (cf. 1,6.20; 24,12 [ἐρρίζωσα] and 23,25), κλάδοι, "branches" (cf. 1,20; 24,16[3x] and 23,25) and κάρποι, "fruits" (cf. 1,16; 24,17 and 23,25 [καρπός]). With these references, Ben Sira not only intends to place the two female figures in relation to each other, but also to present Wisdom as the positive counterpart of the adulterous woman[41]. Another element present in both contexts provides further confirmation: while the adulterous woman is accused of transgressing "the law of the Most High" (23,23), Wisdom instead is identified with "the law that Moses commanded us" (24,23). What the sage intends with the expression "the law of the Most High" (νόμος ὑψίστου) is not made clear in the text. However, we hold with Pancratius C. Beentjes that it does not refer to a concrete commandment (Exod 20,14, for example, or Deut 5,10), but that it has a wider significance, something attested moreover in the other texts where it appears (9,15; 38,34; 41,8; 42,2; 44,20; 49,4)[42]. John J. Collins also aligns himself with this position when—à propos this interpretation—he states: "Sirach's concern is with conformity to tradition in principle, with the attitude of reverence, rather than with legal details"[43].

Let us make a final observation on the adverb οὐθέν ("nothing"), present in the two cola. Its repetition emphasises the radical nature of the conclusion. Both concepts, fear-of-the-Lord and the observance of the Law, exceed all other values Ben Sira wishes to inculcate.

4.2 Function

From our analysis, we deduce that Sir 23,27 functions as a conclusion. It is made clear both by the literary formula used in v. 27bc (a "better"-saying) and by its content (the wordpair fear-of-the-Lord/observance of the law). The combination

---

41 Cf. Marböck, Gesetz und Weisheit, 42; Id., Jesus Sirach, 277; Beentjes, Full Wisdom, 32–33.
42 Cf. Beentjes, Full Wisdom, 33. Differently, Trenchard, View on Women, 102; Schnabel, Law and Wisdom, 47; Skehan–Di Lella, Wisdom, 325.
43 Collins, Jewish Wisdom, 70.

of these two elements with the final position of the verse and the introduction of the "better"-saying (v. 27a) leaves no doubt with regard to this question. Of course, the problem arises when one wants to clarify to what text 23,27 is referring. In other words, for what passage, section or part of the book does it function as a conclusion? To this question there are, in our opinion, six possible solutions, which we present as follows:

a) Sir 23,27 as the conclusion to Sir 23,22–27, the passage on the adulterous woman[44]. The negative tone characterising the description of the woman is softened by the last verse where the excellence of the fear-of-the-Lord and the sweetness involved in the observance of the law get the upper hand. In this way, the sage succeeds in transforming a negative experience like that of the adulterous woman into an effective pedagogic tool.

b) Sir 23,27 as the conclusion to Sir 23,16–27[45], a section devoted to sins of a sexual nature, especially adultery. Our verse, therefore, refers, not only to the adulterous woman but also to the adulterer (23,18–21) and to those who succumb to their passions (23,16–17). It would have the aim of inspiring hope in the face of the dark reality of sin. Put differently, the fear-of-the-Lord and the observance of the Law help a person not to fall into the sins mentioned in this section.

c) Sir 23,27 as the conclusion of Sir 23,7–27[46], a section composed of two quite different passages, one on discipline in speaking (vv. 7–15), the other on sexual passions (vv. 16–27). In this case, the final verse would be a general application addressed to the "future generations". In the introduction one would then find a corresponding general passage, 23,7–8, whose addressees are "sons/disciples". The import of the conclusion, therefore, embraces not only sexual but also verbal sins.

d) Sir 23,27 as the conclusion of Sir 22,27–23,27[47], a section containing warnings about sins that destroy a person, such as sins of the tongue and sins

---

44 BEENTJES, Full Wisdom, 32–33: "Sir. 23:27 has a clear function of summary in reaction to the description of the adulterous woman (Sir. 23:22–26)". According to Murphy, on the other hand, 23,27 has no connection with the previous verses: "It does have the appearance of a sweeping, summary statement" (MURPHY, Proverbial Sayings, 38).

45 ALONSO SCHÖKEL, Eclesiástico, 226; TRENCHARD, View on Women, 96; MACKENZIE, Sirach, 97; COLLINS, Jewish Wisdom, 68–70; SAUER, Jesus Sirach, 176; SCHREINER, Jesus Sirach, 126.128; BALLA, Family, 136: "The comment [she is referring to 23,27] seems almost an expression of hope or perhaps reassurance that whoever fears the Lord and keeps his commandments will be saved from sinning in the way described in 23:16–21.22–26...".

46 HASPECKER, Gottesfurcht, 166 (note that the author follows the Syriac text of 23,27); TRENCHARD, View on Women, 96.

47 WEBER, Sirach, 549; SKEHAN–DI LELLA, Wisdom, 321.326.

of a sexual nature. As Beentjes[48] has demonstrated, the theme of 22,27–23,1 (prayer/tongue) is taken up and developed in 23,7–15 (instruction/tongue) and, in the same way, the theme of 23,2–6 (prayer/passions) is taken up and developed in 23,16–26 (instruction/passions). The purposeful composition of this section highlights the connection between prayer and instruction[49], to which 23,27 implicitly refers. In fact, the fear-of-the-Lord and the observance of the law express the internal and external aspects of the religious spirit, that is, "the devotional and practical sides of religion"[50].

e) Sir 23,27 as the conclusion of Sir 19,20–23,27. At its strategic points, that is, at the beginning (19,20), in the middle (21,11), and at the end (23,23.27), this section contains the three fundamental theological concepts of the book[51]: wisdom, fear-of-God and the Law. Even if 23,27 does not mention wisdom explicitly (the closest occurrence is found in 23,2b), the reference to "knowing" evokes its presence.

f) Sir 23,27, finally, as the conclusion of Sir 1,1–23,27[52]. Since the second part of the book begins in 24,1, our verse resembles Qoh 12,13 since both texts display a close connection between fear-of-the-Lord and observance of his commandments while being concluding verses. While some authors hold that 23,27 can be described as an "elegant conclusion"[53], we propose to read it as a purposeful statement. Between the lines, we can hear the voice of the sage who is instructing his disciples a fundamental lesson: "In short, the indispensable condition for tackling the 'praise of Wisdom' (ch. 24) is to be free from those sins which destroy the person from within. How can this be done? In addition to prayer, the fear-of-the-Lord and the observance of the Law will help you"[54].

The reader now will certainly be confused at the prospect of having to choose between such different proposals. However, they are not mutually exclusive, but rather compatible and even complementary. At the end of our analysis, we believe to have shown that Sir 23,27 is a conclusive verse serving several purposes. This analysis finds confirmation in the connection mentioned above between

48 Beentjes, Sir 22:27–23:6, 144–150.
49 Gilbert, Prayer, 118.
50 MacKenzie, Sirach, 97.
51 Cf. Beentjes, Full Wisdom, 30–32; Marböck, Jesus Sirach, 272.275–276.
52 Peters, Buch, 193; Alonso Schökel, Eclesiástico, 226; Weber, Sirach, 549; Snaith, Ecclesiasticus, 118; Beentjes, Full Wisdom, 32; Morla Asensio, Eclesiástico, 122.
53 Skehan–Di Lella, Wisdom, 326; Murphy, Proverbial Sayings, 38.
54 Balla, Family, 137.

the adulterous woman at the end of the first part of the book (chs. 1– 23) and Lady Wisdom at the beginning of the second part (24,1– 42,12). Sir 23,27 is a hinge: on the one hand, it is conclusive with regard to everything that precedes it and, on the other hand, it opens up before the reader a new horizon of which it is in some way an anticipation.

5 The GkII Addition (Sir 23,28)[55]

It appears that the glossator of GkII was not satisfied with v. 27. In fact, he adds a new verse to our passage with the aim of completing the teaching of the master, which he holds to be insufficient in some way. In the first colon, the glossator proposes an idea—present elsewhere in the book (Sir 1,11.19 and 24,12.16 – 17)— that the relationship with God fills humans with glory. This idea is clarified in the second colon, the content of which recalls Deut 30,20. By means of a link between abundance of days and the fear-of-the-Lord, the author not only clarifies the meaning of "to follow God" (ἀκολουθεῖν θεῷ) in 23,27, but also makes the concluding function more explicit. Length of days in 23,28 refers to 1,12.20 and thus produces the effect of an inclusion.

In conclusion, with this addition on faithfulness to God and the awareness of being accepted by him, the glossator is preparing the transition to the discourse on Wisdom in ch. 24 and then the "Praise of the Ancestors" in chs. 44 – 50. In doing so, however, "he diminished the role of Sir 23,27 within the teaching of Ben Sira"[56]. In other words, the conclusion of the first part of the book is now shifted from 23,27 to 23,28.

---

55 For a detailed analysis of Sir 23,28, cf. BUSSINO, Greek Additions, 361– 368.
56 BUSSINO, Greek Additions, 368.

Ben Sira 24,22—Decoding a Metaphor

The Festschrift dedicated to Friedrich V. Reiterer on the occasion of his 65th birthday[1] opens with a contribution by Pancratius C. Beentjes on Sir 24,19–22[2]. With a few exceptions[3], this little passage has not aroused a great deal of interest among scholars who have generally preferred to study the preceding verses, that is Sir 24,1–17(18), and, particularly, Sir 24,23, the heart of the chapter. I do not intend to repeat here Beentjes's careful analysis in the article just mentioned but only the conclusion which he reaches: "If Lady Wisdom is connected—not identified—with the Torah indeed, then the final verse of her invitation (24,22) at once is crystal-clear: 'He who obeys me will not be ashamed, and those who work with me will not sin'"[4]. Taking its cue from this statement, the present work will seek to determine the meaning and function of Sir 24,22 within the final exhortation (24,19–22) and the composition as a whole (Sir 24). Special attention will be given to the use of metaphors and their decoding.

1 Wisdom's Discourse (Sir 24,1–22)

The poem on Wisdom, the passage that has been commented on more than any other in the book, comes in chapter 24[5]. It is known as the "Praise of Wisdom", a title attested in the majority of Greek manuscripts[6]. Taking his inspiration from Prov 8,1–36, Ben Sira puts a long speech in the mouth of Wisdom in which she praises herself in the midst of her people (Sir 24,1–22)[7]. Beginning in 24,23, the sage takes center stage in order to explain Wisdom's speech (24,23–29) and his mission as the teacher of life (24,30–34). The theological depth of Sir 24, situated precisely half way through the book, has led some authors to consider it as the conclusion of the first part (Sir 1–24); others, however,

---

1 EGGER-WENZEL—SCHÖPFLING—DIEHL (eds.), Weisheit.

2 BEENTJES, Come to me, 1–11.

3 GILBERT, Nutrimento, 51–60; SINNOTT, Personification, 125–127.

4 BEENTJES, Come to me, 10.

5 Among more recent studies, cf. JANOWSKI, Gottes Weisheit, 1–29; NISSINEN, Wisdom as Mediatrix, 377–390; BALLA, Family, 195–206; LEUENBERGER, Gott in Bewegung, 298–304; MARTTILA, Foreign Nations, 80–118.

6 ZIEGLER, Sapientia, 236 (not in the Origenic manuscripts). We do not know if this title (absent from Syr) formed part of the first edition of the book but it is similar to the one which we find at the beginning of the "Praise of the Ancestors" in 44,1: πατέρων ὕμνος (MS B: שבח אבות עולם).

7 On the context in which Wisdom praises herself, cf. MARTTILA, Foreign Nations, 102–103.

https://doi.org/10.1515/9783110492316-020

see it as acting as an introduction to the second part (Sir 24 – 51). A third solution is that suggested by Johannes Marböck according to whom Sir 24 acts a bridge between the two parts[8]. At any rate, it is clear that from chapter 25 to 43 the sage is concerned with themes bound up with the details of everyday life.

Preceded by an introduction (24,1–2), the speech of Wisdom, properly so called (24,3–22), consists of 22 bicola (22 is the number of letters in the Hebrew alphabet). This procedure, often employed by the biblical authors (e. g. Prov 2,1–22; 31,10 –31), enables Ben Sira to focus on the idea of totality, completeness and fullness which is involved in Wisdom (cf. 1,11–30; 6,18 –37; 51,13 –30)[9].

The speech is partly marked out by the double inclusion between vv. 3 – 4 (ἐγώ, 2x) and vv. 16 – 17 (ἐγώ, 2x). The inclusion is only partial because the use of the 1st person singular does not finish in v. 17 but continues as far as v. 22 (ἐν ἐμοί). Added to this is the threefold repetition of the term κληρονομία, at the beginning (v. 7; cf. v. 8d: κατακληρονομέω), the middle (v. 12) and the end of the passage (v. 20). Starting out from these observations, we can distinguish two sections within the speech: one of a narrative character (vv. 3 – 17 +18GkII)[10] in which Wisdom speaks about herself and another in exhortatory mode (vv. 19 – 22) in which she addresses those who desire her.

In the first part of the speech, Wisdom presents herself in continual movement: first, she journeys in space and time (cf. the verbs with the prefix κατα-); then, she concentrates her movements within geographic regions which become more focused, culminating in her occupation of Israel (cf. the triple repetition of the verb ἀνυψόω). This first part is composed of three sections: vv. 3 – 7, vv. 8 – 12 and vv. 13 – 17[11]. Verses 3 – 7 describe the divine origin of Wisdom and her activity in the cosmos (expressed by means of 7 verbs in the aorist). The section ends with a question which Wisdom poses to herself (7b) and which will find its answer in the following verse. Verses 8 – 12 are distinguished by the appearance of the Creator (cf. 8a: ὁ κτίστης ἁπάντων; 8b: ὁ κτίσας με; 9a: ἔκτισέν με) and the presence, in almost every colon, of a circumstantial complement of place (the preposition ἐν + proper or common noun) referring to the dwelling place of Wisdom, that is, the temple in Jerusalem. Finally, verses 13 – 17 are characterised, on the one hand, by the repetition of the comparative adverb ὡς (12x) —almost always in the initial position—which introduces a series of vegetable

---

8 Cf., in this connection, MARBÖCK, Weisheit im Wandel, 41– 44; ID., Structure, 77; ID., Jesus Sirach, 27.

9 Cf. GILBERT, Éloge, 329 – 330.

10 On the Lucianic addition in 24,18, see BUSSINO, Greek Additions, 372– 375.

11 For the literary structure of the passage, cf. GILBERT, Éloge, 326 – 341.

and cultic images referring to Wisdom and, on the other hand, by the presence of several toponyms for the land of Israel.

The second part of the speech is a lively exhortation to listen to and follow Wisdom, a companion in life who offers to all who choose her innumerable benefits and protection against evil. It is precisely to this exhortation that the following paragraphs are devoted.

2 Wisdom's Final Exhortation (Sir 24,19 – 22)

Wisdom's exhortation is only 4 verses, much shorter than her praise of herself. It opens with an invitation which sets the tone for this small unit. In view of the long section in which she exalts herself, it may seem surprising that her speech does not end with a glorification of her greatness, as one might have expected. Instead, Wisdom concentrates on her relationship with her disciples, a relationship that is personal, intimate and profound. Ben Sira describes this connection with a metaphorical language based on multiple biblical allusions.

2.1 Text and Translation

Sir 24 is certainly one of the most, if not the most important text among those for which we cannot make use of a Hebrew text (in addition to Sir 1,1–3,5; 16,28–30,10 apart from some verses, and 38,27–39,14). The desire to have access to the original Hebrew of the text has encouraged some scholars, older and modern, to attempt a reconstruction of the original from the Greek version. This is what was done by Robert Lowth in 1753, Otto F. Fritzsche in 1859 and, later, Patrick W. Skehan in 1979[12]. Although offering thought-provoking results, these texts remain wholly hypothetical and cannot serve as the basis for a careful study of the passage. However, as Martti Nissinen has rightly observed, "even the Greek text clearly reflects the parallelistic structure of the original Hebrew poem, and the lexical associations are easily observable"[13]. Our analysis, therefore, will be made on the basis of the Greek version of Sir 24,19–22 according to

---

12 LOWTH, De sacra poesi, 325; FRITZSCHE, Weisheit, 134–136; SKEHAN, Structure, 374. Cf. also HARṬOM, בן סירא, 87; KAHANA, שמעון בן־סירא, 51; SEGAL, ספר, 146.
13 NISSINEN, Wisdom as Mediatrix, 380.

the edition of Joseph Ziegler[14], which we reproduce in what follows. The Greek text will be accompanied by our translation and by some textual notes which will take account of the Syriac and Latin versions.

19 προσέλθετε πρός με, οἱ ἐπιθυμοῦντές μου,
   καὶ ἀπὸ τῶν γενημάτων μου ἐμπλήσθητε·
20 τὸ γὰρ μνημόσυνόν μου ὑπὲρ τὸ μέλι γλυκύ,
   καὶ ἡ κληρονομία μου ὑπὲρ μέλιτος κηρίον.
21 οἱ ἔσθοντές με ἔτι πεινάσουσιν,
   καὶ οἱ πίνοντές με ἔτι διψήσουσιν.
22 ὁ ὑπακούων μου οὐκ αἰσχυνθήσεται,
   καὶ οἱ ἐργαζόμενοι ἐν ἐμοὶ οὐχ ἁμαρτήσουσιν.

19 Come to me, [15]you who desire me,
   and[16] be filled with my produce[17].
20 For the memory[18] of me is sweeter than honey,
   and my inheritance[19] better than a honeycomb [of honey][20].
21 Those who eat me will still hunger[21],
   and those who drink me will still thirst.
22 He who listens to me will not be put to shame[22]
   and those who put me into practice (lit. work with me) will not miss the mark (lit. sin)[23].

---

14 ZIEGLER, Sapientia, 239. For the Syriac version (Syr), we make use of the edition of CALDUCH-BENAGES—FERRER—LIESEN, Wisdom of the Scribe, 162–163 and, for the Latin (Lat), Biblia sacra, 735; THIELE (ed.), Vetus Latina, 698–699.

15 Codex S, Syr and Lat add "all", which, according to Ziegler, could derive from Matt 11,28 (ZIEGLER, Sapientia, 239).

16 Gilbert understands this καί in a final sense and translates "to be filled with my produce" (GILBERT, Nutrimento, 56: "*per saziarvi dei miei prodotti*").

17 Syr: "And you will delight yourselves (*ttpnqwn*) in my good fruits" (cf. RICKENBACHER, Weisheitsperikopen, 112.124). Lat: *et a generationibus meis implemini*.

18 According to Marböck, instead of μνημόσυνόν one should read μνημοσυνή which is attested by the addition 24,28[Lat] (MARBÖCK, Weisheit im Wandel, 39). Syr: "teaching". Lat: *spiritus*.

19 Syr translates freely: "and for those who inherit me".

20 Ziegler follows Rahlfs in emending κηρου (codex B and S) or κηριου (codex A) to κεριον (ZIEGLER, Sapientia, 239). Lat reads: *super mel et favum* (cf. Ps 18,11[LXX]: ὑπὲρ μέλι καὶ κηρίον) and adds: *Memoria mea in generatione seculorum* (24,28[Lat]). For Peters, *in generatione seculorum* means "bis zu den letzten Geschlechtern" (cf. 24,14[Lat]) (PETERS, Buch, 201).

21 Syr adds "for me" at the end of both the cola. This reading is followed by Rickenbacher (Weisheitsperikopen, 112.125).

22 MS 248 adds δια παντος. Syr: "Whoever listens to me will not fall (*npl*)".

23 Syr translates freely: "and all his works ('*bdwhy*) will not be destroyed (*nthblwn*)". According to Smend, Syr has not really understood the meaning of the verb חטא (cf. 5,15; 7,36; 49,9) (cf. SMEND, Weisheit, 221). Lat adds a further verse (24,31[Lat]) in order to facilitate the passage to the following unit (24,32–47[Lat]) where we hear the voice of the sage: *Qui elucidant* (understood

2.2 Literary Analysis

In addition to the initial imperative προσέλθετε (followed by ἐμπλήσθητε), which marks a neat distinction from the previous passage, Sir 24,19 – 22 is characterised by the concentration of nine pronouns and adjectives in the 1st person singular. Each colon has one, with the exception of the first colon, where there are two. Even if the author never uses the pronoun ἐγώ (cf., by contrast, vv. 3.4.16.17), the "I" of Wisdom dominates the entire exhortation. Not only is she the speaking subject but, in addressing her audience, she employs a self-referential language (come to me, the memory of me, my inheritance). Moreover, her potential hearers/disciples are presented as "those who desire me", "those who eat me", "those who drink me", "those who listen to me" (in the singular in the text) and "those who put me into practice".

From the syntactic point of view, the presence of the conjunction γάρ in v. 20a is important. In our opinion, it governs not only v. 20 but also the following verses. In other words, the invitation to approach Wisdom and to be filled with her fruits in v. 19 is justified in vv. 20 – 22 (cf. the 4 verbs in the future). Consequently, it would be possible to propose the following division into two parts for our passage: Wisdom's invitation (v. 19) and the reasons for it (vv. 20 – 22). However, if we take as point of reference the use of metaphorical language, then we are faced with another twofold structure. The first part comprises vv. 19 – 21, where all the metaphorical expressions are concentrated: Wisdom presents herself as a lover, as a tree or plant which bears fruit, and even as food and drink for nourishment. The second part, on the other hand, is composed of a single verse (v. 22) which, in our view, has the function of decoding the metaphors by way of a final conclusion.

2.3 Wisdom's Metaphorical Self-presentation (Sir 24,19 – 21)

The invitation which Wisdom addresses to her hearers/readers (her potential disciples are understood)[24] is permeated by a metaphorical vocabulary which refers to other passages in the book and in the biblical tradition. As we shall see, Ben Sira employs his metaphors in a very original way. They are often superimposed

---

as the teachers of wisdom) *me vitam aeternam habebunt* (cf. Dan 12,3). In his commentary, Peters observes that this is the only occurrence of the verb *elucidare* in the entire Latin Bible (cf. PETERS, Buch, 201).

24 According to Marttila, we have here a universal invitation (MARTTILA, Foreign Nations, 109), while Gilbert holds that Wisdom is speaking to the people of Israel (GILBERT, Éloge, 335).

upon one another, making it very difficult, almost impossible, to determine their limits. One can say with Jessie Rogers that "he makes imaginative use of metaphors that allow for a variety of free associations with biblical imagery"[25]. This is precisely what happens in Sir 24,19–22.

2.3.1 Sir 24,19

In Sir 24,19a, Wisdom addresses her audience with the vocative "you who desire me" (οἱ ἐπιθυμοῦντές μου). This is not the first time that Ben Sira refers to the relationship between Wisdom and her disciple in terms of desire. It is enough to recall Sir 1,26 (ἐπιθυμήσας σοφίαν διατήρησον ἐντολάς, "if you desire wisdom keep the commandments") or Sir 6,37 (ἡ ἐπιθυμία τῆς σοφίας δοθήσεται σοι, "the desire for wisdom will be given to you"). The latter passage is the conclusion of a poem which presents the picture of the disciple doing his utmost to attain the Wisdom he desires (Sir 6,18–37). This passionate search on the part of the disciple and the numerous trials which he has to overcome evoke the vicissitudes of the experience of love (cf. Sir 4,11–19; 14,20–15,10; 51,13–30)[26]. In the final analysis, desire is that power of the heart which attracts one human being to another. Thus, the woman in the Canticle can say: "I am my beloved's, and his desire is for me" (Cant 7,11)[27].

Beside the love metaphor, there is also the botanical one, and it is a metaphor very dear to Ben Sira. Wisdom/the lover now becomes a thriving tree or plant bearing fruit with which the disciple must fill himself (v. 19b). Behind this image, Maurice Gilbert glimpses "a certain discreet allusion to the tree of life in paradise (Gen 2,17)"[28].

The careful reader is hardly surprised by this language since from the first chapter of the book Ben Sira has referred to the root (1,6.20), fruits (1,16; 6,19; 24,17), branches (1,20; 14,26; 24,16[3x]) and produce (1,17; 6,19; 24,19) of Wisdom. Sir 24,12–17 deserves a special mention, for there this metaphor reaches its maximum development in illustrating the plant cycle of a fruit tree (its roots its growth, its scent, its foliage, its flowers and its fruits), as Alain Fournier-Bidoz has shown[29].

---

25 ROGERS, Wisdom and Creation, 144.
26 Cf. BALLA, Family, 187: "Some of the images used in Sir 6:18–31 potentially have erotic overtones and describe a love affair between wisdom and her lover".
27 Cf. GILBERT, Nutrimento, 54.
28 GILBERT, Nutrimento, 55: "una certa allusione discreta all'albero di vita del paradiso (Gen 2,17)".
29 FOURNIER-BIDOZ, Arbre, 1–10.

In our opinion, the most remarkable aspect of v. 19 is the superimposition of the metaphors. Wisdom's invitation to fill oneself with her produce resonates with the invitation of the woman of the Canticle: "Let my beloved come to his garden, and eat its choicest fruits" (Cant 4,16). The erotic connotations of the Canticle's fruits emerge again in Sir 24,19, where to be filled with the fruits of Wisdom "also implies—in the words of Ibolya Balla—quenching one's desire for an intimate relationship with her"[30]. This intimate relation is also hinted at, even if expressed differently, in Sir 4,15 (MS A): "He who gives heed to me —says Wisdom—will dwell in my inmost chambers [of the house]" (Syr: "within me").

2.3.2 Sir 24,20

Sir 24,20 is the only verse of the passage in which the addressees of the speech are not present, at least explicitly. There remains only the "I" of Wisdom who is revealed by means of two concepts that are fundamental in the thought of Ben Sira: μνημόσυνον, "memory" (17x) and κληρονομία, "inheritance" (17x). Both the memory which the disciple will have of Wisdom (cf. 49,1) and the inheritance which he will receive from her are compared to honey whose sweetness is a pleasure to the taste (cf. Prov 24,13 – 14)[31].

The mention of honey, as Maurice Gilbert suggests, could refer to the blessing of the land in the Pentateuch and so evoke "the land flowing with milk and honey" (Exod 3,8)[32]. However, if we bear in mind the interweaving of the metaphors, it seems to us that the honey metaphor together with that of the fruits echoes the response of the male lover to the invitation of his female beloved in the Canticle of Canticles: "I have come to my garden, my sister, my bride, and I gather my myrrh and my balsam; I eat my honeycomb and my honey, I drink my wine and my milk. Eat, friends, drink; intoxicate yourselves, my dear ones" (Cant 5,1). Balla's interpretation is along the same lines[33]. According to

---

30 BALLA, Family, 204.

31 We should note the lexical links between 24,20 and the pericope on the adulteress: μνημόσυνον (23,26), κληρονομία (23,22), γλυθκύτερον (23,27c). By means of these, a relationship is established between the two female figures: the adulterous woman is presented as the opposite of Wisdom. The links are extended if we take into account chapters 1 and 24 (ρίζα: 1,6.20; 24,12; 23,25a; κλάδοι: 1,20; 23,25b; 24,16[3x] and καρπός: 1,16; 23,25b; 24,17). Cf. MARBÖCK, Weisheit im Wandel, 42; ID., Jesus Sirach, 275.277; BEENTJES, Full Wisdom, 32 – 33; BALLA, Family, 204; CAMP, Ben Sira, 92 – 93; CALDUCH-BENAGES, Pivotal Verse, 195 – 196.

32 GILBERT, Éloge, 336; SINNOTT, Personification, 126. According to Hogan, Ben Sira borrows imagery from Ps 19,11, cf. HOGAN, Theologies in Conflict, 78.

33 BALLA, Family, 204.

her, the sage employs the honey image to describe the sweetness of the relationship between Wisdom and her disciple, the same sweetness which characterises the relationship between the two lovers in the Canticle: "Your lips are oozing with honey, O virgin, O bride; there is milk and honey under your tongue, and the scent of your garments is like the scent of Lebanon" (Cant 4,11). For his part, after observing the contacts between Sir 24,19–20 and the Canticle of Canticles (in addition to some references to the love poetry of the Ancient Near East), Martti Nissinen reaches the following conclusion: "It seems like Lady Wisdom presents herself superior even to the (divine) love praised by the Song of Songs"[34]. One can discuss the significance of this statement, but the expressions employed by Wisdom do indeed confirm her superiority: the memory of her and her inheritance are precisely sweeter than honey (ὑπὲρ τὸ μέλι γλθκύ, ὑπὲρ μέλιτος κηρίον), a sweetness that is superlative, incomparable.

2.3.3 Sir 24,21

In Sir 24,21 the addressees reappear, this time in the guise of dining companions. Wisdom has invited them to a banquet which recalls that of Prov 9,1–6. The hostess opens with these words: "Come, eat my bread and drink the wine which I have prepared for you" (Prov 9,5; cf., also, Isa 25,26; 55,1–3). Already in his first chapter, Ben Sira associates the activity of wisdom with eating and drinking: "The fear-of- the-Lord is the fullness of wisdom; she intoxicates (μεθύσκει) her devotees with her fruits (ἀπὸ τῶν καρπῶν αὐτῆς). She fills their house with desirable things (ἐπιθυμημάτων), and their storehouses with her produce (ἀπὸ τῶν γενημάτῶν αὐτῆς)" (Sir 1,16–17). The same goes for Sir 15,3. Here too, we have the idea of the banquet, even if the food and drink which are provided are of a spiritual order (cf. 4,12–15). Wisdom, personified as a mother and as a virgin bride, nourishes her disciple with "the bread of understanding (לחם שכל, ἄρτον συνέσεως) and the water of wisdom (מי תבונה, ὕδωρ σοφίας)". The association between wisdom and food is also found in Sir 6,19, where the sage invites the disciple to draw near to Wisdom (πρόσελθε αὐτῇ), to wait for her good fruits (τοὺς ἀγαθοὺς καρποὺς αὐτῆς), and, at the same time, to toil to obtain them. The reward will not be long in coming and, like the farmer, the disciple will soon be able to feed on her produce (τῶν γενημάτων αὐτῆς).

In all these texts of Ben Sira, the disciple is invited to nourish himself with the fruits of Wisdom both materially and spiritually. In Sir 24,21, on the other hand, she offers herself as food and drink, something rather unusual (cf. John 6). If we

---

34 NISSINEN, Wisdom as Mediatrix, 383.

go through the pages of the Old Testament, we will not find a single person who presents him or herself as nourishment, as the source of life and salvation. A self-referential speech of this type is found only in the mouth of Wisdom[35]. She is, at one and the same time, the spring and the water, the tree and the fruit. Her products are herself. Wisdom speaks in the first person and speaks of herself so as to invite, exhort, teach, motivate, stimulate, attract and nourish those who desire her and seek to love her. "Her language is the poetic projection of a desire which"—in the words of Paul Beauchamp—"is neither realised nor completely unsatisfied but which already anticipates, even if imperfectly, its realisation"[36].

Normally, eating and drinking satisfy hunger and thirst. However, if the food and drink being consumed is Wisdom herself, then one is never filled[37]. "Even if one is satisfied a little", comments Marko Marttila, "one immediately longs for more"[38]. Continuing to have hunger and thirst after eating and drinking seems something negative or even a contradiction. In the text, however, it has a positive value. According to Gilbert, the fundamental idea in Sir 24,21 is that "the banquet offered by Wisdom is so excellent that whoever tastes it will return without ever again seeking his nourishment elsewhere"[39].

The fact is that the search for Wisdom has no limits. The more one involves oneself with her, the more the desire to meet her increases and the more one realises that one is far from the goal of reaching her. According to Ben Sira's own testimony, this "never ending, inexhaustible but attractive activity"[40] lasts throughout the whole of life: "When I was young and innocent, I kept seeking wisdom. She came to me in her beauty and until the end I will seek her out" (Sir 51,13 – 14 according to 11QPs[a]).

---

35 This idea is inspired by BEAUCHAMP, Personificazione, 208 – 209.
36 BEAUCHAMP, Personificazione, 208: "Il suo linguaggio è la proiezione poetica di un desiderio che non è né appagato né del tutto frustrato, ma che già anticipa, benché in modo imperfetto, il suo appagamento".
37 On the relationship between this verse and the Fourth Gospel (John 4,14; 6,35), cf. GILBERT, Nutrimento, 59; MARTTILA, Foreign Nations, 109 – 110 note 83.
38 MARTTILA, Foreign Nations, 109.
39 GILBERT, Nutrimento, 58 – 59: "Il banchetto offerto dalla Sapienza è così ottimo che colui che lo gusta vi ritornerà sempre senza cercare mai più altrove il suo sostentamento".
40 BEENTJES, Come to me, 7.

3 From Metaphorical to Decoded Language (Sir 24,22)

The metaphorical language which Wisdom has employed in her speech up until now vanishes abruptly. If, in the preceding verses, the metaphorical images and allusions concerning her relationship with her disciples are interwoven to create a rather evocative scenario, in Sir 24,22, they are replaced by a decoded language with a pedagogic purpose. This process of decoding, that is, the passing from metaphorical language to the identification and interpretation of its content, is not a new thing; in fact, it is frequent in biblical texts (cf., e.g. Ps 23; Isa 5,1–7 or Sir 6,18–37). We shall now analyse this process in our verse.

3.1 Two Parallel Verses

From a formal point of view, v. 22 is practically identical to v. 21. Both verses are constructed according to the rules of parallelism, and in both verses this parallelism is synonymous.

21a		οἱ ἔσθοντές	με	ἔτι πεινάσουσιν
21b	καὶ	οἱ πίνοντες	με	ἔτι διψήσουσιν
22a		ὁ ὑπακούων	μου	οὐκ αἰσχυνθήσεται
22b	καὶ	οἱ ἐργαζόμενοι	ἐν ἐμοὶ	οὐχ ἁμαρτήσουσιν

Very striking are the two differences between the verses and within the same verse: the presence of negation in v. 22 (v. 21, by contrast, is formed positively) and the use of the singular in 22a (in v. 21 and in 22b, on the other hand, the 3rd person plural is employed). As for the rest, all the elements correspond perfectly: present participles with the article (subjects), pronouns in the first person (objects) and verbs in the future.

The parallel arrangement of the subjects highlights the correspondence between eating and drinking, on the one hand, and listening and putting into practice on the other. Eating and drinking are two complementary actions as are listening and putting into practice. The former act as nourishment for the body, the latter as formation of the mind and spirit. All four, however, are oriented to the same end: the growth of the person.

As for the parallel arrangement of the verbal forms, it raises an interesting fact: v. 21 is formulated positively but with a negative meaning (the absence of satisfaction), while v. 22 is formulated negatively but with a positive meaning.

Finally, it should be noted that the only element which remains unchanged is the 1st person singular pronoun referring to Wisdom (object complement of all the verbs). It is through it that we are able to glimpse her chameleon-like presence and listen to her authoritative voice.

3.2 Hearing and Putting into Practice

The unusual image of Wisdom offering herself as food and drink disappears all of a sudden. For a moment, the reader remains disconcerted but immediately takes up the thread of the speech. When all is said and done, it is a question of listening to Wisdom and putting her into practice, just as is the case with the father/teacher and his teachings (cf. Prov 5,7; 7,24), or with the Law of the Most High. According to Luis Alonso Schökel, "the two verbs, listen and fulfil, are applied traditionally to the Law: the human being 'observes' the Law when he 'fulfils' it"[41].

Let us linger for a moment on the first element of the wordpair just mentioned, that is "hearing". This is not the first time that Wisdom exhorts her disciples to listen to her. She has done this also in Sir 4,15 (MS A: "Whoever listens to me [שמע לי] will judge nations [or: in truth] and whoever gives heed to me [מאזין לי] will dwell in my inmost chambers") and in the book of Proverbs, specifically in Prov 1,33 ("Whoever listens to me will live in safety and be at ease, without fear of harm"), in Prov 8,32 ("And now, my children, listen to me: happy are those who keep my ways"), and in Prov 8,34 ("Happy is the one who listens to me, watching daily at my gates, waiting beside my doors"). We should note that these three verses, exactly like Sir 24,22, are texts of a concluding character which are intended to influence the hearer in a particular way. Prov 1,33 is the conclusion of Wisdom's first speech (Prov 1,20–33), and Prov 8,32 and 8,34 form part of the conclusion of her second speech (Prov 8,1–36).

We intend now to consider the second element of this wordpair, that is, "putting into practice". The expression οἱ ἐργαζόμενοι ἐν ἐμοί has long given trouble to scholars[42]. How is ἐν ἐμοί to be understood when it refers to Wisdom? In a local sense (in me)[43], an instrumental one (through me)[44], a final one (for

---

41 ALONSO SCHÖKEL, Eclesiástico, 231: "Los dos verbos, escuchar y cumplir, se aplican tradicionalmente a la ley: el hombre "guarda" la ley al "hacerla""; RICKENBACHER, Weisheitsperikopen, 125.

42 Some translate freely according to Syr: "they that serve me" (BOX—OESTERLEY, Book, 399; "wer mir dient" (HAMP, Sirach, 66; SCHREINER, Jesus Sirach, 131).

43 OESTERLEY, Wisdom, 161; SNAITH, Ecclesiasticus, 123; SAUER, Jesus Sirach, 178.

44 BECKER—FABRY—REITEMEYER, Sophia Sirach, 1124.

me)[45], or as a modal complement (with me)[46]? This last option seems to be the most frequent. In fact, in Sir 13,4 we find a similar expression: ἐὰν χρησιμεύσῃς, ἐργᾶται ἐν σοί, "If you are useful, he [the rich man] will work with you" (to profit from it, obviously). However, the translation οἱ ἐργαζόμενοι ἐν ἐμοί in Sir 24,22 with "those who toil/work with me" does not fit the context. Not by chance, although he goes for this translation, Alexander A. Di Lella holds it necessary to give a further explanation: "i.e. those whose obedience to her (i.e. Wisdom) is put into practice"[47].

In our opinion, the fundamental idea of the text is not so much working for wisdom, through wisdom or with her as acting according to her, that is, putting her teachings into practice (we should remember that she appears personified in the text). We agree, therefore, with Otto Rickenbacher, who translates "those who act according to me", even if, within parentheses, he offers another possible translation in which Wisdom becomes the object complement of the verb: "those who do me"[48]. This proposal takes its cue from the translation of Luis Alonso Schökel, behind which we can glimpse the figure of the Law: "he who puts me into practice"[49]. This veiled association between Wisdom and the Law (due to be made clear in the next verse) had already been perceived by Rudolf Smend in his commentary of 1906: "Ultimately, like the law, wisdom can be 'performed'"[50].

Finally, we should mention the translation of Johannes Marböck: "those who strive for me"[51], who places the emphasis on the effort presupposed by the search for Wisdom. Orienting one's life towards her and acting according to her teachings is certainly a laborious task for her disciple (cf. Sir 6,18 – 19), and the testimony of Ben Sira confirms this (cf. Sir 24,34; 36[33Hb],16.18; 51,19).

---

45 GILBERT, Nutrimento, 59.

46 SKEHAN–DI LELLA, Wisdom, 336; WRIGHT, Sirach, 739.

47 SKEHAN–DI LELLA, Wisdom, 336.

48 RICKENBACHER, Weisheitsperikopen, 112: "die mir gemäss handeln (die mich tun)". Cf. Sir 27,9 – 10, where ἀλήθεια and ἄδικα are the object complement of ἐργάζομαι: "Birds will nest with those like them, and truth will come back to those who practise it. A lion lies in wait for prey, so sin for people who practise injustices".

49 ALONSO SCHÖKEL, Eclesiástico, 231: "el que me pone en práctica".

50 SMEND, Weisheit, 221: "Man kann am Ende auch die Weisheit 'tun' wie das Gesetz".

51 MARBÖCK, Weisheit im Wandel, 76: "die sich um mich mühen"; cf. HAMP, Sirach, 635: "wer sich um mich abmüht".

3.3 Shame and Sin/Failure

Listening to and committing oneself to Wisdom are two praiseworthy attitudes, so much so that the disciple who behaves in this way will receive rewards: he will never need to be ashamed and he will not sin (in other words he will not fail in reaching his goals). The first reward has to do with "shame", an important theme in the book of Ben Sira[52]. Even if there is a good kind of shame, which can be described as glory and favour (4,21b), Ben Sira shows himself to be much more concerned with that shame which, in itself, is sin or leads to sin (4,21a), and so must always be avoided. It is to this subject that he dedicates Sir 41,14–42,8, a long section which, according to Josef Haspecker, contains a double decalogue on shame which is "almost like a summary of important topics of wisdom in practical life already covered in the book"[53]. In the first decalogue (Sir 41,14–42,1d), Ben Sira lists the things one must be ashamed of (true shame) and, in Sir 42,1ef–42,8, what one must not be ashamed of (false shame).

We should note that in 9 of the 10 occurrences of αἰσχύνω[54] in the book, the verb is always accompanied by a complement[55]. In some cases, it is a question of being ashamed of sinful things such as sexual immorality before parents (41,17) or of ill-mannered behaviour such as peering into someone else's house (21,22). In other cases, however, we are dealing with not being ashamed of good things (42,1e) such as being oneself (4,20), confessing one's own sins (4,26), protecting a friend (22,25), practising wisdom (51,18) or praising God (51,29). Finally, we should point out 13,5b, the only text in which the object complement of αἰσχύνω is a person: "He [the rich man] will shame you with his foods". Interestingly, the only exception is our passage. In Sir 24,22, the verb αἰσχύνω is used absolutely. Wisdom promises the attentive and obedient disciple that he is not to be ashamed. In our view, the lack of a complement is very suitable to a concluding phrase which avoids details and so favours a broad interpretation of the content. In other words, the good disciple is never to be ashamed, on no occasion and for

---

52 Cf. CAMP, Honor and Shame, 171–187; EAD., Honor, Shame and Hermeneutics, 157–171; EAD., Ben Sira; BOTHA, Ideology of Shame, 353–371; DE SILVA, Wisdom, 433–455; PIWOWAR, Vergogna.

53 HASPECKER, Gottesfurcht, 185: [Der doppelte Dekalog über die Scham] "nimmt sich fast aus wie ein Resumé wichtiger im Buch schon behandelter Themen weisheitsgemässen Verhaltens im praktischen Leben".

54 On 6 occasions, αἰσχύνω translates the Hebrew בוש (4,20.26; 41,17; 42,1; 51,18QPs[a] [הפך in MS B]; 51,29).

55 Note that, in Sir 41,14–42,1d and 42,1ef–42,8, even if the verb αἰσχύνω is mentioned only twice, at the beginning of each unit respectively (41,17; 42,1e), it is implicit in each verse.

no reason. Whoever wants something more concrete can always consult the double decalogue mentioned.

We pass on now to the second reward. The key word is the verb ἀμαρτάνω, which is usually translated with "to sin". But is this the sense which the verb has in Sir 24,22? Again, we find ourselves faced with a problem of translation. The verb ἀμαρτάνω, just like αἰσχύνω, is not accompanied by any complement. In some texts, by means of complements, Ben Sira specifies the kind of sin (19,16; 23,11; 35[32Hb],12), the reason which provokes it (27,1; 42,1) or the person or persons against whom it is committed (7,7; 10,29; 38,15). In others, however, it refers to the act of sinning in a general way (5,4; 7,36; 15,20; 19,4.28; 20,21; 21,1). From a grammatical point of view, Sir 24,22 belongs to the latter group. I repeat, however, are we sure that our verse is speaking of sin at all?

The main Hebrew word corresponding with ἀμαρτάνω is חטא. It is attested thus in the LXX. In Ben Sira, this correspondence is confirmed on only 3 occasions (5,4; 38,15; 42,1). In 7,7 and 10,29, ἀμαρτάνω renders רשע and, in 7,36, שחת. Without the Hebrew text of 24,22, one can only hypothesize as to what verb lies behind ἀμαρτάνω. According to Skehan, we would have here לא יחטאו, which he translates as "will not fail". In this case, just as in Prov 8,36, the verb חטא "has its basic physical sense of falling short, missing the mark, and does not rather convey the derived sense of 'sin'"[56]. Another possibility is that defended by Rudolf Smend. Basing himself on 7,36, he claims that, in 24,22, ἀμαρτάνω renders the Hebrew שחת (Hiphil: "to be corrupt", "to act corruptly")[57]. At any rate, even if the idea of sin could be implicit and is not to be rejected completely, we think that in 24,22 the sense of ἀμαρτάνω is rather that of "missing the mark", that is, failing to achieve the result that was intended[58]. Thus, what we have suggested for αἰσχύνω is applicable to ἀμαρτάνω, that is, the concluding function of the verse is expressed also by the use of terms with broad significance which embrace all the areas of a person's life.

Let us add a final observation. By contrast with Sir 4,11–19, where the rewards awaited by the good disciple are all formulated in the positive, in 24,22, on the other hand, the two promises made by Wisdom are expressed negatively. It is our contention that the two negations before the verbs in the future and in final position confer on Wisdom's speech a judicious and authoritative tone which is reassuring for the disciple (cf. 7,36).

---

56 SKEHAN, Structure, 378.
57 Cf. SMEND, Weisheit, 221. Cf. note 22.
58 CORLEY, Intertextual Study, 159–160: "Proverbs 8 and Sirach 24 both warn against missing the opportunity to gain wisdom, in each case at the end of her first-person speech". The reference is clearly to Prov 8,36 and Sir 24,22.

4 Conclusion

Following our analysis, we can affirm that Sir 24,22 acts as a conclusion, not only to Wisdom's exhortation (24,19 – 22), but to her entire speech in the first person (24,3 – 22). In this case, the method chosen by Ben Sira to conclude the poem has been to decode the metaphor of Wisdom as a fruit tree (together with that of Wisdom as a lover) which he had developed so carefully in the previous verses. The metaphorical language is, then, replaced by a language that is direct and clear but not for this reason any less stimulating and convincing. There is also a note of realism in this conclusion of his. An essential component of listening to Wisdom and putting her into practice (her teachings are understood) is personal effort. Without a fundamental commitment, the disciple will never succeed in reaching these objectives.

At the same time as he decodes Wisdom's metaphors, Ben Sira introduces indirectly the figure of the Law in such a way as to prepare the passage for the following verse. It will be precisely in Sir 24,23 where the close relationship between Wisdom and the Law will come to light. So, then, in addition to its concluding function, Sir 24,22 acts as a transition to the speech of the sage (24,23 – 34) with which chapter 24 finishes.

In 24,1– 22, Ben Sira has chosen a point of view and a voice in order to transmit his message. The point of view and the voice are those of Wisdom, but, behind these, is hidden the figure of the sage and his authority. Perhaps, as Benjamin Wright suggests, we have here the authoritative voice of the ideal sage, "one who embodies Wisdom", with whom Ben Sira identifies himself. The ideal sage (Ben Sira) is an example for the disciples who frequent his school: "His is not simply an example to be imitated, but he is someone to be emulated"[59].

---

59 WRIGHT, Sage as Exemplar, 181; cf. CAMP, Ben Sira, 163 – 168.

Dreams and Folly in Sir 31(34Hb),1–8

Like most people of the ancient Orient the Hebrews believed that dreams were a special means of communication between humans and the divinity[1]. Although the Bible condemns recourse to dreams as an ordinary means of divination (Deut 13,2–6; 18,9–14; Jer 23,25–32; 27,9–10; 29,8), on various occasions it considers them as a vehicle of divine revelation (Gen 28,10–17; 37,5–11; 1 Kgs 9,1–9; cf. Matt 1,20–23; 2,13.22), especially in texts of an apocalyptic nature (Dan 2; 4; 7)[2].

Ben Sira is the only sapiential author who fulminates directly against dreams as a source of information or as a guideline for behaviour, though not without a certain ambiguity (31[34Hb],1–8). Although he cannot deny the positive function of dreams in the tradition, he treats them in the most cursory fashion (31[34Hb],6a). Traditionally Sir 31(34Hb),1–8 is considered as a reaction against mantic traditions and magical practices originating from Hellenistic culture. Such pagan and degrading practices were thought to have infiltrated Palestine in the 2nd century BC and to constitute a serious threat to the moral and religious integrity of the Israelite faithful[3]. There is, however, a growing tendency to interpret Sir 31(34Hb),1–8 as a strong rebuttal by Ben Sira and his school of the apocalyptic movement exemplified in 1 Enoch and Aramaic Levi. According to this interpretation the polemic in the passage provides evidence of some animosity between the two traditions, even if it was not openly expressed. Besides dreams and visions, other points of conflict are the use of the calendar (solar, lunar or both), esoteric knowledge (cosmological speculation, eschatological realities) and the attitude towards the priestly circles that dominated the cult in Jerusalem[4]. To these two interpretations should be added a markedly psychological reading which perceives in Ben Sira's remarks against dreams the psychological and medical realism of the sage[5].

Our study wants to investigate the evident antipathy of Ben Sira for the world of dreams not from the point of view of the social, cultural and political

---

1 Cf. OPPENHEIM, Interpretation of Dreams.

2 Cf. EHRLICH, Traum, esp. 137–149 (dreams as divine manifestation) and 155–170 (ban on dreams in Sacred Scripture); RESCH, Traum; HUSSER, Songe; ID., Dreams; BAR, Letter; and the doctoral dissertation by FLANNERY-DAILEY, Standing at the Heads of Dreamers.

3 SPICQ, Ecclésiastique, 736; HENGEL, Judaism and Hellenism, vol. 1, 240; SKEHAN–DI LELLA, Wisdom, 409; HUSSER, Dreams, 158.

4 ARGALL, 1 Enoch, 81–82; WRIGHT, Puzzle, 140–142; COLLINS, Seers, 391–392; BOCCACCINI, Middle Judaism, 80.86.

5 WISCHMEYER, Kultur, 221–223, esp. 223.

https://doi.org/10.1515/9783110492316-021

context of the time, nor from the postulates of human sciences, but from the doctrinal framework of the book itself. Our principal criteria of interpretation are the teaching which underlies the work of the sage and especially the notion of "wisdom" (in relationship to Law and fear-of-God) which characterises his school.

1 Translation and Textual Notes

As for the Hebrew text of Sir 31(34Hb),1–8, we only have some words of the first verse in MS E which contains in the first leaf 35(32Hb),16–36(33Hb),14b in recto and 36(33Hb),14c–31(34Hb),1 in verso (ENA 3597)[6]. Therefore, our study begins with an analysis of the Greek version[7]. The complete text of the pericope is also found in the Syriac and Latin versions[8].

1 Vain and deceiving hopes are (typical) for the fool
   dreams give wings to the foolish[9].
2 Like one who catches shadows and pursues the wind
   so is he who confides in dreams.
3 A mirror and a dream are similar (things)[10]:
   before a face, the image of a face.
4 Can something pure come from what is impure,
   or something true from what is false?
5 Divinations, auguries and dreams are void,
   like (the mind of) a woman in childbirth producing fantasies.
6 If they are not sent by the Most High as a visitation,
   do not become engrossed in them[11].
7 For dreams have led many astray
   and those who confided in them have fallen.
8 Without deception the Law is (to be) fulfilled,
   wisdom (comes to) perfection in the mouth of a faithful person.

---

6 MARCUS, Fifth Ms, 223–240. See the photographic reproduction between pages 228 and 229.
7 ZIEGLER (ed.), Sapientia.
8 CALDUCH-BENAGES—FERRER—LIESEN, Wisdom of the Scribe; Biblia sacra.
9 In his translation Sauer combines MS E with Gk: "Eitles suchst [du, wenn du auf Trügerisches hoffst], und Träume [beunruhigen törichte Menschen]. Cf. SAUER, Jesus Sirach, 238.
10 Lit. "This according to that is the vision of dreams".
11 Lit. "Do not give your heart/mind/self to them".

31(34Hb),1

The last line of the leaf is very blurred, as Marcus[12] already noted in his edition of MS E: וחלומות / חלת כזב ת.....רֹיק תֹד.... Beentjes[13] follows Marcus except for the third word of the first colon: תוחלת. Segal[14] reconstructs verse 1 as follows:

רק תִּדְרֹ[שׁ] תֹּ[וֹ]חֶלֶת כָּזָב / וַחֲלוֹמוֹת יָפְרִחוּ כְסִילִים

In Syr: "He who seeks vanity (*sryqwt'*), finds falsehood and a dream(world) and idle joy (*sryqt'*)". While verse 1b in Syr is translated freely, verse 1a is closer to Hb than to Gk: κεναὶ ἐλπίδες καὶ ψευδεῖς ἀσυνέτῳ ἀνδρί. According to Minissale[15], Gk does not translate the verb דרש due to its magical connotations (cf. 45,15ab and 46,20a).

31(34Hb),2

Instead of διώκων ἄνεμον Syr reads: "lets a bird fly away", which seems to be an interpolation from 27,18, cf. Prov 9,12[LXX]; and instead of ὁ ἐπέχων ἐνυπνίοις Syr has: "he who believes in a nightly vision (*lḥzw' dlly'*)". Lat reads: *qui attendit ad visa mendacia.*

31(34Hb),3

τοῦτο κατὰ τοῦτο ὅρασις ἐνυπνίων. In Syr: "Thus (it) is (with) a vision and a dream by night". Smend[16] assumes an original זֶה כָזֶה, "the one like the other" (τοῦτο κατὰ τοῦτο, *hoc secundum hoc*) and reads מַרְאָה, "mirror" instead of מַרְאֶה, "vision" (ὅρασις, Syr *ḥzw'*). The second colon corroborates this reading in all versions, since it describes the function of a mirror without naming it: Gk (κατέναντι προσώπου ὁμοίωμα προσώπου), Syr ("in front of a person [appears] the shape of a face") and Lat (*ante faciem hominis similitudo hominis*).

---

12 MARCUS, Fifth Ms, 237.
13 BEENTJES, Book, 107.
14 SEGAL, ספר, 216.
15 MINISSALE, Versione greca, 212.
16 SMEND, Weisheit, 305.

31(34Hb),4

Following Fritzsche[17], Ryssel thinks that the Greek translator read יִטַּהֵר (Hithpael) instead of יִטְחַר (Qal), and therefore translated καθαρισθήσεται instead of καθαρεύσει, a form which in fact goes better with ἀληθεύσει than the first one. Smend, on the other hand, followed by Box–Oesterley[18], holds that the passive καθαρίζεσθαι often signifies "to be clean" as in Sir 23,10; 1 Sam 20,25; Ezek 36,25. Concerning the first colon of Syr: "And could innocence come from a chief of the people?", Edersheim and Ryssel[19] think that the translator divided the words badly and read מֵרֹשׁ עַמּוֹ יִצָּדֵק instead of מֵרָשָׁע מַה יִּצְדָּק. In the second colon "or will he who is a liar, be free from guilt (nzk')?" the Syriac translator possibly interpreted יצדק in his own way.

31(34Hb),5

In Lat the three nouns of verse 5a (μαντεῖαι καὶ οἰωνισμοὶ καὶ ἐνύπνια) are given a qualification (*divinatio erroris*[20] *et auguria mendacia et somnia malefacientium*). For verse 5b, MS 248 presents a variant: ὡς ὠδινούσης φαντάζεται σου ἡ καρδία which corresponds to Lat: *sicut parturientis cor tuum fantasiam patitur*. In Syr, however, the image of the woman in labour does not appear: "and he who believes in them, there is his mind". Perhaps the Greek translator read אִשֶּׁה תְּחוֹלֵל, "a woman in childbirth" instead of אֲשֶׁר תְּחוֹלָל, "what you expect"[21]. If this were the case, the colon would be as follows: "What you expect is what your heart/mind imagines"[22].

31(34Hb),6

For verse 6a, ἐὰν μὴ παρὰ ὑψίστου ἀποσταλῇ, MS 248 reads ἐν σου ἐπισκοπῇ. According to Box–Oesterley, Lat might best represent the original text: *nisi ab Altissimo fuerit emissa visitatio*[23]. Syr strangely omits the negation at the beginning of

---

17 RYSSEL, Sprüche, 400; FRITZSCHE, Weisheit, 191.

18 SMEND, Weisheit, 305; BOX–OESTERLEY, Book, 433.

19 EDERSHEIM, Ecclesiasticus, 169; RYSSEL, Sprüche, 400.

20 HART (ed.), Ecclesiasticus, 186: + *erroris* 𝔏 "reserving the rights of legitimate divination in accordance with [verse] 6 Gr".

21 SMEND, Weisheit, 306; PETERS, Buch, 280.

22 Cf. the saying of R. Jonatan: "A man sees in dreams only those things that his own thoughts suggest to him" (b. Ber. 55b).

23 BOX–OESTERLEY, Sirach, 434: "[Lat] apparently means: unless the dream be followed by some definite and practical consequences, pay no heed to it".

the phrase: "And (even) if from God it is commanded to go astray in nocturnal considerations"[24].

31(34Hb),7

In the first colon, Gk (πολλοὺς γὰρ ἐπλάνησεν τὰ ἐνύπνια) and Lat (*multos enim errare fecerunt somnia*) coincide, while Syr translates freely: "For by dreams many have mistaken the path". The same occurs in the second colon (Gk: καὶ ἐξέπεσον ἐλπίζοντες ἐπ᾽αὐτοῖς; Lat: *et exciderunt sperantes in illis*), where the Syr substitutes "those who hope in them" with the image of the road: "and they have stumbled on their routes". According to Smend[25], Gk read correctly ויכשלו בתוחלתם. Peters[26] on the other hand, favours Syr and mantains that instead of ויכשלו בשבלם, Gk read erroneously ויכשלו בשברם.

31(34Hb),8

In 31(34Hb),8 it is very difficult to establish the precise relation between the two cola. In verse 8a, Gk (ἄνευ ψεύδους συντελεσθήσεται νόμος) and Lat (*sine mendacio consummabitur verbum* [Vulg.: + *legis*]) coincide except for the last word. Syr translates differently: "In a place in which there are no sins, God is pleased". According to Ryssel[27], the translator did not understand the first words of the colon and this error affected the rest of his translation. In verse 8b it would be better to read ἐν στόματι πιστοῦ (πιστῶν in *O-V* 296 – 548 Arm Clem. = *in ore fidelis*). Clement of Alexandria eliminates τελείωσις which Lat translated with the verb *complanabitur*. In the second colon Syr reads "because the wisdom of the evil-doers is verified in the night". Assuming Hb to be וחכמה לפי נאמן כליל (see Segal's commentary)[28], it is probable that the translator read בליל[ה] instead of כליל and לפשע instead of לפי. Smend[29], on the other hand, proposes the Hebrew ופי חכמה כליל נאמן and explains the Syriac version as follows: in the Vorlage of Syr

---

24 SMEND, Weisheit, 306: "Die Auslassung der Negation ist offenbar falsch".

25 SMEND, Weisheit, 306.

26 PETERS, Buch, 280.

27 RYSSEL, Sprüche, 401: "Wahrscheinlich stand im Urtexte: בְּלֹא [שֶׁקֶר] (= ohne, wie z. B. Ps. 17,1) und S machte das בְּ vom Prädikatsverbum abhäng: 'an dem Nicht-Sündigen' und verschob dadurch das Ganze".

28 SEGAL, ספר, 216.

29 SMEND, Weisheit, 307: "Schwerlich war כליל Prädikat zu חכמה, sondern eher Adverbium (wie 37,18) zu נ]אמ[ה, das im Sinne von 46,15 stand und zu פה, nicht zu חכמה gehörte".

ופי would have been substituted with כי and, on the basis of this erroneous reading [ה]בליל, the translator thought it appropriate to add "of the evil-doers" (*d'wl'*).

2 Dreams and Travels

Some authors, like Peters and Spicq[30], sought to discover in Sir 31(34Hb),1–8 a kind of answer to the question in 36(33Hb),33 (directed to the owner) concerning the slave who escaped because of the bad treatment he received: "by what road will you go to look for him?" We believe that the text on the dreams is to be connected not with the preceding text on the servants (36[33Hb],25–33) but rather with the text that follows it and which deals with travels (31[34Hb],9–20)[31]. There seems to be no apparent connection between dreams and travels, but an attentive reading of both texts allows us to detect a *Leitmotiv* which ingeniously compares the deceiving fantasy of dreams with the real and enriching experience of travels. The first is a source of folly, while the latter is a source of wisdom.

On the level of the vocabulary there are six significative points of contact between 31(34Hb),1–8 and 31(34Hb),9–20: ἐλπίς, ἐλπίζω (vv. 1a.15.16b.7b), ἀσύνετος, σύνεσις (vv. 1a.9b.12b), σκιά (vv. 2a.19c), ἐπέχω (vv. 2b.18), πλανάω, ἀποπλανάω (vv. 7a.9a.11.12a), πίπτω, πτῶσις (vv. 7b.19d). All of this vocabulary serves to establish a contrast between the two pericopes. Furthermore, it is noteworthy that πιστός (v. 8b), has a corresponding term in the second pericope: ὁ φοβούμενος κύριον (vv. 14a.16a.17a; cf. 19a).

1. The idle and deceptive hopes (ἐλπίδες, v. 1a) of those who confide (ἐλπίζοντες, v. 7b) in dreams contrast with the consoling hope of those who fear the Lord, for their hope is the Lord himself (vv. 15.16b).

2. The foolish and insensible man (ἀνὴρ ἀσύνετος) is the opposite of the experienced person who has travelled (vv. 9–11) and who, besides having other qualities, speaks with intelligence (σύνεσις). In reality, this person is no other than Ben Sira who, in the 1st person singular, tells us of his experience: he has seen many things on his travels and his understanding (σύνεσις, v. 12b) goes beyond his words, i.e. he has learned more than he could put into words (cf. 39,6.9).

---

30 PETERS, Buch, 279; SPICQ, Ecclésiastique, 734: "[the question in 36(33Hb),3] évoquerait le cas d'un homme recourant aux présages et aux songes pour connaître les choses cachées et fixer sa ligne de conduite".
31 Cf. CALDUCH-BENAGES, Elementos, 289–298; LAVOIE, Ben Sira le voyageur, 37–60.

3. and 4. The person who relies (ἐπέχω, v. 2b) on dreams is one who catches at shadows (σκιά, v. 2a) and pursues wind, while the one who relies (ἐπέχω, v. 18) on the Lord finds in him a shelter from the scorching wind and a shade (σκιά, v. 19c) from the midday sun.

5. If dreams have made many go astray (πλανάω, v. 7a), the person who has travelled (πλανάω, ἀποπλανάω), like Ben Sira, knows many things, speaks with understanding and increases his or her resources (vv. 9a.11.12a).

6. Those who confided in dreams have fallen (πίπτω, to fall in a moral sense, v. 7b). By contrast, the hope of those who fear the Lord is a protection against stumbling, a secure help against falling (ἀπὸ πτώσεως, 19d).

Finally, let us have a closer look at the word πιστός. Sir 31(34Hb),1–8 opens with a negative image, viz. the image of the insensible fool, but closes in a positive vein, viz. with the faithful person (πιστός), whose mouth pronounces wise and sincere words. The faithful person emerges strongly in the teaching about the value of travel, although he goes by various names. Without entering into the discussion about whether the expression τούτων χάριν (v. 13b) refers to the previous verses or the following[32], we note that in Sir 31(34Hb),9–20, Ben Sira, intelligent and experienced, presents himself as the prototype of a faithful person. The sage implicitly identifies with the group of those who fear and love the Lord (cf. vv. 14.16a.17.19a), with the ones who confide in the Saviour and with those who do not trust the unreal world of dreams.

3 Dreams and Deceit

Sir 31(34Hb),1–8 is structured in two distinct parts: in verses 1–5 Ben Sira expounds his doctrine on dreams (vv. 1–3: the fool and his oneiric experiences; vv. 4–5: dreams put on a par with divinatory practices), and in verses 6–8 he warns the disciple against dreams (v. 6: conditional negative counsel; v. 7: justification; v. 8: conclusion). It is noteworthy that the term ἐνύπνια ("natural and therefore deceptive dreams") appears five times in eight verses: vv. 1.2.3.5.7 (cf. ὄνειροι, "oracular dreams", not attested in Sir)[33] and is closely related to the concept of falsehood/deceit which is repeated thrice in the text: in the beginning, middle and at the end (ψευδής, vv. 1a.8; ψεῦδος, v. 4b). The first occurrence

---

32 CALDUCH-BENAGES, Elementos, 293 note 8.
33 According to Husser, this radical distinction between dreams "came into force little by little under the influence of Hellenism, and seems to have been generally accepted in the 2nd century BCE by intellectuals" (HUSSER, Dreams, 102).

refers to the hopes of the fool (v. 1a)[34] which, besides being vain and deceitful, lead to failure (cf. v. 7b), the second alludes implicitly to dreams (v. 4b), and the third alludes to the fulfilment of the Law, which, by contrast, is to be realised "without deceit" (v. 8a).

With the exception of our text, the verb (ψεύδω) and its derivatives (ψευδής, ψεῦδος, ψεύστης) is always mentioned in relationship to the habit of lying—considered to be more grave than robbery—and its irreparable consequences (cf. 7,12–13; 20,24–26; 25,2; 41,17). Ben Sira himself has suffered the attacks of persons without wisdom who contrive lies (51,2.5) without ever thinking about what they are doing (15,8). Lies and foolishness go together in 20,24: "A lie is an ugly blot on a person; it is continually on the lips of the ignorant (ἀπαιδεύ-των)", but keen understanding towers above both: "As the palate tastes the kinds of game, so an intelligent mind (συνετή) detects false words" (33[36Hb],24). In the teaching of Ben Sira, therefore, foolishness and lying are qualities of the fool, while the wise person shuns this shameful habit and stands out through his or her capacity to discern what is true from what is false both in speech and in dreams.

From 31(34Hb),2 onwards the negative quality of dreams is accentuated more and more in a crescendo which culminates in 31(34Hb),5: first, through the images of shadows and wind (cf. Hos 12,2; Qoh 1,14), the mirror (cf. Prov 27,19) and the woman in labour[35]; second, by alluding to the concept of the impure (cf. Job 14,4)[36]; and, lastly, by putting dreams on a par with illicit divinatory practices (cf. Lev 19,26.31; 20,6.27; Deut 18,10–14) that are, according to the sage, "void" (μάταια), unreal and meaningless, idle and without religious meaning. Moreover, the fact that ἐνύπνια (v. 5a) is mentioned after the consultation of oracles in general (μαντεῖα) and of omens based on the observation of birds (οἰωνισμοί) in

---

34 The Syriac version ("He who seeks vanity, finds falsehood and a dream[world] and idle joy") seems to have inspired the saying of R. Simeon ben Yochai: "As there cannot be grain without hay, neither can there be dreams without vanity" (b. Ber. 55a). A Spanish proverb makes that same connection: "Creer en sueños, vanísimo agüero" (Believing in dreams is a vain omen).
35 According to Alonso Schökel (Notas, 311), "Ben Sira apunta un análisis psicológico: son sombras sin cuerpo, viento inconsistente, imagen sin realidad, mentira, fantasía febril". As Morla Asensio (Eclesiástico, 169) comments, "estas imágenes pretenden definir tales actividades [mantic techniques] como engañosas por inaferrables, inconsistentes y reflejo de uno mismo (búsqueda narcisista y egoísta de los propios intereses). Auténticos transtornos pasajeros, como los de la mujer ante la inminencia del parto".
36 Cf. ARGALL, 1 Enoch, 82: "The rhetorical question in 34,4a may imply that visionaries are ritually unclean. Have they separated themselves from the temple?"

particular, favours the interpretation of this term as oneiromancy or divination of the future through dreams (cf. 1 Sam 28,6)[37].

4 A Single Exception

After such a negative presentation, and just before advising the disciple not to pay attention to dreams, the sage mentions a possible exception which contradicts his lapidary judgement in 31(34Hb),1b that "dreams give wings (ἀναπτέρω) to the foolish"[38]. If a particular dream is sent by the Lord, then one should indeed pay attention to it. The fact that Ben Sira is strongly opposed to divinatory practices does not mean that he denies a possible divine manifestation by means of dreams.

Sir 31(34Hb),6a says that no significance should be attributed to dreams "if they are not sent by the Most High as a visitation (ἐν ἐπισκοπῇ)"[39]. In the LXX the terms ἐπισκοπή and ἐπισκέπτω usually signify a "visitation" by the Lord, i.e. a divine intervention in human history for salvation (cf. Gen 21,1; 50,24; Exod 3,16) or for judgement (cf. Isa 10,3; Jer 6,15). The book of Ben Sira takes the same position: in this theological context ἐπισκέπτω and its main Hebrew equivalent פקד signify to "pay attention" (32[35Hb],21c), "judge" (2,14) and "protect with benevolence" (46,14); the noun ἐπισκοπή stands for "the moment of judgement" (18,20) and "divine punishment" (23,24). In 31(34Hb),6a the use of the phrase ἐν ἐπισκοπῇ surprises the reader, for he or she has no information on how to interpret it exactly. Maybe one should think, as Husser suggests, that the word ἐπισκοπή marks the unquestionable divine intervention when a true/ authentic dream is at stake, indicating that God himself is the one who takes the initiative to communicate with the dreamer[40]. Ben Sira wants to underline on the one hand the rarity of such a dream, and on the other, the divine initiative in such an intervention. Probably he is thinking of the passages in the Old Testament in which God reveals his will in a dream (Gen 28,12–16; Dan 2,1–45).

---

37 Cf. HUSSER, Dreams, 157; CRENSHAW, Problem of Theodicy, 57 note 33: "Here Sirach strikes out against those who make free use of dreams in order to predict the future"; HAMP, Sirach, 90: "Falsche Zukunftsschau" (this is the title given by the author to Sir 31[34Hb],1–8); SAUER, Jesus Sirach, 240.

38 According to Argall (1 Enoch and Sirach, 83) and Wright (Putting the Puzzle, 141), this sentence could be directed against the visionary ascents to heaven like that of Enoch (cf. 1 En. 14,8).

39 Instead of the literal translation "as a visitation", Box–Oesterley prefer "providentially" (cf. BOX–OESTERLEY, Sirach, 434).

40 HUSSER, Songe, 203; ID., Dreams, 158.

Before finishing his discourse on dreams, the sage strengthens his argument by appealing to the experience of the past: many were led astray and were lost because they trusted in dreams. Contemporaries of Ben Sira might have known to whom he was referring, but for us it remains an obscure reference (perhaps the sage intended to contrast fools with faithful Abraham, who was led by God by means of a nightly visitation [Gen 15,12–21] and with whom God made an alliance [Sir 44,20; cf. Gen 15,18]). In any case, this appeal to experience achieves its rhetorical and pedagogical function, emphasising his earlier observations.

One problem remains to be solved: How does one distinguish between a true and a false dream? How can one be sure that a dream is sent by the Lord (cf. Job 33,14–15) rather than from existential anxiety (Sir 40,5–7), or as a consequence of gluttony (Sir 34[31Hb],20)? The sage does not answer this question, but his silence suggests that the intelligent disciple will be able to distinguish between a deceptive and a true dream.

5 True Wisdom

In keeping with the objective of his book, Ben Sira concludes his teaching on dreams by recommending a sensible, secure and wise course of action: the sincere fulfilment of the Law, which is the reliable source of revelation[41]. In 31(34Hb),8 two key words of the book appear for the first and only time: νόμος and σοφία related to the idea of fulfilment (συντελεσθήται) and perfection (τελείωσις). To these keywords one should add the faithful person (πιστός), who is understood as the equivalent of one who fears the Lord (ὁ φοβούμενος κύριον)[42]. The intrinsic relationship between the Law and wisdom is a constant theme in the book (1,26; 6,37; 24,23–29), just as is the relationship between the Law, wisdom and fear-of-God (1,26–27; 15,1; 19,20; 21,11). Wisdom consists in fearing the Lord, and fear-of-the-Lord expresses itself in fulfilling the Law. In 31(34Hb),8 the accent does not fall so much on the equivalence of Law and wisdom as on their incompatibility with all that represents deceit, falsehood, inauthenticity, emptiness, or instability. Whereas the Law is fulfilled "without deceit" (i.e. without recourse to dreams that do not come from God and divinatory

---

41 Cf. SAUER, Jesus Sirach, 240: "Für Ben Sira ist die von Gott kommende Offenbarung, die jede Täuschung ausschließt, im Gesetzt zu suchen".
42 Cf. Sir 1,14: Ἀρχὴ σοφίας φοβεῖσθαι τὸν κύριον, καὶ μετὰ πιστῶν ἐν μήτρᾳ συνεκτίσθη αὐτοῖς.

practices)[43], wisdom comes to perfection in the mouth of the faithful, i.e. in sincerity/truth.

From the first verse the sage has linked dreams with the figures of the fool and the insensible (ἀσύνετος, ἄφρων)[44]. The fool not only lacks wisdom but will never be able to achieve it (19,23; 15,7); he thinks of stupidities, speaks in an untimely way and incoherently (16,23; 20,7; 21,18; 27,11); he is curious and tiresome (21,23; 22,15); in short: it is better to avoid his company, for it could lead to one's ruin (22,13; 27,12). The opposite side of the coin is the intelligent person (συνετός) who meditates on proverbs and who knows how to gain a hearing (3,29; 21,16), who knows wisdom and honours whoever has found it (18,28–29), but above all who distinguishes himself or herself by trusting in the Law (36[33Hb],3)[45] and observing its commandments (cf. 35[32Hb],24). Therefore, the sage encourages those who want wisdom to converse with the intelligent and, concretely, to ponder the Law of the Lord with them (9,15).

Ben Sira values human intelligence (10,3; 14,20; 18,28–29; 31[34Hb],9–12). Intelligence, in order to be authentic, must be closely linked with observance of the Law. A complacent kind of intelligence which pretends to achieve a knowledge surpassing one's own capacities is a vain presumption, a folly that could lead to one's downfall (cf. 3,21–24). In 19,24 Ben Sira affirms unmistakably that intelligence loses all its value if it violates the Law: "Better the God-fearing (ἔμφοβος) who lacks understanding (ἡττώμενος ἐν συνέσει) than the highly intelligent (περισσεύων ἐν φρονήσει) who transgresses the Law (παραβαίνων νόμον)". This verse concludes the teaching on true and false wisdom which began in 19,20[46], repeating the parallelism between fear-of-God and fulfilment of the Law: "Full/true wisdom (πᾶσα σοφία)[47] is fear-of-the-Lord (φόβος κυρίου), and in full/true wisdom there is the fulfilment of the law (ποίησις νόμου)". The sage reinforces this teaching by considering the contrary principle: "The knowledge of wickedness (πονηρίας ἐπιστήμη) is not wisdom, nor is there prudence

---

43 Cf. RYSSEL, Sprüche, 401; BOX–OESTERLEY, Sirach, 434; SKEHAN–DI LELLA, Wisdom, 409. For another interpretation (Torah as trustworthy promise), see MARBÖCK, Weisheit im Wandel, 92.

44 Cf. the Spanish proverb: "Creer en sueños es de hombres necios" (Believing in dreams is for foolish people).

45 In 36(33Hb),1–3 the one who fears the Lord, the sage and the intelligent person appear to be synonyms with a markedly theological nuance.

46 Cf. WEBER, Wisdom, 330–348.

47 On the elative meaning of the adjective πᾶσα, cf. BEENTJES, Full Wisdom, 39–40.

(φρόνησις) in the counsel of sinners (19,22)". In other words: "human wisdom without ethical and religious honesty is not authentic wisdom"[48].

In 31(34Hb),8 the conclusion reached by Ben Sira leaves no room for doubt: true wisdom is that religious wisdom which is born from a reciprocal relationship with the Lord and which becomes manifest in the observance of the Law. Dreams and other magical practices have no part in this, for they belong to the phantasmal world of the false and unreal which has nothing to do with the intelligent and sincere search for wisdom.

6 Conclusion

The attitude towards dreams which Ben Sira displays in Sir 31(34Hb),1–8 ties in very well with his sapiential doctrine, in which all postulates directly or indirectly deal with true wisdom, with the sage, and with the adequate means to achieve wisdom. By contrast, special attention is dedicated to false wisdom, foolish and insensible persons as well as to the attitudes which cause foolishness and lead to one's ruin.

– The immediate context of our text shows the contrast between dreams and travels, i.e. between fantasy and reality, between illusory thoughts and real experience, between futility and intelligence. All of this is supported by the personal testimony of the sage, who has profited greatly from his travels.
– Associating belief in dreams with the figure of the fool or insensible person automatically means that focusing on dreams cannot be a part of the sapiential program, and that their equivalence with foolishness is immediate and irreversible.
– The false and inconsistent character of dreams contrasts strongly with stability and truth, which are typical features of the Law. Such falseness and inconsistency stand out negatively against the wisdom of a faithful person who fears the Lord.

Unless they come from the Lord, dreams are an example of false wisdom that is to be avoided in order not to endanger one's personal integrity. Dreams do not figure in the school of the sage, for they teach foolishness. By contrast, observance of the Law is the source of authentic wisdom[49].

---

48 ALONSO SCHÖKEL, Eclesiástico, 210–211.
49 OESTERLEY, Wisdom, 218.

The Hymn to Creation (Sir 42,15 – 43,33): A Polemic Text?

Ben Sira begins the last part of his book with a hymn of praise to the wisdom of God, manifested in nature (Sir 42,15 – 43,33: hymn to creation) and in the history of Israel (Sir 44,1– 49,16: the "Praise of the Ancestors", which leads to Sir 50,1– 24: the glorification of the high priest Simon). With these two compositions in hymnic style, the sage succeeds in harmonising the universal dimension of the creation with the national character of salvation, rooted in Israel (Sir 24,1– 22). Both the creation which embraces the whole of humanity and the important characters of the history of Israel—whether they are heroes or anti-heroes—are different manifestations of the same divine wisdom which encourages its disciples to search for God[1].

1 Introduction

The hymn to creation, or, if you wish, the hymn to the Creator, can be described as "a composition that is successful on the literary level and poetically inspired"[2] in which the sage praises the sovereignty and the supreme wisdom of God manifested in the universe, and invites his hearers/readers to unite themselves to him in this attitude of praise. The majority of commentators on the Book of Sirach as well as those authors who have made a more detailed study of the passage follow this line of interpretation. Johannes Marböck, in his by now classical monograph (1971)[3], studies Sir 42,15 – 43,33 as an essential contribution to the theology of creation expressed in the book. Gian Luigi Prato, in his volume on the problem of theodicy in Ben Sira (1975)[4], highlights the function of the elements in the contemplation of the creation. Twelve years later, Keith W. Burton, in his Glasgow doctoral thesis of 1987, still unpublished[5], proposes the theme of creation (divided into eight sections) as the structuring element of the book. Sir 42,15 – 43,33 is the last of the series. In a study on the connection between wisdom and creation,

---

1 Cf. CALDUCH-BENAGES, Inno al creato, 54.
2 ZAPPELLA, Contemplazione, 41.
3 MARBÖCK, Weisheit im Wandel.
4 PRATO, Problema della teodicea.
5 BURTON, Judaic Doctrine.

https://doi.org/10.1515/9783110492316-022

Leo G. Perdue (1994)[6] concentrates on the metaphor of divine wisdom as the guarantee of the order present in the world ("a world of elegance and wonderment"), a metaphor which, according to him, constitutes the centre of the hymn. More recently, George Sauer (2000) has published an article on the Old Testament background of Sir 42,15–43,33[7] in which he points out all the texts of the tradition from which the sage has derived inspiration in composing his poem.

As far as the composition of the hymn is concerned, despite the multiplicity of proposals that have been advanced, all agree in identifying an introduction which exalts the power of God in creation (42,15–25)[8] and a conclusion which is actually a summons to praise the Creator (43,27–33)[9]. The central part of the hymn dedicated to the individual works of creation (43,1–26) is more debated: some consider it to be unitary; others divide it into two or even three strophes. In his commentary, Alexander Di Lella suggests instead a division of the entire poem into four strophes of 15, 14, 16 and 8 cola respectively: 42,15–25; 43,1–12; 43,13–26; 43,27–33[10].

This study does not intend to take sides in the debate. Instead it will focus on the polemical dimension of the hymn, which presupposes the presence of a group of adversaries who are opposed to the school (51,23: בית מדרש) of the sage. It is probable that Ben Sira would have thought of such a group when he taught the hymn to his disciples. To establish the identity of these people (perhaps belonging to one or maybe more schools of thought) is a difficult undertaking, impossible in practice in so far as these people (groups, communities, schools) are never mentioned explicitly in the hymn to creation or elsewhere in the book. To this we must add the total absence of other sources of information or clues of an historical character which could offer reliable guidance for research.

Perhaps we can catch a glimpse of the adversaries behind the old debate formula (אל תאמר: "do not say") which Ben Sira employs on nine occasions (Sir 5,1–6 [4x]; 11,23.24; 15,11.12; 16,17) and above all in the didactic/hymnic compositions on theodicy (Sir 16,24–17,14; 36[33Hb],7–15; 39,12–35; 42,15–43,33). With the old debate formula is linked the expression "no one can say" repeated three times in Sir 39,12–35 (v. 21a: "what use is this?"; v. 21b: "this is worse than that"; v. 34: "this is bad, what is this?") with which Ben Sira rejects his

6 PERDUE, Wisdom & Creation, 243–290 ("I Covered the Earth like a Mist", Cosmos and History in Ben Sira).

7 SAUER, Hintergrund.

8 MINISSALE, Versione greca, 116–125.

9 CALDUCH-BENAGES, God Creator of All.

10 SKEHAN—DI LELLA, Wisdom, 491.

adversaries' opinions on the thorny problem of theodicy. According to James Crenshaw—the first to have an inkling of any religious controversy in the work of the sage—behind the formulae just mentioned one can hear the voices of the anonymous, implicit opponents of Ben Sira and, even if we cannot identify these people or groups for certain, we can at least discern "the basic thrust of their attack"[11].

As far as the theme of Sir 42,15–43,33, the creation and the Creator, is concerned, there are three areas which could have inspired polemic in the teaching of Ben Sira. The first is the Jewish wisdom tradition, the second is that of the Enochic apocalyptic circles, and the third is Greek-Hellenistic culture. In any case, the possible polemic dimension is not the predominant element of the hymn, certainly less evident than in the other three poems on theodicy[12].

2 The Jewish Wisdom Tradition

As Prato, Di Lella and Sauer, among others, have well noted, Sir 42,15–43,33 is full of references to other biblical texts, among which are the priestly account of the creation in Gen 1 (Ben Sira seems, however, not to have known chapters 2–8 and 10–11 of Genesis), Job 28 and 38–41, and a few Psalms (96; 136; 104; 147; 148 to cite only some)[13]. What is most striking is the original and free use that Ben Sira made of these and other texts. He then avoided them when he considered it convenient[14]. Let us record some examples, always with reference to Gen 1. In the introduction to the hymn in 42,15c, we read: "by the word of God his works [were made]", a clear reference to the creative activity of God as it is presented in the first chapter of Genesis. However, we should observe that at no stage does he allude to the creation in six days, to the first human couple (cf. Sir 17,1–12) or to the Sabbath on which God ceased from his labour. In 42,16, it is suggestive that the sun precedes the moon, as if Ben Sira had wished to correct the naïve picture of the Genesis account which presents the creation of the light (Gen 1,3) before that of the sun (Gen 1,16), which is the principal source of

---

11 CRENSHAW, Problem of Theodicy, 47; COLLINS, Jewish Wisdom, 81.

12 CRENSHAW, Problem of Theodicy, 53: "The final didactic hymn [...] (42,15–43,33) shows a decided advance in the direction of praise over polemic".

13 Cf. also the *Song of the Three Children* in the Greek additions to the Book of Daniel and the hymns of Qumran, esp. 1QH IX, 10–14.

14 For the midrashic use of Gen 1, cf. ALONSO SCHÖKEL, Vision of Man, with reference to DE FRAINE, Loflied.

light in premodern cosmology[15]. In Sir 43,1–10 the creation of the firmament, the sun, the moon, and the stars refers to Gen 1,14–18. Ben Sira follows the same order in the creation of the stars that is found in Genesis. However, he not only devotes much more attention to the moon than to the sun, but he also modifies the meaning of the Genesis text: "And God said, 'Let there be lights in the firmament of the heavens to separate the day from the night; and let them be for signs and for seasons and for days and years, and let them be lights in the firmament of the heavens to give light upon the earth'". While here the sun and the moon serve to distinguish and fix the times and seasons, in the text of Ben Sira this function is reserved only to the moon. Moreover, it is to be noted that in 43,11, Ben Sira describes the rainbow, which embraces the arch of the sky with its splendour, but without mentioning the flood, or Noah, or his covenant with God (Gen 9,12–17).

These are not the only differences which surprise us. Besides these, there are other "polemical notes", to use the words of Crenshaw[16], which seem to be directed against the same wisdom tradition to which Ben Sira is heir. In fact, in 42,21, the sage says of God: "He has established the power of his wisdom, he is the only one from all eternity. There is nothing to be added or taken away, and he has no need of any teacher". This verse seems to reject the idea of a pre-existent Wisdom which in the role of "counsellor"[17] assisted God in the creation of the world (cf. Prov 8,22–31, esp. v. 30). According to Crenshaw, this idea would be the fruit of speculation about personified Wisdom, an idea that Ben Sira rejected because he identified Wisdom with the Law[18]. In the doctrine of the sage, wisdom is present as eternal (1,4.9; 24,9) and pre-existent (1,1b; 24,9b), but, above all, it is described as created by God (1,4.9; 24,9). In the three verses which precede 42,21, Ben Sira praises the unlimited knowledge of God with regard to space and time and the totality of his wisdom: "He searches out the abyss and the heart; he understands all their secrets. For the Most High knows all that may be known, and foresees the things which happen in the world. He reveals what has been and what is to be, and he reveals the most hidden mysteries. No thought is absent from him; no word escapes him" (42,18–20). These statements seem designed to refute Eliphaz the Temanite, witness of the

---

15 Cf. MORLA ASENSIO, Eclesiástico, 208.
16 CRENSHAW, Old Testament Wisdom, 158: "Surprisingly polemical notes can be heard now and again within this hymn".
17 This would be one of the possible interpretations of אמון: intended as a derivation from the Akkadian *ummânu*, "scribe, sage; heavenly scribe" (in Hebrew אָמָן), which the Massoretes vocalised incorrectly. Cf. CLIFFORD, Proverbs, 100–101.
18 CRENSHAW, Old Testament Wisdom, 158.

traditional wisdom, when, in interpreting tendentiously the previous declarations of Job he replies: "And you say, 'What does God know? Can he judge through the deep darkness? Thick clouds enwrap him, so that he does not see, when he walks on the vault of heaven'" (Job 22,13 – 14).

In my opinion, however, Ben Sira is not openly opposing the wisdom tradition of Israel in the hymn to creation but rather he is reformulating it in his own way, emphasising some aspects which he, as teacher, considers useful in teaching his disciples how to appreciate and praise what God had done in creation.

3 The Enochic Apocalyptic Circles

"The classic image of Ben Sira as a representative of the conservative wisdom tradition against advancing Hellenism seems inadequate in expressing the complexity and novelty of his thought"[19]. Thus Gabriele Boccaccini expresses himself at the conclusion of a famous study on the Book of Sirach and its connections with Qoheleth and apocalyptic literature (1993) in which he takes up again and develops the same ideas which he had already published elsewhere in 1986.[20] According to him, Ben Sira, would have been afraid of directly criticizing the instances of the apocalyptic tradition. Such a polemical connection between Ben Sira and 1 Enoch had already been suggested by George W. E. Nickelsburg (1983)—who even sees the poor of Ben Sira's time as possible authors of the Epistle of Enoch—as well as Saul M. Olyan (1987), and Lewis J. Prockter (1990)[21].

The recent studies on the Book of Enoch and, above all, the latest research on the intellectual and sociological characteristics of the group which hides under this literature[22] have demonstrated that Enochic Judaism was, at least in a certain measure, "one of the targets of Sirach's polemic arrows"[23]. Many authors today consider Ben Sira and 1 Enoch not only as two different reactions to the threat of Hellenism, but as the expression of two schools of wisdom that were not only in disagreement but were also rivals (*konkurrierende Schule*). On the other hand, to speak of schools of wisdom in this context raises the

---

19 Boccaccini, Middle Judaism, 125. To the authors cited in the note, we add Hengel, Judaism and Hellenism, vol. 1, 131–175.

20 Boccaccini, Origine del male, 34.

21 Nickelsburg, Social Aspects, 651; Olyan, Ben Sira's Relationship, 279–280; Prockter, Torah as a Fence. Cf. also Marböck, Buch, 367.

22 Cf. Henoch 24 (2002).

23 Boccaccini, Introduction, 11; Nickelsburg, 1 Enoch, 63: "It is possible that Ben Sira is polemicizing against those in the Enochic camp".

question of whether and how these texts might allow us to grasp the nature of the conflict between these groups of Jews[24]. Was Ben Sira—*per impossibile*—the only representative of the wisdom which he promoted in his book, or was he part of a sacerdotal community? Did the authors of the different parts of 1 Enoch consider themselves as belonging to a precise social group or community? To what degree does their view represent the society of the period? All these questions would merit further detailed study. One thing is certain, however: Both in the book of Ben Sira and in 1 Enoch, the identity of the opponents always remains hidden. Despite this, there are some texts in which the antagonism between the two groups is more obvious. For example, in 1 En. 98,15, we read: "Woe to you who write lying words of impiety; for they write their lies that men may hear and not forget their folly; and they will not have peace, but will die a sudden death"[25]. The text is aimed at those who are opposed to the doctrine of the sages. But who are these people? Could they be the followers of Ben Sira, promoters of another type of wisdom? In 1 En. 104,10, the author has in his sights the "many sinners who will alter and distort the words of truth and speak evil words among themselves and lie and concoct great fabrications and write books in their own words". According to Sir 50,27, Ben Sira has written a book of wisdom. Would he, therefore, be one of these sinners?

In his 1992 doctoral thesis, developed at the University of Iowa under the supervision of George E. W. Nickelsburg, Randal A. Argall undertook a new line of research on the connection between Ben Sira and 1 Enoch[26]. After having examined the literary forms and the theological themes of revelation, creation and judgement in both books, Argall arrives at the conclusion that Ben Sira (representative of traditional wisdom) and 1 Enoch (representative of the apocalyptic tradition) were very close both at the level of form and of content. Both the books share themes, literary forms, oral traditions and large perspectives which are explained as deriving from a common background.

In fact, the book of Ben Sira and some parts of 1 Enoch are most probably contemporary. While the majority of scholars are in agreement over the dating of Ben Sira (between 200 and 175 BC), that of 1 Enoch is more disputed. In spite of the difference of opinions on the dating of the different sections of the book, today it is held that the Book of Watchers (1 En. 1–36) and the Book of

---

24 WRIGHT, Sirach and 1 Enoch, 182.
25 Basically, I cite the Book of Enoch in the edition of SPARKS (ed.), Apocryphal Old Testament. For suggestions with regard the English translation of the Italian edition of SACCHI, Apocrifi dell'Antico Testamento, I am grateful to Dr. Michael Tait. English editions/translations may be found in CHARLESWORTH (ed.), Old Testament Pseudepigrapha; NICKELSBURG, 1 Enoch.
26 ARGALL, 1 Enoch and Sirach.

Heavenly Luminaries (1 En. 71–82)—if not the whole, then a good part of it—already existed in the 2nd century BC. The Epistle of Enoch (1 En. 92–105), on the other hand, seems to come from a letter date. Given that the persecution of Antiochus Epiphanes in 167 BC is not mentioned in the Apocalypse of Weeks, which is inserted into the Epistle (1 En. 93,1–10; 91,11–17), it is reasonable to think that chapters 92–105 were completed prior to this date[27]. We have spoken first of similarities, but clearly there are substantial differences with regard to the content of the wisdom revealed (the doctrine of opposites vs. speculative cosmology; temporal judgement for each person vs. catastrophic and universal judgement at the end of time) and, as Argall puts it, "such differences are the stuff of the conflict"[28]. According to him, each of the traditions—represented by Ben Sira and 1 Enoch respectively—sees the other as a rival to be challenged.

In 1997, Benjamin G. Wright published an article[29] in which he holds that Ben Sira is responding polemically to the criticisms of certain groups who questioned the legitimacy of the Jerusalem priesthood in their writings and were opposed to the cult in Jerusalem. These writings are the Book of Watchers, the Book of Heavenly Luminaries and the Aramaic Document of Levi which goes back to the 3rd century BC[30]. Beyond the priesthood and the cult, there are other points at issue between Ben Sira and the apocalyptic circles: dreams and visions, the use of the calendar (solar, lunar or both) and esoteric knowledge (cosmological speculations, eschatological realities). Both Argall and Wright deepened the argument in the first seminar on Enoch held at Sesto Fiorentino in June 2001[31]. I also want to mention the study of Gabriele Boccaccini on Zadokite Judaism and sapiential Judaism[32], and that of Martin Ebner which appeared in 2003. The subtitle reveals Ebner's viewpoint: *Weisheitskonzepte in Konkurrenz*[33].

Argall's comparative study has made clear the similarities and differences between the texts of creation in 1 Enoch and in Ben Sira. He distinguishes between the observable aspects of creation (1 En. 2,1–5,4; 101,1–9; Sir 16,24–17,14; 36(33Hb),7–15; 39,12–35; 42,15–43,33) and the hidden ones (1 En. 12–36; 93,11–14; 72–80; 82,4–20; Sir 1,1–10; 24,3–7)[34]. My contribution is different and more modest. I shall take into consideration only those elements of

---

27 Cf. ARGALL, 1 Enoch and Sirach, 5–7.

28 ARGALL, 1 Enoch and Sirach, 250.

29 WRIGHT, Fear the Lord, which is really an expanded revision of Putting the Puzzle Together.

30 STONE, Enoch, 159 note 2; KUGLER, Patriarch, 222–224.

31 ARGALL, Competing Wisdoms; WRIGHT, Sirach and 1 Enoch, 179–187.

32 BOCCACCINI, Roots, 113–150, esp. 136–137.

33 EBNER, Weisheit.

34 ARGALL, 1 Enoch and Sirach, 99–164 (Part II: "The Creation Theme in 1 Enoch and Sirach").

Sir 42,15 – 43,33 which, in my opinion, allow us to glimpse a polemical dimension against the apocalyptic tradition. Our presentation follows the order of the text.

3.1 The Presence and the Role of the Angels

In 42,17, Ben Sira states: "Not even the holy ones of God are sufficient to declare all his marvels. God has made his hosts strong so that they may stand firm before his glory". Here "the holy ones of God" are the angels who form the heavenly hosts and have the office of standing before God (cf. Deut 33,3; Zech 14,5; Job 15,15; Pss 89,6.8; 103,21; 148,2). This description of the angels, in part negative and, what is more, unique in the book, contrasts strongly with the significant role they perform in 1 Enoch. From the introduction to the Book of Watchers, we learn that God "has come with 10,000 holy ones (angels)" to do justice for the elect and to destroy the wicked (1 En. 1,9). Particular emphasis is given to the figure of Uriel, "one of the holy angels" (1 En. 20,1; 72,1), the angel responsible for all the movements of the stars (1 En. 75,3). In 1 En. 81,5, it is "three holy ones (angels)" who lead Enoch back to earth. Surprisingly, in Sir 42,17, Argall does not discover any trace of polemic (and even believes it appropriate to note this fact) against the role of the angels in the other traditions[35]. We, however, taking account of the context, claim that Ben Sira's observations on the angels are not without motive.

3.2 The Knowledge of God

According to Sir 42,18 – 20, God is the only being to possess total knowledge (v. 18c: "all that may be known", πᾶσαν εἴδεσιν)[36] of the secrets of the universe, of history and of the hearts of humans. This statement of the divine omniscience anticipates the conclusion of the hymn where Ben Sira confesses to having seen only a small part (מעט) of the works of God because many still remain hidden (cf. 43,32). This limited knowledge of his is opposed to the unlimited knowledge of Enoch, to whom the angel Uriel showed everything and made everything manifest (1 En. 80,1). He, in his turn, manifested everything to his son Methuselah so that it was all transmitted from generation to generation (1 En. 82,1). It is

35 Cf. ARGALL, 1 Enoch and Sirach, 144 note 357; differently ALBANI, Astronomie, 151.
36 For the Hebrew, cf. QUIMRON, Notes on the Reading, 230: Yadin reconstructs [ ]דע and Strugnell, following the versions, proposes to read [ת]כל דע. Cf. also pp. 205.220.

appropriate, moreover, to mark out Enoch's declaration concerning his own knowledge: "And I, Enoch, I alone saw the sight, the ends of everything, and no man has seen what I have seen" (1 En. 19,4)[37].

3.3 The Immutability and Obedience of Creation

In Ben Sira's view, the elements of nature "live and endure for ever; all are necessary and all obey (42,23)[38]. The stars are the epitome of this relationship between the Creator and created things: "At a command from God, they occupy their posts and they are untiring in their watches" (43,10). In fact, Ben Sira, good master as he is, often makes reference to the obedience of creation to spur his disciples to a similar attitude in their relations with God (16,24 – 30; 39,28 – 31). The idea of the incorrupt nature of the universe contrasts strongly with the apocalyptic tradition, according to which, at the moment of creation, some stars refused the post assigned to them, upsetting the order of the universe before the fall of the angels. And so it was their disobedience which allowed the entrance of evil into the world. On his otherworldly journey, Enoch reached a deserted place, without water or birds where he saw "stars like great burning mountains". The angel Uriel who accompanied him on his journey explained to him that that place was "the prison of the stars of heaven and the heavenly army". The stars who were turning back and forward over the fire were those who had "transgressed the order of the Lord from the beginning of their rising" because they had not arrived [at their assigned post] at the time [appointed for them] (1 En. 18,14 – 15). In 1 En. 20,3 – 6, the seven rebel stars are bound together above the deserted and fearful place to expiate their sin with a punishment that would last ten thousand years. The same idea is found again in the Book of Heavenly Luminaries. After having described with much care "the law of the stars of heaven", that is to say, all the laws which govern heaven and secure the order

---

37 In Sir 44,16 (MS B), Enoch is remembered as a "sign of knowledge" (אות דעת), while in the Greek tradition he becomes "an example of conversion for the Gentiles" (ὑπόδειγμα μετανοίας ταῖς γενεαῖς), something that cannot possibly be considered a translation error. Cf. Minissale, Versione greca, 221: "Ma poi in 16b G trasforma il testo per attribuire ad Enoch, assimilato ad Elia sulla base della commune assunzione al cielo, una predicazione profetica prima del diluvio, che avrebbe provocato il pentimento degli angeli peccatori (1Enoc 12 – 13)". According to Albani (Astronomie, 149), the Hebrew text has been modified for doctrinal reasons: "Mit der Theologie des Sirachbuches ist es unvereinbar, dass ein Irdischer auch nur annähernd in die Nähe der göttlichen Weisheit gelangt".
38 With MS B and Gk. According to MS Mas: "they are kept for every necessity".

and harmony of the universe (1 En. 79,1–6; 80,1), Enoch notes that this ideal order no longer holds. The whole universe has been upset by the sin of the angels, and so, "in the time of the sinners", order and harmony will vanish and all the things on earth will be changed and will not appear at their appointed time: "The rain will be withheld and heaven will retain it... And the moon will change its customary practice and will not appear at its proper time... And in those days... [the sun] will shine rather more than the laws of light (permit). And many heads of the stars in command (that is, the angels) will go astray and change their course and their activity and not appear at the times established for them" (1 En. 80,2–6). "The presence of such conceptions—Boccaccini claims—makes Ben Sira careful to emphasize the uncorrupted nature of the universe"[39].

3.4 The Sun

After having presented in 42,16 the sun as first witness of the glory of God (MSS B and Mas: "the sun which rises manifests himself to all the creation[40] and the glory of the Lord is over all his works"), in the central part of the hymn, Ben Sira devotes four other verses to it (43,2–5):

> [2] The sun at its rising spreads warmth,
> How marvellous the works of the Lord!
> [3] At midday it parches the land,
> who can resist its heat?
> [4] A blazing furnace smelts metal,
> as a ray of the sun burns the mountain.
> The tongue of the sun consumes the inhabited land
> and its light dazzles the eyes.
> [5] Since great is the Lord who has made it,
> And whose word makes his warrior shine[41].

---

39 Cf. BOCCACCINI, Middle Judaism, 91. The author notes that death as a consequence of the sin of Adam and Eve (cf. Gen 3) is the only variation which Ben Sira admits to have happened in the movement of creation: "From the woman comes the beginning of sin; because of her, all die" (Sir 25,24).

40 In Gk, "The sun which shines sees all from on high" refers to 42,18ab: "He [God] scrutinises the abyss and the heart; he understands all their secrets".

41 Sir 43,5b in MS B (ודבריו ינצח אביריו) is difficult to translate and the scholarly suggestions diverge: "und sein Wort lässt dahineilen seinen gewaltigen Diener" (Smend), "sus órdenes espolean a sus campeones" (Alonso Schökel), "at whose orders it urges on its steeds" (Skehan—Di

The description of the sun is dominated almost throughout (with the exception of vv. 2b and 5ab) by the image of fire and heat (to parch, to blaze, to burn, to consume, to dazzle; warmth, heat, furnace). In fact, this seems to be the only characteristic of the sun which is able to arouse the sage's interest. It is astonishing that Ben Sira does not link the sun to the calendar (cf. by contrast Jub. 2,9 where the sun uniquely fulfils this function). In the Enochic tradition, on the other hand, the laws which regulate the course of the sun are of great importance. At the end of 1 En. 82, a chapter devoted entirely to the greatest star reads: "And thus [the sun] rises and sets; it neither decreases nor rests but runs day and night in (its) chariot. And its light is seven times brighter than that of the moon, but in size the two are equal" (1 En. 72,37). In Sir 43,2–5, Ben Sira not only opposes 1 Enoch but also, as we hinted before, the priestly account of Gen 1,14–15. The fact that the cooperation between the sun and the moon as regards the determination of the dates and the flow of the seasons is completely ignored by Ben Sira can be read in a polemic key. Benjamin G. Wright, taking his cue from an article by Alexander Rofé almost ten years before his own[42], thinks that this silence of Ben Sira is deliberate. He is not prepared to make even an apparent concession to those Jews who, like the author of the Book of Watchers, the Book of Heavenly Luminaries, and the Aramaic Document of Levi, defend the priority of the solar calendar[43].

3.5 The Moon

Ben Sira dedicates three verses to the moon. Different from the sun, the function of the moon consists in fixing the seasons, dates and feasts. It is a question of a more complex function because it is linked to the problem of the calendar:

> [6] And also the moon watches over the times,
> regulator of seasons and eternal sign.
> [7] To it [belong] the solemnities and feasts,
> and when it wanes it resumes its cycle.
> [8] The new moon as its name (indicates) is renewed,

Lella), "and his words make brilliant his mighty ones" (Perdue). The Greek version reads: καὶ ἐν λόγοις αὐτοῦ κατέσπευσεν πορείαν ("and with his words he speeds it on its way").

42 ROFÉ, Onset, esp. 43–44: "In my opinion, it becomes clear that Ben Sira is here polemicizing against an adverse tendency we may define as proto-Essenian" (p. 44).

43 WRIGHT, Fear the Lord, 207–208 (= Putting the Puzzle Together, 137–138). Also the Book of Jubilees and the group of Qumran followed a solar calendar of 364 days. Cf. ALBANI, Rekonstruktion; LIORA, Book of Jubilees.

it is splendid in its phases!
Military signal for the heavenly army of the clouds,
which covers the firmament with its splendour.

The Jewish calendar to which Ben Sira makes reference in this passage is a lunar calendar which establishes the sacred times of the days and months of the year according to the phases of the moon. The function of the moon, therefore, becomes central because it determines the Sabbath, the feasts of pilgrimage, the times of fasting—that is, the liturgical feasts. It is a very important question because it is linked to the different religious groups that were in conflict with one another. To control the calendar is, in a certain way, to control the feasts and religious observances. The Book of Heavenly Luminaries contains the astronomic and cosmological material which stands behind the solar year of 364 days (1 En. 72–82)[44]. For the author, the solar year is superior to the lunar because only with the solar year can the feasts fall on the days truly fixed with regard to the position of the stars in the sky. "Only a liturgy which had feasts on fixed dates—Paolo Sacchi comments—could be in harmony with the cosmos"[45]. More than the intricate explanations of the movement of the stars in heaven, what interest us is those passages which can hide a polemical intention. For example, in 75,2, Enoch mentions "the men who go wrong" in their calculation of the solar year, and in 1 En. 82,4–7 (cf. 80,2) he considers those who do not accept this calendar to be sinners:

> [4]"Blessed are all the righteous, blessed are all those who walk in the way of righteousness, and do not sin like the sinners in the numbering of all their days in which the sun journeys in heaven, coming in and out through the gates for thirty days with the heads over thousands [...] with the four days that are added and which their commanders divide between the four parts of the year. [5]Because of them men go wrong in the reckoning of time since they err and do not know them accurately. [6]In fact, they [the epagomenal days] belong in the reckoning of the year and are truly recorded therein [...] and the year (consequently) is completed in three hundred and sixty-four days. [7]And the account of it is true and the recorded reckoning of it is exact for the lights, the months, the feasts, the seasons of rain and the days Uriel showed me, and he inspired what the Lord of all creation had ordained for me in the power of heaven.

We do not know whether, for the author of these texts, the sinners were Ben Sira and those who followed his teaching. On the other hand, we can observe that Ben Sira attributed the function of fixing and controlling the times solely to the moon, even though he was almost certainly aware of the solar calendar. In

---

44 Cf., in connection with this, ALBANI, Astronomie.
45 SACCHI (ed.), Apocrifi, 597.

spite of the absence of precise indications, we hold it quite probable that Sir 43,6 – 8 is a response to the defenders of the solar calendar.

3.6 The Stars

Ben Sira does not say very much about the stars. He underlines only their beauty and their unconditional obedience to the Creator:

> [9] The glory of the stars is the beauty of heaven
> and their light shines in the heights of the Lord.
> [10] At a command from God, they take their positions
> and they never relax in their watch.

This brief allusion to the stars (cf. 44,21d and 50,6) could reflect an attitude of indifference and perhaps also of rejection on the part of Ben Sira towards astrology, a science very widespread in Israel (and also in the pagan world)[46], as demonstrated by the Enochic tradition, especially the Book of Heavenly Luminaries.

Thanks to the witness of Pseudo-Eupolemus[47], we are aware that the Book of Heavenly Luminaries was also known outside of the elect group, which embraced Enochian principles. In his brief *History of the Jews* (158 BC), the anonymous author eulogizes Enoch, presenting him as the inventor of astrology: "The Greeks, however, say that Atlantes invented astrology and that Atlantes is to be identified with Enoch. Enoch's son was Methuselah, he who is supposed to have received all (wisdom) through the angels of God, and in this way, we have learned (everything)" (frag. 1)[48]. If we can trust this information, then it appears very probable—in agreement with Matthias Albani—that Sir 42,15 – 43,33 is Ben Sira's riposte to the astronomic wisdom which Enoch had received through angelic revelation (1 En. 72– 82) and to the idea of a universal knowledge derived from it[49].

---

46 Cf. Sauer, Hintergrund, 317: "Bezüglich der babylonischen Astrologie ist bekannt, dass Israel die Macht der Sterne und damit die der durch sie repräsentierten Götter depotenzierte, indem alle diese himmlischen Kräfte unter die Verfügungsgewalt Jahwes gebracht wurden. Der griechisch-hellenistischen Astrologie steht Ben Sira vollkommen ablehnend gegenüber".
47 Cited in Albani, Astronomie, 151.
48 The text is preserved in Eusebius of Caesarea, Praep. ev. 9,17,1 – 9.
49 Albani, Astronomie, 152.

4 The Graeco-hellenistic Culture

4.1 Astronomy

The connection of Ben Sira with Greek literature has been amply studied by Theophil Middendorp[50] who has discovered more than a hundred parallels between the word of the sage and Greek literature, the most quoted author being the 6th century (BC) poet Theognis. Middendorp's thesis according to which Ben Sira would be a mediator between Judaism and Hellenism has, however, been contested by Hans Volker Kieweler[51]. As far as the connection with Greek philosophy is concerned, the classical work of Martin Hengel[52] and the recent monograph by Ursel Wicke-Reuter[53] on Ben Sira and Stoicism offer exhaustive coverage. In our study, we intend to refer to the world of science, and particularly astronomy, a science which was developed in Greece in the second half of the 3rd century BC when the Ptolemies were governing Palestine. The famous names are Aristarchus of Samos (who lived to at least after 264), Archimedes (287–212), Eratosthenes (ca. 275–193), the third director of the library of Alexandria and, most famous of all, Apollonius of Perga (262–190) and Conon of Samos, who lived in Alexandria at the court of Ptolemy Euergetes and his wife Berenice.

Among these names, there is a figure who moves between didactic poetry and astronomy: Aratus of Soli (Cilicia)[54], a poet contemporary with Callimachus (born in 315 or 310 and dead before 240 BC) who wrote hymns, epigrams, elegiac poems, funeral laments, but, above all, works of a scientific character, such as *Iatrica*, a poem on medicine, *Canon*, which deals with the harmony of the spheres, or *Astrica* (on the stars) consisting of at least five books. All these works have been lost. Luckily we have his main work, the only one remaining. It is a poem of 1154 hexameters, composed at the request of the ruler of Macedonia, Antigone Gonata. The poem is called *Phaenomena* and is concerned with astronomy and meteorology. Others before him had already written poems on astronomy: Cleostratus of Tenedo, author of an *Astrology* and Alexander Aetolus, himself too author of a *Phaenomena*.

The poem of Aratus had such a success that many after him composed other *Phaenomena* without achieving equal fame. Even many poets wrote commentaries on his poem, which had a great influence on the literature which followed.

---

50 Middendorp, Stellung.
51 Kieweler, Stellung.
52 Hengel, Judaism and Hellenism.
53 Wicke-Reuter, Göttliche Providenz.
54 Easterling–Kenney (eds.), Cambridge History, vol. 1, 598–602.

Aratus was inspired by a treatise in prose by a celebrated mathematician and astronomer of the first half of the 4th century BC, Eudoxus of Cnidus. This work, also called *Phaenomena,* was a precise description of the sky and of the fixed stars with an almanac of their risings and settings, together with temporal prognostications linked to them.

Although not a Stoic work, Aratus' *Phaenomena* begins with a hymn to Zeus (Phaen. lines 1–18) which recalls the famous hymn to Zeus by the philosopher Cleanthes. At the conclusion of the hymn, the poet speaks of having prayed to the god for help in "telling about the stars" in an appropriate way and finally he asks him to guide his song to its end. The first part of the poem (Phaen. lines 19–732) is completely dedicated to the stars which, throughout the year, mark the seasons and scan the work of humans: "All together, though so numerous and so dispersed, the stars are dragged by the movement of heaven, day after day, without interruption, eternally" (Phaen. lines 19–21)[55]. The second part (Phaen. lines 773–1154) treats of the phases of the moon, of the prognostications which start from an examination of the moon and the sun, the atmospheric phenomena and their connection with nature, with the animals and with humans. In short, the poem of Aratus is, in substance, not a technical work, a manual of astronomy, but a very fine poetic composition of scientific content. To use the words of Jean Martin, the poem of Aratus is an invitation to discover gradually the presence and the messages of Zeus in the regular movement of the stars just as in the smaller and less certain events of life on earth[56].

Did Ben Sira know the *Phaenomena* of Aratus or other similar poems? Had he ever read *Astrica*, his vast treatise on the stars or other works of astronomy? Were these works to be found in the library of Alexandria? Had Ben Sira ever been to the capital of Hellenism? Had he visited the famous library founded by Ptolemy I? In the face of these questions we find ourselves in great difficulty because we do not know the answer to them. We can only suggest a few hypotheses.

We have already seen that in his hymn to the creation Ben Sira dedicates only two verses to the stars (Sir 43,9–10)—that which is already highly significant by itself[57]—without ever making any allusion to notions relating to astronomy or meteorology. On the contrary, the sage's interest is quite otherwise. He concentrates on two rather different but complementary aspects: the aesthetic

55 ARATOS, Phénomènes, 2.
56 ARATOS, Phénomènes, LXXXV.
57 In this connection Sauer (Hintergrund, 317) comments: "Dieses Schweigen ist bemerkenswert. Spricht sich doch darin eine Nichtachtung der Sterndeutekunst aus, wie sie rings um Israel seit eh und je geübt worden war [...]. Er verliert über die Sterne kein Wort".

(the beauty of the stars) and the spiritual (their obedience to the Creator). As far as appears, the way in which Ben Sira speaks of the heavenly bodies, especially the stars and of the atmospheric phenomena in Sir 42,15–43,33, does not seem to conceal any criticism of the works of astronomy as such. If, however, we try to read between the lines, perhaps we shall discover a message, or even a warning touch, directed at all those who feel themselves attracted by books which are concerned to explain all the mysteries of the heavens simply by human science. Ben Sira knows that people have always desired to know the secrets of the world and that such curiosity may lead us astray when it does not take account of the Creator and his law (cf. Sir 3,21–24).

4.2 The Astral Cult

In the biblical tradition, the Law, the prophets and the sages all condemn the astral cult. In Deut 4,19, we read: "And beware lest you lift up your eyes to heaven, and when you see the sun and the moon and the stars, all the host of heaven, you be drawn away and worship them and serve them, things which the Lord your God has allotted to all the peoples under the whole heaven" (cf. Jer 8,2; Ezek 8,16; Job 31,26 ff). The astral cult, common in the ancient world, was a widespread practice in the Hellenistic environment of the 2nd century BC, especially at Alexandria in Egypt, cultural capital of Hellenism and seat of a numerous Jewish community. In the Prologue to Sirach, the translator places his literary activity in Egypt, probably in Alexandria, in the thirty eighth year of King Euergetes, almost certainly Ptolemy VII Euergetes Physcon, who reigned in Alexandria in two periods interrupted by a break: from 170 to 164 BC and from 145 to 117 BC. With these dates, we can assume that Ben Sira's grandson began his translation around 132 BC, finishing it about 117 BC, the year of the king's death.

Between the Hebrew text (MSS B and Mas) and the Greek version of Sir 42,15–43,33 there are a few differences which have been studied in a very careful way by Antonino Minissale[58]. We would like to confine our attention to some verses of the hymn where the Greek translation avoids the mythological allusions to the heavens, the sun and the moon: Sir 42,17cd; 43,5ab; 43,6ab; 43,7ab; 43,8ab[59].

---

58 MINISSALE, Versione greca, 116–125 (on 42,15–25).

59 Cf. also Sir 43,25b (MS Mas): "the might of Rahab" (גבורת רהב) becomes in Gk "the creation of sea monsters" (κτίσις κητῶν). The grandson's translation avoids the mention of Rahab, one of the names which the OT attributes to the monster of the ocean (cf. Isa 51,9; Ps 89,11; Job 9,13; 26,12). Cf. SPRONK, Rahab, 1292–1295.

In 42,17ab, both the Hebrew and the Greek texts speak of the holy ones of God (אל י[ו]קדש, τοῖς ἁγίοις κυρίου), that is of his angels who are not able to recount his wonders. In 42,17cd, the two texts differ. While the Hebrew text continues to speak of the angels, using a military metaphor ("God gives strength to his armies/soldiers so that they may stand before him"), the Greek refers to the wonders of God: "the things which the Lord almighty has established so that the universe may be firm through his glory", thus eliminating the military image of the heavenly army.

In 43,5a, the Hebrew and Greek texts coincide: "[For] great is the Lord who has made it" (referred to the sun). Not so in the following colon, 43,5b: "and his word makes his warrior (= the sun) shine" (Hebrew); the Greek text instead eliminates the metaphor of the warrior applied to the sun and speaks simply of its course: "with his words he speeds it on its way".

In 43,6ab Hebrew and Greek differ. While the first underlines the dominion of the moon over time and its divisions ("And also the moon watches over the times, regulator of seasons and eternal sign"), the latter eliminates this idea completely: "and the moon has also its importance which is the indication of the dates and an eternal sign".

The same phenomenon is prominent in 43,7ab. The Hebrew text reads: "To it [belong] the solemnities and feasts, and when it wanes it resumes its cycle", while the Greek has: "from the moon (comes) the sign of the feast; heavenly body which vanishes after its fulness". The translator restricts himself to the view that the moon does not control, but only indicates, the term of the feast.

In 43,8ab, Hebrew and Greek differ once more. The first has: "The new moon (חדש) as its name (indicates) is renewed (מתחדש), it is splendid (נורא) in its phases"; the Greek reads: "the month takes its name from it, increasingly marvelously in its phases". While in the Hebrew the term נורא is attributed to the moon[60], the corresponding Greek θαυμαστῶς describes the growth of the month. Thus, any possible personification of the moon disappears.

How are we to understand these modifications? We can speculate, with Minissale[61], that the Greek translator, aware of an anti-idolatrous concern that was more acute in Alexandria than in Jerusalem, wanted to remove any importance from the sun and the moon for fear that these verses would be read in a mythological key and so promote the astral cult.

---

60 On the other hand, it refers 43,8ab to the month (in fact, חֹדֶשׁ can mean both the new moon and the month), cf. PRATO, Problema della teodicea, 120. It should be noted that the term proper for the moon is יָרֵחַ (43,6a), from which derives also יֶרַח, "month".

61 MINISSALE, Versione greca, 211 note 79.

5 Conclusion

After having studied the polemical dimension of Ben Sira's hymn to the creation within the wisdom tradition, in comparison with the Enochic literature and with the Graeco-hellenistic culture, we can hazard some conclusions.

Despite there being no clear and explicit references to opponents in the text, there are many indications which make us think of the existence of such a group. How are we to explain this position of Ben Sira? Perhaps it could be said that the sage is so committed to his own didactic objectives that he leaves no space in his book for the viewpoint of other contemporary schools/groups of thought. Instead of quoting them directly, he hides them beneath his own viewpoint. From the pedagogic point of view, this is a good choice: when one wants to rebut certain ideas (angelic revelations, speculative cosmologies, the solar calendar, intellectual pride, the astral cult) it is better not to attract the attention of one's disciples directly on to these, but to present one's own opinion in such a way that they are able to make a free decision. Besides, such a context of freedom is a characteristic of the sage's school (cf. Sir 2,1; 6,32–33; 15,15–17).

To take Sir 42,15–43,33 specifically, there is no doubt that we are presented with a contemplation of nature as the source of joy that is both aesthetic and spiritual. The manifestations of beauty and splendour in creation are seen as reflections of the glory of God. On the other hand, the description which Ben Sira gives of the stars (without at all forgetting his silence on some elements), allows us to glimpse a polemic, certainly veiled, against those who do not share his doctrine, especially those points held by him as fundamental for the young in their time of education.

At a general level, although admitting in the sage's work some traces of polemic against apocalyptic thought and the Graeco-hellenistic culture and science[62], we take issue with Boccaccini's view that the book of Ben Sirach was "born with precise polemical intentions"[63]. The principal aim of the sage was never to debate openly with his adversaries, but to instruct his disciples in true wisdom, that is, the fear-of-the-Lord and the observance of the Law.

---

62 Cf., for example, CORLEY, Wisdom versus Apocalyptic.
63 BOCCACCINI, Middle Judaism, 124.

God, Creator of All (Sir 43,27 – 33)

In his programmatic study on the fear-of-God in Ben Sira, Josef Haspecker considers the use of the divine attribute "Creator" as a characteristic element of the book: "The idea of the Creator occupies a very broad place in the image of God found in wisdom teachings and the late Jewish religion. Accordingly, the title of the Creator is very common at this time. This does not mean, however, that it has become a worn coin without a clear profile. Rather, at least in Sirach, the use of this title is quite characteristic"[1]. In his contribution to the Festschrift for Maurice Gilbert[2], Friedrich Reiterer has undertaken an analysis of the non-material level of creation. Before embarking on this specific theme he gives an exhaustive listing of vocabulary pertinent to creation in general which allows us to distinguish seventeen instances in which Ben Sira utilises the title "Creator" or "Maker" with regard to God: בורא (3,16b)[3], עשׂ(ו)ה (7,30a; 10,12b; 35[32Hb],13a; 36[33Hb],13c; 38,15a; 43,5a.11a; 46,13a; 47,8c), יוצר (51,12d), ὁ κτίστης (24,8a), ὁ κτίσας (24,8b); ὁ ποιήσας (4,6b; 39,5b.28d; 47,8d). It goes without saying that these titles make up only a very small part of the vast amount of references to the creational activity of God (nearly one hundred instances).

The goal of this study is to analyse the image which Ben Sira offers of God as Creator in Sir 43,27 – 33. Even though this text does not contain specifically the title Creator or Maker, it is a key passage in the theological construct of the sage especially with regard to the relationship between creation and praise. Before turning our attention to this text, we will first present briefly three different ways of approaching the theme of creation followed by an overall vision based on the most significant texts on creation in the book.

---

1 HASPECKER, Gottesfurcht, 302: "Der Schöpfergedanke nimmt im Gottesbild der Weisheitslehre und der spätjüdischen Religion einen recht breiten Platz ein. Der Schöpfertitel ist dementsprechend in dieser Zeit sehr geläufig. Das bedeutet jedoch nicht, dass er eine abgegriffene Münze ohne klares Profil geworden ist. Vielmehr ist wenigstens bei Sirach die Verwendung dieses Titels durchaus charakteristisch".

2 REITERER, Ebenen, 92.

3 REITERER, Ebenen, 122, erroneously reads בורא in 39,29b.

https://doi.org/10.1515/9783110492316-023

1 The Creator and His Work in Ben Sira

1.1 Three Approaches to the Theme of Creation

On a par with the three major topics of the book: wisdom, fear-of-God and Law (cf. 19,20) the theme of creation stands out as one of the favourite arguments of Ben Sira. It has been studied from various perspectives[4]. In 1975 James L. Crenshaw wrote his well-known article "On the Problem of Theodicy in Sirach: on Human Bondage". While positively evaluating the study of Sir 16,24 – 17,14; 39,12 – 35; 42,15 – 43,33 by Johannes Marböck, Crenshaw pointed out that the texts under consideration had not yet been examined "for the light they throw upon the problem of theodicy"[5].

In the same year Gian Luigi Prato published his doctoral thesis on the problem of theodicy in Ben Sira[6] filling the gap mentioned by Crenshaw. Prato presents a detailed analysis not only of the pericopes under consideration, but also of all texts concerning the principle of double aspect (*composizione dei contrari*) which is related to the theme of creation (*richiamo alle origini*), e.g. Sir 15,11 – 18,14; 36(33Hb),7 – 15; 40,1 – 17; 41,1 – 13 and also 4,20 – 6,17; 9,17 – 11,28. In the context of theodicy creation is considered for two main reasons: to explain how things were at the beginning (in origin) and to understand the various functions assigned by the Creator. This dynamic vision of creation, according to which the created realities reveal themselves more by how they function than by what they are, already existed in the Old Testament tradition. The novelty of Ben Sira, according to Prato, consists in applying this concept of creation to the complex problem of theodicy in all its aspects.

Twelve years later Keith Burton defended a doctoral thesis in Glasgow in which he set out "to examine the formative influences on Sirach's doctrine of creation and the significance of that doctrine in Sirach's thought"[7]. As this thesis remains unpublished and is not readily available I will provide a short outline of this work. It starts with a comparative analysis between Ben Sira and the primordial history (Gen 1– 11), Deutero-Isaiah, some Psalms, Wisdom literature and early Jewish apocalyptic. There follows a study of the principal texts on creation in Ben Sira (1,1 – 10; 15,14 – 20; 16,24 – 17,14; 18,1 – 14; 24; 36[33Hb],7 – 19; 39,16 – 35; 42,15 – 43,33) and the presentation of a scheme in which creation is the

---

4 REITERER, Review, 48 – 54, section 9: "Wisdom, Law and Creation" and section 10: "Creation and Intertestamental Literature".
5 CRENSHAW, Problem of Theodicy, 51.
6 PRATO, Problema della teodicea.
7 BURTON, Judaic Doctrine, 1.

structuring element both for the thought and the book of the sage. In Burton's view, the book consists of eight blocks of creation tradition which together with the eulogy on Simon (in Sir 50), the personal prayer and the autobiographical poem (in Sir 51) constitute the pillars on which the work rests. Burton conceives Sirach's doctrine of creation as a bridge connecting God and Wisdom with human beings. He concludes: "It can be said that Sirach has a distinct doctrine of creation running throughout his whole text, which gives it both form and authority"[8].

Seven years later Leo Perdue dedicated a chapter in his book on wisdom theology to the theme "creation and wisdom" in Ben Sira[9]. He comes to the conclusion that the book presents a rhetorical structure, at times linear and at times concentric, which sustains a well-defined thematic development: "from creation to history to realisation in the new Jerusalem"[10]. According to Perdue, Ben Sira constructs his world view by means of metaphors. For instance, the creation activity of God is expressed by the metaphor of the divine word; the creation of mankind is depicted with images of artistry, and personified Wisdom is associated with the metaphor of fertility. This series of images evokes the image of a sovereign God who, seated on his celestial throne, rules over creation and directs providence by means of his divine word[11].

1.2 Creation in Ben Sira: Synthetic Overview

From the very beginning of his book the sage emphasizes that the Lord, who alone is wise (1,8), after having created wisdom before anything else (1,4) generously distributed her to all living beings and to those who love him (1,9 – 10). In Sir 24 personified Wisdom explains how she roamed the world (24,5 – 6) before ὁ κτίστης ἀπάντων ("the Creator of the universe") commanded her to settle in Israel (24,8cd). Wisdom, however, is not just the first creature of God who presides over the order of creation, but also is the Law revealed to Israel by Moses: "All this is the book of the Covenant of the Most High, the Law which Moses prescribed for us, as an inheritance for the assemblies of Jacob" (24,23). In this way Ben

---

8 BURTON, Judaic Doctrine, 219.
9 PERDUE, Wisdom & Creation, 243 – 290, esp. 248 – 290.
10 PERDUE, Wisdom & Creation, 289.
11 PERDUE, Wisdom & Creation, 290: "These metaphors provide the means by which Ben Sira conveys his understanding of creation. Placed within the rhetorical structures of language, they provoke the imagination to shape a world of beauty and justice in which God rules as creator and sustainer".

Sira outlines the harmony and unity that exists between the natural law of creation and the Law revealed in Sinai; both are manifestations of divine wisdom.

In the long section on the origin of sin, human freedom and divine retribution (Sir 15,11–18,14) Ben Sira articulates his thoughts in answer to some foolish arguments. In reply to the last objection of the fool in Sir 16,17–23 he formulates a poem on the creation of the universe and human beings (Sir 16,24–17,14). His answer comes in the shape of a midrash on the creation accounts in Genesis (Gen 1,1–2,4a and 2,1b–24). In line with the sapiential tradition Ben Sira offers a theology of creation which endorses divine justice. He juxtaposes the celestial beings and the human beings. The stars live in perfect order in the cosmos and in total obedience to the Creator (Sir 16,26–30), and so should the people, who are endowed with freedom and intelligence so that they are responsible for their works, capable of discerning good and evil, and free to accept or reject the commandment of God (Sir 17,1–14). It is remarkable that in Sir 17,11–14 the argument moves from creation to the Sinaitic revelation, which Ben Sira considers to have a universal range[12]. God gave to human beings the Law and an eternal covenant, two elements which are characteristic of the chosen people. The concentration of Sinaitic references at the end of the poem gives the impression that the theophany in Sinai is present in a visible form in the order of creation, or, in the words of John Collins: "Sirach allows no interval between the creation and the giving of the Torah. Rather, he implies that the law was given to humanity from the beginning"[13]. Law is thus part of God's universal wisdom, which is manifest in creation[14].

In Sir 36(33Hb),7–15 Ben Sira has recourse to creation in order to explain the principle of double aspect in creation. Just as there are polarities in the order of the universe (ordinary days, festive days), so also in the human order (some the Lord blesses and exalts, others he curses and humiliates). God's freedom to treat different people differently confounds the disciple who might not even dare to voice his protest: "Why does one human being have better luck than another, if all have been created from clay?" The answer of the sage (God is like a potter who molds the human being as he wants) does not satisfy the disciple, because it implies that the human being is deprived of freedom. Ben Sira then is obliged to refine his discourse on theodicy. Although God created everything in contrasting pairs in a perfect and harmonious balance between good and evil and life and death, it is according to his own choice that a human being becomes a

---

12 Cf. WÉNIN, Création, 147–158, esp. 155–158.
13 COLLINS, Seers, 376.
14 Cf. MARBÖCK, Gesetz und Weisheit, 6.

sinner or a pious person. In reality, God has not robbed anyone of freedom but has arranged that the result of a person's free choice puts him or her on the right or wrong way. This is how Crenshaw understands it, when he affirms: "the decision of what is better is really a discerning of the appropriate time, which Sirach, in contrast to Qoheleth, thinks is open to man"[15].

In Sir 39,12 – 35, classified by Jan Liesen as a didactic hymn or a hymnic wisdom poem[16], Ben Sira returns to the themes of divine justice, divine wisdom and divine providence, situating them in the context of the goodness and profound meaning of creation. If we leave aside the introduction (39,12 – 15) and conclusion (39,32 – 35), the hymn consists of three strophes.

In the first strophe (39,16 – 21) Ben Sira describes the work of God in terms of creation and salvation with special emphasis on the aspect of time. In verse 16 he introduces the insight that he wants to develop: the usefulness of all created reality in so far as it depends on divine dispositions. Appealing to the proper function of and the right time for each thing the sage responds in verse 21 to two objections that question God's control of the universe: "For what is this?" and "This is worse than that".

In the second strophe (39,22 – 27) the goodness of all the work of God is corroborated by a distinction between the just (good) and the sinners (wicked). Some works are destined for salvation and others for punishment. Indeed, the same works are good for the just and bad for sinners. This is the case with the natural elements, with food, and with clothing. The argumentation of Ben Sira has a built-in problem here inasmuch as the concept "work of God" is used with two different meanings: on the one hand, it signifies the creational work of God by which he orders the world; on the other hand, it signifies each created element in the world (see the list in 39,26).

In the third strophe (39,28 – 31) Ben Sira enumerates the cosmic elements which were created for vengeance and judgement and which faithfully obey the Lord's commandment. These personified elements could correspond to a pedagogical intention of the sage, viz. to motivate the disciples to praise the Lord and to fulfill their calling. By this personification Ben Sira seems to return to his initial understanding of the "work of God", but even when the logic of his thoughts remains unconvincing, Ben Sira intends the wisdom poem on the goodness of creation more as a celebration than an argument[17].

---

15 CRENSHAW, Problem of Theodicy, 53.
16 Cf. LIESEN, Full of Praise, 39.
17 Cf. LIESEN, Full of Praise, 276.

2 Sir 43,27–33: Text and Context

2.1 Translation and Textual Notes

The most important text on creation is the long hymn in Sir 42,15 – 43,33 of which we consider the final part in some detail here. Sir 43,27 – 33 is missing in the Masada Scroll (except for some characters at the end of verses 29b and 30b)[18] and in the Syriac version (which skips 43,11 – 33). Thus, our translation is based mainly on the Hebrew text from MS B (and Bmg)[19]. Only when this is lacking or corrupt is the Greek version adduced[20].

43,27	More things like these we shall not add; the last word is: "He is all".
43,28	Let us praise him still, since we cannot fathom (him): He is greater than all his works.
43,29	Awesome is the Lord, very much and his power is admirable.
43,30	You who are praising the Lord, raise your voice as much as you can, for there is still (more). You who are exalting him, renew your strength and do not tire, for you cannot fathom him.
43,31	Who has seen him and can describe (him)? and who will praise him as he is?
43,32	There are (still) many things hidden; I have seen only a little of his works.
43,33	The Lord has made all things and to the pious he has given wisdom.

43,27a. MS B: לא נוסף. Gk: μὴ ἀφικώμεθα translates סוף ("to finish") instead of יסף ("to add"), forming an inclusion with 43,30d.

43,27b. MS B: הוא הכל. Gk: τὸ πᾶν ἐστιν αὐτός. Lat: *Ipse est in omnibus*.

43,28a. MS B: נגד[לה]. Bmg: נגלה. Reconstruction of MS B on the basis of Gk: δοξάζοντες (cf. 43,30a).

---

18 Cf. YADIN, Ben Sira Scroll, 192.
19 Cf. BEENTJES, Book. Without apparent reason Beentjes omits Sir 43,29 – 30 from the text of Masada (120 and 173), while he includes it when describing the contents of the scroll: col. VI: Sir 43,8c–30 (19). See, BEENTJES, Errata et Corrigenda, 376 – 377.
20 Cf. ZIEGLER, Sapientia.

43,29a. MS B: נו]רא ייי מ[אד מאד. Cf. Gk: φοβερὸς κύριος καὶ σφόδρα μέγας. The adjective μέγας echoes the ὁ μέγας of 43,28b.

43,29b. MS B: ונפלאות דבריו. Bmg: גבורתו. MS Mas: תו[... (יו) Adopting the variant of Bmg (Gk: ἡ δυναστεία αὐτοῦ), we read ונפלאת גבורתו, since it fits the context better. The text of the Masada scroll is badly damaged. While Yadin admits the difficulty in determining whether the first character is a *yod* or a *tau*, he decides for a *tau* following the reading in Bmg[21].

43,30a. MS B: מגד]ל[י ייי ה]רימו קול]. Cf. 43,28a.

43,30b. MS B: בכל תוכלו כי יש עוד. MS Mas: ש]אל]... Supposing that the fragment is correctly placed, Yadin reconstructs: בכל תוכלו כי י]ש אל] (cf. Ps 58,12). His interpretation differs greatly from MS B, which according to him "has given rise to many difficulties"[22]. Taking into account the notable difference in meaning between MS B ("... for there still is")[23] and MS Mas ("... for God is") and the fact that the Gk: ὑπερέξει γὰρ καὶ ἔτι is closer to MS B than to Yadin's reconstruction of MS Mas, we prefer to follow MS B.

43,30c. MS B: מרומים תחליפו כח. Bmg: מרוממיו החליפו כח. We prefer to follow Bmg: the form מרומים (MS B) seems to be an error for מרוממיו, ptc. Polel of רום with 3rd per. sg. suf. (Gk: καὶ ὑψοῦντες αὐτόν) and the impv. החליפו (Gk: πληθύνατε) combines better with 43,30a than the future תחליפו of MS B[24].

43,30d. We fill out the text of MS B: כי לא ת' with Bmg: כי לא תח]קרו]. In Gk: οὐ γὰρ μὴ ἀφίκησθε, cf. 43,27a.

43,31ab. Missing in MS B. On the basis of Gk (τίς ἑόρακεν αὐτὸν καὶ ἐκδιηγήσεται; καὶ τίς μεγαλυνεῖ αὐτὸν καθώς ἐστιν), Segal makes the following reconstruction: מי חָזָה אותו וַיְסַפֵּר / וּמִי יְגַדְּלֶנּוּ כַּאֲשֶׁר הוּא.[25] Against the majority of textual

---

21 YADIN, Ben Sira Scroll, 192; SKEHAN—DI LELLA, Wisdom, 490. Cf. by contrast, PRATO, Problema della teodicea, 139; BURTON, Judaic Doctrine, 187–188.
22 YADIN, Ben Sira Scroll, 192.
23 According to Penar, the word עוד is a noun, which means "eternity" and which is used as a divine epithet: "the Eternal", cf. 43,28 (cf. PENAR, Semitic Philology, 73–74). In this case MSS B and Mas have parallel readings.
24 SKEHAN—DI LELLA, Wisdom, 490; PRATO, Problema della teodicea, 140.
25 SEGAL, ספר, 290.

witnesses Skehan follows the reading of codex S and MSS 336 542 753: τὶς γὰρ ἑόρακεν[26].

43,32a. The text of MS B is badly damaged. On the basis of Gk (πολλὰ ἀπόκρυφά ἐστιν μείζονα τούτων), Segal reconstructs רֹב [נִסְתָּרֹות ... מֵ]אֵלֶּה and the edition of Israel Yeivin[27] proposes רוב נ[פ]ל[א] וחז[ק].

43,32b. MS B: ראיתי ("I have seen"). In Gk (ἑωράκαμεν, "we have seen") the inclusion with 42,15b disappears. The edition of Beentjes reads ראתי instead of ראיתי (possibly an error of transcription)[28].

43,33ab. The text of MS B is badly damaged. On the basis of Gk (πάντα γὰρ ἐποίησεν ὁ κύριος καὶ τοῖς εὐσεβέσιν ἔδωκεν σοφίαν), Segal[29] reconstructs as follows: אֶת הַכֹּל [עָשָׂה יְיָ / וְלַ]חֲסִידִים נָתַן חָכְמָה]. Instead of חסידים, Kahana and Di Lella read אנשי חסד (cf. 44,1a)[30].

2.2 Sir 43,27 – 33 in the Context of the Hymn on Creation

Although the majority of interpreters treat Sir 43,27 – 33 as a well-defined literary unit, the problematic character of 43,26 escapes no one. Sir 43,26 is notoriously difficult to integrate into the text both for its position and for its meaning. After the wisdom of God which dominates the ocean and after the sailors who narrate fantastic stories about maritime creatures and sea monsters (43,23 – 25), unexpectedly the figure of a messenger or angel appears. This figure is usually interpreted as a personification of the word of God: "because of him the messenger succeeds (מלאך MS B)[31], and by his words he will do (his) will". For Perdue, the messenger is every element of creation that successfully accomplishes its

---

26 SKEHAN–DI LELLA, Wisdom, 490.

27 SEGAL, ספר, 290 and YEIVIN (ed.), The Book of Ben Sira, 52. Prato follows Segal's proposal, but eliminates the possible lacuna in the text (cf. PRATO, Problema della teodicea, 140). Wright follows YEIVIN (ed.), The Book of Ben Sira, cf. WRIGHT, Fear the Lord, 210 note 68.

28 BEENTJES, Book, 77.

29 SEGAL, ספר, 290. Thus also PRATO, Problema della teodicea, 140.

30 KAHANA, שמעון בן־סירא, 85; SKEHAN–DI LELLA, Wisdom, 496.

31 Some prefer to read מלאכה ("work") instead of מלאך. Cf. HAMP, Sirach, 118: "Um seinetwillen lässt er *die Schöpfung* ihr Ziel erreichen und durch *sein* Wort vollzieht er *seinem* Willen" and BURTON, Judaic Doctrine, 184: "For his own sake He makes his work to prosper".

God-given task. According to him, Sir 43,26 contains a summary statement which initiates the epilogue of the hymn: 43,26 – 30[32].

The obviously conclusive character of 43,27 (note that at the same time it introduces the invitation to praise in vv. 28 – 30) is a sufficient indication for the delimitation of the text. First, the unexpected use of the 1st person plural (also in v. 28)[33] after a very protracted hymn creates a break and changes the tone of the discourse. In this way, the hearers perceive that the sage is preparing for the conclusion. A similar strategy is employed in 2,18, where the sage concludes his exhortations with a 1st person plural remark: "Let us fall into the hands of the Lord and not into the hands of people". Second, the contents of 43,27 clearly indicate that the hymn has finished. The sage not only affirms that he is not going to add any other explanation to what he said before, but also attempts to sum it up in one single phrase: "He is all" (הוא הכל) which forms an inclusion with 43,33a: "The Lord has made all things" (את הכל [עשה] [ייי]). This is his last word (cf. Qoh 12,13).

Sir 43,27 – 33 is, therefore, the conclusion of the hymn on creation (42,15 – 43,33) and serves the same purpose as Sir 50,22 – 24 in relation to the "Praise of the Ancestors" (44,1 – 50,24)[34]. In both texts an invitation to praise (43,30; 50,22) and the gift of wisdom (43,33; 50,23) figure prominently. Besides the conclusion (43,27 – 33: praise to the Creator) the hymnic composition consists of an introduction (42,15 – 25: the power of God in creation) and the central part (43,1 – 26: the marvels of creation)[35]. Although this division is widely accepted, there remains some discussion as to the central part of the hymn. For instance, in view of the content matter A. Minissale, A. Di Lella, and S. Goan prefer to divide 43,1 – 26 into two strophes: 43,1 – 12 (about the sky) and 43,13 – 26 (about the atmospheric phenomena), thus obtaining a more balanced strophic division of the whole[36]. Argall refines this division and distinguishes between the meteorological phenomena (43,13 – 22) and a strophe on the abyss and the sea (43,23 – 26)[37]. Perdue subdivides 42,15 – 25 into three strophes: an announcement of the intent to praise (42,15 – 17), the unfathomable wisdom of God (42,18 – 21),

---

32 PERDUE, Wisdom & Creation, 283. Likewise, HAMP, Sirach, 118.

33 Cf. also Sir 2,18; 8,5 – 7; 24,23; 33(36Hb),1 – 17; 43,24b; 43,32Gk; 44,1; 48,11Gk and 50,22 – 24Gk. On the use of the 1st person (singular and plural) in the book, cf. LIESEN, Strategical Self-References, 63 – 74.

34 On Sir 42,15 – 43,33 and 44,1 – 50,24 with regard to the structure of the book, cf. MARBÖCK, Hohepriester Simon, 215 – 216.

35 Cf. PRATO, Problema della teodicea, 141 – 145.

36 MINISSALE, Siracide, 201 – 208; SKEHAN–DI LELLA, Wisdom, 491 – 496; GOAN, Creation, 82.

37 ARGALL, 1 Enoch and Sirach, 147 – 151.

the beauty and purpose of the created works (42,22– 25); furthermore, he subdivides 43,1– 25 into two strophes: the wonder of sky and moisture (43,1– 22) and the teeming life of the expansive Deep (43,23 – 25)[38].

Accepting the tripartite structure of Sir 42,15 – 43,33 several points of correspondence can be seen between the introduction and the conclusion of the hymn (cf. the hymnic frame in 39,12– 15.32– 35). First, the announcement in 1st person singular with which the sage introduces his new discourse in 42,15 corresponds to the announcement in 1st person plural in 43,27 with which he communicates that the discourse is finished. Second, Ben Sira's plan to narrate what he had seen (חזיתי) in 42,15b, corresponds to the recognition in 43,32b that actually he has seen very little (מעט ראיתי)[39]. Third, God's revelation of the mystery of hidden things in 42,19b (חקר נסתרות, ἴχνη ἀποκρύφων) corresponds to Ben Sira's acknowledgement in 43,32a that many things in creation remain hidden (רוב נסתרות, πολλὰ ἀπόκρυφά). Fourth, God plumbs (חקר) the abyss and the human heart (42,18), but a human being cannot fathom (חקר) God (43,28.30). These terminological correspondences not only manifest the internal unity of the hymn and its fine composition, but also reveal something of the pedagogy of the sage. Through accurate contemplation of creation and humble recognition of one's limitations, Ben Sira leads his disciples to his final goal, i.e. praise of the Creator.

3 Sir 43,27 – 33: Praise to the Creator

3.1 From the Works to the Creator

In the central part of the hymn Ben Sira (43,1– 26) lists one by one the works of God (מעשי אל) with lyrical descriptions of their beauty while at the same time pointing out their specific functions in the universe. First, the sage contemplates the firmament where the brilliant stars are situated, and the two main lights (the sun and the moon) which govern the seasons, and the rainbow which spans the heavenly vault. Then he comes to natural phenomena: lightning, clouds, hail, thunder, wind, storm, snow, frost, north wind, ice, heat and morning dew. In

---

38 Cf. PERDUE, Wisdom & Creation, 278.

39 The acknowledgement of the sage in 43,32, even when it seems to contradict the affirmation of 42,17: "Not even the saints of God (i.e. angels) can narrate his marvels (נפלאות)", in fact only emphasizes how difficult it is for human beings to understand the works (מעשי) of God (the same idea is expressed by the rhetorical questions in 43,31). Cf. by contrast, the Latin version: *Nonne Dominus fecit Sanctos enarrare omnia mirabilia sua?*

the end the terrible ocean is mentioned, a symbol par excellence of anti-creation, which has to bow before the power and wisdom of God. It is noteworthy that the descriptions of the stars (43,1–12) are interlarded with explicit mentions of God (except in case of the moon) celebrating his marvelous creational activity (43,2b.5a.9b.10a.11a.12b). As in 16,26–30 the ever obedient celestial beings in their perfect harmony are Ben Sira's favourite teaching material. From 43,12 onwards direct references to God disappear completely and only indirect references are used (his anger, his power, his word, his wisdom ...).

In 43,27–33 the image of the Lord as Creator takes on a special emphasis: he is no longer considered in relationship to each of the works (as in 43,1–12) but as he is himself. The Lord appears (implicitly or explicitly) at least once in each of the verses of 43,27–33 (in total 17x). Thrice his name is mentioned explicitly (43,29a.30a.33a) and thrice the personal pronoun 3rd per. sg. is used (43,27b.28b.31b). "His works" are mentioned in vv. 28b.32b and "his power" in v. 29b. Furthermore, God is referred to with the direct object "him" (43,30c.30d.31a.31b). In vv. 28a.31a he is understood to be the direct object of the verbs נחקור, נגדלה, and ויספר respectively and in v. 33b he is the subject of נתן.

First, this insistence on God takes on the shape of a series of attributes: his omnipresence (he is all), his greatness (greater than all his works), his transcendence (he is very awesome) and his omnipotence (his power is admirable). All the attributes are expressed in an emphatic way (all, greater than, very much, admirable). This is a way to praise the Creator and to show indirectly the limitation of a human being as creature (43,30–31). The two affirmations of 43,29a in Gk: φοβερός κύριος καὶ σφοδρὰ μέγας are reminiscent of Sir 1,8: εἷς ἐστιν σοφός φοβερὸς σφόδρα, where, also in a context of creation—especially in connection with wisdom—Ben Sira depicts God as the only one who is wise and very awesome, capable of doing things that are beyond human beings: to dominate the universe and to know wisdom.

Second, the insistence on the Creator is indirectly manifest in the limited experience of a human being who cannot fathom him (חקר), nor see him (חזה), nor describe him (ספר). According to Georg Sauer, "the image of God has been refined—and thus made more remote"[40]. Precisely for this reason, for the fact that God is unfathomable, invisible and beyond description, a human being's only possible response is to praise him constantly. Notwithstanding his conviction that no one can praise God as he deserves (lit. כאשר הוא, as he is), the sage invites to praise him unceasingly, without tiring, as much as one can.

---

40 SAUER, Hintergrund, 320: "Das Gottesbild ist verfeinert—und damit in eine grössere Distanz gerückt worden".

Third, the focus on God is evident in the two actions which the sage ascribes to God (making everything and giving wisdom to the pious). These verbs not only summarise the entire hymn, but also establish a link with the opening hymn of the book, where God grants wisdom to those who love him (Sir 1,10).

Luis Alonso Schökel comments: "The final stanza rises from the works to the Creator who synthesizes and surpasses them all"[41]. In other words, in Sir 43,27–33 Ben Sira changes the perspective: first he contemplates the marvels of creation, finding traces of the Creator in them, then he contemplates the Creator of all, inviting everyone to join him in a celebration of praise.

3.2 The Concept of Totality

In Sir 43,27–33 Ben Sira accentuates in a special way the concept of totality. The word כל appears, among other occurrences, in the beginning of the text (v. 27b) as a divine attribute: "He is all" (הוא הכל)[42] and in the end referring to his crea-tional activity: "The Lord has made all things (את הכל)" (v. 33a). Argall affirms that the word "all" in 43,33a should be understood as referring to the polarities of creation[43]. His interpretation of Sir 43,33a is based on his reading of 42,24a (namely instead of שונים, "different" in MS B he follows Yadin's reconstruction of MS Mas: שנים, "two", cf. Syr and Gk). It seems best, however, not to change the text and to understand that what Ben Sira wants to underline in 42,24a with כלם שונים is the variation and diversity of creation instead of its polarity. With regard to 43,33a, the dominant idea of הכל is the totality of creation inas-much as it is a work of God: there is nothing in the universe which has not been created by God. Regarding this word, it is noteworthy that in other parts of the book God is designated as "Creator of all" (18,1; 24,8a; 51,12dHb)[44] and as "God of all" (33[36Hb],1; 50,22aGk)[45]. Another occurrence of הכל comes in the expression "all his works" (כל מעשיו) in 43,28b. It recalls 42,16.24 in the

---

41 ALONSO SCHÖKEL, Eclesiástico, 304: "La estrofa final sube de las obras al Creador que las sintetiza y supera todas".

42 Kaiser understands the personal pronoun as a predicate and הכל as subject and he trans-lates: "Alles ist nur er" instead of "Er ist alles" (KAISER, Rezeption, 49.50); cf. SAUER, Jesus Sir-ach, 296.

43 ARGALL, 1 Enoch and Sirach, 152.

44 Sir 18,1 is text-critically problematic: "He who lives eternally created all things in the same way" (Hb missing). SKEHAN–DI LELLA (Wisdom, 280) follow Syr "judged" (*mtbq'* = ἔκρινεν) in-stead of the Gk (ἔκτισεν) and also PRATO (Problema della teodicea, 293 note 216).

45 For the meaning of this title (אלהי הכל) in 33(36Hb),1, cf. ZAPPELLA, Immagine, 419–420.

introductory part and it is also reminiscent of 1,9; 36(33Hb),15; 39,16.33. Yet another occurrence of הכל shows that the word "all" is not exclusively used for God and his creation. Ben Sira also applies it to human beings in his exhortation to praise God with all their strength (lit. "as much as you can", בכל תוכלו)[46].

The concept of totality is a possible link between the wisdom of Ben Sira and Stoicism. Since the publication of the article by R. Pautrel (1963)[47], the relationship between Ben Sira and Stoic doctrines has not received much attention in biblical research until recent times. In 1998, O. Kaiser wrote an article about the Stoic concept of providence (πρόνοια) and its reception in the book of Ben Sira (cf. note 42), and last year Ursel Wicke-Reuter completed a doctoral thesis on the same subject under the direction of O. Kaiser[48]. It is the phrase of 43,27b "He is all" with its possible pantheistic connotation, probably derived from Stoicism, that continues to attract the attention of interpreters and commentators[49].

The expression הוא הכל, τὸ πᾶν ἐστιν αὐτός, to which Paul Beauchamp dedicated an interesting article[50], already posed difficulties to the commentators of the 19th century when the Hebrew fragments had not yet been discovered. While O. Fritzsche (1859) affirmed without restriction: "There is simply no possibility of a pantheistic form of words", A. Edersheim (1888) considered the expression as "evidently a spurious addition by the younger Siracide"[51]. The line of Fritzsche is followed by R. Smend, A. Eberharter and H. Duesberg[52], and there even have been some interpreters like N. Peters and V. Hamp who thought that Ben Sira wanted to contradict the pantheistic ideas of Hellenism with 43,27b (cf. e.g. the postulates of the mystery religions: *Hermes omnia solus et ter unus; Isis una quae es omnia*)[53]. By contrast, W. Fuss and M. Hengel speak of an "undeniable pantheistic tone" and of "almost 'panthesizing' features" respectively[54]. The majority of commentators (among others G. Box–W. Oesterley, R. Pautrel, J.

---

46 The insistence on "all" is also characteristic of Sir 39,12–35, where כל appears 13x (πᾶν, πάντα, 14x), always (except in v. 19) referring to the works of God in creation.

47 PAUTREL, Stoïcisme, 535–549 and also WINSTON, Theodicy, 239–249.

48 WICKE-REUTER, Göttliche Providenz. Cf. also MARBÖCK, Gerechtigkeit Gottes, 39–43: he studies the concept of totality in Ben Sira and in Stoicism and the plausibility of a contact between the two.

49 Cf. MATTILA, Stoics, 493–495.

50 BEAUCHAMP, Sur deux mots, 15–25.

51 FRITZSCHE, Weisheit, 257: "Von pantheistischer Fassung der Worte kann lediglich keine Rede sein"; EDERSHEIM, Ecclesiasticus, 209.

52 SMEND, Weisheit, 411; EBERHARTER, Buch, 143; DUESBERG, Il est le Tout, 31.

53 PETERS, Buch, 371; HAMP, Sirach, 118.

54 FUSS, Tradition, 307 and HENGEL, Judaism and Hellenism, 146.

Marböck, A. Minissale, A. Di Lella, J. Crenshaw)[55], although admitting that there may be a possible Stoic influence on the choice of words (especially in Gk), maintain that the immediate context (in 43,28 Ben Sira affirms that God is greater than all his works) and also the idea of God the only Creator, which permeates the entire book, eliminate every possible trace of pantheism. Thus P. Beauchamp concludes his study: "He alone is the real 'all'. Apart from God, there is nothing that deserves to be called 'all'"[56].

The interpretation given by C. Spicq (1941), taken up by Di Lella in his commentary of 1987, expresses best what the meaning of τὸ πᾶν ἐστιν αὐτός and its Hebrew equivalent should be: "the whole of creation as a whole and in every last detail can only be explained by God, who is its source and who sustains it constantly"[57]. A similar interpretation is found in the Latin version: *Ipse est in omnibus*. "He is all" means that God is present in all created reality; each of his works carries the same divine stamp but manifests it in its own way[58]. The works of God, both taken as a whole and individually, are a faithful reflection of their Creator[59].

3.3 The Invitation to Praise

"Let us praise (him) still" (נגדלה עוד) is what the sage exclaims in Sir 43,28. This invitation to praise, which is typical of the hymnic style, stands out for its use of the 1st person plural (in agreement with 43,27) and the use of the cohortative. The plural testifies to the communion of the sage with his readers (disciples) and his active participation in what he proposes; as a good pedagogue he practises what he preaches. His invitation to praise has been accompanied from the beginning by the practice of the same (42,15: "I want to remember the works of God and to narrate what I have seen"). Ben Sira invites others to do what he has done and

---

55 Box—Oesterley, Book, 478; Pautrel, Stoïcisme, 543; Marböck, Weisheit im Wandel, 150; Minissale, Siracide, 207; Skehan—Di Lella, Wisdom, 495; Crenshaw, Book, 834.
56 Beauchamp, Sur deux mots, 25: "Le vrai tout, c'est lui seul. En dehors de Dieu, il n'est rien qui mérite le nom de tout". Cf. Wicke-Reuter, Göttliche Providenz, 222–223.
57 Spicq, Ecclésiastique, 798: "Toute la création dans son ensemble et dans les moindres détails ne s'éxplique que par Dieu, qui en est la source et le soutien permanent".
58 Calduch-Benages, Crisol, 249–250.
59 Cf. Marböck, Weisheit im Wandel, 150: "Die Ordnung, die Herrlichkeit, die Weisheit sind nur verschiedene Weisen des Wirkens Gottes, der überall am Werk ist"; Prato, Problema della teodicea, 201: "הכל si riferisce alle maniere con cui Dio si manifesta nel mondo"; Kaiser, Rezeption, 50: "[Alles ist nur ER] bezeichnet ihn aber auch gleichzeitig als den, den all seine Werke bezeugen"; cf. also Reitemeyer, Weisheitslehre, 33.

continues to do till the end of the book (51,1: "I praise you, my God and Saviour"). The cohortative gives emphasis to the intention of the sage and at the same time marks the end of the discourse. The invitation of the sage to praise God is also found in other hymnic texts: in the poem celebrating the goodness of God's works in its beginning and end (39,15.35), in the hymn to the fathers of Israel: between Aaron and Joshua (45,25Hb) and after the praise of Simon the high priest (50,22). It should be noted that, in contrast to 43,28, in all these texts the invitation to praise is formulated with the traditional hymnic imperative in 2nd person plural as in, e.g. Ps 96,1–3.

This hymnic invitation which appears to be a general address (directed to all), actually becomes more particular in 43,30. By means of a participle with vocative meaning the sage addresses a certain group: "you who are praising the Lord", "you who are exalting him" (cf. 2,7–9); this is the group of those who have accepted and put into practice the proposal of the sage. Two texts in the book may clarify the identity of these persons. In 17,6–10 Ben Sira discusses the many creational endowments of human beings: intelligence, discernment of good and evil, inner and outer senses. All these were given "so that they would glorify his marvelous works and praise his holy name" (17,9–10). In other words, Ben Sira holds that human beings are created in order to praise God; their greatness consists therein[60]. In order to praise God, the fact that one needs "eyes and ears that perceive, a mind that understands, a mouth that speaks"[61] goes together well with 15,9–10 where praise is a wise person's response to the gift of wisdom from God (cf. 1,10b). Likewise, in 43,30 "you" designates this group of disciples who love and fear the Lord and who have opted for the way of wisdom. Ben Sira exhorts them to praise for such is the principal task of a sage, and the most adequate way of responding to the mysteries of creation.

Praise also figures in a rhetorical question cast in 3rd person singular: "who will praise him as he is?" (43,31b), which is meant to contrast, again and with more emphasis (cf. 43,28.29.30), the human limitation with the unfathomable mystery of God. Ben Sira himself too is subject to this limitation, due to his human condition. So even when he is full of praise (cf. 39,12.35) he too cannot praise God as he deserves.

---

60 Morla Asensio, Eclesiástico, 91: "La finalidad de la maestría divina en crear un ser aparentemente perfecto es la alabanza. El camino privilegiado del que goza el hombre para manifestar su grandeza es la alabanza".
61 Alonso Schökel, Eclesiástico, 201: "Ojos y oídos que perciben, mente que comprende, boca que proclama".

All persons who are involved in the process of learning wisdom, also partake in an interaction with God through praise: "we" (the sage and his hearers), "you" (disciples), "who?" (anonymous person who can be any human being). The same distinction and interaction of persons (with some variations) occur in 39,12 – 15.32 – 35[62]. All persons involved face an insurmountable difficulty which sets a limit to their praise and forces them to make considerable efforts. This limit is the impenetrable greatness of the mystery of God and his works in creation. Therefore, the sage urges himself and the others to praise the Lord still more.

3.4 The Mysteries of God in Creation

The tension between the unfathomable mysteries of God in creation and the inability of human beings to understand them (cf. Job 5,9; 9,10; 11,7; Is 40,28) is a constant in the book of Ben Sira. The rhetorical questions of 43,31 ("Who has seen him and can describe him? and who will praise him as he is?") are to be answered negatively: No one! These questions contradict the situation which emerges from the context, for after having contemplated and described (part of) the wonders of the Lord, Ben Sira not only praises the Creator, but also invites others to join him in his praise. The same contradiction can be found in Sir 1,1 – 10. In 1,1 – 4, also with the help of rhetorical questions, Ben Sira affirms that no one can completely understand (lit. "measure", ἐξαριθμέω and "explore", ἐξιχνιάζω) the works of God in creation, for to no one the root of wisdom has been revealed, nor does anyone know her secrets (τὰ πανουργεύματα αὐτῆς)[63]. In 1,9 – 10, however, the Lord grants (χορηγέω, "supply") wisdom to those who love him (τοῖς ἀγαπῶσιν αὐτόν)[64]. There exists, therefore, a group of persons who thanks to their profound relationship with God succeed in obtaining wisdom. They are not mentioned explicitly in Sir 18,4 – 7 (Hb missing), which is very close to 43,27 – 33 and 1,1 – 10 in form and content:

18,4 To no one he has given power to proclaim his works,
      and who can explore his mighty deeds?
18,5 Who can measure the power of his greatness?

---

62 Cf. LIESEN, Full of Praise, 95.97, esp. 97.
63 ARGALL (1 Enoch and Sirach, 70 – 71) reconstructs: מערמיה, "her parts" (cf. 43,18, where πανουργεύματα translates מערמים). Likewise, SEGAL, ספר, 3.
64 In Syr: dḥlwhy (= τοῖς φοβουμένοις αὐτόν): this reading is preferred by Haspecker (Gottesfurcht, 51 – 52), Alonso Schökel (Eclesiástico, 146), and Marböck (Weisheit im Wandel, 21).

and who can fully recount his mercies?
18,6   It is not possible to diminish nor to add,
        nor is it possible to explore the wonders of the Lord.
18,7   When a human being finishes, then he begins,
        and when he halts, then he remains stupefied.

Again the rhetorical questions and frank affirmations of the sage insist on the impossibility for a human being to comprehend God (κράτος μεγαλωσύνης αὐτοῦ) and his works in creation (τὰ ἔργα, τὰ μεγαλεῖα, τὰ θαυμάσια). These cannot be proclaimed nor recounted (18,4: ἐξαγγέλλω; cf. 42,17; 43,31: ἐκδιηγεῖσθαι) nor explored (18,4.6; cf. 1,3; 42,18: ἐξιχνιάζω)[65]. To this limitation another one is added: the impossibility to recount his mercies (18,5: ἐκδιηγήσασθαι τὰ ἐλέη αὐτοῦ). Notwithstanding this insistence on human limitations, the end of the poem (18,14) reveals that those who have chosen to follow the way of wisdom and to keep the Law (lit. "the ones who receive instruction" and "who are eager for his decrees") are the recipients of divine pedagogy and mercy. It goes without saying that Ben Sira and his disciples belong to this category.

A halo of mystery surrounds the activity of the Creator in the universe. In 11,4cdHb the sage justifies his exhortation not to ridicule a poor person nor anyone's bitter day with a double affirmation: "for the works of the Lord are marvellous (פלאות, θαυμαστά) and his actions are hidden (נעלם, κρυπτά) from human eyes". In 16,21Gk he affirms: "and [as] a hurricane which a human being cannot grasp, [thus] the majority of his works [remain] concealed (ἐν ἀποκρύφοις)[66]". These texts manifest the existence of a series of mysterious realities in creation which a human being cannot grasp. Also in 3,21–24, in an exhortation to humility and intellectual modesty, the sage mentions "wondrous things" (v. 21a: פלאות, χαλεπώτερα, cf. v. 21b: ἰσχυρότερα) as well as "secret things" (v. 22b: נסתרות, τῶν κρυπτῶν) which are better left alone[67], because they transcend the limits of human comprehension. To try to identify with precision these wondrous and secret things is difficult, since the exhortation of Ben Sira remains very general and vague. Although the majority of interpreters suspects a polemic against cosmogonic and theosophic speculations from Greek philosophy, commentators like L.

65 Cf. Sir 6,27 (ἐξιχνεύω) and 24,8 (ἐξιχνιάζω) referring to wisdom.
66 Gk has added an image which does not exist in the Hebrew text (MS A): "If I sin, no eye will see me, or if I deceive in all secrecy (בכל סתר), who will know [it]?".
67 Cf. 3,21b in MS A: מכוסה ("hidden things") and in MS C: רעים ("bad things"). Against Skehan (cf. SKEHAN—DI LELLA, Wisdom, 159), Argall prefers the reading of MS C especially because of the inclusion with the "evil and erring imaginations" (ומזיונות רעות מתעות) in 3,24b (cf. ARGALL, 1 Enoch and Sirach, 74–75). Cf. the solution of WRIGHT, Fear the Lord, 208 note 63: in 3,21ab he follows MS A for the verbs and MS C for the adjectives.

Prockter and B. Wright discover allusions to mystic and apocalyptic currents within Judaism. More precisely Wright, in his study of the social context of the book of Ben Sira in the light of 1 Enoch and Aramaic Levi, interprets the "wondrous things" as the secrets of creation and the "secret things" as the future events (cf. 42,19; 48,25)[68].

The image of God as creator of unfathomable mysteries clashes with his image in Sir 42,18 – 19: God who explores (חקר, ἐξίχνευσεν) the abyss and the human heart, understands (יתבונן, διενοήθη) all their secrets (בכל מערומיהם, ἐν πανουργεύμασιν αὐτῶν), declares (מחוה, ἀπαγγέλλων) the past and the future, and reveals (מגלה, ἀποκαλύπτων) the most hidden mysteries (חקר נסתרות, ἴχνη ἀποκρύφων)[69]. The fact that God reveals his deepest secrets, if not all then at least part of them (cf. 43,32), implies that someone will be the recipient of this revelation, and will therefore be able to know them. In 39,7 Ben Sira notes that one of the main tasks of the sage is to meditate "on the mysteries of God" (ἐν τοῖς ἀποκρύφοις αὐτοῦ)[70]. A last remark regards 4,18. Here it is Lady Wisdom who as a good teacher, after having put the disciple to the test, announces her recompense: "and I shall reveal my secrets to him" (וגליתי לו מסתרי)[71]. If the pedagogy of God and the pedagogy of Lady Wisdom coincide, it is evident that the revelation of God will not come to naught: there always will be some persons, like Ben Sira and his disciples, who will be disposed to receive it and pass it on to others.

3.5 The Experience of the Sage

Conscious of his limitations Ben Sira recognises that many things remain hidden and indecipherable, and that he has seen only a few of the works of the Lord (cf. 42,15). The use of the verb "to see" (ראה, ὁράω) is reminiscent of two other

---

68 Cf. PROCKTER, Fence, 245 – 252 and WRIGHT, Fear the Lord, 209 – 210. Argall discovers in the secret things of Sir 3,22b an allusion to Dt 29,29a [28a in Hb]: "The hidden things [הנסתרת] belong to the Lord our God" (cf. ARGALL, 1 Enoch and Sirach, 75 – 76) which was already noted by VON RAD, Wesheit in Israel, 372 note 6.

69 Cf. BEAUCHAMP, Sur deux mots, 24: "Cet arrière-fond donne un sens fort à l'ἀποκαλύπτων de Si 42,19. Toute la cosmologie de Ben Sira manifeste à la fois le sens enthousiaste du mystère et la volonté de le contenir".

70 According to Liesen, the expression "on his secrets", in combination with the verb διανοεῖσθαι, probably refers to the wisdom of God and more concretely to his Law (cf. LIESEN, Full of Praise, 83 – 84).

71 In Gk: καὶ ἀποκαλύψει αὐτῷ τὰ κρυπτὰ αὐτῆς (cf. 14,21Gk). Cf. CALDUCH-BENAGES, Prueba, 45.

autobiographical texts, viz. 16,5 and 31[34Hb],11. In a context of controversy with his opponents about sin, freedom and retribution (15,11–16,14) Ben Sira emphasizes his teaching by presenting himself as a witness for it: "Many things like these my eyes have seen" (16,5), and in the text on travelling (31[34Hb],9–17) he appeals again to his own experience: "I have seen many things on my travels" (31[34Hb],11). Both in these texts and in 43,32 the insistence of the sage in giving witness to what he has seen and experienced personally corresponds to a clear pedagogical objective. Ben Sira knows that the testimony of the master's life is an enormously effective way of impressing the disciple.

In 43,32 the many hidden things contrast with the little which Ben Sira has seen; likewise, the hidden part of creation (the invisible things) contrasts with the visible works. In contemplating the universe Ben Sira recognises that he has not exhausted this unfathomable reality. The same idea occurs in Job 26,14 with regard to the foregoing verses: "these are but the fringes of his works; we have heard only a whisper of him; who will understand the thunder of his mighty deeds?". Ben Sira has only touched the fringes of his works, has heard only a whisper, has perceived a spark (cf. Sir 42,22). This fragile and veiled perception of the mystery has brought him to praise the Creator.

Instead of saying anything more about human limitations, Ben Sira concludes his hymn by directing attention towards the Creator. Sir 43,33 contains two affirmations about God which provide an interpretative key for the entire hymn. The first one, "The Lord has made all things" (43,33a) is of indubitably biblical origin (cf. Gen 1,1–2,4a; Is 44,24; 45,7)[72] and can be considered as a confession of faith in God the Creator of the entire universe. According to Burton, 43,33a is a summary statement which not only concludes the final part of the hymn but also resumes the whole doctrine of creation in Ben Sira[73]. The second affirmation, "and to the pious (τοῖς εὐσεβέσιν) he has given wisdom"[74], complements the first by inserting two key concepts of the book (piety/fear-of-God and wisdom), which are thus linked to the creational work of God. The importance attributed to "the pious ones" is noteworthy: through the divine gift of wisdom (cf. 1,10) they acquire a special ability that renders them capable to see part of the works of God and to understand part of the hidden secrets of creation. Ben Sira (and also his disciples) having but followed in the footsteps of his predecessors, presents himself as one of these pious ones. The implications of the

---

72 Cf. BURTON, Judaic Doctrine, 36–38: "The הכל of creation in Sirach and Deuteroisaiah".
73 Cf. BURTON, Judaic Doctrine, 189.
74 According to Argall, the expression ἔδωκεν σοφίαν is a technical term (cf. Sir 6,37d and 1 En. 5,8; 82,2) which goes together with the phrase "[God] reveals the most hidden secrets" of 42,19b (ARGALL, 1 Enoch and Sirach, 72). Cf. WRIGHT, Fear the Lord, 210.

second affirmation of 43,33 have to be seen in the light of what follows: "I wish to praise the men of goodness/piety/fidelity (אנשי חסד), our forefathers, each one in his own time" (44,1). The wisdom which Ben Sira received is the same wisdom which had come to the heroes of the faith, the faithful *par excellence* in history. In this way, the personal testimony of Ben Sira acquires more weight, because it is backed up by the weight and authority of tradition. Ben Sira consciously presents himself, therefore, as a model to be imitated.

4 Conclusion

In the 2nd chapter of his book on wisdom in Israel G. von Rad dedicates some pages to the "Limitations of Wisdom". At a certain point, after having praised the audacity with which Israel tried to understand the wholly unfathomable presence of God, and after having recognised that the sages offered a moving instruction on the mystery of divine government, he notes: "The mystery of God has become an object of study"[75]. Summarising our study of Sir 43,27–33 we could say the same about the entire creation. For Ben Sira and his disciple creation has not only become an object of teaching, but also a motive for praise. In contemplation of the wonders of creation Ben Sira both enjoys and learns from the wisdom of God. Although aware of his limitations, his fine aesthetic and religious sensibility instils in him the desire to praise the Creator of the universe with all his strength.

If creation in its immensity and harmony is the privileged area where God and human beings meet, what image of God does the sage present in these verses? First, God is the absolute Creator of all created reality, which according to the classification of Reiterer includes both *die materielle Ebenen der Schöpfung* (human beings, animals, elements of the universe, concrete persons and many other realities) and *die immaterielle Ebenen* (Wisdom, negative forces such as evil and the devil)[76]. It follows then that God, who is greater than all his works, is present in all and in each one of them. Second, he is an awesome and mighty God, who inspires great respect and who is capable of realising those tasks which are beyond human beings. Third, he is an impenetrable God, invisible, defying description, unfathomable, for, no matter how hard humans try, they cannot penetrate God's mystery, and cannot even praise him

---

75 VON RAD, Weisheit in Israel, 146–147: "Das Geheimnis Gottes ist geradezu zu einem Lehrgegenstand geworden".
76 REITERER, Ebenen, 1.

duly. And finally, he is a wise God who not only created Wisdom but who also poured her out on all his works; a wise God who is especially generous to the pious ones to whom he gives Wisdom. In this way, these can perceive something of his works and know part of his mysteries. This is the experience which Ben Sira wanted to inculcate: praise God, the Creator of all, for there always will be reasons to praise him.

Bibliography

AICHHORN, Wolfgang—KRONBERGER, Helmut, The Nature of Emotions. A Psychological Perspective. In: Renate EGGER-WENZEL—Jeremy CORLEY (eds.), Emotions from Ben Sira to Paul (DCLY 2011), Berlin—Boston: Walter de Gruyter, 2012, 515–525.

ALBANI, Matthias, Astronomie und Schöpfungsglaube. Untersuchungen zum Astronomischen Henochbuch (WMANT 68), Neukirchen—Vluyn: Neukirchener, 1994.

ALBANI, Matthias, Zur Rekonstruktion eines verdrängten Konzepts: Der 364-Tage-Kalender in der gegenwärtigen Forschung. In: ID.—Jörg FREY—Armin LANGE (eds.), Studies in the Book of Jubilees (TSAJ 65), Tübingen: Mohr Siebeck, 1997, 79–125.

ALONSO SCHÖKEL, Luis, Diccionario bíblico hebreo-español. Edición preparada por Víctor Morla y Vicente Collado, Madrid: Trotta, 1994.

ALONSO SCHÖKEL, Luis, Notas exegéticas al Eclesiástico (Ben Sira): EstBíb 54 (1995) 299–312.

ALONSO SCHÖKEL, Luis, Proverbios y Eclesiástico (Los Libros Sagrados 8.1), Madrid: Cristiandad, 1968.

ALONSO SCHÖKEL, Luis, Símbolos matrimoniales en la Biblia, Estella (Navarra): Verbo Divino, 1997.

ALONSO SCHÖKEL, Luis, The Vision of Man in Sirach 16,24–17,14. In: John G. GAMMIE—Walter A. BRUEGGEMANN—W. Lee HUMPHREYS, et al. (eds.), Israelite Wisdom. Theological and Literary Essays in Honor of Samuel Terrien, Missoula, MT: Scholars Press, 1978, 235–245.

ALONSO SCHÖKEL, Luis—José VÍLCHEZ LÍNDEZ, Proverbios (NBE. Comentario teológico y literario. Sapienciales 1), Madrid: Cristiandad, 1984.

ARATOS, Phénomènes, tome I. Texte établi, traduit et commenté par Jean Martin (Collection des Universités de France), Paris: Les Belles Lettres, 1998.

ARCHER, Leonie, Her Price is Beyond Rubies. The Jewish Woman in Graeco-Roman Palestine (JSOTSup 60), Sheffield: JSOT Press, 1990.

ARGALL, Randal A., 1 Enoch and Sirach. A Comparative Literary and Conceptual Analysis of the Themes of Revelation, Creation and Judgment (SBLEJL 8), Atlanta GA: Scholars Press, 1995.

ARGALL, Randal A., Competing Wisdoms: 1 Enoch and Sirach: Hen 24 (2002) 169–178.

BAARDA, Tjitze, The Sentences of the Syriac Menander (Third Century A.D.): A New Translation and Introduction. In: James H. CHARLESWORTH (ed.), The Old Testament Pseudepigrapha, vol. 2: Expansions of the "Old Testament" and Legends, Wisdom and Philosophical Literature, Prayers, Psalms and Odes, Fragments of Lost Judeo-Hellenistic Works, Garden City, N.Y.: Doubleday, 1985, 583–606.

BACHER, Wilhelm, Notes on the Cambridge Fragments of Ecclesiasticus: JQR 12 (1899–1900) 272–290.

BALLA, Ibolya, Attitudes toward Sexuality in the Book of Ben Sira (Ph.D. diss., Murdoch University, Perth, Australia, 2008).

BALLA, Ibolya, Ben Sira on Family, Gender and Sexuality (DCLS 8), Berlin—New York: Walter de Gruyter, 2011.

BALLA, Ibolya, Ben Sira/Sirach. In: William LOADER, The Pseudepigrapha on Sexuality. Attitudes towards Sexuality in Apocalypses, Testaments, Legends, Wisdom and Related Literature, Grand Rapids, MI—Cambridge, U.K.: Eerdmans, 2011, 362–398.

https://doi.org/10.1515/9783110492316-024

BAR, Shaul, A Letter That Has Not Been Read. Dreams in the Hebrew Bible. Translated by Lenn J. Schramm (Monographs of the Hebrew Union College 25), Cincinnati: Hebrew Union College Press, 2001.

BARTHÉLEMY, Dominique—Otto RICKENBACHER, Konkordanz zum hebräischen Sirach mit syrisch-hebräischem Index, Göttingen: Vandenhoeck & Ruprecht, 1973.

BAUCKHAM, Richard J., James, 1 and 2 Peter, Jude. In: Donald A. CARSON—Hugh G.M. WILLIAMSON (eds.), It is Written: Scripture Citing Scripture. Essays in Honour of Barnabas Lindars, Cambridge: Cambridge University Press, 1988, 303–317.

BEAUCHAMP, Paul, La personificazione della Sapienza in Proverbi 8,22–31: genesi e orientamento. In: Giuseppe BELLIA—Angelo PASSARO (eds.), Il Libro dei Proverbi. Tradizione, redazione, teologia, Casale Monferrato (AL): Piemme, 1999, 191–209.

BEAUCHAMP, Paul, Sur deux mots de l'Ecclésiastique (Sir 43,27b). In: Joseph DORÉ—Christoph THEOBALD (eds.), Penser la foi. Recherches en théologie aujourd'hui. Mélanges offerts à Joseph Moingt, Paris: Cerf, 1993, 15–25.

BECKER, Eve-Marie—Heinz-Josef FABRY—Michael REITEMEYER, Sophia Sirach. In: Wolfgang KRAUS—Martin KARRER (eds.), Septuaginta Deutsch. Das griechische Alte Testament in deutscher Übersetzung, Stuttgart: Deutsche Bibelgesellschaft, 2009, 1090–1163.

BEENTJES, Pancratius C., The Book of Ben Sira and Deuteronomistic Heritage. A Critical Approach. In: Hanne VON WEISSENBERG—Juha PAKKALA—Marko MARTTILA (eds.), Changes in Scripture. Rewriting and Interpreting Authoritative Traditions in the Second Temple Period (BZAW 419), Berlin: Walter de Gruyter, 2011, 275–296 = in: ID., "With All Your Soul Fear the Lord" (Sir. 7:27), 125–142.

BEENTJES, Pancratius C. (ed.), The Book of Ben Sira in Hebrew. A Text Edition of all Extant Hebrew Manuscripts & A Synopsis of all Parallel Hebrew Ben Sira Texts (VTS 68), Leiden: Brill, 1997.

BEENTJES, Pancratius C., The Book of Ben Sira in Hebrew. Preliminary Remarks Towards a New Text Edition and Synopsis. in: Actes du Troisième Colloque International: "Bible et Informatique: interprétation, herméneutique, compétence informatique", Tübingen 26–30 août 1991 (Travaux de Linguistique Quantitative 49; Paris–Genève: Champion–Slatkine, 1992) 471–484.

BEENTJES, Pancratius C., "The Countries Marvelled at You". King Solomon in Ben Sira 47:12–22: Bijdr 45 (1984) 6–14 = in: ID., "Happy the One Who Meditates on Wisdom" (Sir. 14,20), 135–144.

BEENTJES, Pancratius C., "Come to me, you who desire me...": Lady Wisdom's Invitation in Ben Sira 24:19–22. In: Renate EGGER-WENZEL—Karin SCHÖPFLING—Johannes Friedrich DIEHL (eds.), Weisheit als Lebensgrundlage. Festschrift für Friedrich V. Reiterer zum 65. Geburtstag (DCLS 15), Berlin: Walter de Gruyter, 2013, 1–11 = in: ID., "With All Your Soul Fear the Lord" (Sir. 7:27), 31–39.

BEENTJES, Pancratius C., Errata et Corrigenda. In: Renate EGGER-WENZEL (ed.), Ben Sira's God. Proceedings of the International Ben Sira Conference Durham—Ushaw College 2001 (BZAW 321), Berlin—New York: Walter de Gruyter, 2002, 375–377.

BEENTJES, Pancratius C., "Full Wisdom is Fear of the Lord": Ben Sira 19,20–20,32: Context, Composition and Concept: EstBíb 47 (1989) 27–45 = in: ID., "Happy is the One Who Meditates on Wisdom" (Sir. 14,20), 87–106.

BEENTJES, Pancratius C., "Happy the One Who Meditates on Wisdom" (Sir.14,20). Collected Essays on the Book of Ben Sira (CBET 43), Leuven: Peeters, 2006.

BEENTJES, Pancratius C., Hezekiah and Isaiah. A Study on Ben Sira xlviii, 15–25. In: Adam S.
VAN DER WOUDE (ed.), New Avenues in the Study of the Old Testament. A Collection of
Old Testament Studies Published on the Occasion of the Fiftieth Anniversary of the
Oudtestamentische Werkgezelschap and the Retirement of Prof. Dr. M.J. Mulder (OTS
25), Leiden: Brill, 1989, 77–88 = in: ID., "Happy the One Who Meditates on Wisdom"
(Sir. 14,20), 145–158.

BEENTJES, Pancratius C., Inverted Quotations in the Bible. A Neglected Stylistic Pattern: Bib
63 (1982) 506–523.

BEENTJES, Pancratius C., Jesus Sirach 7:1–17. Kanttekeningen bij de structuur en de tekst van
een verwaarloosde passage: Bijdr 41 (1980) 251–259.

BEENTJES, Pancratius C., Jesus, zoon van Sirach (Cahiers voor levensverdieping 41), Averbode:
Altiora, 1982.

BEENTJES, Pancratius C., Portrayals of David in Deuterocanonical and Cognate Literature. In:
Hermann LICHTENBERGER—Ulrike MITTMANN-RICHERT (eds.), Biblical Figures in
Deuterocanonical and Cognate Literature (DCLY 2008), Berlin: Walter de Gruyter 2009,
165–181 = in: ID., "With All Your Soul Fear The Lord" (Sir. 7:27), 175–189.

BEENTJES, Pancratius C., Prophets and Prophecy in the Book of Ben Sira. In: Michael E. Floyd
—Robert D. Haak (eds.), Prophets, Prophecy and Prophetic Texts in Second Temple
Judaism (LHB/OTS 427), New York: T&T Clark, 2006, 135–150 = in: ID., "Happy the One
Who Meditates on Wisdom" (Sir. 14,20), 207–229.

BEENTJES, Pancratius C., Sir 22:27–23:6 in zijn Context: Bijdr 39 (1978) 144–151.

BEENTJES, Pancratius C., "Sweet is His Memory, Like Honey to the Palate". King Josiah in Ben
Sira 49,1–4: BZ 34 (1990) 262–266 = in: ID., "Happy the One Who Meditates on
Wisdom" (Sir. 14,20), 159–165.

BEENTJES, Pancratius C., Theodicy in the Wisdom of Ben Sira. In: Antti LAATO—Johannes
Cornelis DE MOOR (eds.), Theodicy in the World of the Bible, Leiden—Boston: Brill,
2003, 509–524 = in: ID., "Happy the One Who Meditates on Wisdom" (Sir. 14,20),
265–279.

BEENTJES, Pancratius C., Tradition and Transformation in the Book of Chronicles (SSN 52),
Leiden: Brill, 2008.

BEENTJES, Pancratius C., "With All Your Soul Fear the Lord" (Sir. 7:27) Collected Essays on the
Book of Ben Sira II (CBET 87), Leuven: Peeters, 2017.

BEGG, Christopher T., Ben Sirach's Non-mention of Ezra: BN 42 (1988) 14–18.

BERGANT, Dianne, Israel's Wisdom Literature. A Liberation-Critical Reading, Minneapolis:
Fortress, 1997.

BERGMANN, Claudia D., Childbirth as a Metaphor for Crisis in the Hebrew Bible and in 1 QH
11:1–18 (BZAW 382), Berlin: Walter de Gruyter, 2009.

BERMAN, Joshua, The 'Sword of Mouths' (Jud. III 16; Ps. CXLIX 6; Prov. V 4): A Metaphor and
Its Ancient Near East Context: VT 52 (2002) 291–303.

Biblia sacra iuxta latinam vulgatam versionem ad codicum fidem. XII, Sapientia Salomonis,
Liber Hiesu filii Sirach / iussu Pauli PP. VI cura et studio monachorum Abbatiae
pontificiae Sancti Hieronymi in urbe ordinis Sancti Benedicti edita; cum praefationibus
et variis capitulorum seriebus, Rome: Typis Polyglottis Vaticanis, 1964.

Biblia Sacra iuxta vulgatam versionem, Stuttgart: Deutsche Bibelgesellschaft, ⁴1994.

BOCCACCINI, Gabriele, Introduction: The Rediscovery of Enochic Judaism and the Enoch
Seminar: Hen 24 (2002) 9–13.

BOCCACCINI, Gabriele, L'origine del male, libertà dell'uomo e retribuzione nella Sapienza di Ben Sira: Hen 8 (1986) 1–35.

BOCCACCINI, Gabriele, Middle Judaism: Jewish Thought 300 B.E.C. to 200 C.E. With a Foreword by James. H. Charlesworth, Minneapolis: Fortress, 1991 = Italian trans.: Il Medio Giudaismo. Per una storia del pensiero giudaico tra il terzo secolo a.e.v. e il secondo secolo e.v. (Radici 14), Genova: Marietti, 1993.

BOCCACCINI, Gabriele, Roots of Rabbinic Judaism. An Intellectual History from Ezechiel to Daniel, Grand Rapids, MI–Cambridge, U.K.: Eerdmans, 2002.

BOCCACCINI, Gabriele, Where Does Ben Sira Belong? The Canon, Literary Genre, Intellectual Movement, and Social Group of a Zadokite Document. In: Géza G. XERAVITS–József ZSENGELLÉR (eds.), Studies in the Book of Ben Sira. Papers of the Third International Conference on the Deuterocanonical Books, Shime'on Centre, Pápa, Hungary, 18–20 May, 2006 (JSJSup 127), Leiden: Brill, 2008, 21–41.

BOGAERT, Pierre-Maurice, Les formes anciennes du livre d'Esther. Réflexions sur les livres bibliques à traditions multiples à l'occasion de la publication du texte de l'ancienne version latine: RTL 40 (2009) 66–77.

BOON, Antonius, Dissertatio exegetico-theologica, de Jacobi Epistolae cum Siracidae libro, sapientia dicto, convenientia, Groningen: apud R. J. Shierbeck, 1860.

BOROWSKI, Oded, Animals in the Literature of Syria-Palestine. In: Billie Jean COLLINS (ed.), A History of the Animal World in the Ancient Near East (Handbook of Oriental Studies. Section 1: The Near and the Middle East 64), Leiden: Brill, 2002, 289–306.

BOROWSKI, Oded., Every Living Thing. Daily Use of Animals in Ancient Israel, Walnut Creek, CA: Alta Mira, 1998.

BOTHA, Phil J., The Ideology of Shame in the Wisdom of Ben Sira: Ecclesiasticus 41,14–42,8: OTE 9 (1996) 353–371.

BOX, George H. – William O.E. OESTERLEY, The Book of Sirach. In: Robert H. CHARLES (ed.), The Apocrypha and Pseudepigrapha of the Old Testament in English: with Introductions and Critical and Explanatory Notes to the Several Books, vol. 1: Apocrypha, Oxford: Clarendon, 1968, repr. of the 1st ed. 1913, 268–517.

BRAUDE, William G. (trans.), The Midrash on Psalms (Yale Judaica Series 13), New Haven: Yale University Press, ³1976.

BRETSCHNEIDER, Karl Gottlieb, Liber Jesu Siracidae graece ad fidem codicum et versionum emendatus et perpetua annotatione illustratus, Ratisbon: Apud Montagium et Weissium, 1806.

BROCKMÖLLER, Katrin, "Eine Frau der Stärke—wer findet sie?" Exegetische Analysen und intertextuelle Lektüren zu Spr 31,10–31 (BBB 147), Berlin: Philo, 2004.

BÜCHLER, Adolf, Die Tobiaden und die Oniaden im II. Makkabäerbuche und in der verwandtenjüdisch-hellenistischen Literatur. Untersuchungen zur Geschichte der Juden von 220–160 und zur jüdischen Literatur. In: VI. Jahresbericht der Israelitisch-theologischen Lehranstalt in Wien für das Schuljahr 1898/99, Wien: Verlag der israelitisch-theologischen Lehranstalt, 1899 (repr. Hildesheim: Georg Olms, 1975).

BURTON, Keith W., Ben Sira and the Judaic Doctrine of Creation (Ph.D. diss., University of Glasgow, 1987).

BUSSINO, Severino, The Greek Additions in the Book of Ben Sira. Translated from the Italian by Michael Tait (AnBib 203), Rome: Gregorian & Biblical Press, 2013.

CALDUCH-BENAGES, Nuria, The Absence of Named Women from Ben Sira's Praise of the Ancestors. In: Jeremy CORLEY—Harm VAN GROL (eds.), Rewriting Biblical History. Essays on Chronicles and Ben Sira in Honour of Pancratius C. Beentjes (DCLS 7), Berlin: Walter de Gruyter, 2011, 301–317.

CALDUCH-BENAGES, Nuria, Animal Imagery in the Hebrew Text of Ben Sirach. In: Jan JOOSTEN —Jean-Sébastien REY (eds.), The Texts and Versions of the Book of Ben Sira. Transmission and Interpretation (JSJSup 150), Leiden: Brill, 2011, 55–71.

CALDUCH-BENAGES, Nuria, Aromas, fragancias y perfumes en el Sirácida. In: EAD.—Jacques VERMEYLEN (eds.), Treasures of Wisdom. Studies in Ben Sira and the Book of Wisdom. Festschrift M. Gilbert (BETL 143), Leuven: University Press—Peeters, 1999, 15–30 = in: EAD., Pan de sensatez y agua de sabiduría. Estudios sobre el libro de Ben Sira (ABE. Artículos selectos 1), Estella (Navarra): Verbo Divino, 2019, 85–102.

CALDUCH-BENAGES, Nuria, Ben Sira 2,1–18 y el Nuevo Testamento: EstBíb 53 (1995) 305–316 = in: EAD., Pan de sensatez y agua de sabiduría, 351–362.

CALDUCH-BENAGES, Nuria, Ben Sira 2,1–18 y los Padres de la Iglesia: EstBíb 61 (2003) 199–215 = in: EAD., Pan de sensatez y agua de sabiduría, 363–380.

CALDUCH-BENAGES, Nuria, Ben Sira 23:27—A Pivotal Verse. In: EAD. (ed.), Wisdom for Life. Essays Offered to Honor Prof. Maurice Gilbert, SJ on the Occasion of His Eightieth Birthday (BZAW 445), Berlin—Boston: Walter de Gruyter, 2014, 186–200.

CALDUCH-BENAGES, Nuria, Ben Sira 24:22—Decoding a Metaphor. In: Irmtraud FISCHER— Andrea TASCHL-ERBER (eds.), Vermittelte Gegenwart. Konzeptionen der Gottespräsenz von der Zeit des Zweiten Tempels bis zum anfang des 2. Jh. n.Chr. (WUNT 367), Tübingen: Mohr Siebeck, 2016, 57–72.

CALDUCH-BENAGES, Nuria, Ben Sira y el canon de las Escrituras: Greg 78 (1997) 359–370 = in: EAD., Pan de sensatez y agua de sabiduría, 19–31.

CALDUCH-BENAGES, Nuria, Ben Sira y las mujeres: Reseña Bíblica 41 (2004) 37–44.

CALDUCH-BENAGES, Nuria, "Cut Her Away from Your Flesh". Divorce in Ben Sira. In: Géza G. XERAVITS—József ZSENGELLÉR (eds.), Studies in the Book of Ben Sira. Papers of the Third International Conference on the Deuterocanonical Books, Shime'on Centre, Pápa, Hungary, 18–20 May, 2006 (JSJSup 127), Leiden: Brill, 2008, 81–95.

CALDUCH-BENAGES, Nuria, Elementos de inculturación helenista en el libro de Ben Sira: los viajes, EstBíb 54 (1996) 289–298 = in: EAD., Pan de sensatez y agua de sabiduría, 235–244.

CALDUCH-BENAGES, Nuria, En el crisol de la prueba. Estudio exegético de Sir 2,1–18 (ABE 32), Estella (Navarra): Verbo Divino, 1997.

CALDUCH-BENAGES, Nuria, Garment Imagery in the Book of Ben Sira. In: Markus WITTE—Sven BEHNKE (eds.), The Metaphorical Use of Language in Deuterocanonical and Cognate Literature (DCLY 2014/15), Berlin: Walter de Gruyter, 2015, 257–278.

CALDUCH-BENAGES, Nuria, Gli ornamenti sacerdotali nel Siracide. Studio del vocabolario. In: Simonetta GRAZIANI (ed.) with the collaboration of M.C. Casaburi and G. Lacerenza, Studi sul Vicino Oriente Antico dedicati alla memoria di Luigi Cagni (Istituto Universitario Orientale. Dipartimento di Studi Asiatici. Series Minor 61), Napoli: Istituto Orientale di Napoli, 2000, 1319–1339.

CALDUCH-BENAGES, Nuria, God Creator of All (Sir 43,27–33). In: Renate EGGER-WENZEL (ed.), Ben Sira's God. Proceedings of the International Ben Sira Conference, Durham—Ushaw College 2001 (BZAW 321), Berlin—New York: Walter de Gruyter, 2002, 79–117.

CALDUCH-BENAGES, Nuria, La mujer en la versión siríaca (Peshitta) de Ben Sira. ¿Sesgos de género?. In: Jesús CAMPOS SANTIAGO—Víctor PASTOR JULIÁN (eds.), Congreso Internacional "Biblia, memoria histórica y encrucijada de culturas", Zamora: Asociación Bíblica Española, 2004, 686–693.

CALDUCH-BENAGES, Nuria, La Sabiduría y la prueba en Sir 4,11–19: EstBíb 49 (1991) 25–48 = in: EAD., Pan de sensatez y agua de sabiduría, 173–199.

CALDUCH-BENAGES, Nuria, Le vesti di Aronne, simbolo cultuale (Sir 45,6–22): ParSpV 60 (2009) 69–81.

CALDUCH-BENAGES, Nuria, L'inno al creato in Ben Sira (Sir 42,15–43,33): ParSpV 44 (2001) 51–66.

CALDUCH-BENAGES, Nuria, Trial Motif in the Book of Ben Sira, with Special Reference to 2,1–6. In: Pancratius C. BEENTJES (ed.), The Book of Ben Sira in Modern Research. Proceedings of the First International Ben Sira Conference 28–31 July 1996 Soesterberg, Netherlands (BZAW 255), Berlin—New York: Walter de Gruyter, 1997, 135–151.

CALDUCH-BENAGES, Nuria, Un gioiello di Sapienza. Leggendo Siracide 2 (Cammini nello Spirito. Sezione biblica 45), Milano: Paoline, 2001.

CALDUCH-BENAGES, Nuria, A Wordplay on the Term *mûsar* (Sir 6,22). In: Renate EGGER-WENZEL—Karin SCHÖPFLIN—Johannes F. DIEHL (eds.), Weisheit als Lebensgrundlage. Festschrift für Friedrich V. Reiterer zum 65. Geburtstag (DCLS 15), Berlin—Boston: Walter de Gruyter, 2013, 13–26.

CALDUCH-BENAGES, Nuria—Joan FERRER—Jan LIESEN, La Sabiduría del Escriba. Wisdom of the Scribe. Edición diplomática de la versión siríaca (Peshitta) del libro de Ben Sira según el Códice Ambrosiano con traducción española e inglesa. Diplomatic Edition of the Syriac Version (Peshitta) of the Book of Ben Sira according to Codex Ambrosianus, with Translations in Spanish and English (Biblioteca Midrásica 26), Estella (Navarra): Verbo Divino, 2003, ²2015, rev. ed.

CAMP, Claudia V., Ben Sira and the Men Who Handle Books. Gender and the Rise of Canon-Consciousness (Hebrew Bible Monographs 50), Sheffield: Sheffield Phoenix, 2013.

CAMP, Claudia V., Honor and Shame in Ben Sira: Anthropological and Theological Reflections. In: Pancratius C. BEENTJES (ed.), The Book of Ben Sira in Modern Research. Proceedings of the First International Ben Sira Conference 28–31 July 1996 Soesterberg, Netherlands (BZAW 255), Berlin: Walter de Gruyter 1997, 171–187.

CAMP, Claudia V., Honor, Shame and Hermeneutics of Ben Sira's MsC. In: Michael L. BARRÉ (ed.), Wisdom, You Are My Sister. Studies in Honor of Roland E. Murphy on the Occasion of His Eightieth Birthday (CBQMS 29), Washington, DC: The Catholic Biblical Association of America, 1997, 157–171.

CAMP, Claudia V., Understanding a Patriarchy. Women in Second Century Jerusalem through the Eyes of Ben Sira. In: Amy-Jill LEVINE (ed.), "Women Like This". New Perspectives on Jewish Women in the Greco-Roman World (SBLEJL 1), Atlanta, GA: Scholars Press, 1991, 1–39.

CAMPBELL, Ken M. (ed.), Marriage and Family in the Biblical World, Downers Grove, IL: InterVarsity Press, 2003.

CERFAUX, Lucien, Les sources scripturaires de Mt XI,25–30: ETL 31 (1955) 331–342.

CHAINE, Joseph, L'épître de saint Jacques (ÉBib), Paris: Gabalda, 1927.

CHARLES, Robert H. (ed.), The Apocrypha and Pseudepigrapha of the Old Testament in English: with Introductions and Critical and Explanatory Notes to the Several Books, vol. 1: Apocrypha, Oxford: Clarendon, 1968, reprint of the 1st ed. 1913.

CHARLESWORTH, James H. (ed.), The Old Testament Pseudepigrapha, vol. 1: Apocalyptic Literature and Testaments, Garden City, NY: Doubleday, 1983.

CLEMENTS, Ronald E., Wisdom in Theology (The Didsbury Lectures 1989), Carlisle: The Pater Noster Press, 1992.

CLIFFORD, Richard J., Proverbs (OTL), Louisville, KY—London: Westminster John Knox, 1999.

COGGINS, Richard J., Sirach (Guides to the Apocrypha and Pseudepigrapha 6), Sheffield: Sheffield Academic, 1998.

COHEN, Boaz, Jewish and Roman Law. A Comparative Study, vol. 1, New York: The Jewish Theological Seminary of America, 1966.

COHEN, Harold R. (Chaim), Biblical Hapax Legomena in the Light of the Akkadia and Ugaritic (SBLDS 37), Missoula, MT: Scholars Press, 1978.

COLLINS, Billie Jean (ed.), A History of the Animal World in the Ancient Near East (Handbook of Oriental Studies. Section 1: The Near and the Middle East 64), Leiden: Brill, 2002.

COLLINS, John J., Jewish Wisdom in the Hellenistic Age (OTL), Louisville, KY: Westminster John Knox, 1997.

COLLINS, John J., Marriage, Divorce and Family in Second Temple Judaism. In: Leo G. PERDUE —Joseph BLENKINSOPP—John J. COLLINS—Carol MEYERS (eds.), Families in Ancient Israel (The Family, Religion, and Culture), Louisville, KY: Westminster John Knox, 1997, 104–162.

COLLINS, John J., Seers, Sybils and Sages in Hellenistic-Roman Judaism (JSJSup 54), Leiden: Brill, 1997.

COLSON, Francis H. (trans.), Philo with an English Translation by F. H. Colson, volume 6 (The Loeb Classical Library), Cambridge, MA: Harvard University Press; London: William Heinemann, 1935, repr. 1950.

CORLEY, Jeremy, Ben Sira's Teaching on Friendship (BJS 316), Providence, RI: Brown University Press, 2001.

CORLEY, Jeremy, An Intertextual Study of Proverbs and Ben Sira. In: ID.—Vincent SKEMP (eds.), Intertextual Studies in Ben Sira and Tobit. Essays in Honor of Alexander A. Di Lella, O.F.M. (CBQMS 38), Washington, DC: The Catholic Biblical Association of America, 2005, 155–182.

CORLEY, Jeremy, The Portrait of Samuel in Hebrew Ben Sira 46:13–20. In: Hermann LICHTENBERGER—Ulrike MITTMANN-RICHERT (eds.), Biblical Figures in Deuterocanonical and Cognate Literature (DCLY 2008), Berlin: Walter de Gruyter 2009, 31–56.

CORLEY, Jeremy, Similes and Sound Patterns as Rhetorical Tools in Two Hebrew Wisdom Books. In: Archibald L.H.M. VAN WIERINGEN (ed.), Verborgen Lezers (Theologische Perspectieven. Supplement Series Deel 2), Bergambacht: Uitgeverij 2VM, 2011, 94–128.

CORLEY, Jeremy, Sirach 44:1–15 as Introduction to the Praise of the Ancestors. In: Géza G. XERAVITS—József ZSENGELLÉR (eds.), Studies in the Book of Ben Sira. Papers of the Third International Conference on the Deuterocanonical Books, Shime'on Centre, Pápa, Hungary, 18–20 May, 2006 (JSJSup 127), Leiden: Brill, 2008, 151–181.

CORLEY, Jeremy, Wisdom versus Apocalyptic and Science in Sirach 1,1–10. In: Florentino GARCÍA MARTÍNEZ (ed.), Wisdom and Apocalypticism in the Dead Sea Scrolls and in the Biblical Tradition (BETL 168), Leuven: Peeters, 2003, 269–286.

CRASS, Alban, La symbolique du vêtement dans la Bible. Pour une théologie du vêtement (Lire la Bible 172), Paris: Cerf, 2011.

CRENSHAW, James L., The Book of Sirach. Introduction, Commentary, and Reflections. In: The New Interpreter's Bible, vol. 5, Nashville: Abingdon, 1997, 601–867.

CRENSHAW, James L., Education in Ancient Israel: JBL 104 (1985) 601–615 = ID., Urgent Advice and Probing Questions. Collected Writings on Old Testament Wisdom, Macon, GA: Mercer University Press, 1995, 235–249.

CRENSHAW, James L., Old Testament Wisdom. An Introduction. Revised and Enlarged, Louisville, KY: Westminster John Knox, 1998 (1st ed. London, 1982).

CRENSHAW, James L., The Problem of Theodicy in Sirach: On Human Bondage: JBL 94 (1975) 47–64.

CRENSHAW, James L., The Restraint of Reason. The Humility of Prayer. In: ID. (ed.), Urgent Advice and Probing Questions. Collected Writings on Old Testament Wisdom, Macon, GA: Mercer University Press, 1995, 206–221.

CRENSHAW, James L., The Sage in Proverbs. In: John G. GAMMIE—Leo G. PERDUE (eds.), The Sage in Israel and the Ancient Near East, Winona Lake, IN: Eisenbrauns, 1990, 205–216.

DA SILVA, Aldina, La symbolique des rêves et des vêtements dans l'histoire de Joseph et de ses frères (Héritage et projet 52), Saint-Laurent: Fides, 1994.

DAVIDS, Peter H., The Epistle of James (NIGTC), Exeter: Paternoster, 1982.

DAVIDS, Peter H., The Pseudepigrapha in the Catholic Epistles. In: James H. CHARLESWORTH—Craig A. EVANS (eds.), The Pseudepigrapha and Early Biblical Interpretation (JSPSup 14), Sheffield: Sheffield Academic, 1993, 228–245.

DAVIDS, Peter H., Tradition and Citation in the Epistle of James. In: W. Ward GASQUE—William Sanford LASOR (eds.), Scripture, Tradition and Interpretation. Essays Presented to Everett F. Harrison by His Students and Colleagues in Honor of His Seventy-fifth Birthday, Grand Rapids, MI—Cambridge, U.K.: Eerdmans, 1978, 113–126.

DAVIDSON, Andrew B., Sirach's Judgment of Women: ExpTim 6 (1894/95) 402–404.

DE FRAINE, Jan, Het Loflied op de menselijke waardigheid in Eccli 17,1–14: Bijdr 11 (1950) 10–23.

DE SILVA, David A., The Wisdom of Ben Sira: Honor, Shame and the Maintenance of the Values of a Minority Culture: CBQ 58 (1997) 433–455.

DE VAUX, Roland Guérin, Ancient Israel: Its Life and Institutions, London: Darton Longman & Todd, 1961 = French orig., Les institutions de l'Ancien Testament, 2 vols., Paris: Cerf, 1958.

DEIST, Ferdinand E., The Material Culture of the Bible. An Introduction. Edited with a Preface by Robert P. Carroll (The Biblical Seminar 70), Sheffield: Sheffield Academic, 2000.

DELL, Katharine J., The Use of Animal Imagery in the Psalms and Wisdom Literature: SJT 53 (2000) 275–291.

DESEČAR, Alejandro J., La necedad en Sirac 23,12–15: SBFLA 20 (1970) 264–272.

DI LELLA, Alexander A., Ben Sira's Praise of the Ancestors of Old (Sir 44–49). The History of Israel as Parenetic Apologetics. In: Nuria CALDUCH-BENAGES—Jan LIESEN (eds.), History and Identity. How Israel's Later Authors Viewed Its Earlier History (DCLY 2006), Berlin: Walter de Gruyter, 2006, 151–167.

DI LELLA, Alexander A., Fear of the Lord and Belief and Hope in the Lord amid Trials: Sirach 2:1–18. In: Michael L. BARRÉ (ed.), Wisdom, You Are My Sister. Studies in Honor of

Roland E. Murphy on the Occasion of His Eightieth Birthday (CBQMS 29), Washington, DC: The Catholic Biblical Association of America, 1997, 188–204.

DI LELLA, Alexander A., Fear of the Lord as Wisdom: Ben Sira 1,11–30. In: Pancratius C. BEENTJES (ed.), The Book of Ben Sira in Modern Research. Proceedings of the First International Ben Sira Conference, 28–31 July 1996, Soesterberg, Netherlands (BZAW 255), Berlin–New York: Walter de Gruyter, 1997, 113–133.

DI LELLA, Alexander A., The Hebrew Text of Ben Sira. A Text-Critical and Historical Study (Studies in Classical Literature 1), The Hague: Mouton and Co., 1966.

DI LELLA, Alexander A., The Newly Discovered Sixth Manuscript of Ben Sira from the Cairo Geniza: Bib 69 (1988) 226–238.

DI LELLA, Alexander A., The Search for Wisdom in Ben Sira. In: Jack C. KNIGHT–Lawrence A. SINCLAIR (eds.), The Psalms and Other Studies on the Old Testament. Presented to Joseph I. Hunt Professor of Old Testament and Hebrew on His Seventieth Birthday, Nashotah, WI: Nashotah House Seminary, 1990, 185–196.

DUESBERG, Hilaire—Irénée FRANSEN, Ecclesiastico (La Sacra Bibbia volgata latina e traduzione italiana dai testi originali illustrate con note critiche e commentate a cura di Mons. Salvatore Garofalo. Antico Testamento sotto la direzione di P. Giovanni Rinaldi C. R. S.), Turin–Rome: Marietti, 1966.

DUESBERG, Hilaire—Irénée FRANSEN, Les scribes inspirés. Introduction aux livres sapientiaux de la Bible, Abbaye de Maredsous: Éditions de Maredsous, 1965.

DUESBERG, Hilaire, Il est le Tout. Siracide 43,27–33: BVC 54 (1963) 29–32.

DUGGAN, Michael W., Ezra, Scribe and Priest, and the Concerns of Ben Sira. In: Jeremy CORLEY—Vincent SKEMP (eds.), Intertextual Studies in Ben Sira and Tobit. Essays in Honor of Alexander A. Di Lella, O.F.M. (CBQMS 38), Washington, DC: The Catholic Biblical Association of America, 2005, 201–210.

DUMOULIN, Pierre, La parabole de la veuve, de Ben Sira 35,11–24 à Luc 18,1–8. In: Nuria CALDUCH-BENAGES—Jacques VERMEYLEN (eds.), Treasures of Wisdom. Studies in Ben Sira and in the Book of Wisdom. Festschrift M. Gilbert (BETL 143), Leuven: University Press—Peeters, 1999, 169–179.

EASTERLING, Pat E.—KENNEY, Edward J. (eds.), The Cambridge History of Classical Literature, vol. 1: Greek Literature, Cambridge: Cambridge University Press, 1985.

EATON, John H., The Circle of Creation. Animals in the Light of the Bible, London: SCM Press, 1995.

EBERHARTER, Andreas, Das Buch Jesus Sirach oder Ecclesiasticus (Die Heilige Schrift des Alten Testaments 6.5), Bonn: Hanstein, 1925.

EBNER, Martin, "Wo findet die Weisheit ihren Ort?" Weisheitskonzepte in Konkurrenz. In: Martin FASSNACHT—Aandreas LEINHÄUPL-WILKE—Stefan LÜCKING (eds.), Die Weisheit—Ursprünge und Rezeption. Festschrift für Karl Löning zum 65. Geburtstag (NTA.NF 44), Münster, 2003, 70–103.

EDERSHEIM, Alfred, Ecclesiasticus. In: Henry WACE (ed.), The Holy Bible according to the Authorized Version (A.D. 1611). Apocrypha, vol. 2, London: John Murray, 1888, 1–239.

EGGER-WENZEL, Renate, "Denn harte Knechtschaft und Schande ist es, wenn eine Frau ihren Mann ernährt" (Sir 25,22). In: EAD.—Ingrid KRAMMER (eds.), Der Einzelne und seine Gemeinschaft (BZAW 270), Berlin: Walter de Gruyter, 1998, 23–49.

EGGER-WENZEL, Renate, Ein neues Sira-Fragment des MS C: BN 138 (2008) 107–114.

EGGER-WENZEL, Renate, Josiah and His Prophet(s) in Chronicles and Ben Sira: An Intertextual Comparison. In: Jeremy CORLEY—Harm VAN GROL (eds.), Rewriting Biblical History. Essays on Chronicles and Ben Sira in Honour of Pancratius C. Beentjes (DCLS 7), Berlin: Walter de Gruyter, 2011, 231–256.

EGGER-WENZEL, Renate, Spricht Ben Sira von Polygamie?. In: Arno BUSCHMANN (ed.), Jahrbuch der Universität Salzburg 1993–1995, München—Eichenau: Roman Kovar, 1996, 57–64.

EGGER-WENZEL, Renate—Jeremy CORLEY (eds.), Emotions from Ben Sira to Paul (DCLY 2011), Berlin—Boston: Walter de Gruyter, 2012.

EGGER-WENZEL, Renate—Karin SCHÖPFLING—Johannes Friedrich DIEHL (eds.), Weisheit als Lebensgrundlage. Festschrift für Friedrich V. Reiterer zum 65. Geburtstag (DCLS 15), Berlin: Walter de Gruyter, 2013.

EHRLICH, Ernst Ludwig, Der Traum im Alten Testament (BZAW 73), Berlin: Walter de Gruyter, 1953.

EICHHORN, Johann Gottfried, Einleitung in die Apokryphischen Schriften des Alten Testaments, vol. 4, Leipzig: Weidmann, 1795.

EISENBAUM, Pamela M., The Jewish Heroes of Christian History. Hebrews 11 in Literary Context (SBLDS 156), Atlanta: Scholars Press, 1997.

ELIZUR, Shulamit, A New Fragment from the Hebrew Text of the Book of Ben Sira: Tarbiz 76 (2008) 17–28 (in Hebrew).

ELIZUR, Shulamit, Two New Leaves of the Hebrew Version of Ben Sira: DSD 17 (2010) 13–29.

ELIZUR, Shulamit—Michael RAND, A New Fragment of the Book of Ben Sira: DSD 18 (2011) 200–205.

ELLIS, E. Earle, Paul's Use of the Old Testament, Grand Rapids, MI: Baker, ³1991.

ELLIS, Teresa Ann, "Gender" in the Book of Ben Sira. Divine Wisdom, Erotic Poetry, and the Garden of Eden (BZAW 453), Berlin—New York: Walter de Gruyter, 2013.

ELLIS, Teresa Ann, Is Eve the 'Woman' in Sirach 25:24?: CBQ 73 (2011) 723–742.

EPSTEIN, Ezekiel Isidore (ed.), The Babylonian Talmud. Seder Nashim, London: Soncino, 1936.

FALK, Ze'ev W., Hebrew Law in Biblical Times. An Introductio, Provo, UT—Winona Lake, IN: Eisenbrauns, ²2001.

FASCE, Silvana, La lode del medico nel libro biblico del Siracide, Genoa: ECIG, 2009.

FELIKS, Yehuda, Nature and Man in the Bible, London—Jerusalem—New York: Soncino, 1981.

FEUILLET, André, Jésus et la Sagesse divine d'après les Évangiles synoptiques: RB 62 (1955) 161–196.

FISCHER, Irmtraud—Ursula RAPP—Johannes SCHILLER (eds.), Auf den Spuren der schriftgelehrten Weisen. Festschrift für Johannes Marböck (BZAW 331), Berlin: Walter de Gruyter, 2003.

FLANNERY-DAILEY, Frances L., Standing at the Heads of Dreamers. A Study of Dreams in Late Second Temple Judaism and Early Christianity (Ph.D. diss., The University of Iowa 2000).

FORTI, Tova L., Animal Imagery in the Book of Proverbs (VTS 118), Leiden—Boston, MA: Brill, 2008.

FORTI, Tova L., Animal Images in the Didactic Rhetoric of the Book of Proverbs: Bib 77 (1996) 48–63.

FORTI, Tova L., Bee's Honey—From Realia to Metaphor in Biblical Wisdom Literature: VT 56 (2006) 327–341.

FOURNIER-BIDOZ, Alain, L'arbre et la demeure en Siracide xxiv, 10–17: VT 34 (1984) 1–10.

Fox, Michael V., Proverbs 1–9. A New Translation with Introduction and Commentary (AB 18 A), New York: Doubleday, 2000.

Fox, Michael V., Proverbs 10–31. A New Translation with Introduction and Commentary (AB 18B), New Haven–London: Yale University Press, 2009.

Fragnelli, Pietro M., Siracide. In: Luciano Pacomio (ed.), La Bibbia Piemme, Casale Monferrato (AL): Piemme, 1995, 1571–1666 = Id., Un uomo saggio istruisce il suo popolo. Invito alla lettura del Siracide, Rome: Pontificio Seminario Romano, n.d.

Frankemölle, Hubert, Zum Thema des Jakobusbriefes im Kontext der Rezeption von Sir 2,1–18 und 15,11–20: BN 48 (1989) 21–47.

Freedman, Harry–Maurice Simon (eds.), Midrash Rabbah Translated into English with Notes, Glossary and Indices under the Editorship of Rabbi Dr. Harry Freedman and Maurice Simon, London: Soncino, ³1961.

Fritzsche, Otto F., Die Weisheit Jesus-Sirach's. Erklärt und übersetzt (Kurzgefaßtes exegetisches Handbuch zu den Apokryphen des Alten Testaments 5), Leipzig: S. Hirzel, ⁴1859.

Fuss, Werner, Tradition und Komposition im Buche Jesus Sirach (Ph.D. diss., University of Tübingen, 1963.

Gammie, John G., The Sage in Sirach. In: Id.—Leo G. Perdue (eds.), The Sage in Israel and the Ancient Near East, Winona Lake, IN: Eisenbrauns, 1990, 355–372.

Gaspar, Joseph W., Social Ideas in the Wisdom Literature of the Old Testament (The Catholic University Studies in Sacred Theology 2.8), Washington, DC: The Catholic University of America Press, 1947.

Gilbert, Maurice, Ben Sira et la femme: RTL 7 (1976) 426–442 = in: Id., Ben Sira. Recueil d'études—Collected Essays (BETL 264), Peeters: Leuven—Paris—Walpole, MA, 2014, 249–264.

Gilbert, Maurice, Ben Sira, Reader of Genesis 1–11. In: Jeremy Corley—Vincent Skemp (eds.), Intertextual Studies in Ben Sira and Tobit. Essays in Honor of Alexander A. Di Lella, O.F.M. (CBQMS 38), Washington, DC: The Catholic Biblical Association of America, 2005, 89–99 = in: Id., Ben Sira. Recueil d'études—Collected Essays, 301–310.

Gilbert, Maurice, God, Sin and Mercy: Sirach 15:11–18:14. In: Renate Egger-Wenzel (ed.), Ben Sira's God. Proceedings of the International Ben Sira Conference Durham—Ushaw College 2001 (BZAW 321) Berlin—New York: Walter de Gruyter, 2002, 118–135 = in: Id., Ben Sira. Recueil d'études—Collected Essays, 123–141.

Gilbert, Maurice, Introduction au livre de Ben Sira ou Siracide ou Ecclésiastique, Rome: Pontifical Biblical Institute, 1985.

Gilbert, Maurice, Jesus Sirach: RAC 17 (1996) 888–904 ("Christliche Rezeption des Sirach-Buches").

Gilbert, Maurice, La Sapienza si offre come nutrimento (Sir 24,19–22): ParSpV 7 (1983) 51–60.

Gilbert, Maurice, La sequela della Sapienza, lettura di Sir 6,23–31: ParSpV 2 (1980) 53–70.

Gilbert, Maurice, L'action de grâce de Ben Sira (Sir 51,1–12). In: Raymond Kuntzmann (ed.), Ce Dieu qui vient. Études sur l'Ancien et le Nouveau Testament offertes au Professeur Bernard Renaud à l'occasion de son soixante-cinquième anniversaire (LD 159), Paris: Cerf, 1995, 231–242 = in: Id., Ben Sira. Recueil d'études—Collected Essays, 181–190.

Gilbert, Maurice, L'Ecclésiastique: Quel texte? Quelle autorité?: RB 94 (1987) 233–250 = in: Id., Ben Sira. Recueil d'études—Collected Essays, 23–37.

GILBERT, Maurice, L'"éloge de la Sagesse" (Siracide 24): RTL 5 (1974) 326–348 = in: ID., Ben Sira. Recueil d'études—Collected Essays, 143–164.

GILBERT, Maurice, L'enseignement des sages: le Siracide. In: Jean AUNEAU (ed.), Les Psaumes et les autres Écrits (Petite bibliothèque des sciences bibliques. Ancien Testament 5), Paris: Desclée de Brouwer, 1990, 308–318.

GILBERT, Maurice, Les cinq livres de Sages. Proverbes, Job, Qohélet, Ben Sira, Sagesse (Lire la Bible 129), Paris: Cerf, 2003.

GILBERT, Maurice, Où en sont les études sur le Siracide?: Bib 92 (2011) 161–181 = in: ID., Ben Sira. Recueil d'études—Collected Essays, 349–366.

GILBERT, Maurice, Prayer in the Book of Ben Sira. Function and Relevance. In: Renate EGGER-WENZEL—Jeremy CORLEY (eds.), Prayer from Tobit to Qumran. Inaugural Conference of the ISDCL at Salzburg, Austria, 5–9 July 2003 (DCLY 2004), Berlin—New York: Walter de Gruyter, 2004, 117–135 = in: ID., Ben Sira. Recueil d'études—Collected Essays, 265–280.

GILBERT, Maurice, The Review of History in Ben Sira 44–50 and Wisdom 10–19. In: Jeremy CORLEY—Harm VAN GROL (eds.), Rewriting Biblical History. Essays on Chronicles and Ben Sira in Honour of Pancratius C. Beentjes (DCLS 7), Berlin: Walter de Gruyter, 2011, 319–334 = in: ID., Ben Sira. Recueil d'études—Collected Essays, 331–345.

GILBERT, Maurice, Sexualité. In: DBSup 12 (1996) 1016–1043.

GILBERT, Maurice, Siracide. In: DBSup 12 (1996) 1390–1402.

GILBERT, Maurice, The Vetus Latina of Ecclesiasticus. In: Géza G. XERAVITS—József ZSENGELLÉR (eds.), Studies in the Book of Ben Sira. Papers of the Third International Conference on the Deuterocanonical Books, Shime'on Centre, Pápa, Hungary, 18–20 May, 2006 (JSJSup 127), Leiden: Brill, 2008, 1–9 = in: ID., Ben Sira. Recueil d'études—Collected Essays, 49–58.

GILLMAYR-BUCHER, Susanne, Emotion und Kommunikation. In: Christian FREVEL (ed.), Biblische Anthropologie. Neue Einsichten aus dem Alten Testament (QD 237), Freiburg et al.: Herder, 2010, 279–290.

GLÜCK, Janus J., Paronomasia in Biblical Literature: Semitics 1 (1970) 50–78.

GOAN, Seán, Creation in Ben Sira: MilS 36 (1995) 75–85.

GOLDSTEIN, Jonathan A., The Tales of the Tobiads. In: Jacob NEUSNER (ed.), Christianity, Judaism and Other Greco-Roman Cults, vol. 3: Judaism before 70 (SJLA 12.3), Leiden: Brill, 1975, 85–123.

GORDIS, Robert, The Social Background of Wisdom Literature: HUCA 18 (1943/44) 77–118 = in: ID., Poets, Prophets and Sages. Essays in Biblical Interpretation, Bloomington, IN: Indiana University Press, 1971, 160–197.

GRANADOS, Carlos, La humildad, camino del amor. Análisis estructural y semántico de Eclo 7: EstBíb 62 (2004) 155–169.

GREENFIELD, Jonas C., Ben Sira 42.9–10 and its Talmudic Paraphrase. In: Philip R. DAVIES—Richard T. WHITE (eds.), A Tribute to Geza Vermes. Essays on Jewish and Christian Literature and History (JSOTSup 100), Sheffield: Sheffield Academic, 1990, 167–173.

GREENFIELD, Jonas C.—Michael E. STONE—Esther ESHEL, The Aramaic Levi Document. Edition, Translation, Commentary (SVTP 19), Leiden: Brill, 2004.

HADOT, Jean, Penchant mauvais et volonté libre dans la Sagesse de Ben Sira, Brussels: Presses universitaires de Bruxelles, 1970.

HAMP, Vinzenz, Sirach (Die Heilige Schrift in deutscher Übersetzung. Echter Bibel: Das Alte Testament 13.2), Würzburg: Echter, 1951.

HANSON, Anthony T., The Use of the Old Testament in the Epistle of James [Seminar Report]: NTS 25 (1979) 526–527.

HARRISON, A. Robin W., The Law of Athens, vol. 1: The Family and Property (Bristol Classical Paperbacks), London: Bristol Classical Press, 1997 (1st ed. Oxford, 1968).

HART, John H. A. (ed.), Ecclesiasticus. The Greek Text of Codex 248, Cambridge: Cambridge University Press, 1909.

HARŢOM, Elijahu Shmuel, הספרים החיצונים כרך ד' בן סירא, Tel Aviv: Yavneh Publishing House, 1963.

HASPECKER, Josef, Gottesfurcht bei Jesus Sirach. Ihre religiöse Struktur und ihre literarische und doktrinäre Bedeutung (AnBib 30), Rome: Pontifical Biblical Institute, 1967.

HAULOTTE, Edgar, Symbolique du vêtement selon la Bible (Théologie 65), Paris: Aubier, 1966.

HEATON, Eric William, The School Tradition of the Old Testament (The Bampton Lectures for 1994), Oxford: Oxford University Press, 1994.

HENGEL, Martin, Judaism and Hellenism. Studies in Their Encounter in Palestine during the Early Hellenistic Period, 2 vols., Philadelphia: Fortress, 1974 = German orig., Judentum und Hellenismus. Studien zu ihrer Begegnung unter besonderer Berücksichtigung Palästinas bis zur Mitte des 2. Jh.s. v. Chr. (WUNT 10), Tübingen: Mohr Siebeck, ²1973.

HILDESHEIM, Ralph, "Bis dass ein Prophet aufstand wie Feuer". Untersuchungen zum Prophetenverständnis des Ben Sira in Sir 48,1–49,16 (TThSt 58), Trier: Paulinus, 1996.

HÖFFKEN, Peter, Jesus Sirachs Darstellung der Interaktion des Königs Hiskija und des Propheten Jesaja (Sir 48:17–25): JSJ 31 (2000) 162–175.

HÖFFKEN, Peter, Warum schwieg Jesus Sirach über Esra?: ZAW 87 (1975) 184–202.

HOGAN, Karina Martin, Theologies in Conflict in 4 Ezra. Wisdom Debate and Apocalyptic Solution (JSJSup 130), Leiden: Brill, 2008.

HUSSER, Jean-Marie, Dreams and Dream Narratives in the Biblical World. Translated by Jill M. Munro (The Biblical Seminar 63), Sheffield: Sheffield Academic, 1999.

HUSSER, Jean-Marie, Le songe et la parole. Étude sur le rêve et sa fonction dans l'ancien Israël (BZAW 210), Berlin: Walter de Gruyter, 1994.

ILAN, Tal, Integrating Jewish Women into Second Temple History (TSAJ 76), Tübingen: Mohr Siebeck, 1999.

ILAN, Tal, Notes and Observations on a Newly Published Divorce Bill from the Judean Desert: HTR 89 (1996) 195–202.

ILAN, Tal, Notes on the Distribution of Women's Names in Palestine in the Second Temple and Mishnaic Periods: JJS 40 (1989) 186–200.

INSTONE-BREWER, David, Divorce and Remarriage in the Bible. The Social and Literary Context, Grand Rapids, MI–Cambridge, U.K.: Eisenbrauns, 2002.

IRWIN, William H., Fear of God, the Analogy of Friendship and Ben Sira's Theodicy: Bib 76 (1995) 551–559.

JANOWSKI, Bernd, Gottes Weisheit in Jerusalem. Sirach 24 und die biblische Schekina-Theologie. In: Hermann LICHTENBERGER—Ulrike MITTMANN-RICHERT (eds.), Biblical Figures in Deuterocanonical and Cognate Literature (DCLY 2008), Berlin: Walter de Gruyter, 2009, 1–29.

JEDLOWSKI, Paolo, La sociología y la memoria colectiva. In: Alberto ROSA RIVERO—Guglielmo BELLELLI—David BAKHURST (eds.), Memoria colectiva e identidad nacional (Ensayo/ Pensamiento 23), Madrid: Biblioteca Nueva, 2000, 123–134.

JOHNSON, Luke Timothy, The Letter of James. A New Translation with Introduction and Commentary (AB 37 A), New York: Doubleday, 1995.

JÜNGLING, Hans-Winfried, Vatermetaphorik und Müttermemoria. In: Irmtraud FISCHER—Ursula RAPP—Johannes SCHILLER (eds.), Auf den Spuren der schriftgelehrten Weisen. Festschrift für Johannes Marböck (BZAW 331), Berlin: Walter de Gruyter, 2003, 77–95.

KAHANA, Avraham, הספרים החיצונים כרך ב' שמעון בן־סירא מבוא, Tel Aviv: Masadah Publishing House, ²1955–56.

KAISER, Otto, Covenant and Law in Ben Sira. In: Andrew D. H. MAYES—Robin B. SALTERS (eds.), Covenant as Context. Essays in Honour of E.W. Nicholson, Oxford: Oxford University Press, 2003, 235–260.

KAISER, Otto, Die Rezeption der stoischen Providenz bei Ben Sira: JNSL 24 (1998) 41–54.

KAISER, Otto, Weisheit für das Leben. Das Buch Jesus Sirach. Übersetzt und eingeleitet, Stuttgart: Radius, 2005.

KEARNS, Conleth, The Expanded Text of Ecclesiasticus. Its Teaching on the Future Life as a Clue to Its Origin. Enlarged with a Biographical Sketch of Kearns by Gerard Norton, an Introduction to Kearns' Dissertation by Maurice Gilbert and Bibliographical Updates (1951–2010) by Nuria Calduch-Benages (ed. Pancratius C. BEENTJES; DCLS 11), Berlin—New York: Walter de Gruyter, 2011.

KIEWELER, Hans Volker, Benehmen bei Tisch. In: Renate EGGER-WENZEL—Ingrid KRAMMER (eds.), Der Einzelne und seine Gemeinschaft bei Ben Sira (BZAW 270), Berlin: Walter de Gruyter, 1998, 191–215.

KIEWELER, Hans Volker, Die Stellung Jesu Ben Siras zwischen Judentum und Hellenismus. Eine Auseinandersetzung mit Th. Middendorp (BEATAJ 30), Frankfurt am Mein: Peter Lang, 1992.

KIRK, Alan K., Social and Cultural Memory. In: ID.—Tom THATCHER (eds.), Memory, Tradition and Text. Uses of the Past in Early Christianity (SemeiaSt 52), Leiden: Brill, 2005, 1–24.

KLEER, Martin, "Der Liebliche Sänger der Psalmen Israels". Untersuchungen zu David als Dichter und Beter der Psalmen (BBB 108), Bodenheim: Philo, 1996.

KNABENBAUER, Joseph, Commentarius in Ecclesiasticum cum appendice: textus "Ecclesiastici" hebraeus descriptus secundum fragmenta nuper reperta cum notis et versione litterali latina (Cursus Scripturae Sacra in Vet. Test. pars II, in libros didacticos VI), Paris: Lethielleux, 1902.

KORN, Joachim Hans, Πειρασμός. Die Versuchung des Gläubigen in der griechischen Bibel (BWANT 72), Stuttgart: Kohlhammer, 1937.

KOSCHAKER, Paul, Neue keilschriftliche Rechtsurkunden aus der El-Amarna Zeit (ASAW 36.5), Leipzig: Hirzel, 1928.

KRÜGER, Paul A., On Emotions and the Expression of Emotions in the Old Testament: A Few Introductory Remarks: BZ 48 (2004) 213–228.

KUGLER, Robert A., From Patriarch to Priest. The Levi-Priestly Tradition from Aramaic Levi to Testament of Levi (SBLEJL 9), Atlanta, GA: Scholars Press, 1996.

KURZ, William S., Intertextual Use of Sirach 48.1–16 in Plotting Luke-Acts. In: Craig A. EVANS—W. Richard STEGNER (eds.), The Gospels and the Scriptures of Israel (JSNTSup 104), Sheffield: Sheffield Academic, 1994, 308–324.

LAMBERT, Gustave, "Mon joug est aisé et mon fardeau léger". Note d'exégèse: NRT 77 (1955) 963–969.

LAVOIE, Jean-Jacques, Ben Sira le voyageur ou la difficile rencontre avec l'hellénisme: ScEs 52 (2000) 37–60.

LEE, Thomas R., Studies in the Form of Sirach 44–50 (SBLDS 75), Atlanta, GA: Scholars Press, 1986.

LEMAIRE, André, The Sage in School and Temple. In: John G. GAMMIE—Leo G. PERDUE (eds.), The Sage in Israel and the Ancient Near East, Winona Lake, IN: Eisenbrauns, 1990, 165–181.

LESLEY, Michael J., Exegetical Wiles: 4Q184 as Scriptural Interpretation. In: George J. BROOKE, et al. (eds.), The Scrolls and Biblical Traditions: Proceedings of the Seventh Meeting of the IOQS in Helsinki (STDJ 103), Leiden: Brill, 2012, 107–142.

LEUENBERGER, Martin, Gott in Bewegung. Religions- und theologie-geschichtliche Beiträge zu Gottesvorstellungen im Alten Testament (FAT 76), Tübingen: Mohr Siebeck, 2011.

LEVENE, David S., Theology and Non-Theology in the Rabbinic Ben Sira. In: Renate EGGER-WENZEL (ed.), Ben Sira's God. Proceedings of the International Ben Sira Conference Durham—Ushaw College 2001 (BZAW 321), Berlin: Walter de Gruyter 2002, 305–320.

LÉVI, Israel, L'Ecclésiastique ou la Sagesse de Jésus, fils de Sira. Texte original hébreu édité, traduit et commenté par Israel Lévi. Seconde Partie (Bibliothèque de l'École des Hautes Études. Sciences religieuses 10.2), Paris: Leroux, 1901.

LÉVI, Israel, L'Ecclésiastique ou la Sagesse de Jésus, fils de Sira. Texte original hébreu. Première Partie (Bibliothèque de l'École des Hautes Études. Sciences religieuses 10.1), Paris: Leroux, 1898.

LEVISON, Jack, Is Eve to Blame? A Contextual Analysis of Sirach 25:24: CBQ 47 (1985) 617–623.

LEWIS, Jack P., What Do We Mean by Jabneh?: JBR 32 (1964) 125–132.

LEWIS, Naphtali—Yigael YADIN—Jonas C. GREENFIELD (eds.), The Documents from the Bar Kokhba Period in the Cave of the Letters. Greek Papiry edited by Naphtali Lewis; Aramaic and Nabatean Signatures and Subscriptions edited by Yigael Yadin and Jonas C. Greenfield (Judean Desert Studies), Jerusalem: Israel Exploration Society, 1989.

LICHTENBERGER, Hermann—Ulrike MITTMANN-RICHERT (eds.), Biblical Figures in Deuterocanonical and Cognate Literature (DCLY 2008), Berlin: Walter de Gruyter, 2009.

LICHTHEIM, Miriam, Late Egyptian Wisdom Literature in the International Context: A Study of Demotic Instructions (OBO 52), Fribourg: Universitätsverlag; Göttingen: Vandenhoeck & Ruprecht, 1983.

LIESEN, Jan, Full of Praise. An Exegetical Study of Sir 39,12–35 (JSJSup 64), Leiden: Brill, 2000.

LIESEN, Jan, Strategical Self-references in Ben Sira. In: Nuria CALDUCH-BENAGES—Jacques VERMEYLEN (eds.), Treasures of Wisdom. Studies in Ben Sira and in the Book of Wisdom. Festschrift M. Gilbert (BETL 143), Leuven: University Press—Peeters, 1999, 63–74.

LINDENBERGER, James M., The Aramaic Proverbs of Ahiqar (The Johns Hopkins New Eastern Studies), Baltimore: The Johns Hopkins University Press, 1983.

LIORA, Ravid, The Book of Jubilees and Its Calendar. A Reexamination: DSD 10 (2003) 371–394.

LIPIŃSKI, Edward, Marriage and Divorce in the Judaism of the Persian Period: Trans 4 (1991) 63–71.

LOWTH, Robert, De sacra poesi Hebraeorum praelectiones academicae Oxonii habitae: subjicitur metricae harianae brevis confutation: et oratio crewiana. Notas et epimetra adjecit Ioannes David Michaelis. Pars prior. Editio secunda, Göttingen: Ioan. Christ. Dieterich, 1770 (1st ed., Oxford: Clarendon, 1753).

MACK, Burton L., Wisdom and the Hebrew Epic. Ben Sira's Hymn in Praise of the Fathers (Chicago Studies in the History of Judaism), Chicago: University of Chicago Press, 1985.

MACKENZIE, Roderick A.F., Sirach (OTMes 19), Wilmington, DE: Michael Glazier, 1983.

MARBÖCK, Johannes, Das Buch Jesus Sirach. In: Erich ZENGER et al. (ed.), Einleitung in das Alte Testament, dritte, neu bearbeitete und erweiterte Auflage (Kohlhammer Studienbücher Theologie 1.1), Stuttgart—Berlin—Köln: Kohlhammer, 1998, 363–370.

MARBÖCK, Johannes, Davids Erbe in gewandelter Zeit (Sir 47,1–11): TPQ 130 (1982) 43–49 = in: ID., Gottes Weisheit unter uns. Zur Theologie des Buches Sirach (ed. Irmtraud FISCHER; HBS 6), Freiburg im Breisgau et al.: Herder, 1995, 124–132.

MARBÖCK, Johannes, Der Hohepriester Simon in Sir 50. Ein Beitrag zur Bedeutung von Priestertum und Kult im Sirachbuch. In: Nuria CALDUCH-BENAGES—Jacques VERMEYLEN (eds.), Treasures of Wisdom. Studies in Ben Sira and in the Book of Wisdom. Festschrift M. Gilbert (BETL 143), Leuven: University Press—Peeters, 1999, 215–229 = in: ID., Weisheit und Frömmigkeit. Studien zur alttestamentlichen Literatur der Spätzeit (ÖBS 29), Fankfurt am Main et al.: Peter Lang, 2006, 155–168.

MARBÖCK, Johannes, Gerechtigkeit Gottes und Leben nach dem Sirachbuch. Ein Antwortversuch in seinem Kontext. In: Jörg JEREMIAS (ed.), Gerechtigkeit und Leben im hellenistischer Zeitalter (BZAW 296), Berlin: Walter de Gruyter, 2001, 21–52 = in: ID., Weisheit und Frömmigkeit, 173–197.

MARBÖCK, Johannes, Gesetz und Weisheit. Zum Verständnis des Gesetzes bei Jesus Ben Sira: BN NF 20 (1976) 1–21 = in: ID., Gottes Weisheit unter uns, 52–72.

MARBÖCK, Johannes, Jesaja in Sirach 48,15–25. Zum Prophetenverständnis in der späten Weisheit. In: Reinhard G. KRATZ—Thomas KRÜGER—Konrad SCHMID (eds.), Schriftauslegung in der Schrift. Festschrift für Odil Hannes Steck zu seinem 65. Geburtstag (BZAW 300), Berlin: Walter de Gruyter, 2000, 305–319 = in: ID., Weisheit und Frömmigkeit, 121–135.

MARBÖCK, Johannes, Jesus Sirach 1–23 (HThK.AT), Freiburg im Breisgau: Herder, 2010.

MARBÖCK, Johannes, Macht und Mächtige im Buch Jesus Sirach. Ein Beitrag zur politischen Ethik in der Weisheitsliteratur des Alten Testaments. In: Otto KIMMINICH—Alfred KLOSE—Leopold NEUHOLD (eds.), Mit Realismus und Leidenschaft. Ethik im Dienst einer humanen Welt. Für Valentin Zsifkovits zum 60. Geburtstag, Graz: Schnider, 1993, 364–371 = in: ID., Gottes Weisheit unter uns, 185–194.

MARBÖCK, Johannes, Structure and Redaction History in the Book of Ben Sira. Review and Prospects. In: Pancratius C. BEENTJES (ed.), The Book of Ben Sira in Modern Research. Proceedings of the First International Ben Sira Conference 28–31 July 1996 Soesterberg, Netherlands (BZAW 255), Berlin: Walter de Gruyter, 1997, 61–79 = in: ID., Weisheit und Frömmigkeit, 31–45.

MARBÖCK, Johannes, Weisheit im Wandel. Untersuchungen zur Weisheitstheologie bei Ben Sira (BBB 37), Bonn: Peter Hanstein, 1971.

MARBÖCK, Johannes, Weisheit im Wandel. Untersuchungen zur Weisheitstheologie bei Ben Sira. Mit Nachwort und Bibliographie (BZAW 272), Berlin—New York: Walter de Gruyter, ^{2}1999.

MARCONI, Gilberto, La lettera di Giacomo (Commenti biblici), Rome: Borla, 1990.

MARCUS, Joseph, A Fifth Ms of Ben Sira: JQR 21 (1931) 223–240.

MARCUS, Joseph, The Newly Discovered Original Hebrew of Ben Sira (Ecclesiasticus xxxii,16–xxxiv,1): The Fifth Manuscript and a Prosodic Version of Ben Sira (Ecclesiasticus xxii,22–xxiii,9): JQR 21 (1930/31) 223–240.

MARGOLIS, Max L., Ecclus. 7,6d: ZAW 25 (1905) 323.

MARGULIES, Heinrich, Das Rätsel der Biene im Alten Testament: VT 24 (1974) 56–76.

MARTTILA, Marko, Foreign Nations in the Wisdom of Ben Sira. A Jewish Sage between Opposition and Assimilation (DCLS 13), Berlin: Walter de Gruyter, 2012, 80–118.

MATTILA, Sharon L., Ben Sira and the Stoics: a Reexamination of the Evidence: JBL 119 (2000) 473–501.

MAYOR, Joseph B., The Epistle of Saint James. The Greek Text with Introduction, Notes and Comments, London: Macmillan, 1892.

McCONVERY, Brendan, Ben Sira's 'Praise of the Physician' (Sir 38,1–15) in the Light of Some Hippocratic Writings. In: Ciaran O'CALLAGHAN (ed.), Proceedings of the Irish Biblical Association 21 (1998) 62–86.

McKINLAY, Judith E., Gendering Wisdom the Host: Biblical Invitations to Eat and Drink (JSOTSup 216; GCT 4), Sheffield: Sheffield Academic, 1996, 160–178.

MEYERS, Carol, Miriam the Musician. In: Athalya BRENNER (ed.), A Feminist Companion to Exodus to Deuteronomy (FCB 6), Sheffield: Sheffield Academic, 1994, 207–230.

MIDDENDORP, Theophil, Die Stellung Jesu Ben Siras zwischen Judentum und Hellenismus, Leiden: Brill, 1973.

MINISSALE, Antonino, La versione greca del Siracide. Confronto tra testo ebraico e versione greca alla luce del metodo midrascico-targumico (AnBib 133), Rome: Pontifical Biblical Institute, 1995.

MINISSALE, Antonino, Siracide (Ecclesiastico). Versione, introduzione, note (Nuovissima Versione della Bibbia 23), Rome: Paoline, ²1990.

MINISSALE, Antonino, Siracide. Le radici nella tradizione (LoB 1.17), Brescia: Queriniana, 1988.

MINISSALE, Antonino, The Metaphor of "Falling": Hermeneutic Key to the Book of Sirach. In: Angelo PASSARO—Giuseppe BELLIA (eds.), The Wisdom of Ben Sira. Studies on Tradition, Redaction and Theology (DCLS 1), Berlin—New York: Waltwer de Gruyter, 2008, 253–275.

MOPSIK, Charles, La Sagesse de ben Sira. Traduction de l'hébreu, introduction et annotation par Charles Mopsik (Collection "Les Dix Paroles"), Paris: Verdier, 2003.

MORLA ASENSIO, Víctor, Eclesiástico. Texto y Comentario (El Mensaje del Antiguo Testamento 20), Estella (Navarra): Verbo Divino et al., 1992.

MURAOKA, Takamitsu, A Greek-English Lexicon of the Septuagint, Leuven—Dudley, MA: Peeters, 2009.

MURPHY, Roland E., Proverbial Sayings/'Better'-Sayings in Sirach. In: Nuria CALDUCH-BENAGES —Jacques VERMEYLEN (eds.), Treasures of Wisdom. Studies on Ben Sira and the Book of Wisdom. Festschrift M. Gilbert (BETL 143), Leuven: University Press—Peeters, 1999, 31–40.

MURRAY, J. Kohn, The Trauma of Isaac: JBL 26 (1991/92) 96–104.

NAUCK, August, Tragicorum Graecorum Fragmenta: Supplementum adiecit Bruno Snell, Hildesheim: Olms, 1964.

NEUDECKER, Reinhard, Das "Ehescheidungsgesetzt" von Dtn 24,1–4 nach altjüdischer Auslegung. Ein Beitrag zum Verständnis der neutestamentlichen Aussagen zur Ehescheidung: Bib 75 (1994) 350–387.

NICKELSBURG, George W. E., 1 Enoch. A Commentary on the Book of 1 Enoch, Chapters 1–36 (Hermeneia), Minneapolis: Fortress, 2001.

NICKELSBURG, George W. E., Social Aspects of Palestinian Jewish Apocalypticism. In: David HELLHOLM (ed.), Apocalypticism in the Mediterranean World and the Near East, Tübingen: Mohr Siebeck, ²1989 (1st ed., 1983) 641–654.

NISSINEN, Martti, Wisdom as Mediatrix in Sirach 24: Ben Sira, Love, Lyrics, and Prophecy. In: Mikko LUUKKO—Saana SVÄRD—Raija MATTILA (eds.), Of God(s), Trees, Kings, and Scholars. Neo-Assyrian and Related Studies in Honor of Simo Parpola (Studia Orientalia 106), Helsinki: Finnish Oriental Society, 2009, 377–390.

NUTKOWICZ, Hélène, A propos du verbe *sn'* dans les contrats de marriage judéo-araméens d'Éléphantine: Trans 28 (2004) 165–173.

OESTERLEY, William O. E., The Wisdom of Jesus the Son of Sirach, or Ecclesiasticus in the Revised Version with Introduction and Notes (The Cambridge Bible for Schools and Colleges), Cambridge: Cambridge University Press, 1912.

OKOYE, John I., Speech in Ben Sira with Special Reference to 5,9–6,1 (EHS.T 535), Frankfurt am Main: Peter Lang, 1995.

OLYAN, Saul M., Ben Sira's Relationship to the Priesthood: HTR 80 (1987) 261–286.

OPPENHEIM, A. Leo, The Interpretation of Dreams in the Ancient Near East. With a Translation of an Assyrian Dream-Book (TAPS.NS 46.3), Philadelphia: The American Philosophical Society, 1956.

PAJARDI, Piero, Un giurista legge la Bibbia. Ricerche e meditazioni di un giurista cattolico sui valori giuridici del messaggio biblico ed evangelico, Padua: Cedam, ²1990.

PALMISANO, Maria Carmela, Siracide. Introduzione, traduzione e commento (Nuova versione della Bibbia dai testi antichi 34), San Paolo: Cinisello Balsamo (MI), 2016.

PALMISANO, Maria Carmela, Sulla recente scoperta di due nuovi fogli ebraici del ms C del libro del Siracide: Bogoslovni vestnik 70 (2010) 517–529.

PAUTREL, Raymond, Ben Sira et le Stoïcisme: RSR 51 (1963) 535–549.

PAZ, Sarit, Drums, Women and Goddesses. Drumming and Gender in Iron Age II Israel (OBO 232), Fribourg: Academic Press; Göttingen: Vandenhoeck & Ruprecht, 2007.

PENAR, Tadeusz, Northwest Semitic Philology and the Hebrew Fragments of Ben Sira (BibOr 28), Rome: Pontifical Biblical Institute, 1975.

PERDUE, Leo G., Cosmology and the Social Order in the Wisdom Tradition. In: ID.—John G. GAMMIE (eds.), The Sage in Israel and the Ancient Near East, Winona Lake, IN: Eisenbrauns, 1990, 457–478.

PERDUE, Leo G., The Social Character of Parenesis and Paraenetic Literature: Semeia 50 (1990) 5–39.

PERDUE, Leo G., Wisdom & Creation. The Theology of Wisdom Literature, Nashville: Abingdon, 1994.

PETERCA, Vladimir, Das Porträt Salomo's bei Ben Sirach (47,12–22). Ein Beiträg zu der Midraschexegese. In: Matthias AUGUSTIN—Klaus-Dietrich SCHUNCK (eds.), Wünschet Jerusalem Frieden (BEATAJ 13), Frankfurt am Main: Peter Lang, 1988, 457–463.

PETERS, Norbert, Das Buch Jesus Sirach oder Ecclesiasticus. Übersetzt und erklärt (EHAT 25), Münster: Aschendorff, 1913.

PETERS, Norbert, Das "etymologische Rätsel". Ecclesiasticus 6,22(23): TQ 80 (1898) 94–98.

PETERS, Norbert, Der jüngst wieder aufgefundene hebräische Text des Buches Ecclesiasticus. Untersucht, herausgegeben, übersetzt und mit kritischen Noten versehen von Norbert Peters, Freiburg im Breisgau: Herder, 1902.

PETERS, Norbert, Liber Iesu filii Sirach sive Ecclesiasticus hebraice secundum codices nuper repertos vocalibus adornatus addita versione latina cum glossario hebraico-latino, Freiburg im Breisgau: Herder, 1905.

PETRAGLIO, Renzo, Figli e Padri. Lettori, copisti e traduttori cristiani di Ben Sirac. In: Letture cristiane dei Libri Sapienziali (Studia Ephemeridis "Augustinianum" 37), Rome: Institutum Patristicum "Augustinianum", 1992, 489–504.

PETRAGLIO, Renzo, Il potere in Siracide e in Sapienza: PaVi 23 (1978) 280–301.

PETRAGLIO, Renzo, Il libro che contamina le mani. Ben Sirac rilegge il libro e la storia di Israele (Theologia 4), Palermo: Augustinus, 1993.

PETRAGLIO, Renzo, Le Siracide et l'Ancien Testament. Relectures et tendences: Apocrypha 8 (1997) 287–302.

PIWOWAR, Andrzej, La vergogna come criterio della fama perpetua. Studio esegetico-teologico di Sir 40,1–42,14. Dissertazione per il Dottorato nella Facoltà di teologia della Pontificia Università Gregoriana, Katowice: [s.n.], 2006.

POCK, Johann-Ignaz, Sapientia Salomonis. Hieronymus' Exegese des Weisheitsbuches im Licht der Tradition (Dissertationen der Karl-Franzens-Universität Graz 89), Graz: Technische Universität Graz, 1992.

POMEROY, Sarah B., Women in Hellenistic Egypt. From Alexander to Cleopatra, New York: Schocken, 1984.

PRATO, Gian Luigi, Il problema della teodicea in Ben Sira. Composizione dei contrari e richiamo alle origini (AnBib 65), Rome: Pontifical Biblical Institute, 1975.

PRATO, Gian Luigi, La lumière interprète de la sagesse dans la tradition textuelle de Ben Sira. In: Maurice GILBERT (ed.), La Sagesse de l'Ancien Testament (BETL 51), Leuven: University Press—Peeters, ²1990, 317–346.

PRÉAUX, Claire, Le monde hellinistique. La Grece et l'Orient de la mort d'Alexandre à la conquête de la Grece (323–146 av. J.C.), vol. 2 (Nouvelle Clio. L'histoire et ses problèmes 6 bis), Paris: Presses Universitaires de France, 1978.

PROCKTER, Lewis J., Torah as a Fence against Apocalyptic Speculation: Ben Sira 3,17–24. In: David ASSAF (ed.), Proceedings of the Tenth World Congress of Jewish Studies (Jerusalem, August 16–24, 1989), Division A: The Bible and Its World, Jerusalem: Magnes Press, 1990, 245–252.

PUECH, Émile, Ben Sira and Qumran. In: Angelo PASSARO—Giuseppe BELLIA (eds.), The Wisdom of Ben Sira. Studies on Tradition, Redaction, and Theology (DCLS 1), Berlin—New York: Walter de Gruyter, 2008, 79–118.

QIMRON, Elisha, The Dead Sea Scrolls: The Hebrew Writings, vol. 1, Jerusalem: Yad Ben-Zvi Press, 2010 (in Hebrew).

QUIMRON, Elisha, Notes on the Reading. In: Masada VI. Yigael Yadin Excavations 1963–1965. Final Reports. Yigael Yadin, The Ben Sira Scroll from Masada. With Notes on the Reading by Elisha Qimron and Bibliography by Florentino García Martínez (The Masada Reports), Jerusalem: Israel Exploration Society—The Hebrew University of Jerusalem, 1999, 227–231.

Rahlfs, Alfred (ed.), Septuaginta. Id est Vetus Testamentum graece iuxta LXX interpretes edidit Alfred Rahlfs, Stuttgart: Deutsche Bibelgesellschaft, 1979.

Reitemeyer, Michael, Weisheitslehre als Gotteslob. Psalmentheologie im Buch Jesus Sirach (BBB 127), Berlin–Wien: Philo, 2000.

Reiterer, Friedrich V., "Urtext" und Übersetzungen. Sprachstudie über Sir 44,16–45,26 als Beitrag zu Siraforschung (ATSAT 12), St. Ottilien: EOS, 1980.

Reiterer, Friedrich V., Aaron's Polyvalent Role according to Ben Sira. In: Jeremy Corley–Harm van Grol (eds.), Rewriting Biblical History. Essays on Chronicles and Ben Sira in Honour of Pancratius C. Beentjes (DCLS 7), Berlin: Walter de Gruyter, 2011, 27–56.

Reiterer, Friedrich V., Der Pentateuch in der spätbiblischen Weisheit Sirachs. In: Otto Eckart–Jurie LeRoux (eds.), A Critical Study of the Pentateuch. An Encounter Between Europe and Africa (Altes Testament und Moderne 20), Münster: LIT Verlag, 2005, 160–180.

Reiterer, Friedrich V., Die immateriellen Ebenen der Schöpfung bei Ben Sira. In: Nuria Calduch-Benages–Jacques Vermeylen (eds.), Treasures of Wisdom. Studies in Ben Sira and in the Book of Wisdom. Festschrift M. Gilbert (BETL 143), Leuven: University Press–Peeters, 1999, 91–127.

Reiterer, Friedrich V., Gelungene Freundschaft als tragende Säule einer Gesellschaft. Exegetische Untersuchung von Sir 25,1–11. In: Id. (ed.), Freundschaft bei Ben Sira. Beiträge des Symposions zu Ben Sira Salzburg 1995 (BZAW 244), Berlin–New York: Walter de Gruyter, 1996, 133–169.

Reiterer, Friedrich V., Gott, Vater und Herr meines Lebens. Eine poetisch-stilistische Analyse von Sir 22,27–23,6 als Verständnisgrundlage des Gebetes. In: Renate Egger-Wenzel–Jeremy Corley (eds.), Prayer from Tobit to Qumran. Inaugural Conference of the ISDCL at Salzburg, Austria, 5–9 July 2003 (DCLY 2004), Berlin–New York: Walter de Gruyter, 2004, 137–170.

Reiterer, Friedrich V., The Influence of the Book of Exodus on Ben Sira. In: Jeremy Corley–Vincent Skemp (eds.), Intertextual Studies in Ben Sira and Tobit. Essays in Honor of Alexander A. Di Lella, O.F.M. (CBQMS 38), Washington DC: The Catholic Biblical Association of America, 2005, 100–117.

Reiterer, Friedrich V., Review of Recent Research on the Book of Ben Sira (1980–1996). In: Pancratius C. Beentjes (ed.), The Book of Ben Sira in Modern Research. Proceedings of the First International Ben Sira Conference 28–31 July 1996 Soesterberg, Netherlands (BZAW 255), Berlin: Walter de Gruyter, 1997, 48–54.

Resch, Andreas, Der Traum im Heilsplan Gottes. Deutung und Bedeutung des Traums im Alten Testament, Freiburg im Breisgau: Herder, 1964.

Rey, Jean-Sébastien, 4QInstruction: sagesse et eschatologie (STDJ 81), Leiden–Boston: Brill, 2009.

Rey, Jean-Sébastien., Un nouveau bifeuillet du manuscrit C de la Genizah du Caire. In: Hans Ausloos–Bénédicte Lemmelijn–Marc Vervenne (eds.), Florilegium Lovaniense. Studies in Septuagint and Textual Criticism in Honour of Florentino García Martínez (BETL 224), Leuven–Paris–Dudley, MA: Peeters, 2008, 387–416.

Reymond, Eric D., New Hebrew Text of Ben Sira Chapter 1 in MsA (T-S 12.863): RevQ 105 (2015) 83–98.

Reymond, Eric D., Sirach 40,18–27 as 'Tôb-Spruch': Bib 82 (2001) 84–92.

REYMOND, Eric D., Wordplay in the Hebrew to Ben Sira. In: Jean-Sébastien REY—Jan JOOSTEN (eds.), The Texts and Versions of the Book of Ben Sira. Transmission and Interpretation (JSJSup 150), Leiden: Brill, 2011, 37–53.

RICKENBACHER, Otto, Weisheitsperikopen bei Ben Sira (OBO 1), Freiburg Schweiz: Universitätsverlag; Göttingen: Vandenhoeck & Ruprecht, 1973.

RIEDE, Peter, Im Spiegel der Tiere. Studien zum Verhältnis von Mensch und Tier im alten Israel (OBO 187), Freiburg Schweiz: Universitätsverlag; Göttingen: Vandenhoeck & Ruprecht, 2002.

RIMBACH, James A., Animal Imagery in the Old Testament. Some Aspects of Hebrew Poetics (Ph.D. diss., Johns Hopkins University, 1972).

RINALDI, Giovanni, "Onus meum leve". Osservazioni su Ecclesiastico 51 (v. 26, Volg. 34) e Matteo 11,25–30: BeO 9 (1967) 13–23.

ROFÉ, Alexander, The Onset of Sects in Postexilic Judaism: Neglected Evidence from the Sepuagint, Trito-Isaiah, Ben Sira, and Malachi. In: Jacob NEUSNER—Ernest S. FRERICHS—Peder BORGEN—Richard HORSLEY (eds.), The Social World of Formative Christianity and Judaism. Essays in Tribute to Howard Clark Kee, Philadelphia: Fortress, 1988, 39–49.

ROGERS, Jessie F., "As ploughing and reaping draw near to her". A Reading of Sirach 6:18–37: OTE 13 (2000) 364–379.

ROGERS, Jessie F., Wisdom and Creation in Sirach 24: JNSL 22 (1996) 141–156.

ROSALDO, Michelle Z., Toward an Anthropology of Self and Feeling. In: Richard A. SHWEDER—Robert A. LeVINE (eds.), Culture Theory: Essays on Mind, Self, and Emotion, Cambridge: Cambridge University Press, 1984, 137–157.

ROSSETTI, Marco, Le aggiunte ebraiche e greche a Sir 16,1–16: Sal 64 (2002) 607–648.

ROTH, Martha T., Babylonian Marriage Agreements: 7th–3rd Centuries B.C. (AOAT 222), Neukirchen-Vluyn: Verlag Butzon & Bercker Kevelaer, 1989.

RÜGER, Hans Peter, Le Siracide: un livre à la frontière du canon. In: Jean-Daniel KAESTLI—Otto WERMELINGER (eds.), Le canon de l'Ancien Testament. Sa formation et son histoire, Genève: Labor et Fides, 1984, 47–67.

RÜGER, Hans Peter, Text und Textform im hebräischen Sirach. Untersuchungen zur Textgeschichte und Textkritik der hebräischen Sirachfragmente aus der Kairoer Geniza (BZAW 112), Berlin: Walter de Gruyter, 1970.

RYSSEL, Victor, Die Sprüche Jesus' des Sohnes Sirachs. In: Emil KAUTZSCH (ed.), Die Apokryphen und Pseudepigraphen des Alten Testaments, vol. 1, Tübingen: Mohr Siebeck, 1900, 230–475.

SACCHI, Paolo, Apocrifi dell'Antico Testamento. In: Pietro ROSSANO (ed.), Classici delle Religioni, vol. 2: La religione ebraica, Turin: UTET, 1981.

SANDERS, Jack T., Ben Sira and Demotic Wisdom (SBLMS 28), Chico, CA: Scholars Press, 1983.

SANDERS, Jack T., Ben Sira's Ethics of Caution: HUCA 50 (1979) 73–106.

SANDERS, Jack T., A Hellenistic Egyptian Parallel to Ben Sira: JBL 97 (1978) 257–258.

SARACINO, Francesco, La Sapienza e la vita: Sir 4,11–19: RivB 29 (1981) 257–272.

SAUER, Georg, Der traditionsgeschichtliche Hintergrund von Ben Sira 42,15–43,33. In: Axel GRAUPNER—Holger DELKURT—Alexander B. ERNST unter Mitarbeit von Lutz Aupperle (eds.), Verbindungslinien. Festschrift für Werner Schmidt zum 65. Geburtstag, Neukirchen-Vluyn: Neukirchener, 2000, 311–321.

SAUER, Georg, Jesus Sirach/Ben Sira (ATD Apokryphen 1), Göttingen: Vandenhoeck & Ruprecht, 2000.

SCHECHTER, Solomon—Charles TAYLOR (eds.), The Wisdom of Ben Sira. Portions of the Book Ecclesiasticus from Hebrew Manuscripts in the Cairo Genizah Collection Presented to the University of Cambridge by the Editors, Cambridge: Cambridge University Press, 1899.

SCHEIBER, Alexander, A Leaf of the Fourth (sic; read Sixth) Manuscript of the Ben Sira from the Geniza: Magyar Könyvszemle 98 (1982) 179–182.

SCHMITT, Armin, Enkomien in griechischer Literatur. In: Irmtraud FISCHER—Ursula RAPP—Johannes SCHILLER (eds.), Auf den Spuren der schriftgelehrten Weisen. Festschrift für Johannes Marböck (BZAW 331), Berlin: Walter de Gruyter, 2003, 359–381.

SCHNABEL, Eckhard J., Law and Wisdom from Ben Sira to Paul. A Tradition Historical Enquiry into the Relation of Law, Wisdom, and Ethics (WUNT 2. Reihe 16), Tübingen: Mohr Siebeck, 1985.

SCHOCHET, Elijah J., Animal Life in Jewish Tradition. Attitudes and Relationships, New York: KTAV, 1984.

SCHRÄDER, Lutz, Leiden und Gerechtigkeit. Studien zu Theologie und Textgeschichte des Sirachbuches (BET 27), Frankfurt am Main: Peter Lang, 1994.

SCHREINER, Josef, Jesus Sirach 1–24 (NEB. Kommentar zum Alten Testament mit der Einheitsübersetzung 38), Würzburg: Echter, 2002.

SCHROER, Silvia—Thomas STAUBLI, Biblische Emotionswelten: Katechetische Blätter 132 (2007) 44–49.

SCHROER, Silvia, Die Weisheit hat ihr Haus gebaut. Studien zur Gestalt der Sophia in den biblischen Schriften, Mainz: Matthias-Grünewald, 1996; ET: Wisdom Has Built Her House. Studies on the Figure of Sophia in the Bible, Collegeville, MN: Liturgical Press, 2000.

SEGAL, Moseh Z., ספר בן סירא השלם, Jerusalem: Bialik Foundation, [4]1997.

SEGER, Nicolas, L'utilisation de la polysémie des racines hébraïques chez Ben Sira (Ph.D. diss., Université de Strasbourg 2—Marc Bloch, 2005).

SINNOTT, Alice M., The Personification of Wisdom (SOTSMS), Aldershot, U.K.—Burlington, VT: Ashgate, 2005, 125–127.

SKA, Jean-Louis, L'Éloge des Pères dans le Siracide (Si 44–50) et le canon de l'Ancien Testament. In: Nuria CALDUCH-BENAGES—Jacques VERMEYLEN (eds.), Treasures of Wisdom. Studies in Ben Sira and in the Book of Wisdom. Festschrift M. Gilbert (BETL 143), Leuven: University Press—Peeters, 1999, 181–193.

SKEHAN, Patrick W., Structure in Poems on Wisdom: Proverbs 8 and Sir 24: CBQ 41 (1979) 365–379.

SKEHAN, Patrick W., The Acrostic Poem in Sirach 51:13–30: HTR 64 (1971) 387–400.

SKEHAN, Patrick W.—Alexander A. DI LELLA, The Wisdom of Ben Sira. A New Translation with Notes by Patrick W. Skehan. Introduction and Commentary by Alexander A. Di Lella (AB 39), New York: Doubleday, 1987.

SMEND, Rudolf, Die Weisheit des Jesus Sirach erklärt, Berlin: Reimer, 1906.

SMITH, Mark S., The Heart and Innards in Israelite Emotional Expressions: Notes from Anthropology and Psychobiology: JBL 117 (1998) 427–436.

SMITS, Wilhelm, Ecclesiasticus vulgatae editionis versione belgica. Notis grammaticalibus, literalibus, criticis & c. praemisso prolegomeno, elucidatus, authore F. Wilhelmo Smits,

Antverpiae et Amstelodami: apud Alexandrum Everaerts et apud Gerardum Tielenburg, 1749.

SNAITH, John G., Ecclesiasticus or The Wisdom of Jesus, Son of Sirach (CNEB), Cambridge: Cambridge University Press, 1974.

SPARKS, Hedley F. D. (ed.), The Apocryphal Old Testament, Oxford: Oxford University Press, 1984, 169–319.

SPATAFORA, Andrea, Intelligent or Sensible Woman (Sir 25:8)?: Thf 31 (2000) 267–281.

SPICQ, Ceslas, L'Ecclésiastique. In: Louis PIROT—Albert CLAMER (eds.), La Sainte Bible. Texte latin et traduction française d'après les textes originaux avec un commentaire exégétique et théologique, vol. 6, Paris: Letouzey & Ané, 1951, 529–841.

SPICQ, Ceslas, Le Siracide et la structure littéraire du Prologue de saint Jean. In: René DUSSAUD et al. (eds.), Mémorial Lagrange, Paris: Gabalda, 1940, 183–195.

SPICQ, Ceslas, Les épîtres pastorales (ÉBib), Paris: Gabalda, ⁴1969.

SPRONK, Klaas, Rahab. In: Karel VAN DER TORN—Bob BECKING—Pieter W. VAN DER HORST (eds.), Dictionary of Deities and Demons in the Bible, Leiden—New York—Köln: Brill, 1995, 1292–1295.

STADELMANN, Helge, Ben Sira als Schriftgelehrter: eine Untersuchung zum Berufsbild des vormakkabäischen Sofer unter Berücksichtigung seines Verhältnisses zu Priester-, Propheten- und Weisheitslehrertum (WUNT 2. Reihe 6), Tübingen: Mohr Siebeck, 1980.

STONE, Michael E., Enoch, Aramaic Levi and Sectarian Origins: JSJ 19 (1988) 159–170.

STRAWN, Brent A., What is Stronger than a Lion? Leonine Image and Metaphor in the Hebrew Bible and the Ancient Near East (OBO 212), Fribourg: Academic Press; Göttingen: Vandenhoeck & Ruprecht, 2005.

STROTMANN, Angelika, Das Buch Jesus Sirach: über die schwierige Beziehung zwischen göttlicher Weisheit und konkreten Frauen in einer androzentrischen Schrift. In: Luise SCHOTTROFF—Marie-Teres WACKER (eds.), Kompendium Feministische Bibelauslegung, Gütersloh: Gütersloher Verlagshaus, 1998, ²1999, rev. ed., 428–440.

STROTMANN, Angelika, Sirach (Ecclesiasticus): On the Difficult Relation between Divine Wisdom and Real Women in an Androcentric Document. In: Luise SCHOTTROFF—Marie-Teres WACKER (eds.), Feminist Biblical Interpretation: A Compendium of Critical Commentary on the Books of the Bible and Related Literature, Grand Rapids, MI—Cambridge, U.K.: Eerdmans, 2012, 539–554.

STUMMER, Friedrich, "Via peccantium complanata lapidibus" (Eccli 21,11). In: Bonifatius FISCHER—Virgil FIALA (eds.), Colligere Fragmenta. Festschrift Alban Dold zum 70. Geburtstag am 7.7.1952 (Texte und Arbeiten I.2), Beuron in Hollenzollern: Beuroner Kunstverlag, 1952, 40–44.

SUNDBERG, Albert C., The Old Testament of the Early Church (HTS 20), Cambridge, MA: Harvard University Press, 1964.

SWETNAM, James, Jesus and Isaac in the Light of the Aqedah. A Study of the Epistle to the Hebrews (AnBib 94), Rome: Pontifical Biblical Institute, 1981.

TAIT, Michael, Jesus, the Divine Bridegroom, in Mark 2:18–22: Mark's Christology upgraded (AnBib 185), Rome: Gregorian & Biblical Press, 2010.

TCHERIKOVER, Victor, Hellenistic Civilization and the Jews, Philadelphia: The Jewish Publication Society of America, 1961 (New York, ⁶1982).

THACKERAY, Henry St. J. (trans.), Josephus with an English Translation by H. St. J. Thackeray, vol. 4: Jewish Antiquities, Books II–IV (The Loeb Classical Library), London: William Heinemann; New York: G. P. Putnam's Sons, 1930.

THIELE, Walter (ed.), Sirach (Ecclesiasticus), (Vetus Latina. Die Reste der altlateinischen Bibel 11.2), Freiburg im Breisgau: Herder, 1987–2005.

TOLONI, Giancarlo, La riforma di Giosia nell'ottica di Ben Sira. Ideologia e storia in Sir 49,2a: RivB 47 (1999) 257–276.

TRENCH, Richard C., Proverbs and Their Lessons, London: Routledge, 1861 (1st ed., 1857).

TRENCHARD, Warren C., Ben Sira's View of Women. A Literary Analysis (BJS 38), Chico, CA: Scholars Press, 1982.

TRUBLET, Jacques, Constitution et clôture du canon hébraïque. In: Christoph THÉOBALD (ed.), Le canon des Écritures. Études historiques, exégétiques et systématiques (LD 140), Paris: Cerf, 1990, 77–187.

UEBERSCHAER, Franz, Weisheit aus der Begegnung. Bildung nach dem Buch Ben Sira (BZAW 379), Berlin–New York: Walter de Gruyter, 2007.

URBANZ, Werner, Emotionen mit Gott–Aspekte aus den Gebetsaussagen im Sirachbuch. In: Renate EGGER-WENZEL–Jeremy CORLEY (eds.), Emotions from Ben Sira to Paul (DCLY 2011), Berlin–Boston: Walter de Gruyter, 2012, 133–158.

URBANZ, Werner, Gebet im Sirachbuch. Zur Terminologie von Klage und Lob in der griechischen Texttradition (HBB 60), Freiburg et al.: Herder, 2009.

URBANZ, Werner, Jeremia–ein Prophet am Ende. Anmerkungen zu Sir 49,4–7. In: Franz GRUBER – Christoph NIEMAND – Ferdinand REISINGER et al. (eds.), Geistes-Gegenwart. Vom Lesen, Denken und Sagen des Glaubens. Festschrift für Peter Hofer, Franz Hubmann und Hanjo Sauer (LPTB 17), Frankfurt am Main: Peter Lang, 2009, 121–136.

VACCARI, Alberto, I libri poetici della Bibbia tradotti dai testi originali e annotati, Rome: Pontifical Biblical Institute, 1925.

VAN BROEKHOVEN, Harold, Wisdom and World. The Functions of Wisdom Imagery in Sirach, Pseudo-Solomon and Colossians (Ph.D. diss., Boston University, 1988).

VAN LEEUWEN, Raymond C., Proverbs 30:21–23: JBL 105 (1986) 599–610.

VAN PEURSEN, Wido T., The Verbal System in the Hebrew Text of Ben Sira (Studies in Semitic Languages and Linguistics 41), Leiden: Brill, 2004.

VAN WOLDE, Ellen, Sentiments as Culturally Constructed Emotions: Anger and Love in the Hebrew Bible: BibInt 16 (2008) 1–24.

VANDERLIP, Vera F., The Four Greek Hymns of Isidorus and the Cult of Isis (ASP 12), Toronto: Hakkert, 1972.

VATTIONI, Francesco, Ecclesiastico, testo ebraico con apparato critico e versione greca, latina e siriaca (Pubblicazioni del Seminario di Semitistica. Testi 1), Napoli: Istituto Orientale di Napoli, 1968.

VATTIONI, Francesco, San Gerolamo e l'Ecclesiastico: VetChr 4 (1967) 131–149.

VEIJOLA, Timo, Law and Wisdom. The Deuteronomistic Heritage in Ben Sira's Teaching of the Law. In: ID. (ed.), Leben nach Weisung. Exegetische und historische Studien zum AT (FRLANT 224), Göttingen: Vandenhoeck & Ruprecht, 2008, 144–164.

VELLA, José, Eclesiástico. In: PROFESORES DE LA COMPAÑÍA DE JESÚS (eds.), La Sagrada Escritura. Texto y Comentario. Antiguo Testamento, vol. 5 (BAC 312. Sección 1. Sagradas Escrituras), Madrid: Biblioteca de Autores Cristianos, 1970.

VON RAD, Gerhard, Wesheit in Israel, Neukirchen: Neukirchener, 1970.

Vox, Onofrio (ed.), Carmi di Teocrito e dei poeti bucolici greci minori (Classici greci), Turin: UTET, 1997.

WACHSMUTH, Curt – Otto HENSE (eds.), Ioannis Stobaei Anthologium, vol. 4: Anthologii libri quarti partem priorem ab Ottone Hense editam continens, Berlin: Weidman, 1909.

WAGNER, Andreas (ed.), Anthropologische Aufbrüche. Alttestamentliche und interdisziplinäre Zugänge zur historischen Anthropologie (FRLANT 232), Göttingen: Vandenhoeck & Ruprecht, 2009.

WAGNER, Andreas, Emotionen, Gefühle und Sprache im Alten Testament (Kleine Untersuchungen zur Sprache des Alten Testaments und seiner Umwelt 7), Waltrop: Spenner, 2006.

WAGNER, Christian, Die Septuaginta-Hapaxlegomena im Buch Jesus Sirach (BZAW 282), Berlin —New York: Walter de Gruyter, 1999.

WAINWRIGHT, Elaine M., Gendering Healing both Human and Divine: The Case of Sirach 38,1–15. In: Paul McKECHNIE—Philippe GUILLAUME (eds.), Ptolemy II Philadelphus and His World (Mnemosyne Supplements. History and Archeology of Classical Antiquity 300), Leiden—Boston: Brill, 2008, 257–272.

WALTKE, Bruce W., The Book of Proverbs. Chapters 15–31 (NICOT), Grand Rapids, MI— Cambridge, U.K.: Eerdmans, 2005.

WATANABE, Chikako E., Animal Symbolism in Mesopotamia. A Contextual Approach (WOO 1), Vienna: Institut für Orientalistik, 2002.

WEBER, Kathleen, Wisdom False and True (Sir 19,20–30): Bib 77 (1996) 330–348.

WEBER, Thomas H., Sirach. In: Raymond E. BROWN—John A. FITZMYER—Roland E. MURPHY (eds.), The Jerome Biblical Commentary, vol. 1, Englewood Cliffs, NJ: Prentice Hall, 1968, 541–555.

WÉNIN, André, De la création à l'alliance sinaïtique. La logique de Si 16,26–17,14. In: Nuria CALDUCH-BENAGES—Jacques VERMEYLEN (eds.), Treasures of Wisdom. Studies in Ben Sira and in the Book of Wisdom. Festschrift M. Gilbert (BETL 143), Leuven: University Press— Peeters, 1999, 147–158.

WEST, Martin L. (ed.), Hesiod, Works and Days: Edited with Prolegomena and Commentary by M. L. West, Oxford: Clarendon, 1978.

WEST, Martin L. (ed.), Iambi et elegi graeci ante Alexandrum cantata, vol. 1: Archilochus, Hipponax, Theognidea, Oxford: Oxford University Press, ^{2}1989.

WESTERMANN, Claus, Genesis (BKAT 1/2), Neukirchen-Vluyn: Neukirchener, 1981.

WICKE-REUTER, Ursel, Göttliche Providenz und menschliche Verantwortung bei Ben Sira und in der Frühen Stoa (BZAW 298), Berlin—New York: Walter de Gruyter, 2000.

WILLI-PLEIN, Ina, Die Versuchung steht am Schluss. Inhalt und Ziel der Versuchung Abrahams nach der Erzählung in Gen 22: TZ 48 (1992) 100–108.

WINSTON, David, Theodicy in Ben Sira and Stoic Philosophy. In: Ruth LINK-SALINGER (ed.), Of Scholars, Savants and Their Texts. Studies in Philosophy and Religious Thought. Essays in Honor of Arthur Hyman, New York: Peter Lang, 1989, 239–249.

WINTER, Paul, Some Observations on the Language of the Birth and Infancy Stories of the Third Gospel: NTS 1 (1954) 111–121.

WISCHMEYER, Oda, Die Kultur des Buches Jesus Sirach (BZNW 77), Berlin—New York: Walter de Gruyter, 1995.

WISCHMEYER, Oda, Gut und Böse. Antithetisches Denken im Neuen Testament und bei Jesus Sirach. In: Nuria CALDUCH-BENAGES—Jacques VERMEYLEN (eds.), Treasures of Wisdom.

Studies in Ben Sira and the Book of Wisdom. Festschrift M. Gilbert (BETL 143), Leuven: University Press—Peeters, 1999, 120–136.

WITTE, Markus, "Mose, sein Andenken sei zum Segen" (Sir 45,1). Das Mosebild des Sirachbuchs: BN 107 (2001) 161–186 = in: ID., Texte und Kontexte des Sirachbuchs. Gesammelte Studien zu Ben Sira und zur frühjüdischen Weiheit (FAT 98), Tübingen: Mohr Siebeck, 2015, 123–149.

WRIGHT III, Benjamin G. III, B. Sanhedrin 100b and Rabbinic Knowledge of Ben Sira. In: Nuria CALDUCH-BENAGES—Jacques VERMEYLEN (eds.), Treasures of Wisdom. Studies in Ben Sira and in the Book of Wisdom. Festschrift M. Gilbert (BETL 143), Leuven: University Press—Peeters, 1999, 41–50 = in: ID., Praise Israel for Wisdom and Instruction. Essays on Ben Sira and Wisdom, the Letter of Aristea and the Septuagint (JSJSup 131), Leiden: Brill, 2008, 183–193.

WRIGHT, Benjamin G. III, Ben Sira and the Sage as Exemplar. In: ID., Praise Israel for Wisdom and Instruction, 165–182.

WRIGHT, Benjamin G. III, The Use and Interpretation of Biblical Tradition in Ben Sira's Praise of the Ancestors. In: Géza G. XERAVITS—József ZSENGELLÉR (eds.), Studies in the Book of Ben Sira. Papers of the Third International Conference on the Deuterocanonical Books, Shime'on Centre, Pápa, Hungary, 18–20 May, 2006 (JSJSup 127), Leiden: Brill, 2008, 183–207.

WRIGHT, Benjamin G. III, "Fear the Lord and Honor the Priest". Ben Sira as Defender of the Jerusalem Priesthood. In: Pancratius C. BEENTJES (ed.), The Book of Ben Sira in Modern Research. Proceedings of the First International Ben Sira Conference 28–31 July 1996 Soesterberg, Netherlands (BZAW 255), Berlin: Walter de Gruyter, 1997, 189–222 = in: ID., Praise Israel for Wisdom and Instruction, 97–126.

WRIGHT, Benjamin G. III, Putting the Puzzle Together: Some Suggestions Concerning the Social Location of the Wisdom of Ben Sira (SBLSP 1996), Atlanta: Scholars Press, 1996, 133–149 = in: ID.—Lawrence M. WILLS (eds.), Conflicted Boundaries and Wisdom and Apocalipticism (SBLSymS 35), Atlanta: Society of Biblical Literature, 2005, 89–112.

WRIGHT, Benjamin G. III, Sirach and 1 Enoch: Some Further Considerations: Hen 24 (2002) 179–187.

WRIGHT, Benjamin G. III, Sirach. In: Albert PIETERSMA—Benjamin G. WRIGHT (eds.), A New English Translation of the Septuagint and the Other Greek Translations Traditionally Included under that Title, Oxford: Oxford University Press, 2007, 715–762.

XERAVITS, Géza G., The Figure of David in the Book of Ben Sira: Hen 23 (2001) 27–38.

XERAVITS, Géza G.—ZSENGELLÉR, József (eds.), Studies in the Book of Ben Sira. Papers of the Third International Conference on the Deuterocanonical Books, Shime'on Centre, Pápa, Hungary, 18–20 May, 2006 (JSJSup 127), Leiden: Brill 2008.

YADIN, Yigael, The Ben Sira Scroll from Masada. With Introduction, Emendations and Commentary, Jerusalem: The Israel Exploration Society—The Shrine of the Book, 1965.

YADIN, Yigael, The Ben Sira Scroll from Masada. With Notes on the Reading by Elisha Qimron and Bibliography by Florentino García Martínez. In: Masada VI: Yigael Yadin Excavations 1963–1965. Final Reports (The Masada Reports), Jerusalem: The Israel Exploration Society—Hebrew University of Jerusalem, 1999, rev. ed., 151–252.

YARON, Reuven, On Divorce in Old Testament Times: RIDA 4 (1957) 117–128.

YEIVIN, Israel (ed.), The Book of Ben Sira. Text, Concordance and an Analysis of the Vocabulary. With an English foreword by Ze'ev Ben-Ḥayyim (The Historical Dictionary of the Hebrew Bible), Jerusalem: Academy of the Hebrew Language and the Shrine of the Book, 1973.

YODER, Christine R., Wisdom as a Woman of Substance. A Socioeconomic Reading of Proverbs 1–9 and 31,10–31 (BZAW 304), Berlin: Walter de Gruyter, 2003.

ZAPFF, Burkard M., Jesus Sirach, 25–51 (NEB. Kommentar zum Alten Testament mit der Einheitsübersetzung 39), Würzburg: Echter, 2010.

ZAPFF, Burkard M., Sir 38,1–15 als Beispiel der Verknüpfung von Tradition und Innovation bei Jesus Sirach: Bib 92 (2011) 347–367.

ZAPPELLA, Marco, L'immagine d'Israele in Sir 33(36),1–19 secondo il Ms ebraico B e la tradizione manoscritta greca. Analisi letteraria e lessicale: RivB 42 (1994) 409–446.

ZAPPELLA, Marco, La contemplazione sapienziale di Dio creatore (Sir 42–43): PaVi 48 (2003) 40–44.

ZIEGLER, Joseph (ed.), Sapientia Iesu Filii Sirach (Septuaginta. Vetus Testamentum Graecum auctoritate Societatis Litterarum Gottingensis editum 12.2), Göttingen: Vandenhoeck & Ruprecht, ²1980.

ZORELL, Franz (ed.), Lexicon hebraicum Veteris Testamenti, Rome: Pontifical Biblical Institute, 1984.

Index of Authors

https://doi.org/10.1515/9783110492316-025

Index of References

Old Testament

https://doi.org/10.1515/9783110492316-026

New Testament

1 Corinthians
  1 Cor 9,25: 128

Hebrews
  Heb 11,11: 87

James
  Jas 1,1: 159
  Jas 1,2 – 12: 158
  Jas 1,2 – 3: 162
  Jas 1,2: 163

Jas 1,8: 160
Jas 1,8.12: 161
Jas 1,13 – 18: 158
Jas 1,19 – 27: 158
Jas 2,15: 161
Jas 3,8: 160
Jas 4,8: 160

1 Peter
  1 Pet 1,7: 162
  1 Pet 3,6: 87

Old Testament Pseudepigrapha

Ahiqar
  Ahiqar 5: 78
  Ahiqar 9: 71
  Ahiqar 184: 74
  Ahiqar 186: 74

Aramaic Levi
  Aramaic Levi, ch. 6: 197

Jubilees
  Jub. 2,9: 252
  Jub. 17,7: 37
  Jub. 19,8: 37

1 Enoch
  1 En. 1 – 36: 247
  1 En. 1,9: 249
  1 En. 2,1 – 5,4: 248
  1 En. 5,8: 278
  1 En. 12 – 36: 248
  1 En. 12 – 13: 250
  1 En. 14,8: 238
  1 En. 18,14 – 15: 250
  1 En. 19,4: 250
  1 En. 20,1: 249

1 En. 20,3 – 6: 250
1 En. 71 – 82: 248
1 En. 72 – 82: 253
1 En. 72 – 80: 248
1 En. 72,1: 249
1 En. 72,37: 252
1 En. 75,2: 253
1 En. 75,3: 249
1 En. 79,1 – 6: 251
1 En. 80,1: 249, 251
1 En. 80,2: 253
1 En. 80,2 – 6: 251
1 En. 81,5: 249
1 En. 82: 252
1 En. 82,1: 249
1 En. 82,2: 278
1 En. 82,4 – 20: 248
1 En. 82,4 – 7: 253
1 En. 91,11 – 17: 248
1 En. 92 – 105: 248
1 En. 93,1 – 10: 248
1 En. 93,11 – 14: 248
1 En. 98,15: 247
1 En. 101,1 – 9: 248
1 En. 104,10: 247

Dead Sea Scrolls and Related Texts

Mishnah, Tosefta and Talmud

Other Rabbinic Works

Apostolic Fathers

Nag Hammadi Codices

New Testament Pseudepigrapha

Apostolic Constitutions and Canons
  Apos. Con. 7,12,1: 71

Hellenistic Jewish Literature

FLAVIUS JOSEPHUS
Antiquitates Judaicae
  A.J. 3,6 – 7: 152
  A.J. 3,179 – 180: 134
  A.J. 4,253: 64, 68
  A.J. 14,300: 106
  A.J. 15,11: 68
  A.J. 18,17: 68
Bellum Judaicum
  B.J. 1,477: 106
  B.J. 4,37: 29
Contra Apionem
  C. Ap. 1,38 – 41: 6
Vita
  Vita 426: 64

PHILO OF ALEXANDRIA
De Abrahamo
  Abr. 65: 36
De ebrietate
  Ebr. 158: 36
De migratione Abrahami
  Migr. 216 – 218: 36
De Vita Mosis
  Mos. 1,181 – 185: 152
  Mos. 2,117 – 118: 134
De specialibus legibus
  Spec. 1,84 – 85: 134
  Spec. 3,30: 64

Early Christian Sources/Fathers of the Church

ATHANASIUS
Epistulae festales
  Ep. fest. 39: 10
Epistula ad episcopos Aegypti et Libyae
  Ep. Aeg. Lib. 3: 11
Orationes contra Arianos
  C. Ar. 2,79: 11

AUGUSTINE
De gratia et libero arbitrio
  Grat. 1,2,3: 22
De scriptura sancta speculum
  Spec. 240: 22

BASIL THE GREAT
Homiliae
  Hom. 21: 175

CLEMENT OF ALEXANDRIA
Paedagogus
  Paed. 2,98,2: 22
  Paed. 3,58,2: 9

CYPRIAN
Ad Quirinum testimonia adversus Judaeos
  Test. 2,1: 22

CYRIL
Catechesis mystagogicae
  Catech. myst. 5,17: 10

EPIPHANIUS
Panarion (Adversus haereses)
  Pan. 33,8: 11
  Pan. 42,11: 11
  Pan. 76,22: 11
De mensuribus et ponderibus
  Mens. et pond. 4: 11

Greek and Roman Authors

Egyptian Literature

Index of Subjects

https://doi.org/10.1515/9783110492316-027